YOURS FOR THE UNION

The Civil War Letters of

John W. Chase

First Massachusetts Light Artillery

YOURS FOR THE UNION

The Civil War Letters of

John W. Chase

First Massachusetts Light Artillery

Edited by

John S. Collier & Bonnie B. Collier

Fordham University Press
New York
2004

The North's Civil War Series, No. 29
ISSN 1089-8719

Library of Congress Cataloging-in-Publication Data
Chase, John W. (John Webster), b. 1825.
Yours for the Union : the Civil War letters of John W. Chase, First Massachusetts Light Artillery / John S. and Bonnie B. Collier, editors.-- 1st ed.
p. cm.
Includes index.
ISBN 0-8232-2303-5 (Hardcover)
1. Chase, John W. (John Webster), b. 1825--Correspondence. 2. United States. Army. Massachusetts Light Artillery Battery, 1st (1861-1864) 3. Massachusetts--History--Civil War, 1861-1865--Personal narratives. 4. United States--History--Civil War, 1861-1865--Personal narratives. 5. Massachusetts--History--Civil War, 1861-1865--Regimental histories. 6. United States--History--Civil War, 1861-1865--Regimental histories. 7. United States--History--Civil War, 1861-1865--Artillery operations. 8. Soldiers--Massachusetts--Correspondence. 9. Roxbury (Boston, Mass.)--Biography. 10. Boston (Mass.)--Biography. I. Collier, John S. II. Collier, Bonnie B. III. Title.
E513.81st .C48 2004
973.7'81--dc22

2003024722

Printed in the United States of America
07 06 05 04 5 4 3 2 1
First edition

Table of Contents

Illustrations

Illustration Credits

AJB	*The Story of the First Massachusetts Light Battery,* by A. J. Bennett, Deland and Barta, Boston, Mass., 1886
CFC	Chase or Collier family collection
HW	*Harper's Weekly,* Vol. VI, No. 265, January 25, 1862; Vol. VIII, No. 393, July 9, 1864
JSC/BBC	John S. Collier and Bonnie B. Collier
LC	Library of Congress p. 18, Memory series; p. 75, LC-USZ62-11096; p. 90, LC-B8171-0334; p. 92, LC-B817-7143; p. 120, LC-USZC4-5817; p. 130, LC-B813-6377; p. 131, LC-USZ62-47450 & LC-USZ62-66840; p. 133, LC-USZ62-126493; p. 150, LC-B817-7085; p. 156, LC-USZ62-14724; p. 168, LC-USZ62-100749; p. 179, LC-USZC4-5629; p. 195, LC-USZ62-12799; p. 214, LC-USZ62-14638; p. 223, LC-B8171-7471; p. 234, LC-USZ62-119121; p. 280, LC-USZ62-103217; p. 287, LC-B813-1467; p. 303, LC-USZ62-7034; p. 314, LC-B817-7161; p. 320, LC-USZ62-101466; p. 325, LC-B811-1051; p. 333, LC-USZC4-2393; p. 365, LC-B482-4012; p. 366, LC-USZ62-14914; p. 368, LC-USZC2-3761; p. 370, LC-USZ62-15163; p. 371, LC-B811-2564; p. 394, LC-USZ62-7052
LJ	*History of the Sixth New Hampshire Regiment*, by Lyman Jackman, Republican Press Assoc., Concord, N. H., 1891
NA	National Archives p. 2, B-5294; p. 224, American Originals; p. 266, 66-G-19G-15; p. 312, pension records; p. 358, 165-SB-26; p. 401, pension records; p. 426, 79-CWC-3F-22; p. 430, B-443

NEHGS	Engraved for the New England Historic Genealogical Society by F. T. Stuart, Boston, Mass., 1868
RCG	*Roxbury City Gazette,* Vol. 2, No. 14, July 31, 1862.
TGM	*The Granite Monthly,* Vol. XXVI, No. 3, March 1899
USAMHI	U.S. Army Military History Institute, Carlisle, Pennsylvania p. 22, Vol. 95-4873; p. 128, RG98S-CWP20.99; p. 200, RG98S-CWP216.70; p. 263 & p. 407, Vol. 95-4874; p. 427, Vol. 95-4872

Acknowledgments

We are grateful to the previous generations of the Chase family who recognized the historical, or, perhaps, sentimental value of these letters and saved them.

We want to acknowledge the effort of Margaret Johnston Collier who typed the initial transcriptions of the letters years ago and who contributed several of the family photographs. We also want to acknowledge the contributions of family photographs by Dorothy Chase Barthlemes, Mary Chase Barker, and Joyce Barker Rowe.

John & Bonnie Collier

PORTER'S LIGHT BATTERY
1st Massachusetts
LIGHT ARTILLERY.
The U. S. Christian Commission
Mr Samuel S Chase
THE WAR FOR THE UNION
OUR CAUSE IS JUST
Mr Samuel S Chase
Roxbury
U. S. Christian Commission
SOLDIER'S LETTER.
WASHINGTON AUG 26 D.C.
Mr Samuel S Ch
Roxbury

CFC

Introduction

While he was a soldier in the Union army during the Civil War, John W. Chase wrote frequent letters to his older brother, Samuel S. Chase, back in Roxbury, Massachusetts. He patriotically signed several of his letters "Yours for the Union," which explains in part why he left friends and family to join the Union army. One hundred and seventy-two of those letters have survived and live on to describe John Chase's experiences and thoughts from October 1861 until the war ended in April 1865.

In plain language, his letters reflect the view of the war from the perspective of a common soldier rather than from an officer or a journalist or an historian. His letters portray a man who is trying to provide for his children, maintain his finances, and obtain food and clothing to supplement his meager rations, all while marching in the dust and the mud and fighting a war. His letters reveal his patriotism and his enthusiasm for preserving the Union, but as the war went on, his increasing cynicism becomes apparent and his criticism of the Union officers and the leadership in Washington grows more intense. His occasionally crude language reveals his strong opinions about abolition and, especially, abolitionist politicians. As a soldier in the Army of the Potomac, Chase was present at most of the major battles fought in the East. John Chase's state of mind reflects that of the Union army after each discouraging defeat or encouraging victory.

This collection of letters is not a sanitized or heroic memoir, and there are better and more complete descriptions of the battles and of the military strategies of the competing armies. Instead, these letters chronicle the experiences of one common soldier in the Union army.

John enlisted for three years as a private in the First Massachusetts Light Artillery, in Boston, on August 28, 1861, and reported for duty on September 2, 1861. He was appointed corporal (chief of caisson) on October 9, 1861, promoted to sergeant on June 9, 1863, and promoted to 1st sergeant on September 7, 1863. He reenlisted on December 23, 1863, at Brandy Station, Virginia. He was attached to the Fifth Maine Battery on October 3, 1864, when the First Massachusetts Battery was dissolved at the expiration of the men's three-year terms of enlistment. He was transferred to the Ninth Massachusetts Battery on March 28, 1865. He mustered out on April 26, 1865, at age 39, near Petersburg, Virginia, two weeks after Lee's surrender near Appomattox Court House.

John Webster Chase's pension records list his name erroneously as John Webber Chase, an error probably made by the law firm handling the pension application by his widow. He was almost certainly named after Daniel Webster, who was a prominent member of Congress at the time of John's birth in 1825.

The letters are presented here in their entirety as written by John W. Chase, with only the following minor editing. The original spellings have been maintained where they appear repeatedly, except that "ss" has been substituted for the old style "fs." Punctuation was rare, with no periods to end sentences and only occasional capitalizations to start them; however, Chase used other capitalizations liberally. We have added capitalized first letters of sentences and periods for readability, but made no attempt otherwise to punctuate the letters.

A few letters were written in black ink, but most were written in pencil on blue-lined paper. A couple of letters were written in a reddish ink that was made from local berries. Although his handwriting was moderately legible, it was very difficult to distinguish between some letters. We have used brackets [ ] for editors' additions.

This collection of letters, which fills one shoe box, was passed down through the family. Sam probably gave them to John's son, George, who lived in Stratham, New Hampshire, after John died.

When George died, they went to his younger daughter, Mary Chase Hatch, who also lived in Stratham. Mary had heart damage from scarlet fever, which led to an early death. The letters were retrieved from Mary's attic by her older sister, Pearl Chase Johnston, only a year or two before the house was destroyed by fire. Pearl left the letters with her daughter, Margaret Johnston Collier, who transcribed them. Margaret also loaned them to Bruce Catton, who quoted from them in his book, *This Hallowed Ground*. Margaret's son, John S. Collier, John W. Chase's great-great-grandson, along with his wife, Bonnie Baldwin Collier, verified and edited the transcriptions, collected the photographs, and did additional research to create this book.

There are many people mentioned in John Chase's letters. The following is a list of his friends and family mentioned most frequently, and their ages in 1861:

Brother	Samuel S. Chase (44)
Lizzie	Sam's wife, Elizabeth (42)
Asher	Sam and Lizzie's son (20)
William	Lizzie's brother, William Curtis (45)
Hitty	William's wife, Mehitable (41)
Mrs. Curtis	Lizzie's mother, Betsy (65)
Mary	John's daughter (14)
Charley	John's son (10)
George	John's son (7)
Sarah	John's daughter (4)
Mary	John's sister, Mary Littlefield (49)
Eliza	Mary Littlefield's daughter (21)
Levi	John's brother, Levi Chase (38)
Pricilla	Levi's wife, Priscilla (35)
Sis	John's sister, Sarah Littlefield (54)
Horatio Littlefield	Sarah Littlefield's son (21)

Susie Smith	Sarah Littlefield's daughter (20)
Harry Smith	Susie Smith's husband, William H. Smith (25)
George Head	The widower of John's youngest sister, Susan, who died in 1860 (37)
Father	Andrew Chase (74)
Mother	John's mother, Sarah, died in 1856. John called both his stepmother, Hannah, and his mother-in-law, Mary Marston, "Mother"
Emily	Emily Grindell lived with William and Hitty Curtis's family. She was a dressmaker for the family (28)
Mace	Probably John Wilder May, who became City Solicitor for Roxbury in 1864 (43)
Langdon	John Langdon Jewell (47) and Sophia (Marston) Jewell (41), the sister of John's late wife, cared for three of John's children
Lydston	Alfred Lydston (41), Sam's coworker

John W. Chase's Family

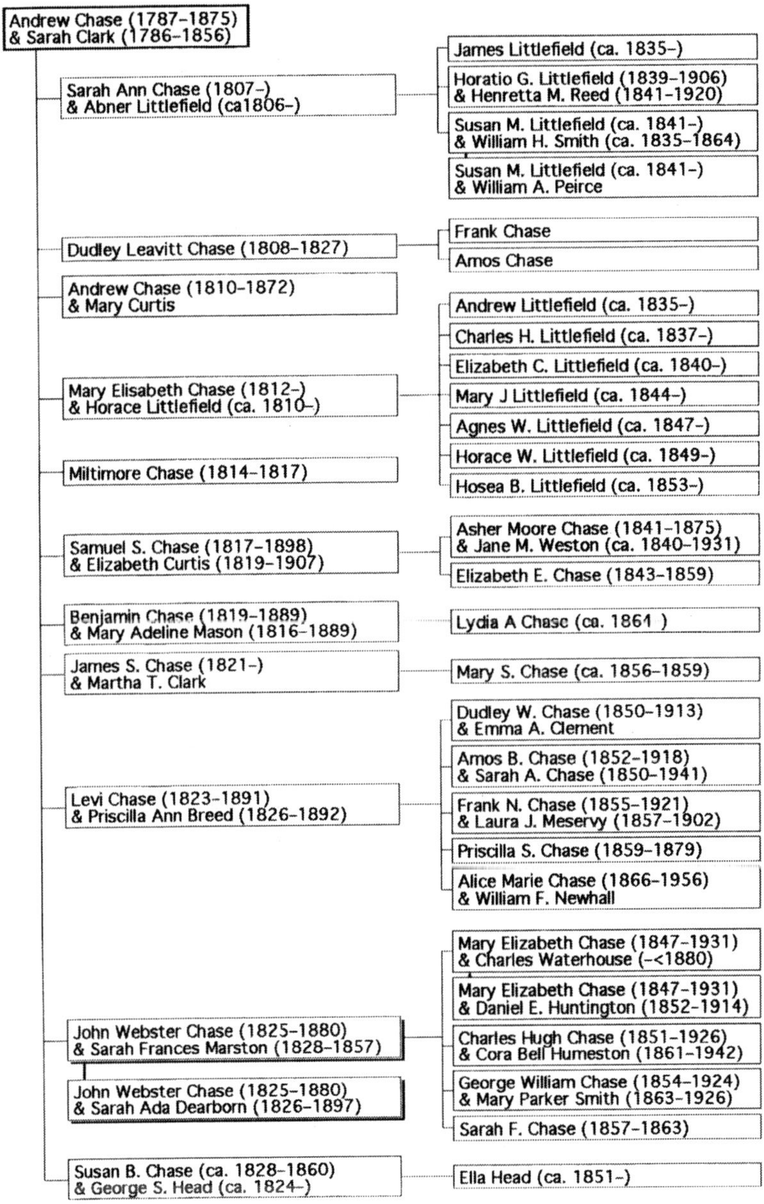

Prologue

John Webster Chase was born in 1825, in Roxbury, Massachusetts, which was then a town located just outside of Boston. He was the tenth of eleven children of Andrew and Sarah Clark Chase, who were both from Stratham, New Hampshire. John Chase was the seventh generation of Chase in New England since Aquila Chase came from England in 1640. John's grandfather, Major Dudley Leavitt Chase, fought in the Revolutionary War in Colonel Alex Scammel's Third New Hampshire Continental Regiment. Dudley was also the owner of Chase's Tavern in Stratham, which had been owned by his father, Thomas, and then his mother, Love, before him. John's father was a carpenter and, later, a farmer. John and his brothers, Samuel and Benjamin, were also carpenters.

Andrew Chase moved his family from Roxbury back to Stratham when John was still a boy. John Chase married Sarah Frances Marston in 1847, in nearby Hampton, New Hampshire, when he was 22. They lived and raised their family in Stratham, where John worked as a mechanic and a carpenter. Sarah died at the age of 28, a few days after the birth of their fourth child, in 1857. In 1860, John was living in Stratham with his father and stepmother, Hannah, working as a house carpenter. (John's mother had died in 1856.) Three of John's children, Mary, age 12, George, 6, and Sarah, 3, were living in Stratham with Sophia Marston Jewell and John Langdon Jewell, John's wife's sister and her husband. John's older son, Charles, age 9, was living with his maternal grandparents, Thomas and Mary Marston, in nearby North Hampton. By 1861, John had moved back to Roxbury, where his brother Sam lived with his wife and son, Asher. John enlisted in the First Massachusetts Light Artillery in Boston at age 36, in August 1861.

John Chase's Travel Routes in Chapter 1:
October 1861 to April 1862

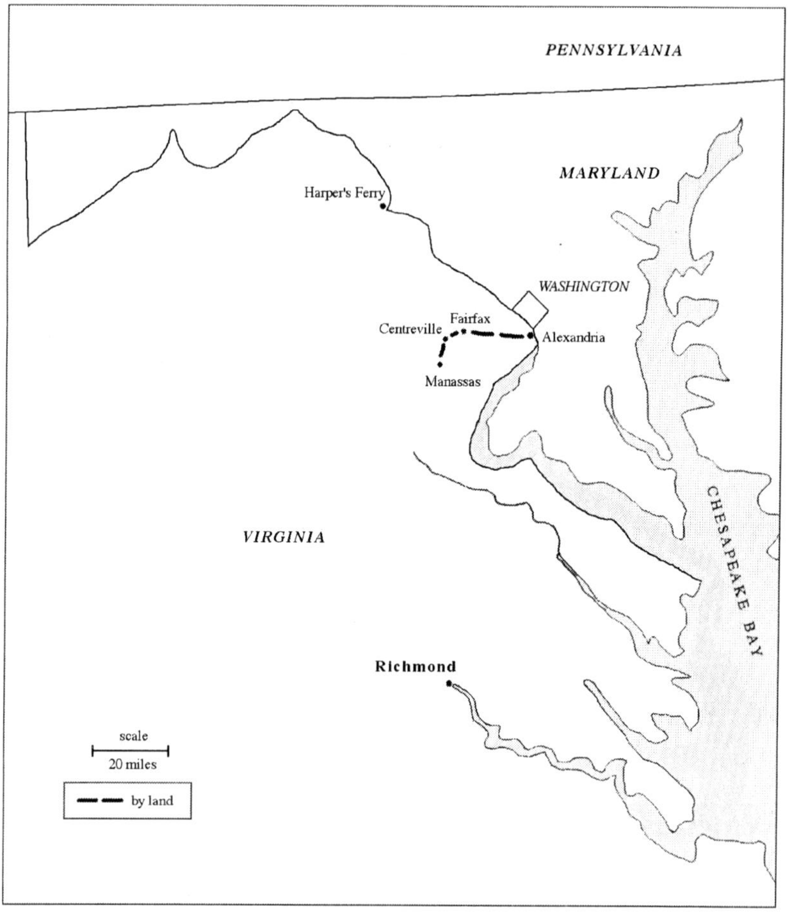

JSC/BBC

CHAPTER 1
Alexandria

Following the defeat of the Union army at the First Battle of Bull Run, the Army of the Potomac is encamped near Fairfax Seminary just north of Alexandria, Virginia. With many new three-year recruits, including John Chase, to replace the men who had enlisted for only ninety days, the army is being drilled under its new commander, General George B. McClellan.[1] *Chase describes the life of drilling and waiting.*

Alexandria
October 16th 1861

Dear Brother

I received your letter today and was very happy to hear from you it being the first letter that I have received from any one since I came out here. I have written some four or five letters but I suppose they will come some time or other at least I hope so. We left Washington last Monday and came to this place. It is some twelve miles from Washington and three from Alexandria City. It is a first rate Camping place. We have got one of the best wells of water that I have seen since I left New Hampshire. Captain Arnolds Battery[2] dug it out. They have been here since the Bull Run battle in which they were engaged. They are regulars. We are now with Franklins

[1] President Lincoln replaced General Winfield Scott with General McClellan as general-in-chief on Nov. 1, 1861.
[2] Captain Richard Arnold of the Fifth U.S. Artillery.

Brigade.[3] It is made up of New York & New Jersey troops mostly. You can have no idea of the number of troops there is in and around Washington. It is a perfect muster field. In coming here it was Camp after Camp. We passed Fort Ellsworth and just got a glimpse at the celebrated Marshall House where Ellsworth[4] was Killed. It is a fine country where we are now and if it was not for cursed war I should like to live here. I think if they could have a lot of New England farmers settle here they could show them how to raise a heap of stuff but war has left its mark all along where we have been since we came from Washington. Some splendid [houses] were destroyed and beautifull parks turned into cattle pens for the army but I suppose that this is but the beginning of what it will be. I hope when it is done it will be a permanent thing and the Question settled that there is such a thing as a Union.

The Marshall House NA

I expect we shall leave here in a day or two as our folks are trying to shell the enemy out of the woods some fourteen miles from us. We are in the advance wing of the army. We are on the direct road to Fairfax and Munsons Hill is in sight of us. We heard the cannonading here Yesterday. It begins to look squally around. Well if it must come let it come. I hope Capt Porters Battery[5] will do their duty and as for myself as an humble member I want to do my duty as

[3] General William B. Franklin's division consisted of four artillery companies, three brigades of four infantry companies, and one cavalry unit.
[4] Colonel Ephraim Elmer Ellsworth, a friend of President Lincoln, was killed by the proprietor of the Marshall House hotel when he removed a Confederate flag flying from its roof. The proprietor, James T. Jackson, was then killed by one of Ellsworth's men. Ellsworth became the North's first martyr, and Jackson became the South's.
[5] Captain Josiah Porter.

a soldier and a man and if I fall I hope it will be in front of the enemy and not running away from them and if I die I think I have friends enough at home that will take care of those I have left behind. I should like to see the children once more. I shall "put my trust in God and Keep my powder dry." I forget to tell you that we have changed four of our guns the two rifled and the smooth bores and have got four Parrot guns whose range is seven miles so they say. We have got 150 rounds of shot and shell in each of our cassons and I have to open the cassons every day and dry the ammunition and sit right on the carriage myself and not trust it to any guard. I have been over and seen the 1st Regiment of Massachusetts. I saw Horatio Littlefield.[6] He looks first rate. I was there the day that George Curtis was there but I did not see him but I did see Col Cowdin and Ben Perley Poor. I saw the Regt Drill and have a Dress Parade. They drill first rate and live first rate. We have lived rather tough but the living is improving and I think now we have got away from Washington we shall live better. At any rate I am glad we have got out of that Brick Yard for it was nothing but Clay. We have

Captain Josiah Porter AJB

[6] Horatio Littlefield, age 21, was the son of John's sister, Sarah Littlefield. He was a private in the First Massachusetts Infantry.

plenty of music for there is Infantry encamped all around us and the Bands play every night.

If any one inquires for me tell them I am on the sacred soil of old Virginia and hope when I get off of it that this trouble will have come to an end and the Stars & Stripes float in every State of the Union. I saw a secession flag over to the first Regiment that they captured while they were gone down the river. They were gone four weeks and got back a few days before I was over there. It is the only one I have seen. They had it hoisted union down and the Stars and Stripes waving over it. I also visited the New Hampshire 2d and saw Lieut Smith[7] and the boys from Stratham. I ran away the day I went over and was marched up to head quarters the next morning and got a talking too by the Seargeant Major who said if I done so again he would take the stripes off my shoulders but I guess he is not quite big enough to do that. My health is first rate. I was a little sick coming from New York to Amboy but since then I have been first rate. We have not a case of sickness yet only some that was brought on themselves by their own imprudencies. Folletts Battery came into Washington the day before we came away. They camped right by the side of us and Wilsons Regiment went over to George Town but I believe I have written about as much as you will want to read for it is rather a tough place to write in a tent with a dozen men around You some singing and some a dancing. You had ought to see them when the letters come. They sound the Assembly and then the clerk reads off the names of those that have letters. My under lip began to drop to cry but when my name was called I felt better.

I hope you will write often for you do not know how good it is to get a letter from your friends when you are in an enemies country. Give my love to Mary and let me know how to direct a letter to her and I will write to her. Give my respects to every body that wants to hear from me and after you read this send it up to Stratham. I want you to send me out some Postage Stamps for we shall not get any money till next month and I want you to send me some envelopes

[7] William (Harry) Smith was the husband of John's niece, Susie, who was the daughter of John's sister, Sarah Littlefield.

and some writing paper and tell Elizabeth to send me out some hankerchiefs if not to much trouble. Send me out some tobacco for I am dead broke and that is hard to get any way. Send the postage stamps in a letter and the other stuff by Express and I will try and renumerate you when we get paid off. I have just been to roll call and in one half hour we shall have to go to bed and get up at half past five in the morning and roll call at six.

I will just [say] to the folks in Stratham that I am just as happy as a man can be that is away from home and friends. I would not be without those minitures for a big sum. I take a great deal comfort in looking at them and those have seen them think it is a good looking family and I think so too. I have got my hair shaved snug to my head and my whiskers fixed in the Zouave style. I dont know as you would know me. I look about ten years older than I did when I came out here. Charles French[8] & Winslow send their respects to you. Winslow and I sleep side by side on the sacred Soil of Old Virginia. We sleep snug togeather so as to have both blankets over us. He is a first rate man but he must growl as all old Sailors clame that privaledge but I wish the whole Battery was made up of just such men but I believe we have got a better lot of men than Folletts after all the fuss. I wish we had a good united states officer with us. I dont think we have got but one real smart officer but he is just as smart as the next one but I have run on rather a long story and will close by bidding you good night.

Yours for the Union
Corp John W Chase

Love to Emily.[9]

* * * * * * * * * *

[8] Charles W. French, a sergeant in the First Massachusetts Battery, was from Stratham, New Hampshire.

[9] Emily Grindell was a 28-year-old dressmaker who resided with the family of Sam's wife's brother, William Curtis.

Alexandria Va
Oct 20th [1861]

Dear Brother

Having nothing to do and feeling rather sleepy I thought I would sit down and write and see if I could get waked up. We have had no drill now for three days and it make time hang heavy on our hands. It has rained two days the most of the time and a rainy day in camp is a rather dull affair. To day it is cool and pleasant. I have always thought that in the South they had a very even temperature but as far as we have gone it is as bad as ever I felt it in New England for it will be hot enough one day to roast you and the next just the reverse and the third day rain for sure and when it does rain here it rains and then the mud ye Gods a brick yard is nothing to be compared with it.

We dont have much excitement here for we do not dare to go a great ways out of camp for we are liable to be ordered to march at any time. We go around amongst the other Regiments some and see them drill and hear the music and get all the news we can. There is a fort about a mile from us and we go up there considerable. It is called Fort Taylor and you get a fine view of Washington and the country around it. It will be a rusher when they get it done. They captured a Sesesh Baloon Friday about a mile below us [interlined: (proved to be a camp story)] and yesterday one of the pickets of the Maine 5th captured a spy. He was dressed in womans clothes and was horse back. I saw him go by the camp to the slave pen in Alexandria. He will probably get his neck stretched. They have skermishes amongst the pickets almost every day and the other night we could see the shells flying through the air. It looked kind of like fourth of July. There is lots of game around here rabbits and partridges and plover. We borrow a gun sometimes and go out and get a mess.

The land arround where we are encamped belonged to Gen Lee. His house is just above us. It is a splendid residence and he owned an immense amount of land around here and good land too. I dont think you would wonder so much at the troops fireing into one another if you were out here for it is woods all around here. They have cut off hundreds of acres. There will be a patch of 7 or 8 acres and it will be surrounded with woods.

I have not had but one letter since I have been out here and have wrote a dozen but I expect to get some tomorrow. I want you to write just as often as you can and send me some papers for reading [is] rather scarce and when we are laying around a paper would work in quite handy. Give my love to all the folks and tell Emily that I should like a loaf of brown bread. We had beans for breakfast this morning and they were first rate. We built a brick oven yesterday. Got the bricks from an old chimney in an old house that was standing near the camp. We have just got orders to pack up and be ready to start at an hours notice but what is up I cannot tell. In fact what is going on you know better there than we do here.

The way we make our beds we take a lot of cedar boughs and spread on the ground and then spread our rubber blankets on them and sleep like a pig. I have gained four lbs since I came from Camp Cameron. I will put one of our feathers in this letter.

Yours
J W Chase

Tell Asher to write.

We had our first frost here the very night you did I think it is colder here nights than it is in New England.

* * * * * * * * * * *

Alexandria Va
Oct 28th 1861

Dear Brother

I received your letter today and was very glad to hear from you. I began to think that I was never going to have another letter from that part of the country for I have written four to Stratham and have not got an answer from them yet but I have this to comfort me if they dont write I shall not have to write to them but I think if they knew how [much] it [meant] to get a letter from home that they would try and write. I should like to hear from the children for I have not heard from them since before I came away from Boston. We still remain at Alexandria about 4 miles from the city. We have had two alarms and got all hitched up ready for a start but I begin to think we are got up to see how quick we can get ready but they have always found us on hand. We have a Battery of regulars right on the other side of the street and we can just knock them as high as a kite on drill. We had a review yesterday and the Major said we was the best drilled Battery in the division.

I had got this far and was ordered out for a knapsack drill the first we have had since we have been out here. We have not been worked very hard since we have been here but when we do get a drill we get a rough one. I begin to think some times that we are not going to get a lick at the rebels. One thing I am sure of if we do not advance in the course of four weeks we shall not make one this winter for they tell me here that then the rainy season sets in and they say that we have not seen any rain yet but I dont know what it can be for the roads are now almost as bad as they are there in the spring and if it is as bad as they say it is no 6 horses can draw any peice or casson over these roads but if they do have a fight I hope we shall be reckoned in for I want to see what we are made of and try them Parrotts and see if they will do what they say they will but I think that the policy is to starve the devils out. I went yesterday to visit a Fort just out of Alexandria. They have got 6, 64 pounders mounted besides a park of light Artillery. It is a gay place. You can see miles all around. We have a fort above us and one below us. I dont [think] they intend to retreat into Washington again.

Our waggons went away yesterday and visited a secession farm and brought with other teams that were with them one hundred loads of hay and they go again tomorrow after corn. They went 3 miles into the enemys country. I wish you could be out there and see the camps of an evening when the camp fires are lit up it looks like a city. We have some pretty good times. I dont know as I have been home sick a minute since I came out. I should like to see the children and the folks but I think I should be lonesome up to Stratham now.

I want you to give my respects to all the folks and I will write again when I get the box and before if it dont come soon. Friend Winslow is hauled up with the Rheumitism but thinks he is getting better. Charles French is first rate and tell Elizabeth that horse he rides cant be beat in no Battery. I want you to write as often as you can for a letter is better than gold out here. The first part of this letter that is wrote with a pencil I wrote a week ago. I should have sent it before but I had no postage stamp nor could I get one. I did have a dollar bill but could not get it changed without a discount and I would not stand it.

Tell Hitty[10] I am very much obliged to her and also all the other friends and I hope there friendship will not be misplaced.

Yours for the Union
John W Chase

Direct as before.
This ink is home made. We make it out of garget berries.[11]

* * * * * * * * * * *

Alexandria
Nov 7th 1861

Dear Brother

I suppose you begin to think it is about time to hear from the box you sent me. I received it last night it being directed to Washington and our teams not going over there and they being quite smart about it they would not Forward it until they got an order from the Captain but I have got it all right and am much oblidged to you and all the rest that helped to make it up for tobacco was getting awful short around the camp and I have not had a decent smoke untill last night for a fortnight but to day they are paying off and the boys are happy as clams at high water and I expect some of them are happier now than they will be after there money is gone for there is plenty of

[10] William and Hitty (Mahitable) Curtis were Sam's wife's brother and his wife.
[11] Garget berries were the same as poke berries.

sharpers of all kinds here to take all they can get hold of. I received a letter from my Mary last week and she wrote that she never got the two letters that I wrote to her and also said that she never knew whether I succeeded in getting the Bounty from the State. I have written to her that I suppose I was to have it as you have never wrote to the contrary. If there is any trouble about it I wish you would let me know about it and then I can write to her and let her know about it. I cant give you much news in the war line as we are still in the old place and for all I can see we are likely to stay here. We have got our tent fixed so that we can have a fire in it and are as comfortable as can be expected for Soldiers. We have made a change in the man that drawed our provision for us and we are living first rate now just as well as I want too. They drill us a little more than they did when we first came out here. That is when it dont rain. Rainy days we dont do anything but loaf. They are drilling us now in dismounting the Guns and Carriages and it is a little might like work I tell you but I like it better and better every day. I never done anything yet that I like so well as I do Soldiering but perhaps when we get into a fight I shall not like it so well but I feel as though I was ready for the devils and when I read the account of the battle at Edwards ferry I thought I should like to have been there and had a lick at them. I see by the papers that Massachusetts troops are cracked up very high but I have not seen any troops yet that looked any better or drilled any better than New York troops or any better Boys. They are just as good hearted set of men as ever I saw. We have six Regiments of them around us and they are rats I tell you at least they are my style.

I have just been in and got my pay $26,31 cts and I have sent $20,00 of it to you which I want you to send up to Stratham to Langdon.[12] I have sent it by Major Mason the Paymaster that paid us off. He will take about 2,000 from this Battery and as much more from Folletts and I suppose it will be very welcome to a good many familys at any rate. I think it will be by mine at any rate.

I want you to give my love to all the folks and Emily amongst the

[12] Langdon Jewell was the husband of John's sister-in-law, Sophia. They were caring for three of John's children, Mary, age 14, George, age 7, and Sarah, age 4.

rest. I want you to write as soon as you get this and tell Asher[13] to send just as many papers as he feels to for reading matter is always acceptable out here. I have been looking for a letter from Levi[14] but have not got it yet. I dont know why I have always got yours regularly and I dont know why his should miss. Friend Winslow has gone to the hospital. We have two men there with the Rheumitism and we have three more that have it slightly. The dews here are bad. If men are not very careful the fever and Augue[15] is rather prevalant but I dont think it will trouble me as I am too lazy to shake but to be serious all I ask is health and I am ready to fight when called for.

Yours truly
John W Chase to
Samuel S Chase

The money you had better send to the General. Let him send it to Stratham without someone is going down that will take it. That is when you get it.

Dear Brother

I had got my letter all wrote and was just a going to post it when the welcome cry of letters came and I went out with the rest and got one from you and was very much pleased for I found that it explained what I wanted to know in the other sheet as to the money that I have sent you. If it is not needed for the children and I dont suppose it will be as long as I get the Bounty from the state I should like very well to have it invested for me. I thought six dollars would do me for two months as it is not much that we actualy need out here without we are sick. In that case a little money works in very well but as long as I am well if I can get tobacco enough and enough writing Materials I am all right. As to Clothing I am very well supplied at present but some of the Regiments out are not so well supplied as we are. I have not seen a Regiment here that had near so

[13] Asher Chase was Sam and Elizabeth Chase's 20-year-old son.
[14] Levi Chase was John Chase's 38-year-old brother.
[15] Malaria.

good overcoats as we have got. In fact some of them have got none at all but the Government is doing all they can for them. I wish you would see what you can get a rubber coat for and if they dont come to high I think I will have one for there is so much wet weather here that a coat would work in very well on guard nights. As to the tobacco it is first rate and the other stuff was just what I wanted. Tell Emily that I am very much oblidged to her for those hankerchiefs and I hope that when I come back if I should be so lucky I shall find her settled down with a small family around her.

As for the climate here I agree with you for I think it colder here nights than it is in New England. At any rate I find it cold enough guard nights. Tell Elizabeth that young mans name is Richardson that led the horse up to her. He is the same one that cleaned the Parasol for her and it was his Mother that gave us the Bibles and he is just as good a fellow as ever lived. As for the Horse he is looking as well as could be expected for all of our horses look a little tough for they have to stand out in the storms and cold and then we have been rather short of feed and have to go a foraging for corn and hay for we cannot get any thing from Washington on account of the Blockade of the Potomac. I am going to try and get a pass to Alexandria and see the Marshall House and get a relic. If I succeed I will write and send you a peice.

Yours
John W Chase

I am very sorry to hear that Mrs Rollins is failing. I am in hopes she will yet recover and live years yet.

Speaking of whiskey there is no trouble about getting it. I wish there was for I dont think that it is any benefit to either Officers or men. I have seen officers out here that were so drunk they could hardly walk and I have seen others that had full enough for there benefit. I have not drinked but one glass of liquor since I came to Washington but I could have got plenty of it if I wanted but I have come to the conclusion that the less whiskey I drink the more money I shall have and I guess it will be as well for my health. At any rate I am going to try it a little while longer. I find I am gaining in weight and I dont want to do anything that will put me back. I want you to say to the Stratham folks that if they have not wrote that I shall not write again untill they do for I have not got time. If they have written I dont see why I should not receive them as well as yours. I have got one paper from Levi and a letter from Sis[16] and that is all. I should not advise Levi to enlist for I dont think he had ought to leave his family and another thing if a man is coming out here he wants to make up his mind to keep sober or else it is a hard place for him for if they get drunk they not only punish him with guard duty but they also fine him besides. I believe I have written all I can think of. At any rate I written as much as you can read for I am in rather a hard place to write for there is all kinds of games going on playing cards and most every thing else. We have some of the New York 16th in here and they are gay Boys.

so good night
Yours John

Tell Asher I received his papers for which I am much oblidged. Let me know when you get the money.

* * * * * * * * * * *

Alexandria
Nov 14th 1861

Dear Brother

I received your letter to day and take this chance to answer it. We have just got back from a grand review of this division. There was 12 Reg of infantry and 3 Batterys and one Reg of cavalry which makes Gen Franklins division. We were reviewed by Gen McClellan and his staff and for once I got a fair look of the Gen and he looked like a man that was not afraid of the cry of on to Richmond. He has got an

[16] Sis was John's sister, Sarah Ann Littlefield.

HARPER'S WEEKLY. A JOURNAL OF CIVILIZATION

Vol. VI.—No. 265.] NEW YORK, SATURDAY, JANUARY 25, 1862. [SINGLE COPIES SIX CENTS. $2.50 PER YEAR IN ADVANCE.

"LITTLE MAC" OUT AGAIN.

General George B. McClellan in *Harper's Weekly*, January 25, 1862 HW eye like a hawk. I looked him right in the eye and he done the same by me. I was bound to see what he looked like and I think I should know him if I should see him again. It was a bully review. The Infantry looked and marched finely. We think we have got just as good a division as there is out and Franklin they say is a tryer. He told our Captain last night that he need not be afraid but what he would have a chance to fight for if there was any fighting done in this part he was bound to be reckond in and I suppose if he is there we shall be. We have moved our camp a short distance. We have gone into an oak grove and intend to make it winter quarters. It is a first rate place out of the way of the wind and makes it a great deal better for the horses. We are going to patch up and bye boards for floors and then it will be gay as a lark. The Gen tells us if we have to go out to fight we shall take no tents with us and that encourages us to fix up a little. We had to cut down the trees to make a park for our peices and we had some work for a few days. I tell you soldiering is not all play but I think I can stand it if I am well and I have not been sick but one day since I have been here and that I think was caused by eating too much for I thought when we were first paid off I would indulge in a few extras and as the nigger said I could not have it but I believe I am all right now but if you send out a box I want you to send me a box of Rochelle powders[17] for I cant bye a box out here short of a dollar and I think you had better send it to Alexandria and direct your letters there also. I have not got only two papers from you since I have been here and the other boys are troubled the same way. One in our tent has six sent him every week. Sometimes he gets them and sometimes he dont but you can put some in the Box if you are a mind to. I got a letter from Thomas [Ham?] from Stratham to day and he wrote me that Pricilla[18] had written to me but I have not seen it yet. I have two in Stratham that I write too besides my own folks and I get answers from them and I dont see why the others should miss. I wrote two last week to Sis and have not got an answer yet. I should like to hear from my children if it is a possible thing but if I

[17] A laxative.

[18] Priscilla Chase was the wife of John's brother Levi.

cannot I suppose I shall have to bear it but it is rather hard. I shall write to you every week if it is a possible thing and I want you to do the same. My letters I know are not very interesting for we dont begin to see what the infantry see for they go out on picket and scouting and it is fun to hear them relate there adventures when they get back but I shall try and keep you informed of my whereabouts and when any thing turns up that I think will interest you I shall try and relate it in my feeble manner as uncle Noah used to say. I shall write to Stratham again tomorrow and if I cant get any answer to that I shall begin to think it is no use. Tell Ben I would write to him but I thought that he could find out all I had to say by going to your house but if he will write I will write to him. In regard to the money you understood me right and I wrote to Mary to that effect and I told her in case anything happened to them that they wanted more they could write to you and you would send it to them. I thought as you done the other business for me that you had better have charge of it all. I dont suppose the Paymaster will get to Boston next week but I am not afraid but what he will do the honest thing. You spoke of putting some potatoes in the box. We do get potatoes out here and good ones too but if some kind friend wants to send me a box of sardines tell them they would be very acceptable. Our Captain had a Proclamation for Thanksgiveing sent him and we intend to have a big dinner that day if nothing happens. Friend Winslow was up to see us yesterday. He thinks he is gaining. He is anxious to get out of the hospital although he says everything is well conducted but he feels lonesome.

Corporal Covell has been promoted to Gunner although he ranks the same. You know it is a step more towards promotion. Getting paid off was the result of taking the stripes off of one Gunner and one Chief of the Casson because if they had not been paid off they would not have got drunk and if they had not got drunk Covell would not been Gunner nor M. Green Chief of the Casson but such is the fact. I have not lost mine yet and God forbid that Rum should be the means of my losing them and I know if I dont drink any I shall not get drunk.

They begin to put it to the boys now when they dont do about right and I for one am glad of it for I think it will be all the better for those that want to do about right and you know if we dont have discipline we cannot have good soldiers.

I want you to give my love to all my friends and tell Emily that I will hope now that she will not get married at all and that I think that dress must be very handsome. I have pinned it up right over my bunk and it will often remind me of the good old times when she and Sarah F was with you and if you write to Sarah send her my love and best wishes.

yours for the union
J W Chase

I want Asher to get me a song called Annie Lyle. He can get one down to Partridges in Hanover Street for a cent and you can put it in a letter. We have great sings out here.

* * * * * * * * * *

Camp Revere Alexandria
Nov 20, 61

Dear Brother

I received your letter of the 15th tuesday night and sent down the same evening for the box but it did not come and I sent down to day and did not get it but you must not fret for boxes are often 8 and more days comeing and I should not have wrote but I thought you would want to hear. I answered your other letter the same day that I got it so you must not blame me for not getting an answer for you may rest assured that I shall write to you if I dont write to any body else but when I get the box I shall write again if it is tomorrow which I suppose you know is Thanksgiveing. We had a Proclamation with a letter from Gov Andrews[19] read to us last Sunday night at roll call and I tell you there was more than one wet eye when it was read for I suppose it made the boys think of home. I know it did me and I

[19] Governor John A. Andrew, an ardent abolitionist, was governor of Massachusetts during the war.

A New song call'd

ANNIE LISLE

Down where the waving willow
Neath the sunbeams smile,
Shadow'd o'er the murmering waters,
Dwelt sweet Anie Lisle,
Pure as the farest lily,
Never thouget of guilt,
Had its home within the bosome
Of lov'd Annie Lisle

CHORUS—

Wave willows murmur waters
Go'den sunbeams smile,
Earthly music cannot waken,
Lovely Annie Lisle,

Sweet came the hallow'd chiming
Of the sabbath bell,
Borne on the morning breezes,
Down the woody dell,
On a bed of pain & anguish,
Lay dear Annie Lisle,
Chang'd were the lovely featnres,
Gone the happy smile,

Toll bells of sabbath morning
I shal never more,
Hear your sweet & holy music;
On this earthly sho e,
Forms clad in heavenly beauty,
Look on me and smile,
Waiting for the longing sp rit,
Of your Annie Lisle,

Raisme in yourarms dear mother
Let me once more look,
On thegreen & waving willows
And the flowing brook,
Hark those stra ns of angel music
From the choirs above,
Dearest mother I am going,
Truly God is love,

P. Brereton, 1, Lr, Exchange St

Annie Lisle LC

suppose it did others. It has got to be a review here now about three times a week and to day has been what we call one of the reviews. We went out about 5 miles and had a grand review by Gen Mc and the President but I suppose the papers will give you an account and I will not try too but when any body says there was not one hundred thousand men there then I say they are no judge. I wish Samuel you could have been there. I never expected to see such an amount of troops together and the way I felt was just this. For Gods sake lets us make a grab at them fellows and see if we can stand them a hand or not but I suppose we have got to wait until somebody says go but I think that this review means something but whether it will be the means of getting us out of this wilderness or not remains to be proved. We had the New Hampshire Battery there and if they are not some for nine then I would not say so. We were only two miles from the rebels pickets were only two miles from us and you know I should just like to have made an advance and tried our luck. The Gen made a good appearance and I think he can chew as much tobacco as I can for the way he was chewing to day was a caution to anti tobacco chewers. The President was with him and I thought he looked kind of care worn and I dont wonder at it for God knows to look at that army and that only a part of the Grand Army was enough to make any one think that any body must have some care. I shall send you with this a picture and I want you to send it up to Mary. That is my Mary when you get a chance. I was on police duty the day I had it taken for missing a roll call and I thought I would have it taken in character. I had a dog at my feet but the artist only got a black spot and I could not get time to have it taken over for I had to wait three hours to have it taken but you can imagine there is a dog there and that will do just as well. We are going to have a Thanksgiveing dinner tomorrow. The boys have put in 25 cents apeice and are going to have a tuck out and myself and two others have stole a couple of chickens and they are out picking them now and we Intend to have a big time private. Give my love to all the folks Emily Included and excuse the [shortness of] this for too night is a busy [one].

I will write again as soon as I get the box.

From John W. Chase

The light is out.

* * * * * * * * * *

Camp Revere Alexandria
Nov 22nd 1861

Dear Brother

I received the box and contents this afternoon and have made an investigation of the contents this evening at supper and the conclusion is in my tent that whoever cooked the stuff was some pumpkins. I gave Richardson and French there pies for which they return there thanks and I also return mine to whoever in any way contributed to fill it up. The old saying is a true one that we dont know our friends untill we try them and I think I have proved mine very well and I hope that I may always prove worthy of there friendship and as the boys say out here never go back on them. Winslow is still in the hospital but he comes up once in a while to see us and I shall keep some for him for I think more of him than any other man in the Battery for he is just my style. As you remark in your letter it would have been pleasant to have had it the day you had yours but the boys had a dinner. They put in 25 cents apeice and had turkey and pies and had a very good dinner. For my part with four others we went in on our own hook. We had as good a pair of chickens as ever I saw and a plum pudding. We cooked it our selves. It took us about all day to do it but we enjoyed it first rate. Probably we did not do it up in so that it would have suited your appetite but we thought it was a big thing. We stole the chickens of an old secesh that has got a son in the rebel army and went up to the same place and begged some sage to put in the stuffing (for we had them stuffed we did). I wrote you in my last that we had a big review. I wish you could have seen it. It was up to baileys cross roads near munsons hill and is quite near the rebels. The most of the boys thought when we started that it was for a fight for we took our ambulances with us and all the Infantry took 40 rounds of powder and Ball but everything passed of well. One officer fell off his horse and broke his leg and that was all the accident that I have heard of. I thought when we were up there that day that it meant something and I think so still for the New York 16th and the Maine 5th camped right beside us are under marching orders and our left section with the two howitzers got orders at 12 o clock last night and left here at 1/2 past four this morning. There was a regiment of cavalry and two reg of Infantry went with them but where they are gone nobody knows. They took there blankets and coats with them so I suppose they intend to be gone at least one night and to night they tell us we must be ready to start at any moment. There has been cannonading going on all day in the direction of Fairfax but we have had no report that we could put any confidence in but as you may suppose we are very anxious to hear. The boys were sorry that we could not all go together but you know in military you have to obey orders but I believe we shall have a chance at them before long and if we do and I am numbered among those that fall I have one thing to ask of you and that is to remember these little ones I have left behind. I should like to live for there sake but Gods will be done. There has been two buried right by the side of our camp since Sunday and one sent home to New York. They all belonged to the new york 16th. One of them was on duty Wendsday and was buried to night at sunset. He died with the phistic[20] or tissic just as you are a mind to spell it.

I received a letter from my Mary to day and one from Eliza[21] last Sunday but have never got one from Pricilla but I wrote to her last week. I heard that she had written and I thought I would write to her. I believe I have got all the letters that have been sent me but hers and I dont understand it. By some means or other I dont get the papers that you sent me and I dont know as it is any use sending them for if I can get the letters I can get along and it is no use to send them if I cannot get them. Much oblidged to you for the papers in the box. I

[20] The phthistic was tuberculosis.
[21] Eliza was the daughter of John's sister, Mary.Littlefield.

have had a half dozen after them now for reading is getting kind of scarce.

There was a man killed by his Captain in the New York 31st last week. He was a little drunk and gave the Captain some back talk and the Captain being drunk run him through with his sword. He stabbed him three times so you see that they get rum out here for all the talk but that is a tough Reg the toughest that I know of around us and the 16th is the best one. They are from the northern part of the state and are most all country boys and good ones at that. I saw the Mass 14th and 9th in the review and they looked Bully. Blenker[22] was there with his Brigade and they looked as dutch as sour crout. They all had a sprig of box in there caps. I dont know what it was for but I suppose they do. The Manchester Battery was there. They are about as large a set of men as ever I saw together and I found some amongst them that I knew. Follett[23] was there and I dont think that he goes without his rum by the looks of him but his Battery looked and appeared well but we thought that we looked as well as any of them and was very highly complimented. The three Batterys in our division fired the salute and that you know is something to brag of. We were drilled to day by Capt Platt. He has command of these three Compys and he told our Capt after we got through that the Cannoneers and drivers done well but he did not say anything about the Officers. McCartney[24] was off with the left Section and I

Captain Follett USAMHI

[22] General Louis Blenker, a former New York businessman who was born in Germany, led a brigade manned almost exclusively of recent German immigrants.
[23] Captain Dexter H. Follett commanded the Third Massachusetts Light Artillery.
[24] First Lieutenant William H. McCartney was in command of the right section of the First Massachusetts Battery.

tell you when he is gone the Officers are all gone in my opinion that is for drill. The others are good men but they are too easy for the benefit of the men. Mc you will recollect was our Lieut but I suppose they thought he was the best man to go with them. I wish we had West Point men for officers for I have been over to the Regulars so much that I have come to conclusion that they know there Business and they look after the men better than the Volunteer officers do and dont work them any harder and I dont think so hard.

I suppose you have got my picture. I want you to send it up to Sis when you get a chance. You need not bother to send it by mail. I want you to write as soon as you get this and let me know if you have got it and the money too. I am not out of tobacco yet and will write when I am and when you send it want you to send me a box of Rochell Powders. I wrote you to send them in this box but you did not get the letter but I wrote the same day I got yours requesting me to write. Some times it take 4 days for a letter to come and some times we get them the next day after they are mailed. Give my love to every body and tell Emily I am very much oblidged to her. I liked to have forgotten to state that every thing came save but the pickels. The bottle broke but did not do any damage for the papers soaked up the vinegar so that it done no hurt at all.

Receive this with the thanks of your Brother.

J. W. Chase

I have had another meal off the thanksgiveing and find it tastes better and better. I am going to keep the turkey untill next Thursday and have another thanksgiveing. If you go up to Fathers[25] I want you to give my love to all the folks and tell them I should like to [be] with them and probably my mind will wander up that way.

The other boys got home last night. They went out 3 miles beyond our pickets and they drove the rebels off but did not get a chance to draw a bead on them. They were fortifying a place there. That was what they were sent out for. It is raining here great guns

[25] John and Sam's father, Andrew Chase, lived in Stratham, New Hampshire.

and our camp is all afloat but I begin to get used to such things now. I shall write to Father and Mary to day and if you go up you tell them to answer them.

Good Bye for the present
John W Chase

* * * * * * * * * * *

Camp Revere Alexandria
Sunday Nov 24th 1861

Dear Brother

I now sit down on the strength of a plum pudding which we have just devoured. I thought before I received that box of good things that we were living very well but since I got that I am disgusted with goverment food but I guess I shall come to it again after the contents are used up. There is 12 of us in our tent and we had pudding enough to give us all quite a good meal and the boys all unite in sending there thanks to the ladies that made them. There was 8 boxes came the same night that mine did and 6 the next day so that we have lived high for the last few days and our appetites were all in order to appreciate the good things sent us by our friends. I wrote up to my Mary yesterday that you was going up to Hampshire to Thanksgiveing and I wanted her to see if somebody did not want to give me a blanket and if they did you would take charge of it and send it out to me. Also some stockings. At any rate I want you to get one also two pairs of drawers and one of these jackets such as we used to work in. I want one that is not too thick to wear under my blouse for they are so thin that they are not warm enough and you can take some money and pay for them without some of these friends to the Soldiers wants to give them to a poor old Soger. The fact is I must have something to wear if we are going to stay in this God forsaken country for I believe it is colder than it is there. At any rate I know it is a good deal muddier here. Our camp is about half leg deep this morning. I have been in hopes we should get out of here and go on further South but I dont know but what we shall have to stay here all winter. At any rate I want to be provided for it for I dont want to get sick for if they do have a fight I want to be with the rest of the boys.

The day that I wrote you they had gone away. It seems they went out to drive away some rebels that were fortifying themselves out in Springfield but when they got there the rebels had left but the people told them that the rebel cavalry were there in the morning. The Section went 4 miles through the woods and had to cut there way. The Infantry left them and went another way and they [went] outside of our pickets. Rather poor management you will think I suppose and so thought Gen Harney who came up with our little squad and asked where the infantry was. Mc told him they had cleared out and left them. What says he nobody to protect you. Damn the New Jersey fellows he says. I will give them three days rations and send them to hell. He is a rough old duck and has only one arm but I guess he knows his bis I do. They passed through the camp of the 12th Alabama who left it last week and they found a board and mark on it [we] are the 12th Alabama 1200 men good for any 12,000 Yankees. I rather think they would have a good time. At any rate I wish they would just march this division up that way and that is just about what we could turn out and give us a chance to have a little skirmish so as to see what we could do. The boys said there was a lot of places that looked like new made graves and they judged there had been a good deal of sickness with them and I should think it quite likely for I dont believe that they can stand this climate so well as northern men and there is considerable sickness among our troops. The 16th New York have buried four men this week but our Company stand it pretty well so far.

You can put some tobacco in the box when you send it and dont forget those Rochelle powders and if you get this before you go up country I want you to tell Mary to beg me a peice of cheese among some of the cheese makers. I think a good deal of that cheese for that is something that will keep and any little relish of that kind tastes awful good. You can send the box to Alexandria and if we are ordered off there will be orders to forward things to us. I believe I have written about all I can think of for I have written so many letters this last week that I am about out of Ideas and I dont suppose you want me to draw on the imagination for the sake of making out a long letter. I have finally received the papers. I got eight in one day. I think they must have been blockaded on the road. No letter from Pricilla and you ask her if she has written.

Give my love to all the folks and tell Emily that pudding was very nice indeed and tell William and his wife that I will express my opinion of the turkey and cranberry sauce in my next letter for I have not eaten it yet. I wrote to Sis that I going to send her some morning glory seeds in a letter but I forgot to put them in but I will try and think of them next time. I will put some in this for you. I dont know as they will grow in a union country but you can try them.

From your Brother
John W Chase

* * * * * * * * * *

Camp Revere Alexandria
Dec 1st 1861

Dear Brother

I began to think that I was not a going to hear from you last week but Saturday brought me a double letter. The reason we did not get our letters before they sent ours to the first New York Battery and tried to send all theirs here but our mail carrier found out they did not belong to us and told them so but it came round all right and safe. I was in hopes that you would not send another box untill you received my last letter for I suppose you have received another by this. I supposed you was going up to Hampshire to Thanksgiveing and I had wrote to Sis for some things and I thought you could send them but if you have sent it is all right and if you have not why then it is all right but when you do send one I want you to send me a salt fish and two or three candles. I received a letter from Mrs Goodwin yesterday. It was a good long one and a very good letter. She wrote me that they were going to send me a box at Christmas. I also got a letter from Levi and one from Langdon and one from Sis this week so you see I have been well supplied this week and I think I ought to be for I have been writing all the time this last week for I have been off duty on account of eating to much and have had nothing else to do but I am well and hearty now and have got the turkey left yet for I dont mean to eat that until Winslow comes back which I suppose will be next week for he was up here yesterday and said he should if the doctor would let him. He thinks he is as well as he ever was. I spoke to him about having the picture taken and he said he was willing. I suppose It will cost a dollar to have them taken full length. I went over to day to have one taken with French but the artist was fixing up things and could not take them but we shall try it again in a day or two. He said he would pay for mine for the sake of having them together and I thought I could not do any better and we shall also try and get the dog. He is no secesh dog but in for the union. I am much oblidged for the postage stamps but I was not out for the Captain had a lot and I bought some of him but postage stamps are just as good as money out here but they cant come any 10 cent games on the boys of this Battery but it is a good deal as you say. Some of the sutlers[26] and pedlars would take a mans heart if they could sell it and I am afraid that a good many of the officers are more on their make than any love they have for their country but I like our officers well. They dont of course suit me all the time but I think they are as good as they will average. I suppose you know that Follett has resigned and his fourth lieutenant is booked for a Court Martial. What his crime is I dont know but I suppose the papers will tell you. One of our boy was court martialed yesterday but I have not heard the verdict yet but I tell you they are rough on the boys out here when they do get a lick at them but it dont trouble me any for I know if I do my duty it will be all right and I believe the stricter the discipline the better it will be for us. The stricter the better I say. Levi wrote me that some of the folks up there did not believe that I

[26] Sutlers were camp-following shopkeepers that sold food and clothing, etc., to the soldiers at inflated prices. Each regiment was allowed one sutler.

liked out here so well as I pretend I do. Well perhaps I am a damn fool and dont know what I do like but I dont happen to see it in light myself for in the first place when I enlisted I done it I believe with the Idea that we were not comeing out here to play Soldier but to fight when I was called upon to do so and I can truly say that if it needs my life to free my country from this Rebellion I am willing to let it go but I am not downhearted about that at all for I think that worse things than death can happen to a man and if I ever do get into a fight my prayer is that I may do my duty and if I dont you need never expect to see me that way again even if I should live for I should be ashamed to meet those friends that have been so kind to me since I have been out here and no man that way will ever have the priveldge of saying there goes a coward and as for being out here I never was so well contented in my life in no place that ever I was in to be sure. There is a good many things that are not so pleasant but I never got into a place yet but what there was. The most that troubles me here is the mud and rain but we have got a board floor now to sleep on and an old fashioned fire place built and we have it just as gay as they make them. I should like to have Elizabeth out here and take her round to the different camps. She would think that there was troops enough around here to eat up the Southern Army niggers and I dont know what is up but the way they have put the troops up above us the last week is a caution and the story is that we are going to have a fight but I suppose that Gen McClellan knows and I am of the opinion that if he does make a move he wont do it without he is pretty sure of going into the king row. I should say that there was 150000 troops within a circuit of 20 miles around here but what it means of course we cant tell for you know Soldiers are not supposed to know much any way but I suppose that after Congress gets together that some thing will be done. One thing we do know that is that the rebels are falling back but I suppose they think to draw us on to Manassas again but I think if they do that we shall not stop there but go a little farther at least I hope so.

I wish it was so that you could come out here this winter and it seems as though you might in some of those excursion trains. You could see the great Capitol of the Nation and more Soldiers than you ever did before but I suppose you know your own business best. If we dont have to leave here I mean to try and get over to Washington one day after Congress meets for I have not had a furlough yet and I begin to think it is about my turn.

You must give my love to all the folks and excuse this letter for we are full of company this afternoon and can hardly get room to move much more to write. I expect there would be some sputtering if you had to write crowded up as we are and as many gabs a going but we have to put up with it for you know we think that our Brother Soldiers friends are our friends and we are all glad to see them and talk with them.

I am going to write to Eliza to night if the candle holds out. They keep us rather short on light but we make out pretty well by buying one once in a while. Give my best respects to Mace and all the rest.

J W Chase

Tell Elizabeth she was mistaken about the vinegar hurting the things in the box for the rags soaked up all the vinegar and perhaps if it had hurt them a little I should not eat so much. I have some of the cheese left now for I am kind of stingy of that for it suits my taste very well. We had some indian Johnny cakes last night for supper. Baked them in those tin pans. I dont think I shall send them back for we can buy a little indian meal and we can just bake them in our fire place. I suppose if she was out here she would think we did keep our dishes so clean as we might but the box makes me a very good cupboard. Before I got that I had to keep them under my head but we are not so particular as we might be I suppose. I wrote down east last week and I am in hopes to hear from there before long. Tell Emily that I remain about the same and hope she is. I should like to see her and see if I could worry her any now. I have worn my bracelet off and have got it safe in my pocket book. I shall hang on to that for I want to know what it means if I ever get back again. I am going to write to Langdon in a day or two and he may want some of that money I sent you for he can not collect a note I left with him. The money is at the Mayors office in Boston. If you have not got it you can get it by calling there.

Write Soon. Good Bye for the present.

* * * * * * * * * *

Camp Revere Alexandria Va
Dec 6th 1861

Dear Brother

I received your letter to day which I was anxiously looking for and I will commence by answering your inquiries about Mr Coy. He is in our detatchment. As to what he has wrote home the facts are just these. When we first came out here we had a quartermaster that did not know his business. He was a first rate fellow but could not keep a hotel and we lived a little rough but I made out to stand and probably he could if had thought so but he is like some others I suppose he thought he could send home a good story and get some money and some thing to eat and it would pay. He has had both sent him but he sent home money when he was paid off. He has not drinked much since he has been out here but he is always growling about his comeing and you know when a man is not satisfied with his lot he is hard to please. As to what he wrote about McCartney it is a damn lie. The right half of the Battery that comes directly under him I will bet money two thirds will say they like him better than any other officer in the Company but some of the loafers that dont know anything and dont want to dont like him for he is just the man to put a man through if he thinks he is trying to shirk and that is just the man that I like. He uses rather hard language some times but he is just a good hearted a man as ever was made. At any rate he suits me and that is all I care about. When I write to you I intend to write what I believe to be truth for when I came out here I did not expect to fare as well for grub but the most of the time we have had enough. Our Orderley Sargeant draws the grub for us now and we are liveing very well. There is some things that we can not get now that we did when we first came out here. Potatoes & beans for instance but our Orderley says we shall have what he can get and enough of it but I have lived so far and gained on it and I guess if we never live any worse we shall not die of starvation but I did not come out to find fault and I think if I want anything that I can get it without writing anything home to worry folks out of it for I dont think they would take much comfort to be thinking that I was starving to death. I think when I get some thing more to keep me warm I shall go it. But I dont want you to say anything about Coy that will implicate me any for he is behaveing a good deal better now than when he first joined the Battery for he used to be drunk all the time then but he has not drinked but very little now and I dont want to say anything about him for I think when he is steady he is a pretty good kind of a man. I am glad to hear you talk of comeing out here and I think you will see Soldiers enough if you dont happen to see a Review and we never know more than a day or two before hand when we are going to have one but the talk seems to be now that we shall shortly have a different kind of a one from what we have been having. Our Orderly told me to day that it takes 30,000 more loaves of bread for the troops on this side of the Potomac than it did last week and still they come. We could hear the drumming last night. They were marching all night long so you can judge whether there is any troops around here or not and I hope we shall get a chance to have a hack at the rebels before the fun is all over. We had the reports of the battles that have been fought lately read to us last night at roll call and there was a little noise for a spell you had better believe. I kind of think that the boy will spoil if we dont have a fight soon but I suppose we shall have to wait untill the little General says the word for I dont think he intends to have another failure if he can help it. I had a letter from my Mary yesterday and she said that George wanted to know if I had killed a man yet.

Winslow has got back with us. He is quite well now but I am afraid that so much wet weather will bring him down again. We had roast chicken for dinner to day at his expense. He received a box yesterday with a pair of chickens and a duck and other fixings and

George Chase CFC

among the rest a pint of whiskey and a pint of gin. I indulged in a nipper of gin and I pronounced it good. The first since I left that part of the country. As for that dog that Elizabeth wants to know about it is one that French brought out with him. He is a big black one and weighs 75 lbs. He sleeps at my back and he is a bully dog I tell you and he can clean out any Secesh dog there is in this part of the country.

I suppose you saw an account of a scrape that some of our men had with the rebels when they were out a foraging. If you did it is a damn lie and if we knew who wrote it we would just clean him out for we dont want any such stories wrote home to trouble folks nor no credit untill we earn it. I could fill a sheet every day if I should write all the camp stories that are going the rounds but I know you can get lies enough in the papers without my writing any to you. There was a little peice in the Saturday Gazette stating that when we passed the President at the big review he turned to Mc and said that is the best Battery I have seen yet. Well we did look kind of bully that day. We had our over coats on and turned the capes back and buttoned the corners together so that it showed the red and it looked first rate. The Idea was original with us but I taken notice that Folletts & the Manchester Battery saw the point very quick and it was not long before theirs was fixed the same way. We had a big drill to day you had ought to seen us when we came in. We were all covered with mud for it was muddy as the devil. It will freeze here a little nights and about the middle of the day it is awful I tell you and we have to recite lessons out of the Instructions book twice a week to the officers that is we non commissioned fellows and next week we have got to be examined before Capt Platt of the regulars. Dont know how we shall come out but hope for the best. They or rather he thinks that is necessary for officers to know how to do it right and I suppose it is. I want to for one and I want them that is over to know too. I want you to give my respects to all the folks and tell them I am not sick of Soldiering yet for I like better and better every day. I will write again when I get the box and before too if it dont come next week. One of our boys got one to day that started the 20th. He had a roast turkey and some other things in it. They were all spoiled but I suppose the salt fish will keep. Mary wrote me that she was going to send me a box and I wrote to her not to send any thing rich for it made me sick and I had rather have some thing that would keep a spell. Give me good plain food and I am all right. I will get some different envelopes. I guess I can find some for they have most all kind out here.

Saturday Morning

Have just been to breakfast. Had roast duck and fried pork bread and coffee so you see we are on our good feed. Most to high for sogers. I hope I shall not get sick for Winslow has got a good nice ham and two salt fish. I have not eaten my turkey yet so you can guess that I am not quite starveing yet but I thought that would keep and I might want it more some other time.

We have got to wash up the gun carriages and cassons to day. Have to go through with it every Saturday and Inspection every Sunday.

Give my love to Emily and all the rest of the folks and tell them we are comeing out all right one of these days so good bye for this time.

From your Brother
J W Chase

I have just been to supper and had the turkey served up. Winslow acted as boss as I was busy writing. It was first rate at any rate we all pronounced it so and we think we are good judges. I am glad to hear that Mace is reelected. I read in the Herald that Hunneman was nominated by the Constitutional Union and Democrats.[27] I think them partys must be growing small by the vote that Hunnemans got. I suppose Mace will kick Sam Felton now if he says anything too him Impudent.

I want you to tell Emily I am sorry to hear she has the heart complaint. I used to think I had it but I have got bravely over it now but dont know but what I should have a relapse if I should chance to come back to New England for I have not seen a woman since I left there that I think would give it to a man.

I have come to the conclusion that there will not be much fighting done in this section this winter without Congress forces the Gen into but I think he is the man that will not allow even Congress to tell him his business but I suppose some of them begin to think it is costing a good deal of money and I guess most any body would think so if they could be here a little while and see the baggage trains go along some times 200 in a string and to look around here and see the men and horses it looks as though somebody had some bills to pay but I think McClellans policy is to do as little fighting as possible but I for one am willing to leave it with him.

I had a letter from Pricilla to day and have got well booked up. She thinks my picture is a good one but thinks it looks haggard as they all do that come out here. I cant say that I think that we look haggard for I think I look pretty rugged. Winslow is setting by my side blowing about the Corporal and I shall have to close soon to have an argument. He sends his respects to you and says when he comes back he hopes he shall have the pleasure of meeting you again. He often speaks of going in to Haywards down to the depot. He is a first rate man a regular growler but if he likes a man he likes him and if he dont he will soon find it out. He went up to the 18th with me yesterday and a good many of them are acquainted with him

[27] The Constitutional Union party was an outgrowth of the former anti-Catholic, anti-immigrant, "Know Nothing," American party. To try to avoid disunion, it had taken no stand in the election of 1860, for or against slavery. Southern Democrats strongly supported slavery, even at the cost of disunion, while northern Democrats tolerated slavery to try to preserve the Union. Republicans strongly opposed slavery, and many supported the use of force, if necessary, to preserve the Union.

and they told me that there was no danger of his ever deserting a man as long as there was life in him but he blows me as much as he wants too. He says I am no Corporal because I wont put on the stripes but some of these fellows put on so many airs with there stripes that I am rather disgusted and I dont think I can afford to put out a dollar to have them put on.

I want you to tell John Davis that I got some books that I suppose came from him and I am oblidged to him. They were directed in this way give these books to Jack Chase a member of your Battery J F Davis and I concluded they must come from Salty Davis. Respects to all the folks and tell them I am not home sick a mite nor dont mean to be.

J W Chase

* * * * * * * * * *

Camp Revere Alexandria
December 15th 1861

Dear Brother

I received your letter last night and take the first chance to answer it for I went a visiting yesterday and did not get home untill dark and then had to go to work and fix up my bunk for they had been policeing the tents and I found my bed and boards piled out into the open air and this forenoon we have been out for inspection and the Doctor has been here and examined us and our quarters yesterday. I went up about five miles above where we are. Went as far as there was any encampments and visited the 18th 29th Mass Regs and Folletts and the Manchester Batteries. The 18th is a bully Reg and they have got a new french uniform like the french Chasseurs. It is a gay looking rig. They have also got new tents and camp equipage and a complete outfit all from france. It is a big thing I tell you. They have picket tents they can carry on there knapsacks. The knapsacks are made of goat skin with the hair on. I saw one all packed with tent and all on it. I think I should have hard work to put the stuff back in its place if I should go to work and take it out. The whole concern is a present from Prince de Joinville[28] and three Regt have the same. The other two are one from New York and one from Michigan. I also visited the camp of the Garabaldis. There camp is all trimmed up for Christmas and it beats all the evergreen trimming that ever I saw. Great arches 20 ft high with eagles Stars and most all kind of devices on them you can think of. I thought when I was looking at it how Elizabeth would admired it if she could see it. I wish she could come out here and visit the different camp. I am afraid she would think we thought more of fixing up our quarters than we did of fighting but you know it is a good deal better for the men to be at work than it is laying around in there bunks and it takes up there mind and makes them feel gay and happy still but now I have given you the bright side I will write you some of the stern realities of Army discipline.

Last Friday we were ordered out that is our Division to witness the execution of a spy. He belonged to a cavalry Comp attached to this division from New York. The troops were formed in three sides of a square in two ranks about eight paces apart and first came a waggon containing a coffin and behind that the prisoner in an open waggon with a priest by his side and behind him twelve men of his Comp on foot with Carbines eleven of them loaded with ball and one with blank cartridge and the rest of his Comp brought up the rear. They came in on the right of the square and went all the way round and brought him into the centre the bands playing a dead march. They then seated him on his coffin and blindfolded him. The officer then formed the men that shot him about four paces in front of him and dropped his hankerchief and that was the last of the deserter. The troops were then formed in column and marched by him as he lay on the ground. He had four balls through his head that I saw and I suppose there were more in the other parts of his body. I suppose some of the folks will think it was rather hard but I cant say that I felt any ways bad for him. I never felt as though I should want to see any one hung but I did want to see him shot for according to his own

[28] François Ferdinand Philippe Louis Marie was an observer of the war for the government of France. He was the son of the former king of France, Louis Philippe d'Orleans. He was also a sketch artist and watercolorist of war scenes.

confession he enlisted with the intention of deserting and I could just stand all day and see such men as those shot and I think I could help shoot them with a bold hand but his race is run and I hope every other traitor will share the same fate.

We have had beautiful weather here the last week. Frosty nights but splendid days but I am afraid it will not last much longer for it begin to grow thick now as night approches and looks as though we were going to have a storm. We have had visitors from Cambridge here the last week. The Mayor and one of the Alderman and a young mans Father from Boston. They came round and see us all and as we had a good dinner of Roast Beef that day we were in pretty good spirits. We are living very well now for we have had four boxes come into our tent within a week and when we get any thing we generally distribute a part of it and then we have bought a linen and had a feed on that. I calculate I can stand it a spell longer as far as grub is concerned. You did not say in your letter whether you had sent the box or got the money but I took it for granted that you had.

I have got to write to Eliza to night. I received a letter from her yesterday. She wanted me to ask you if you had forgotten her. She said the General weighed 211 lbs. I think he will do but I must close or I shall have to make her letter Short as I have got to answer hers and Pricillas to night if I can.

So good bye for this time
John

* * * * * * * * * * *

Camp Revere Alexandria
Dec 22nd 1861

Dear Brother

I received your letter to day and was very happy to hear that you was still around. You need not fear but what you will get a letter from me every week for when I dont write to you I shall not write to any one and I dont intend it shall be my fault if you dont get one that is if it is possible for me to write. This last week we have been pretty busy for we have been building sheds for our horses and I have been at work at the old trade. It seemed kind of natural. We shall move some time this week if the weather is pleasant and I shall be glad when the fuss is over for I think it will be quite an improvement on this camp. Our sheds are built so as to form three sides of a square two hundred feet on each side and the back side of the regulars makes the other side and we are going to have our tents inside of the square and I think it must be pretty warm and we are going to have stoves in our tents so you see we go in for comfort but the weather lately has been such that we did not need much fire but to day it is cooler and it feels like snow but I am in hopes it will keep away untill we get moved and fixed up a little and I suppose by the time we get well settled we shall have to move again for that has been the way so far but I dont care if they will only move us farther south for I am getting sick of this part of the country and want to be on the move if we have to fight our way through.

I have not got the box yet. There was seven came last night and they had only been on the road four days but the other Corporal in our detatchment had one that was three weeks comeing and it had a big turkey and lots of stuff in it and it was most all spoilt. It made us feel kind of bad to have to throw it away but it was no use but I am in hopes that mine will be here this week for if it is going to be cold I shall want them. I shall send the receipt down by the Orderly Seargeant tomorrow and see what he can do with it and I guess it will come all right yet. Langdon wrote to me about that money. The fact is when I came away I left some money for him with my Mary but some how or other there was a misunderstanding about it and the money was used for another purpose and then I left a note and the man agreed to pay it in a month and he has not paid it yet so you see take it all together it brought me in debt for the Childrens board more than I knew anything about for I wrote to Langdon twice and he never got the letters but he finally did get one and he wrote me how it was and I told him to write to you and you would send him some. You can send him what you have on hand after paying for the things. They cant have only what there is. It was always my luck if I owed a man anything they wanted it but if some of them owed me they thought I did not want it but I dont say this to complain of Langdon for he has been a good friend to me and I want him to have every cent that is due him. He wrote me that he was short on account of his boy going to house keeping and you know how it is with Farmers. They want to keep there crop for a good price and I dont know as I blame them. I suppose that pay day will be around again soon and then I am in hopes to send you some more for I mean to try and keep out of debt if I can and I want the children taken care of and God only knows where I could get them to be as well situated as they are now. They are all I have to live for now and I want them to remember they have a Father that has not forgotten them because he is out of there sight. I suppose I shall have some stockings when I get the box from Mary as Sis wrote me that I was going to have some sent me and I could drawed my drawers out here but I have had about enough of Goverment Clothes and I think I can do better than to buy underclothes of them at there prices. I should like to get hold of some of these army contractors and hang them on a tree for some of the stuff they make up for Soldiers is not worth one half we are charged for it. What would you think of three dollars for a blouse such as we had out at Camp Cameron. That is the price sent out here from Mass and you know we are charged with everything we had there and they charge it to the General Gov but our Clerk would not make out the clothing list by the prices sent out for he said he knew it could not be right. Take one of the shirts worn by the Regulars and it is worth two that we have and about the same by there other clothes but the next time we get any we shall get the same as they do. I suppose the only objection I have to there shirts is they are white and I dont think they look as well as grey but I am hopes that when I get what you have sent I shall have enough to last me this winter and I know I shall have outside clothes enough for if we are going to stay here all winter I dont think we shall do much drilling and shall not wear out so many as we otherwise should but if we have any fighting to do we may get a chance to wear out some in the cause. The boys out here talk as though they did not care whether England went to war with us or not for they think then that we shall surely get a chance to try our guns and courage too. The most of the excitement out here is the talk about Gen McClellan for it seems that some of the wise men seem to think he is not the man. They could not do a worse thing in my opinion than to remove him for as far as I have had a chance to inform myself the rank and file think he is just the man to lead us on to victory WHEN HE GETS READY and not when Horace Greely[29] says go or any other nigger lover. For my part I think he is just the man and the kind of a man that can keep a Hotel and I am in hopes that reason and not passion may rule in the council of the nation but I must draw to a close for it is my night to take the guard and I have got to get up at midnight and I shall want a little sleep and it has begun to rain so you see I shall have it kind of rough. Winslow has got a cold and he is growling around. He says if you come out here he will try and get you a drink. French and Covell are well and in fact we have but one man that is sick to amount to anything. You must give my love to all the folks and tell them I am not down hearted yet. I am bound to go in for the union. Much obliged to Lizzie for the words of that song and hope she will not get down hearted because Henny is gone away but try and enjoy herself as well as she can under the circumstances. I shall write just as soon as I get the Box.

yours for the union
J W Chase

* * * * * * * * * *

Camp Revere Alexandria Va
Dec 26th 1861

Dear Brother

I sit down to let you know that I received the box to night and found every thing all right for all it has been about three weeks a comeing but the trouble seems to be at the office in Washington.

[29] Horace Greeley was the editor of the *New York Tribune*, and was a strong and influential abolitionist.

Some of our men went over there last Tuesday and found 25 boxes for the Battery and yesterday there was five of them came over and to day there was 20 more and they say there is more to come. It has been a great time for boxes this week. There was over two hundred went up to the ninth Regt to day. There Lieut Col would not let them come until after Christmas but I guess they made out to have a good time without them. Some of our boys was up there yesterday and I had an invitation but the other Corporal was off and the Seargeant intended to go and I got skun out of it but I mean to go up there New Years if it is possible. They have got there Camp trimmed up in great shape and the news that Col Corcoran[30] had escaped from the rebels makes them feel about as good as it is possible for men to feel. I think if they had kept him and hung him that they would marched on to the rebels whether they had got orders or not for the Celtic blood was up. Christmas was the dullest day I have seen since I have been out here for a good many of our boys was off and we had an order from head quarters to have no drilling nor labor without such as was actually necessary and I was loafing around Camp all day but the New York troop around us had a big time. The 16th had there Camp with Chinese lanterns last night and they had a big time generally but all the amusement I had was a little pistol shooting. Winslow and myself started out a foraging for a little whiskey but did not make a raise for everything was dry and we could not get down to Alexandria for we had no pass and the road was full of the Provost Guard and them are the fellows that Soldiers dont like to meddle with much without he has a taste for the Guard house. We had a dinner of roast beef yesterday with sweet potatoes and cranberry sauce and apple dumplings for supper but as Father used to say we dont live so every day but he would appreciate a good dinner I reckon if he was out here and I reckon he would eat it if it did not have just the right scald on it but I make out to live and shant find any fault if we always live as well as we do now but I am getting tired of this hanging around camp and doing nothing for I [am]

[30] Colonel Michael Corcoran of the Sixty-ninth New York Infantry, "The Fighting Irish."

getting too lazy to turn over. We have not had a drill now for a fortnight but have been building stables but have not moved our camp yet but think some of going tomorrow if it is fair and I shall be glad when we get settled down once more for it is something of a job to get everything fixed up so as to have it handy and I hope the next time we move it will be for a fight for I want to do something to get the rust off but perhaps I shall be as glad to get out of it but I came out here to fight and I want a chance to try it on but I suppose we shall have to wait untill they tell us to go for I suppose there is bigger heads than mine at work. If there is not I pity them. One of our Seargants a signal Seargant that is in favor with the powers that be went to day to Mount Vernon and he brought home a few holly leaves and a few small stones that he brought from the walk around the tomb. He gave me one which I enclose thinking perhaps it might be acceptable at this time. He says it is almost impossible to bring off anything in the shape of a relic and the Agent says if he should let every one that wants bring away a peice of the shrubbery there would not be a bush left on the place. I hope if I live to have a chance to visit it myself before I come back but you know it is no use for a common Soldier to think of travelling around much without he has an influence with those in authority which I dont happen to have but I may live to get out of it and if I do I mean to see some of this part [of] the country. You spoke about sending a bird home. I have not seen a bird since I have been here but plover and I guess it would be hard work to catch one of them. I have been thinking of sending her an Opussum but did not know as she would fancy such a pet. We had three in camp at one time but we have had a good many visitors here from Boston and vicinity lately and they have cleaned us out but they will probably hunt some more the next good moon.

We had a pretty high wind and a big rain here last Sunday night and I thought that blanket would be very acceptable but with overcoats and Winslow and my blankets we laid as warm as a bug in a rug. I have not laid cold a night yet and I think with the extra blanket I can go it now just but that night the wind blowed so I thought the old tent would be over but it made out to stand although some of them blowed down but could not have any fire for the sparks flew. Some were afraid we should get our tents on fire but you know we must have some troubles in this world and Soldiers must expect to have there share.

I want you to tell William I am much oblidged to him for that Cheese and Asher for the tobacco and to all the others that done anything towards making up the box and hope they take the comfort in bestowing that I do in receiving, If they do they will take a good deal. The Frock is a good one and the blanket will answer just as good a purpose as a thicker one. I shall try it to night but the weather here is a devilish sight more Changeable than it is in New England for some times it changes about four times a day and these fools cant or wont tell you whether the weather is very cold here or not. I dont think they know enough to last them over night any way. I want you to give my love to all the folk and tell Mace I will tell him something I want him to send me the next time you send a box.

I want you to come out here if it a possible thing but if Johnny Bull[31] pitches in I suppose you will have a chance to see Soldiers enough without comeing here but tell the folks the boys out here are not frightened with talk and think we can just clean them out if they pitch in but I am not a going to brag but tell them all that I feel as though I was ready to go in for God and my Country so good Bye for the present.

J W Chase

Friday Morning

Put on the new drawers and frock and find them very comfortable for we are haveing one of the Secesh winds and it blows so we cant have any fire so we have to pile on the clothes.

Tell Mr Adams I shall think of him wet nights when I am on guard and I am very much oblidged to him. Last night at mid night I was woke up by the band serenading Gen Franklin and they closed with sweet home and I thought how many of us never will see that

[31] The British.

place again but I hope if we never meet here we may meet in heaven.

This extract that I enclose is true as Gospel. [No enclosure found.]

* * * * * * * * * * *

Envelope of January 2, 1862 CFC

Camp Revere Alexandria
Jan 2nd 1862

Dear Brother

I have just finished reading your letter for I have been off all day. I got a pass and went over to the New Hamp 5th and then went to Alexandria with a Capt Murray of Portsmouth belonging to that Reg and I reckon I had a pretty good time. It is the first time I have been to the city since I have been here and I dont care much about going there again for it is a kind of a God Forsaken looking place but it is filling up with Eastern men that have come out here to trade with the Soldiers. I suppose you have got the letter that I wrote you about the box. I find the frock works in quite handy but the weather is not very severe here yet. Yesterday I was running around in my shirt sleeves and to day we wanted overcoats on so you can judge that the climate here is not very even. I think Old New England is rather before it yet I do myself. I am going to write now and ask a little advice. I received a letter from my Mary to night and she wrote me she did not go to school this winter because they did not think they had a very good master. Now I dont want to judge anyone wrong but last winter it was just the same and I begin to think that they want her to help do the work for last winter they had no hired girl and this winter Henny has gone to keeping house and they keep no girl now. I have always paid them just what they said was right for the Childrens board. I know it has always been a small sum but if I pay any one what they say is right then I expect it is right and it appears to me a girl 14 years of age ought to go to school all she can for god knows I cannot afford to send her to school without is to a common school if I should live and I feel as though she should improve every chance for her education is not very great at present and when I read the letter I was a little mad but thought I would not write to her untill I cooled off and thought I would just ask your opinion about it. I dont want you say anything about it to anyone for you know a few words would be multiplied if they should happen to hear them and I may be jealous for nothing but you know my Children is all I have to live for now and I am a good ways from them now but I want you to write as soon as you get this and let me know what you think of it and I shall not write to her untill I hear from you. We were mustered in last Tuesday and probably shall be paid off in a few days and then I shall have the picture taken and I am going to have one taken for Eliza. We have got moved into our new camp and have got pretty well fixed up now but I suppose by the time we get fixed up to suit us we shall have to move again but I hope if we do it will be for a fight but I dont know as ever we shall have a chance to immortalize ourselves any way. Only on reviews. We get enough of them. So many that I have got tired of them but I suppose it is no use to find any fault with the powers that be.

The Irish out here dont feel very well because the trouble between England and this country is settled but I rather think it is best to lick old Jeff and his minions first. One of our Regts left us to day. They have gone to join Burnsides[32] expedition. It is said that he wanted this Battery to go with him but I suppose they think it is better to keep us loafing here and doing nothing.

I shall enclose with this a peice that I cut out of a paper that was in the box you sent me I want you to keep it for me if ever I come back. [No enclosure found.] I want it to look at and read to remember Philadelphia Ladies by. I thought I was about as tough a fellow as there was out but I cant read that peice and think of the attentions paid to us at that time without pipeing my eye a little mite. If everything that is wrote was as true as that peice it would be different than it is now but I must close for I dont feel very happy to night besides being awful tired so give my love to all and tell them I am not going to give up yet.

J W Chase

Write as soon as you get this and keep shady.

* * * * * * * * * *

Camp Revere Alexandria
January 9th 1862

Dear Brother

I have just finished reading your letter and thought I would sit down and write you a few lines. I dont feel much like writing for we were paid off Tuesday and there has not been much sleep in this camp since but I am in hopes the excitement will begin to die away for they have got about a dozen in the guard house and some of the worst ones on the spare wheel and that generally stops there noise. You will find enclosed in this letter a check for fifteen dollars which will be paid at the Mayors office in Boston & the Book went this morning and you can get the money just as soon as you are a mind to go after it. I should have sent twenty but I am oweing a little bill up in Hampshire and thought I would send it up in a letter and I want to

[32] General Ambrose E. Burnside led a successful campaign in coastal North Carolina.

go over to Washington and stop a couple of days for if we are going to stay around here I want to do something to amuse myself for I am getting sick and tired laying around here doing nothing but loafing. I dont wonder you are sick of reading the lies in the papers for they know just as much about it as you do. I was in hopes we should go in Burnsides expedition. There was four divisions went from around Washington and two Batterys and several detached companies from this side but I guess if we get any farther South we shall have to go by the way of Manassas gap but I hope we shall get to Richmond some way before long for I want to see this thing settled one way or the other. The talk here now is that within ten days we shall make a move but I have heard that story so many times that I begin to grow tired of it but I know for the last few days we have done more to get into fighting order. They have been distributing pistols and fixing up generally so that now we are all ready and waiting for the word go and I hope when we do go we shall go right through in good shape.

If you go up to Stratham I should like to have you talk to my Mary and tell her that she ought to go to school and you can talk her into I guess and not have them mistrust that ever I wrote anything to you about it. I am willing she should stay with Langdon and rather she should stay there than anywheres but I want her to go to school and improve her chance now for Learning for I know now is the time. I shall write to her to night and tell her so. Tell Mr Seaverns that Coye got his box and I had a slice of ham and a peice of pie out of it and I thought the ham was about the thing I did. Coye sent home 20 dollars so you see he dont fool away all his money. I dont think he will ever make a great Soldier for it is almost impossible to learn him anything. He seems to be willing enough but he cant seem to learn. Winslow and myself are going to have that picture taken next Sunday if nothing happens. I had a letter from Eliza to day. She is still at North Berwick. I want you to give my respects to all the folks and tell them I am rugged as a bear. The men in our tent were weighed the other day and we averaged 160 lbs each and had gained on an average 10 lbs so you see that Soldiering agrees with us. Most every man in the Comp has gained but there are some that have fell away. Covell is sick and in the hospital. He has the inflamation of the bowels but he is getting better. We have all sorts of weather here now. Since I wrote before it has been cold and we had about two inches of snow but last night it rained and to day it is as muddy as ever you saw it I guess and you are in danger of losing your boots in the mud but it is warm enough to day to go in your shirt sleeves. Give my love to Emily and write as soon as you can. You must excuse this writeing for I have a man by the side of me that has been to happy hollow and they are rather jolly so good bye.

From J W Chase

* * * * * * * * * *

Camp Revere Alexandria
Jan 11th 1862

Dear Brother

I have just been over and had the pictures taken and you will find them enclosed here. The photograph is one that Winslow had taken in Boston before he came away. You must excuse the dress for the mud is about knee deep and we dont like to dress up more than we can help but they all say here that they are first rate pictures. I am going to have one taken for Eliza and I shall send it to you and let you send it up. Winslow says you must not make fun of his cap for it was so small that he could not make it set anywheres on his head but I am not going to make any excuses about mine for it is hard work to get a picture taken here there is so many rushing in to get one and the accomodations are not quite as good as they are in Boston but it is the best I could do. My health is first rate and if it was not for this devilish mud it would be lovely for the weather over head is first rate. Give my love to all the folks and let me know when you get the pictures. The Secessionists tried to blow up the Hospital in Alexandria but I suppose you will see an account of there damned works in the papers and I will not write it. If I could have my way I would burn the place down for I believe there is just as much Secesh

Ben Winslow and John Chase CFC

there as there is in Richmond and I think they have borne enough from the devils.

Hopeing soon to hear from you I will close.

J W Chase

* * * * * * * * * * *

Camp Revere Alexandria
Jan 16th 1862

Dear Brother

I received your letter to day and was glad to hear that you still live. I sent the likeness to you last Sunday and did not intend to write again untill I heard from that but did not know as you would get it so I thought I would sit down and write a few lines and send you another picture one that I intend for Mrs. Goodwin or at least I had it taken for her but I am going to have another taken if I can ever get a chance but it is as much as your life is worth to get a picture taken. I was down to Alexandria and went into the Marshall House. They have opened a place there to take miniatures but they take mean pictures. It is the name of the place that makes them go any way but I thought I should rather send a good picture if I could get it and I think I have got it but perhaps the next one will be better. At any rate I want you to keep them both untill I send you word where to send them for I want to send one up country and I want to send a good one for perhaps it will be the last chance that I shall have to send one and I want to improve the chance.

You want to know how I like my coat. I like it first rate. I have a chance to try it several times and it answered every purpose. There has two or three of our boys that have got new ones they bought out here and I would not swap with them. The tobacco is very good. It dont make much odds to us out here for it is a good deal better than any we get here. I thought I had written all about the contents of the box before but I got one from Exeter about the same time and have written so many letters that I get them mixed sometimes for I write a letter most every day but I am going to cut off some of my correspondents for I dont think it pays to have quite so many. Somehow or other I cannot get a letter from Pricilla. I have not heard from her for a month. I have written to her twice and to Father twice but I get a letter from my Mary every week and I have another person up there that writes once a fortnight so I get pretty well posted up. It was true about there trying to blow up the hospital and they have burnt a couple of houses near our camp within a week. I tell you there is Secesh enough around here if it was not for the Soldiers there are around here to keep the devils down and one night they cut the picket rope of the cavalry and let there horses loose but they found it out in season so they did not make much by the operation. There is not much chance for them to play any games here but it shows what they would do if they could. Things continue here about the same and so is the weather. We have had a little snow since I wrote last and now it is as muddy as usual. The mittens are about the thing and I had a pair sent me from Stratham so I am pretty well supplied now. I got the papers you sent before but have not got them this week but probably they will come in due season. Covell still continues sick and I am afraid he will not get any better very soon but still he may. Winslow and French are well. Winslow says he shall try and keep out of the doctors hands and thinks he can if he can get enough to eat but he has to have his regular growls. He says you must not make fun of his picture because if he is handsome he cant help it. You must give my love to all the folks and tell Mace that I will tell him what I want sometime but I am so lazy now that I dont want anything but they tell us if we dont move next week we have got to go to drilling with the Infantry and have some sham fights so I suppose they mean to make us do something for our money. I shall write again when I send the other picture so I will close this scrawl.

From your Brother
J W Chase

Write soon.

* * * * * * * * * * *

Camp Revere Alexandria
Jan 23d 1862

Dear Brother

I have just received your letter and thought haveing nothing else to do I would sit down and answer it. We still remain in the same place and for all I can see we are likely to stay here although we have stories here every day that we are going to leave and go on an expedition or make an advance or some other cock and bull story but I have got so that I dont pay any attention to them for I feel as though the man at the head knows best and when he says go I am ready to start not that I would have you think that I am satisfied with this way of spending our time for I think it is the hardest life I ever lived for it is just the same day after day and there is no comfort in going around for the mud is so bad that it is hard work to walk around. It is now over a week since we have seen the sun and there is not much more prospect of it now than there was a week ago and our tents look like so many hog pens for it is impossible to keep them clean and bye the way I think we have got the meanest tents there is out for they leak like seives and it is not so pleasant to wake up and find your ear full of water as a good many might suppose but I suppose those that furnished them made a good job of it and damn little they care whether the Soldiers are wet or dry. My [opinion] of the men that furnish the clothes and cam[p equip]age for the Soldiers is rather small and if I could [have my] way with them they would fare rather hard but I [have come] to the conclusion that Soldiers are bound to [be] robbed and them that steal the most from them are the best fellows.

The health of the men as a general thing is good. We have some cases of the Rheumitis and we have discharged two men with it and I have suffered some with it but it has not been bad enough to disable me from duty and my side has troubled me considerable lately but I think that is brought on by laying still so much and am in hopes it will soon be so that we can drill and see if that will not cure it.

One of our men was killed last monday. He drove one of the teams and was after wood. He had just unlocked the wheels and his team started and he ran to catch them and slipped and the wheels ran over him. He only lived about a half an hour. The Company voted unanimously to send the body home and he was sent home last Tuesday. It cost ninety dollars for the coffin and for his passage home. The coffin cost fifty. His name was Henry Carpenter and he belonged to Lowell and was married but a short time before he enlisted. He was a first rate fellow. I dont think he had an enemy in the Battery. The night before he was killed he was in our tent and was saying he would give a hundred dollars to get home for he had just got a letter from his wife and heard that his wifes mother was dead and she was about crazy and he was very down hearted about it but poor fellow he is gone and little he thought he would get home so soon. He is the first and God only knows who the next will be.

I have not got the other picture yet and it seems as though the fates were against me for I have been over a half a dozen times and got no picture yet but I shall try once more and if I dont succeed then I will give it up. I am glad you like yours and I think you would like the original if you knew him as well as I do although he is no man worshiper nor mealy mouthed gentleman but is a man that if he likes you he does and if he dont why he dont I reckon. I shall enclose with this one of Gen Franklin and it is a first rate likeness. [No enclosure found.] Did not know but what you would like to see our General. You speak about not hearing from Stratham. I have not heard from Levi since November and dont know whether they are dead or alive. I had a letter from John Scammon and he said the folks are all well so I suppose they are alive but there is one thing about it. They will not hear from me untill they do write for I have got enough

General William B. Franklin AJB

to do to write to those that will write to me.

I received the papers to day and see the Democracy of Hampshire still live. Bully for them say I. I reckon the people will get there eyes open one of these days and take the Gov in to there own hands and then I think there will be a change in the affairs of the nation but let Politics go untill the rebels are cleaned out and the states once more brought together and then go in. Winslow and French send there best respects to you. I read the last part of your letter to the boys in the tent and they say we will and if they will only give us a chance to try it on you shall hear a good account from the first Detachment for you must know that we have got promoted and take the right of the Battery and we just allow that we are the Bully Detachment of the First Mass Light Battery or any other Battery there is around these parts but I will stop blowing and I guess writing. You must give my love to all the folks and if you write to Mrs Lenter give her lots of love from me and remember me to Emily and tell her that I go in for union. So good bye for this time.

From Your Brother
John W Chase

PS Has Charley Blodgett gone for a Soldier and how is Lydston? On his rum or off?

* * * * * * * * * *

Camp Revere Alexandria
Jan 30th 1862

Dear Brother

I received your letter this forenoon and now sit down to answer for that is about all we have to do now a days to amuse ourselves is to read and write. I will try and give you a faint Idea of how we pass our time. The Reville sounds at six A M when we fall in for roll call then we have a pot of coffee after which the stable call sounds when the drivers have to clean the horses and the cannoneers clean out the stables and feed them then the recall when we fall in and have another roll call are dismissed and have Breakfast then the water call when the horses have to be watered then guard mounting. Well it is now got to be half past eight and we lie down and wait for the boys with the Baltimore Clipper send that and wait for letters which generally get along about eleven o clock then stable call at noon when we feed the horses again. At half past twelve dinner call and then we loaf around untill half past three when we turn out and fall in for another roll call and march to the stables again when the drivers clean and water the horses and the cannoneers police the stables and feed them. At sunset the retreat is sounded and we fall in for another Roll call then the Non Com recite their lessons then supper call then at eight tattoo and another roll call. At half past eight taps when out goes the lights and we roll ourselves up in our blankets and try and go to sleep but that being impossible with me I generaly lie awake until ten talking with Winslow and hearing the bands play and we have just some of the best bands out here there is out. The New York 31st has got a rouser I tell you then there is the 16th 27th and 32nd and the New Jersey 2nd and we are in hearing of them all so you see we have a plenty of music but the weather has been such this month that they dont get out so much as they used for I dont think we have had four pleasant days this month and to day it is raining as usual and I think if I ever get back into old New England I will not find any fault with the weather or mud. Mr Damrell was here a few days ago from Boston and he had been down where the Mass 1st and 11th were and he said there was more mud there than we had and if that is the case God pity I say for I dont see how they travel around but thank God January is most gone and they say here that February is generally a pleasant month but I dont know how it will prove but one thing I know it cannot be much worse. One of our Secesh neighbors was arrested in Alexandria yesterday and they have sent him on to view the prospect from fort Warren. One of the men in our tent has his wife out here and she boards with this mans wifes mother and he has been saying all along he thought he was a rank Secesh at heart and so it proved. He was arrested in the first place for charging a percentage in changing the bills we are paid off in and he was fined

20 dollars and that led them to watch Mr Secesh and now he is arrested for haveing communication with the rebels and in my opinion there are plenty more of them that ought to served in the same manner. There is more Secesh than union amongst the people around here in my opinion and they are makeing money out of this war but if I could have my way I would smoke them out.

I had two letters from Stratham to day but have not heard anything from Levi or Fathers folks for three weeks. Neither have I heard from Eliza but I saw a letter from Exeter to day stateing that she was down east yet and I directed my last to Exeter so I suppose she has not got it. I got a pass to day to go down to the city and have a picture taken but it rained so I would not go and they have got the small pox in the Regt where I had the others taken and they dont like to have us go into that Regt very well and I dont suppose it is hardly proper but I am in hopes to get one for her soon. At any rate I will do the best I can for her. I want you if you go to Stratham to carry that one I sent you up and give it to Mother[33] and tell her to give the one she has to Charley.[34] That is if she likes this one any better but if not give the one you have to him.

The story is going round the camp to day that we are going to lose Lieut McCartney but how true it is I cannot say. They say he is going to take command of the 5th Battery that is now in Washington. He has been over there for three days but I hope he will not go but if he does you need not be surprised to hear that Corporal Chase has gone too for if it is a possible thing I shall get transfered and I know several others that will too. I suppose if he leaves Sleeper[35] will take command of our Section. He is what they call in Boston a devilish good fellow but he dont suit me like Mac. He is my man for [he] can just keep a hotel he can but I hope he will not go. Since I wrote you last Covell has gone home on a furlough for twenty days and he told me he would call out and see you if he could get a chance. I dont

---

[33] John's mother died in 1856. Mother refers to his late wife's mother.

[34] John's son, Charley, age 10, was living with his maternal grandparents, Thomas and Mary Marston.

[35] Lieutenant J. Henry Sleeper was in command of the left section of the First Massachusetts Battery.

Thomas and Mary Leavitt Marston CFC

know as I can find anything more to write of any consequence and I believe I will dry up but remember me to all the folks and tell Lydston he would have hard work to get his regular rum out here. Two of our Boys were comeing up from town yesterday and the guard stopped them and took away two bottles of gin. So you see we have to run a blockade to get it into camp. They have such spells once in a while and then it plays out like every thing else. Give my respects to Mace and tell him I hope he will have lots of Aty work and plenty of whiskey.

So good bye untill next week and then if nothing happens you will hear from me again.

From your Brother
J W Chase

* * * * * * * * * * *

Camp Revere Alexandria Va
February 6th 1862

Dear Brother

I received your letter this forenoon and after eating a hearty dinner of pea soup I sit down to answer it. I am glad to hear that you are all well and sorry to hear that Asher has lost his place for I was in hopes he had a place that he would keep but I suppose business is so dull the merchants must curtail there expenses some how but I hope he will be lucky enough to obtain some place for I think as you do that Loafing is rather poor business for a young man but I dont know as I can say much for we dont do much here but Loaf without is to take care of the horses. We have been out once this week to practice and were a going again to day but it is the same old story rain. Yesterday was a beautiful day and I began to be in hopes that we were going to get some good weather but it proved otherwise for to day the rain is pouring down with a perfect looseness and I begin to think that it rains here all the time.

I dont know as I can write any news for we dont get much here only what we get from the papers and we see a good deal more in them than is true. I saw in the papers last week about the small pox in the camp around us and I supposed the New York 16th was half of them sick with it but come to inquire of there Major he said they had not had a case but they bury about four every week that die with something but I expect they have got it somewhere around us as we were ordered to the Doctors to be vaccinated and they are putting all the soldiers around here through the same process. We had quite a snow storm here Sunday and Sunday night and Monday. The Col of the New York 31st turned out his Regt and they had a Sham fight with snow balls and it was a big thing. They had the bugles out and went through all the movements in regular military style and you had ought to have seen some of the officers that they dont like very well. Perhaps they did not get much snow balled <u>oh no</u> but everything passed off in good shape and they had a big time I tell you.

Speaking about rum being the means of those men getting into trouble I am afraid that rum causing a good deal of trouble and as long as OFFICERS are allowed to transport rum into camp privates will get it and I have yet to learn why it is any worse for a private to get drunk than it is for a man with a commission for I have seen officers just as drunk as ever I did a private and I think a little drunker. As for myself I have not drank much rum since I have been out here although there is plenty of it around us that we can get but Winslow and myself generally travel together and we rather think it is best not to have much to do with it but he says tell your Brother if we ever get back to Boston we will all three have one drink together if agreeable. I received two letters from Stratham to day and they wrote that Levis children all had the measles but the rest of the folks were all well. Mrs Goodwin wanted me to ask you if you had forgotten her. As to the pay for that picture I think you had better keep it at present as I may want it more some other time as I have stamps and money enough to last me untill next pay day if we get paid as regularly as we have before. Some of the men out here tell me there familys have a good deal of trouble about the Bounty the state pays but as you never said any thing about I did not know how it was.

You must give my respects to all enquireing friends and tell them I am anxiously waiting to hear the word Forward either toward Richmond or else to Boston for I am sick and tired of this doing nothing but we live in hopes.

So good bye for this time
John W Chase

You need not fear about the rebels getting any of my letters that I receive for I generally use them for kindling the fire.

Tell Elizabeth she must not get excited about the war but keep cool but I think myself if they would hang some of the traitors and a few nigger worshipers it would be a benefit to the country.

Love to Emily &C.

* * * * * * * * * *

Camp Revere Alexandria Va
February 13th 1862

Dear Brother

I squat myself down this evening to answer your letter which I received to day. Was glad to hear you still keep up good courage. Expect to night you feel very jubilant. If you dont you are different from us here for if you had been here to day you would thought there had been a Presidential Election for the way the cheers went up for Burnside and his gallant boys was a caution to all rebels and I for one say Glory to God and the Soldiers.

I see by the papers there is a good many predictions about an advance but in my opinion they know but little about it but I find as the weather grows better and the mud grows less that the drills begin to grow plentier. All the Infantry around us are fireing at target and going into the bayonet exercise and the batteries begin to practice fireing shell. We have been out twice this week and I tell you it is good fun. I never believed before that you could see a ball when it come out of a gun but you just can and some times you can follow a ball untill it strikes and it is very pretty to see them burst but I expect the fun is a good deal more to see them go away from you than it is to see them comeing towards you but I tell you Artillery practice is a big thing to learn and I reckon the most of the Batteries out here need a good deal of practice yet to be good Artillerists but I think we improve but should rather trust to grape and cannister than to shell for that is what rakes them down I tell you.

There has two Regt gone from here this week and one Battery. Expect they have gone up along somewhere but dont know certain. We can hear the guns banging away down the Potomac to night. Probably some tug is comeing up with hay and grain. There was some came up last night. I think the rebels are worse gunners than we are for they dont seem to hurt anything and we can hear them banging away most every night but let them fire away. It costs something for them to fire them big fellows and the more they waste the more it will cost them. I received a letter from George Chase[36] to

[36] Not John Chase's son, otherwise unknown.

day and he seems to think that there is as many Democrats that supports the President as there is of the Republicans and he seems to think that union rather predominates and niggers is down. Well that is about the thing I reckon.

I also got a letter from Pricilla and Levi and I have found out why I came out here and the reason is because Miss Horn got married. Glad I have found out why I come. I always thought I came here because I wanted to help put down this rebellion and try and sustain the constitution but Stratham people always did like to talk about me and I suppose they always will and if they can take any comfort in it I suppose I had ought to be willing for you know they are a christian people up there and never do any thing wrong <u>oh no never</u>.

I suppose you have seen the account of takeing the minister out of the church at Alexandria last Sunday. Well they have tried twice to burn the church down and they had a row down there last night but I have not got the particulars but I was on guard and I heard the muskets fireing and the signals going up and I came to the conclusion that something was up. I think we shall have to burn the cursed hole down yet for it is rotten with Secesh and I was down there last week and I heard men talk it right out loud. At any rate if a man had talked so in Boston last spring they would have mobbed him and I think the best way is to clean them out as you go and make sure work of it but I must bring this to a close for the Bands are all playing and the men are cheering and I must go out before roll call and see some of the fun.

Give my love to all the folks and tell Lizzie I will try and kill one rebel for her if I have to shoot one right here for I think I can find some without going a great ways for I have no faith in any of these fellows around here. Give my love to Mace and I hope you will find lots of work to do and good pay. Tell the folks I am well and all ready to go in lemons. It is a splendid night here to night and I must go out and hear the music so good night.

From your Aff Brother
John W Chase

* * * * * * * * * *

Camp Revere Alexandria Va
February 20th 1862

Dear Brother

Yours of the 16th was received to day and found me up to my knees in mud digging out our tents for since I last wrote it has snowed and rained about all the time but to day it is clear and windy and we have been trying to clean up a little. Very pleasant this liveing with a pond of water for a floor. We have a ditch around our tent a foot deep and the same in width but some how the water will find its way under our bunks and we find rubber blankets very convenient in this part of Dixie.

We have had a good deal of excitement here this week and Saturday we are going to have a regular jubilee as they tell us the whole division has got to turn out. I hope the wind will continue to blow so as to dry up the mud for I think if it dont dry up we should look more like mud diggers than Soldiers. The good news continues to come and the troops on this side of the Potomac are at fever heat. Three Regt left yesterday for Kentucky and Gen Franklin is trying hard for this whole division to go but the man at Washington called Mac seems to do pretty much as he pleases about sending troops away and sends them that he thinks he can spare but the men here are afraid they will not have chance to immortalize themselves but "I dont see it" for I think there will have to be a fight in Virginia just to punish the devils and learn them what to expect in case they should rebel again.

I saw Capt Dudleys[37] promotion in the papers and thought of you knowing that you used to be very intimate but I think you have very good reasons for staying at home but I wish it was so that you could have come out for I think you would like it first rate judging by myself and I think if I was a Major I should like a good deal better I do. The 16th New York have just come in off picket and they report two hundred rebel Soldiers have come within our lines since the

[37] Captain Albion M. Dudley of Co. K, Fifty-eighth Massachusetts Infantry.

capture of Roanoke[38] and say they look rather tough ragged and dirty. The rebels say it is no use. They might as well desert as to stay and get whipped. So you see the damn curs have got there tails down and I think in about a couple of months we shall have them pretty well cleaned out.

There is a couple of familys right snug to our camp and our boys go over there every day after we get the news and report but they would not believe it at first but now all they will say is why dont you take Manassas. I rather think we shall take there old huts down over there heads some fine night if they dont stop some of there gab but they have cooled awfully the last few days and begin to think that yankees are most too much for snuff chewers and I reckon they will find it out one of these days to there sorrow.

I had a letter from down east this week. Mary writes she is well and all the rest of the folks and says she goes in for the war heavy. I also received one from my Mary and she wanted to know if I was willing she should come to Boston the first of May and make a visit and I wrote her I was if I could find a place for her to stop and I want you to ask Elizabeth if she will take charge of her if she should come for you know she is young and will want some one to look after her a little and if she will do it I will be very much oblidged and will try and kill one rebel for her if I have to get into a fight single handed for I think I should like to kill several of the yellow skinned devils that I know around here. I was sorry to hear that Asher was sick and hope he will get over it soon. The measles and small pox is prevailing in the army around here some but I hope it will not spread much as they keep it pretty close now.

You must give my respects to all the folks and tell Emily she must hurrah for Gen McClellan for he is the man that is going to whip the rebels and then whip the English if they dont stop bragging and blowing so much. Remember me to Mace and all that wants to hear from me. Winslow sends his respects.

From John W Chase

[38] Roanoke Island, North Carolina.

* * * * * * * * * *

Camp Revere Alexandria Va
February 28th 1862

Dear Brother

I began to look with anxious eyes for your weekly letter as it generally gets along Thursday but this week it waited untill Friday but I have got it and read it although it was hard work for we have so many assemblies now a days that it keeps us busy about all the time and to day being the last day of the month we have been mustered for pay but the Capt seems to think that we shall not get paid so promptly as we have before but I guess Abe will not go back on us now because we are getting rather short and they do tell us that we have got to move. Orders were read yesterday to reduce our stock in our knapsacks to the smallest compress that is allowed and the officers to have nothing but a valise and Regt will only be allowed four Waggons each so you see they are bringing things down kind of fine. Well I dont happen to be troubled with much extra baggage. Only my blanket and frock and I will just bet that I am Soldier enough to contrive some way to carry them for I tell you there is a chance for a man to learn somethings that he never knew before and after six months schooling I dont happen to be quite so green as I was when I first enlisted and I begin to think I know most as much as those that were out three months. In fact we tell the boys when they begin to relate there three months stories thats played out but to be serious I think that the Army of the Potomac is about to move and in fact some of it has moved and I expect before long that you will hear something from us in the shape of war news and instead of the all quiet on the banks of the Potomac it will be a fight in Virginia and I say for one let it come for I am just vain enough to believe that we can just clean them out from here and that at the word go for I think there are men in this part of the Army that can fight just as well as the Western troops although Greely seems to think we are not in so good a state for an advance now as we were last Dec but I dont happen to see it for I know as far as our own Co is concerned we knew but little about our business when we came out here and I think we have learnt something this winter but editors must have something to talk about so they talk about the army. You probably see a good deal in the papers about the drunkenness in this army. Now I will bet the men in the army of the Potomac dont drink half the rum that the same number of men do at home and you will not see so many drunken Soldiers in Alexandria as you will drunken men in Exeter on an average and I think that the morals of the men in the army are about as good as the morals of any the citys but let them talk. They cant hurt anybody just yet. You spoke about the weather with you last Monday. Well here we had rain in the morning then it cleared off very warm and calm. About ten o clock it came up squally and the wind blew a hurricane and blew down all our tents but two and blew the roof off of our stables but towards night the wind went down and we made out to raise our tents up again but ours looks rather the worse for wear and we can lie in our beds and study the stars but it gives us a good ventilation and that you know is very benificial. That night the ground froze harder than it has before this winter and that is the way we have it. Now first cold and then warm and rainy and windy. I think the weather changes here oftener than it does with you.

I got a letter from Mother to day and it done me more good than a Sutlers pie for I tell you Sam a letter from home out here is like cold water to a thirsty soul and you have my warmest thanks for the kind letters you have sent me and the other favors you and other friends have confered on me but I suppose my other Brothers think they are well rid of me but perhaps if I ever get back I shall have a chance to tell them what I think of them for let others think of Soldiers as they will I think they are just as good as other folks and I am not sorry that I went for a Soldier yet and I hope to have a chance to try my courage with the chivalry of the South and if I fall I shall not be much of a loss only to my children and I have faith to believe my friends will not see them suffer. I wish you would write Levi a letter for from what I learn he is worse than he ever was before and perhaps you might have a little influence over him.

I want you the next time you write to send me a few stamps as I am out and about out of change and I dont want to be without a cent in my pocket for it makes a man feel kind of mean and I want you to buy me a couple of lbs of tobacco and send it out and pay yourself out of the money that I shall send home when we are paid off.

Give my love to Mace and all the rest of the folks. Tell them I am well. Only a cold in my head and a hoarseness that was brought on shouting for the victorys down South.

So hopeing this will find you and yours in good health I will close.

yours for his country
John W Chase

PS Respects to Emily.

* * * * * * * * * * *

Alexandria Camp Revere
March 7th 1862

Dear Brother

I received yours to day and take the earliest opportunity to answer. We still hang on at the old camp but are all packed ready for a start and we are expecting every day to get orders to march and for one I dont care how quick for if we have got to fight I want to do it and have the fuss over with and either lick the devils or get licked for the fact is I am getting rusty but they are kind of taking the rust off now by drilling us and the way Mac puts us through the mud is a caution. I think if you could see us some times when we come in you would have hard work to recognize me from any body else for about all you can see is mud. We have had to day a drill with Infantry and fire blanks and there was some kicking amongst the horses but the ground was hard for it froze here last night quite hard and the weather is cold to day but pleasant for a wonder. Two Regt of our division have gone away to day but where of course we cannot tell. There has another Battery come over and camped right by the side of us and yesterday there was eight come over from Washington with a lot of Ambulances so you see the Army is trying to move and Banks,s[39] end of it has commenced and I suppose our turn will come next and I hope by the time you get this we shall have got off. The Infantry here have all got little tents just big enough for two men to get under and about three feet high and they have got some kind of a shelter for us different from our tents but I have not seen it as it is not yet unpacked and we have all got rubber ponchos so you see Samuel looks after the welfare of his men if the Comissary dont. They tell us now we shall not get paid before the first of Aprill for some of the Western troops have not been paid for five months. If such is the case I am willing to wait for I think they had ought to be seen to first for God knows they have had some hard work to do out there.

I got a letter from Eliza to day. She says they are all well and Dudley has got married and gone on a wedding tour. Hope he will have a good time and not have an attack of Rheumitis. I have had no letter from Mary this week and dont know what to think of it as she has never failed before of writeing every week but the devil has been to pay with our letters this week and yesterday we got no mail at all and perhaps hers has stopped on the way and I may get it yet. At least I should like to but perhaps now they have got some money they think it is no use to write. I am glad the weed is comeing for of all the stuff they have here it would kill anybody but a Soldier and they can hardly stand it. Much oblidged for your good intentions but if I can get tobacco and postage stamp enough I reckon I can live although there is a good many things we should like but I find it is about as well to have as little stuff round as you can get along with for extras are only a trouble. Give my respects to all the folks. Tell William that I intend to come back and try that Demijohn again before three years are gone and drink success to the union. Glad to hear that Asher is better and hope he will soon be around again. So

[39] General Nathaniel P. Banks was a former governor of Massachusetts, who was in command of Union troops in the Shenandoah Valley of Virginia.

hopeing soon to have a good fight I will close.

From
J W Chase

* * * * * * * * * * *

Fairfax Court House Va
Mar 13th 1862

Dear Brother

I dont wait to get your letter this week before writeing but take this chance as I dont know when I shall get another. We left the old camp Monday morning at 5 o clock expecting to go on to Manassas but it seems the rebels concluded not to wait for us and we got as far as this place and stopped but are expecting every hour to move. The rebels it seems have burnt a bridge and the pontoon train went up this morning and I expect we shall soon follow them. There is some Soldiers around here you had better believe. I thought I had seen quite an army before but it warnt a circumstance. I have seen more Cavalry the last three days than I ever expected to see in my life and still they come and Batterys enough to cover the Common all over. The boys dont like this stopping at all and I guess there never was so many disapointed men in one day before as there was that day when they found they had left Manassas but never mind we will find them yet and drive them out of these holes. There is any quantity of Contrabands[40] comeing this way. I asked one of them if there was any rebels where he come from he said dare was some but dey were lebeing berry fast. He came from beyond Centreville. I suppose you get all the news and I will only say I am well and happy as a clam. My courage grows better every day and I did not feel a mite like going home the day we started but think I should if I had belonged to an Infantry Co. This lugging a gun knapsack grub and 60 rounds of ammunition is enough to kill a horse much more a man. Some of the 22nd that CRACK REG so much talked of threw away there

[40] Fugitive slaves.

knapsacks and some of them did not get in till this morning. I tell you Sam the proof of the pudding is in the eating and puffs in news papers is not going to help a Regt reputation any now but they have got to come up to the scratch to get any honor. The 16th N York came in with us and will flank us if we ever do fight and I just bet they are the boys to do it. At any rate they are the boys that will live if Mr Secesh has any Cattle pens or any thing else that is eatable and they think the first Mass Battery is about the thing and we are always welcome in there camp and if there is any thing good we get it. I shall have to narrow my correspondence down now for I find that writing on a march is working under difficulties but I shall try and keep you posted and you must Inform the rest. I had a letter from Langdon last week and one from Mary and our mail is going down tomorrow again. I have not got the tobacco yet but dont know whether it has come or not. Direct your letters to Washington and they will be forwarded.

Give my love to everybody but nigger Worshipers. I have none for them. I enclose with this a document I got out of the celebrated Fairfax Courthouse. Thought you might like it for its age. Tell Lizzie I expect to get a chance at a rebel for her now. I have got my pistol well loaded.

From Your Brother John

LOVE TO EMILY.

Friday morning

Wet and nasty and the boys is around the camp fires for we have no tents and things are kind of dismal. Covell thinks a little of Uncle Johns Improved would not go bad. Our officers went to Manassas yesterday and brought back some swords and knifes that looked as though they were made in the year one. They have all been burnt as the rebels set fire to every thing they left. I dont know when you will get [this] as our mails are not very regular but you must write and I will do the same. You will get them some time.

good morning
John

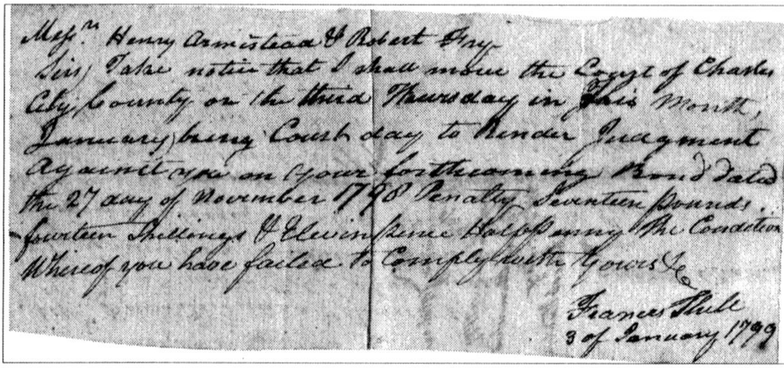

Relic from Fairfax Court House CFC

[The relic from Fairfax Court House is a document that reads:]

Messrs Henry Armistead & Robert Fry
Sirs Take notice that I shall move the Court of Charles
City County on the third Thursday in This month,
January being Court day to Render Judgment
Against you on your forthcoming Bond dated
the 27 day of November 1798 Penalty Seventeen Pounds
fourteen Shillings & Elevin pence Halfpenny The Condition
Whereof you have failed to Comply with Yours &C
Frances Shell
3 of January 1799

[The reverse side reads:]

Shell
vs } Notice
Armistead & Fry
4 of January 1799
Henry Armistead & Ro. Fry
Jacob Vaider

* * * * * * * * * * *

Camp Revere Alexandria Va
March 29th 1862

Dear Brother

I suppose you begin to think it is about time to hear from me and I thought I would sit down and let you know that I still live. The box arrived safe last Wednesday and I am much oblidged to Mace for the cure all and those that tried it think it would be hard to beat that remedy for the complaints for which it was recommended and the fishes did not go bad. In fact the box take it all in all was quite a God send for me and you must thank Mace for me and tell him if it is possible for me to obtain what he wants he shall have it but I have come to the conclusion that this division is not expected to do any fighting but is to be kept for a show as we have been Reviewed four times since we came back from Fairfax on. The whole of McDowells command was reviewed consisting of Franklins Smiths McCalls and Kings[41] divisions making between forty and fifty thousand men. We have had Lord Lyons[42] and all the rest of the great men to see us and then we have had brigade drills and Battery drills in any quantity so you see we have not laid still much but I begin to grow sick of this cleaning up carriages and harnesses and uniforms and I think if they dont want us to fight they had better send us home. They are sending any quantity of troops down the river. Porters and Hentzlemans[43] command have all gone and they are still sending them and there is any quantity of them left now. They come from all directions and I think if they concentrate them at any one point there will be enough to do something. Norfolk I expect is the point aimed at now but of course it is all guess work. We are told every day that we shall go next but I have got so that I dont place much dependence on what I hear but I hope we shall get away from this place soon for I am sick and tired of it and want to go somewheres else and exhibit ourselves if that is what we are intended for the weather is quite cold here and

[41] General Irvin McDowell headed a corps composed of divisions headed by Generals William B. Franklin, William F. Smith, G. A. McCall, and Rufus King.

[42] Lord Richard Lyons was the British minister to the United States.

[43] Generals Fitz-John Porter and Samuel P. Heintzelman commanded army corps under General McClellan's Army of the Potomac.

to day we are haveing a snow storm and as we have no stoves in our tents it makes it quite uncomfortable but thank God summer is comeing and then I hope it will be warmer. I suppose you are all looking with anxious eyes to see what this branch of the army is going to do and I hope before another week rolls around that we shall have possesion of Norfolk and have the Merrimac[44] in our hands for I think it is a disgrace to the nation to have all this army doing nothing when they are all ready and willing to go for there is men enough here to clean them out if they will only give us somebody to lead us on and if we dont have posession of Norfolk and Richmond in a fortnight we had ought to be ashamed of ourselves.

I had a letter from Eliza, Sewall and Susie Smith. It took all three of them to write it. I also had one from Mary this week. The folks are all well. As usual you must give my respects to all the folks. Tell them I am well and hearty as a buck and feel as if I wanted to fight some body or some thing for I am getting rusty. I am much oblidged for those papers for reading was getting scarce and they have been all around the camp.

good bye
From John

* * * * * * * * * *

April 6th 1862
Manassas Sunday night

Dear Brother

I have been looking all day for the man with the letters thinking I should get one from you but it did not make its appearance so I thought I would sit down and write to you but dont know when you will get it as we are now on the Advance and letter writing is prohibited in a measure but I am going to write and trust to luck in getting it to you.

We left camp Friday morning and a beautiful morning it was and

---

[44] The USS *Merrimac* had been converted into the ironclad CSS *Virginia* by the Confederate navy to break the Union naval blockade.

that night we arrived at Centreville heights where we took possesion of some of the good log huts that Mr. Rebel had built and stopped all night. The next morning the Reville was sounded at four o clock and we started about six and it rained like the devil. We arrived at this place at noon and of all the rough roads that ever I travelled that was the worst. We passed the Bull Run stream at Mitchells ford the place where the Mass 1st had the skirmish. The bridge was gone and we had to get over the best way we could. After we arrived here we waited untill three o clock for orders and we were ordered to camp. We started on about a half mile and camped in the woods. This morning we hitched up and came back a little ways and went into a log cabin where if nothing happens I expect to pass the night and I am in hopes mr Rebel will keep away for I feel as though I could sleep without [waking]. The railroad is running to this place and beyond. They are pouring the troops in with a rush. The Infantry most of it comes in the cars. Tomorrow we expect to start again and go on when God and McDowell only knows and they wont tell but I hope where we shall see the foe. There are scouts of Rebel cavalry around here and last night the Cols orderly of the 15th NY was shot and three horses taken from him so you see we dont care about going a great ways from camp. The rebels had first rate quarters here and according to appearances plenty to eat and do with and when any body says they could not made a big stand at Centreville it shows they dont know anything about it but of course you get all this in the papers. I wish you could be here and see it. The road from Manassas to Centreville is truly sickening. Dead horses and everything else scattered along the road. You can see enough to make a man sick of war and not want to see a fight. Relics are scarce articles that is any that is good for anything as the Cavalry go on ahead and have the first pick. I could not find even a rebel button and I dont think there is more than 6 in the whole company but I reckon we shall see relics enough before we get through. The boys are well and hearty and I dont find many weak kneed ones but some few as we advance begin to be troubled with it. Winslow wants to be remembered to you and thinks that Soldiering is not just the thing for a mans health. 10

crackers a day and salt junk dont make him fat yet.

We signed the pay roll the day before we left camp and were going to be paid off the next day but alas we had to leave and the boys are out of money and out of tobacco and I found plenty of customers for mine. I have a little left and I have to keep it hid for this being on a march without tobacco is up hill work. Give my love to all the folks and write for I shall get the letters some time If I live and I will try and keep you posted as to my whereabouts. I shall send this the first chance so good bye as I hear the first call for roll call.

John

Six months to day we arrived at Washington and the night we stopped at Centreville was the first I have lain in a house.

* * * * * * * * * *

Milford Va
Apr 10/62

Dear Brother

I have had no letter from you for a fortnight but I have concluded to write every chance I get and having a chance to send tomorrow I thought it best to improve it. I got a letter from Eliza and one from Susie Smith to day and had answered them both and thought I might as well keep on. When I wrote you last we were at Manassas which we left Tuesday morning and came as far as this place which is about six miles. It was raining hard when we left and continued to rain and snow until this morning but this PM it cleared off and now the sun is shining bright and the mud is up to your knees. We were obliged to stop here on account of the streams being so high we could not cross and to day it is still higher and I dont know when we shall move but I hope before long for I want to be at it. We or I had rather a hard time getting here. The Casson under my charge got stuck and it was three hours before we got it out and we had on ten horses but we made out at last and such looking critters as I and Winslow was you never saw. I had on a pair of rubber leggings and my old rubber coat and it was

Artillery, by Edwin Forbes LC

mud from one end to the other and the mud was a regular brick color. There was one battery came on yesterday and they had to take the ammunition boxes off in order to get out at all so you can see how much these folks know that have been talking about an advance all winter for the mud in some places now is up to the axle-tree and it is not a circumstance to what it has been. The infantry part of our division is ahead about five miles and last night they found five of the 16th N.Y. tied to a tree with there throats cut and their tongues cut out. The pickets found them so you see it is rather risky moving a great ways from camp but the cavalry go out foraging and the way the pigs and hens come in to their camp is a caution. The fact is we are bound to live if we have to steal for this living on ten crackers a day is not just the thing I tell you. The snow storm rather shook my love for the Union for come to camp out such weather it takes hold and I should like to have a Regt of nigger worshippers out here and tramp them over the road and then have them sleep under a poncho in wet clothes and wet blankets. I am inclined to think they would want to sell out but thank God the glorious sun once more shines and I feel as patriotic as ever and am ready to fight or march or give three cheers for the President and McClellan and three more for the old flag but it kind of makes the rheumatiz stick out this wet and cold weather but I hope we shall not get anything worse but I expect we shall soon have business and plenty of it but I want you to write and send this to Mary.

After Supper 7 P.M. Just been to supper fried potatoes and boiled ham hard bread and coffee without sugar no thanks to our officers however for it. We stole it and cooked it and eat it but we have killed an ox to day and I guess we are all right. You must give my love to all the folks. Tell them I am gay and happy by spells. No Paymaster yet and no signs of any. Rather think Sam has gone back on us. Shall soon feel compelled to steal some tobacco for I am getting nervous. Remember me to Emily and all the rest and tell them I remain

John W Chase
vulgarly called Jack

* * * * * * * * * * *

Alexandria Va
April 15th 62

Dear Brother

I suppose you will be surprised to see my letter hailing from this city but it happens so we are once more back to this place but I expect we leave it tomorrow as our peices are loaded and we load our horses to day and I expect we shall go tomorrow. I wrote you at Milford. We left that same Afternoon and went on about four miles where one of Franklins staff rode up and ordered us back to Alexandria to take the boat for Yorktown as Gen McClellan had telegraphed to the President twice to let him have Franklins Division come to him. So you see we think we are some pumkins to be sent for by the little Gen and the whole Division were much pleased and gave three rousing cheers for they dont like McDowell at all as they dont think he done right last summer at Bull Run and all the Infantry in this Division but one Regt were in that fight. I dont pretend to know anything about it but there is one thing about it. I had rather be

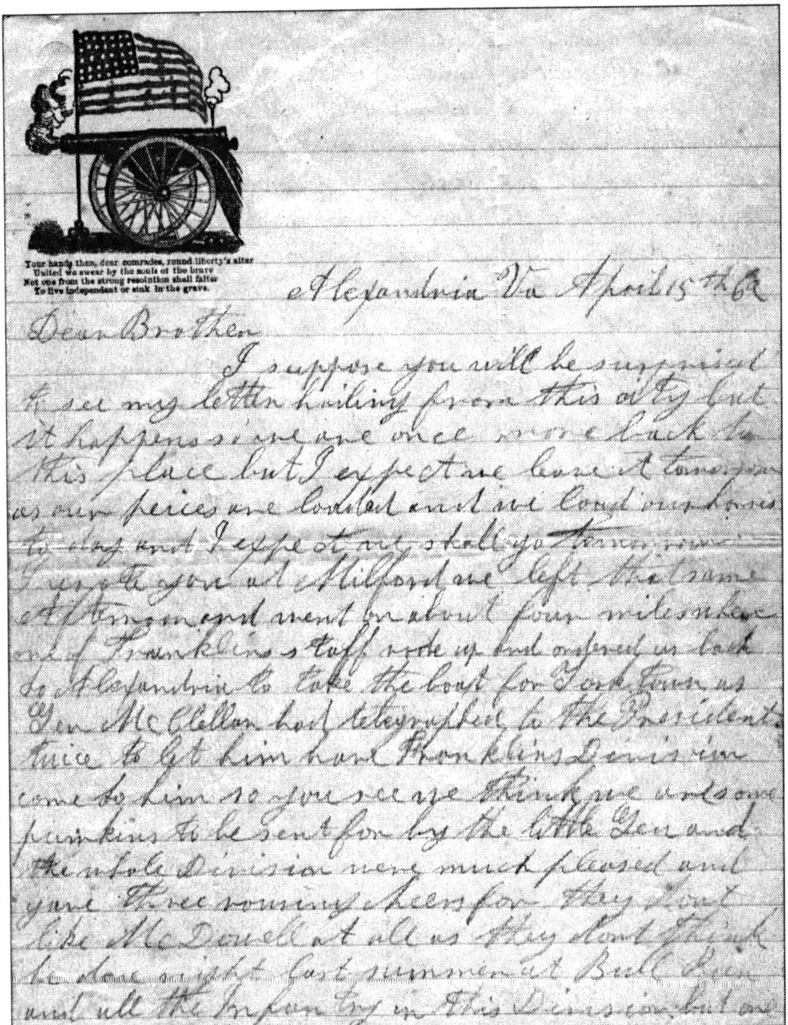
Your hands then, dear comrades, round liberty's altar
United we swear by the souls of the brave
Not one from the strong resolution shall falter
To live independent or sink in the grave.

Alexandria Va April 15th 62

Dear Brother

I suppose you will be surprised to see my letter hailing from this city but it happens so we are once more back to this place but I expect we leave it tomorrow as our pieces are loaded and we load our horses to day and I expect we shall go tomorrow. I wrote you at Milford we left the same afternoon and went on about four miles when one of Franklins staff rode up and ordered us back to Alexandria to take the boat for York Town as Gen McClellan had telegraphed to the President twice to get him have Franklins Division come to him so you see we think we are some pumkins to be sent for by the little Gen and the whole Division were much pleased and gave three rousing cheers for they dont like McDowell at all as they dont think he done right last summer at Bull Run and all the Infantry in this Division but one

Letter of April 15, 1862 CFC

where the little Gen is and risk it for I tell you I have great faith in Abraham and George B and the men of this division are willing to go where he will lead them. I think we have got just as good a division Gen as there is out and I know we have got just as good Brigadiers as anybody else especially Gen Kearney[45] of the Jersey Brigade. He has got but one arm but he is a whole man I tell you and a tough one at that. He is what I call a gentleman and that is more than you can say of a good many of the fools that holds Commissions and Capt Arnold who has command of the four Batteries is another of the same kind and will speak to a private just as politely as he will to a General and I tell you he looks after us like a Father and if there is a chance to get us a shelter when we are on a march he is bound to do it. We all like him very much. We had rather a rough march out to Manassas and back but I dont regret it much for I saw enough to pay me. It is surpriseing to me how the rebels came to leave that place for any one that says they were not well fortified is a liar for at Centreville they had a clean sweep for four miles all around and to have got possession must cost an immense loss of life & when you hear folks telling about there being starved out you just tell them I dont see it for there was any quantity of meat and flour left in the cabins. In one I was in there was a barrel of roast chickens that they left in there flight. They were liveing better than the union troops ever began to and according to the appearance had everything to make them comfortable. All the Cabins and there was any quantity of them had good fireplaces in them and according to the looks of things the men cooked for themselves and I wish we could do the same way. Winslow and I do cook a good deal and we have got coffee and some other things laid in. I have got a coffee pot I found at Centreville. It is a good one that and a knife and fork I found is all the relics I brought back. You tell Elizabeth I will send her a relic if we ever do have a fight and I live and I think I shant be much of anything else but a relic if I get back for I find this thing is kind of useing me up. I have the cramp a good deal but my general health is first rate and I feel determined to stick her out as long as I can stand on my legs. I dont feel any mind to give up at all and I am bound to put her through.

We were paid off yesterday. Our Captain was advised not to pay

[45] General Philip Kearney had lost an arm in the Mexican War.

us untill we were aboard the boat but he told them he had a company he could trust and he was going [to]. He made us a speech & we gave him three rousing cheers and the boys are behaveing first rate. There is some drunken ones as a matter of course for you see we are right in the city and there is any quantity of rum. I shall enclose a check in this for fifteen dollars and it will be payable at the Mayors office in Boston. I want you to get it & pay yourselve for the tobacco you sent me and send Mary five dollars for her own use. I dont know whether she will come to Roxbury or not but she can probably find a use for the money. I want you to get a copy of that picture I sent you and send it to Mary down east as she wanted one and I dont have much time to get one here and send it to her with my love and tell her I have not forgotten her if I have not wrote and will write some time but I cant get much chance to write now adays. Give my love to everybody that wants to hear from me and write as often as you can. I got a letter from you Sunday and that is the first since the 28th of March so good bye for this time and I hope the next time I write I shall be able to give you an account of a fight at Yorktown.

[Unsigned]

[The caption under a cannon and flag on the stationery reads:]

Your hands then, dear comrades, round liberty's altar
United we swear by the souls of the brave
Not one from the strong resolution shall falter
To live independent or sink in the grave.

* * * * * * * * * *

John Chase's Travel Routes in Chapter 2: April 1862 to August 1862

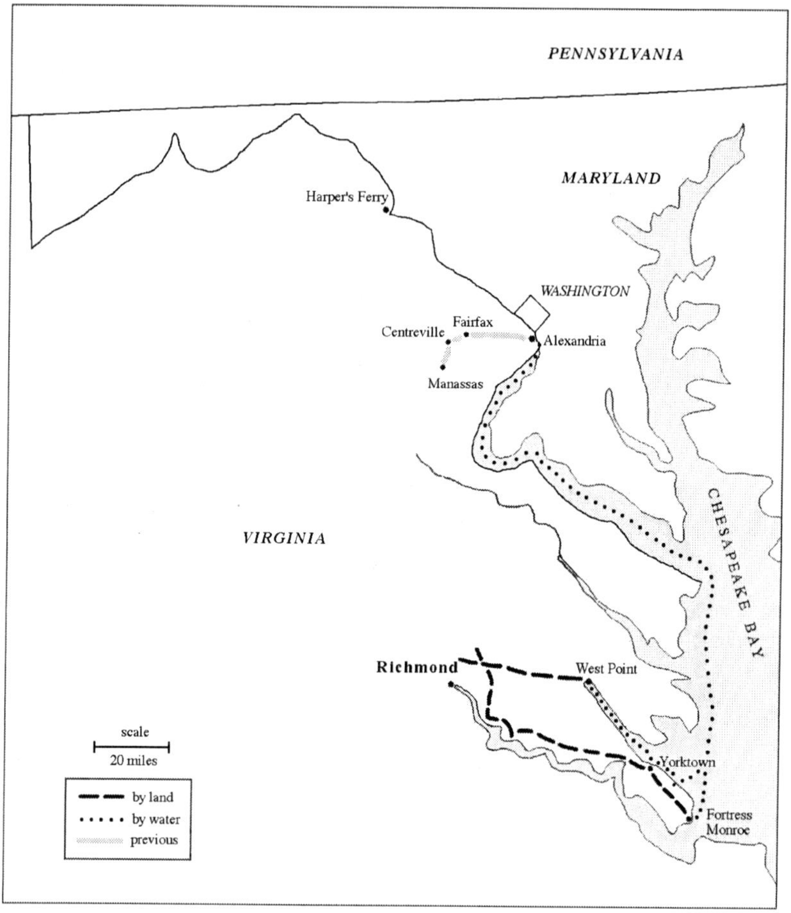

JSC/BBC

CHAPTER 2

The Peninsula Campaign

Invading the south, the Army of the Potomac begins the Peninsula Campaign in the spring of 1862. Union troops steam down the Potomac River and the Chesapeake Bay to the Yorktown, Virginia, area. When the Confederates abandon Yorktown, the Union army moves quickly past Williamsburg to the outskirts of Richmond, where they are repelled by the Confederate army under its new commander, General Robert E. Lee. Chase describes his experiences at the fight at West Point, Virginia, and during the Seven Days' Battles.

Shipping Point Va
Apr 20th 1862

Dear Brother

Being on guard to night and haveing time and place to write I thought best to improve the chance. I received your last letter the day we went Aboard the transport which brought us here. We dropped down the River about two miles the same night (Thursday) and the next morning at five we bid Farewell to Alexandria to come to this place which is about twenty miles from Fortress Monroe & seven from York Town and 160 from Washington. We arrived here Saturday P M about three o clock and are still on board the vessel (Sunday night) and where or when we are going to leave it is more than I can tell but I expect here but it would not surprise me any to hear we were going to New Orleans or any where else. In fact I have got so I am not surprised at any orders we get for I find a Soldier has no business to think much about anything and the less he knows the better he is off.

We had a beautiful passage down the Potomac. It was calm and pleasant and I think I shall be well paid for my Soldiering just in seeing that beautiful river. There are some houses on the banks and the peach trees were all in bloom and looked very lovely. Mount Vernon is the only place of much note and that looks just like the pictures of it and it is a very beautiful place.

We were brought down with a Steamer and two Schooners the Battery being aboard the Steam and the men and horses on board the Schooners the Steamer towing them. There was about two hundred vessels in all. The Nelly Baker Nantasket Mystic and a number of others from Boston and the boys almost began to think we were in Boston Harbor. The Mass first is in camp about a mile from here and I am in hopes to see some of them before long but I have not been ashore yet.

I want you to tell Lizzie I have lost that Bracelet I had it in my pocket book and expect I pulled it out with a bill some time. I never was so sorry for anything in my life and think I had rather lost an arm and I have always been very careful of it and dont see how it could have got out but I cannot find it and I suppose it must have gone that way but you must tell her not to blame me for I was very much hurried the day we came away and I was buying some things to bring with me and I expect I lost it then. I was in hopes to kept it untill I come back so as to have got the history but it is gone and it is just about my luck for I never could keep any thing I cared for.

I want you to give my love to all the folks. Tell them my health and courage is good and I hope soon to have a chance to try the latter at the takeing of York Town. Winslow is well and still growls and I think if he could not he would be sick. Remember me to William and Mace and all the rest of the folks and write often but I dont know when you will get this for I have not found out any thing about the Mail yet but perhaps you will get it some time and I am in hopes to get them from you but I must close and relieve the guard.

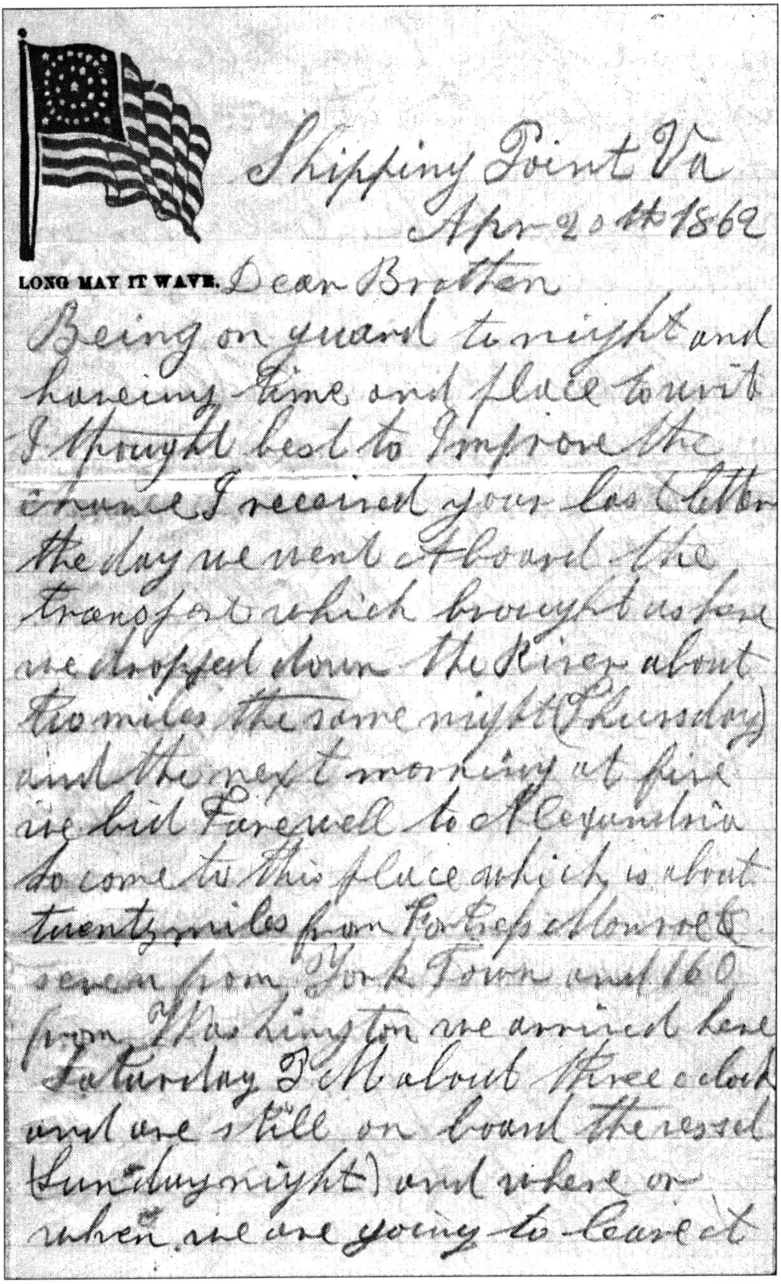

LONG MAY IT WAVE.

Shipping Point Va
Apr 20th 1862

Dear Brother
Being on guard tonight and haveing time and place to writ I thought best to improve the chance I received your las letter the day we went Aboard the transport which brought us here we dropped down the River about two miles the same night (Thursday) and the next morning at five we bid Farewell to Alexandria to come to this place which is about twenty miles from Fortress Monroe & seven from York Town and 160 from Washington we arrived here Saturday P.M about three oclock and are still on board the vessel (Sunday night) and where or when we are going to leave it

Letter of April 20, 1862 CFC

Monday Morning Apr 21st

It is a wet and nasty morning and no signs of leaving the vessel yet but I am in hopes we shall get off to day for our horses are getting tired of it and I reckon the poor critters will be glad to get off. I am going to send this on shore morning and I expect it will start to day so good bye. I will write again in the course of a week if it is so I can but I hope before that time York Town will be ours and all the rest of Virginia.

John

Direct to First Mass Battery
Franklins Division
Washington DC

* * * * * * * * * * *

Ship Point Va
April 27th 1862

Dear Brother

I received yours of the 20th with three from Hampshire from Pricilla Susie Smith and Eliza. You did not state in your letter whether you got the receipt for the money I sent you or not but I expect you did as you say you got the letter. I had a letter from Mary this week and she thinks she shall not come to Boston this spring but you can send her the five dollars. She will probably find a use for it. She says she is going to wait till I get home. Pray God she may not have to wait long for I begin to grow tired of this kind of a life. It will do well enough for three months or so but it has kind of played out with me and I find the other boys are growing sick of soldiering. I have been up to the Mass first and NH 2nd to day. The first were out on picket and I did not see many of them. I saw James Miller and Horatio Littlefield. Horatio was building a tomb as they had four dead men. They were killed in a skirmish they had night before last. I suppose you see the account of it. They received a great deal of

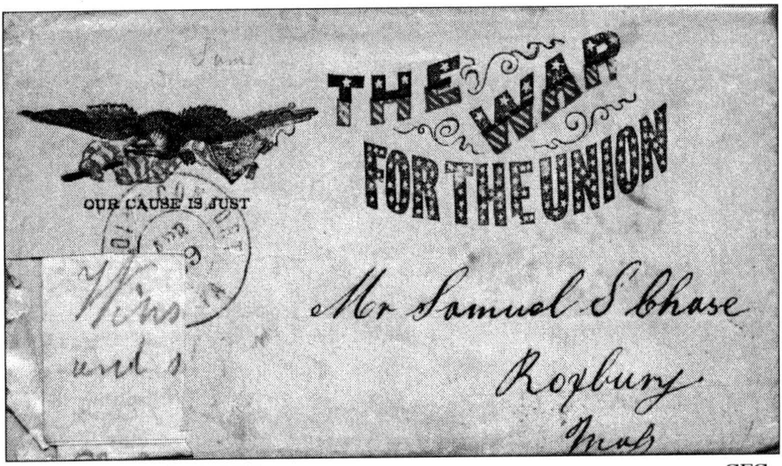

Envelope of April 27, 1862 CFC

praise for there conduct. They say they charged the rebels like veterans. I have always said the Mass 1st and NH 2nd could not be beat and I have no reason to alter my opinion. I saw a good many in the NH I knew and I find they are all anxious to have the thing settled. They feel as I do they dont want to go home untill the thing is finished up but they dont care how quick it is settled. They all feel confident they can clean the devils out and have the fullest confidence in McClellan. They have to work like dogs. Go out on picket one night and work on the forts the next but they bear it like heroes. Not a murmur out of them but I am afraid it will tell on them for the climate is enough to kill the devil and the water is enough to sicken a cat. We dig a hole anywheres to get water out of for it is all alike. It is nothing but swamp from here to York Town and it is a nasty place for white men. I expect we shall leave here tomorrow and go to Gloucester Point. I suppose you have seen maps in the papers and you can easily find the location. I expect we shall open the ball there and I expect before another week rolls around there will be some fighting done that will astonish the Rebels.

You must give my love to all the folks and excuse the shortness of this letter as I have got three more to write to night. I have received eight this week and think I must answer part of them. So

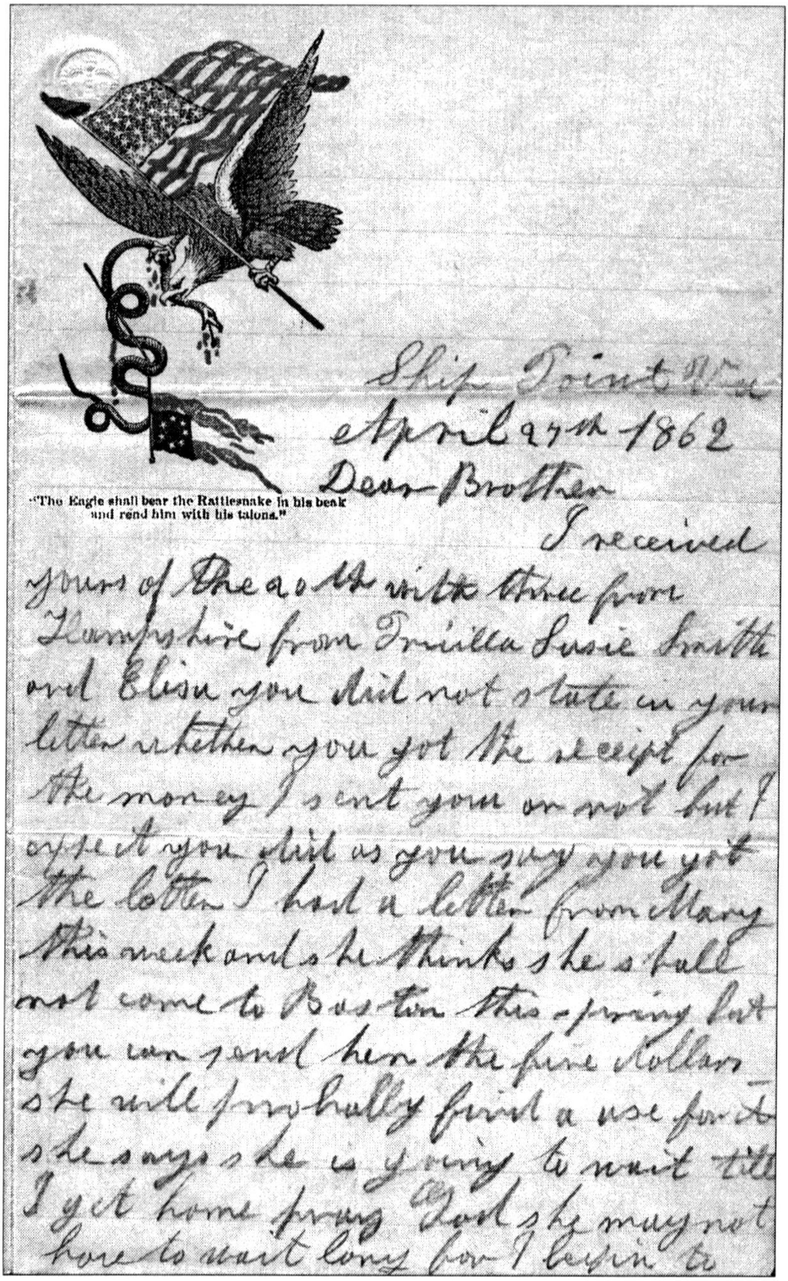

Ship Point Va
April 27th 1862
Dear Brother
I received yours of the 20th with three from Hampshire from Priscilla Susie Smith and Eliza you did not state in your letter whether you got the receipt for the money I sent you or not but I expect you did as you say you got the letter I had a letter from Mary this week and she thinks she shall not come to Boston this spring but you can send her the five dollars she will probably find a use for it she says she is going to wait till I get home for god she may not have to wait long for I begin to

Letter of April 27, 1862 CFC

hopeing we shall take York Town this week I bid you adieu.
J W Chase

Winslow sends his respects and says he will not sleep on the common anyway.

* * * * * * * * * * *

Ship Point Near Yorktown
May 3d 1862

Dear Brother

I have been watching for the mail all this afternoon for I expected letters from you and Mary but Instead of that I got one from you and one from the School Marm but we must be grateful for small favors out here. I dont think Mary had ought to exposed me if I have got a School Marm for a correspondent but I never could do any thing on the sly and if there is any trouble about it Eliza has agreed to back it. You must tell Miss Grindell that I dont believe she is a real native but if she is she is such a little ways into the state that she is about equal to New Hampshire women. She is an Abolitionist and she is trying to make one of me but I am afraid she has got a hard subject for the more I see of niggers the less I think of them. They have a lot of Contrabands here and the Government is feeding and clotheing them and they try to make them help unload the vessels that come here with forage and grub but it is more work to get them to do anything than it is to do it yourself but still I am open to conviction and perhaps Miss Laura will be able to make an impression on my dark mind. At any rate I think she is a smart girl and I like her style. All but the nigger. Tell Emily that I dont want her to think that I am going to forget her if I do write to a School Marm for I shall certainly remember her the first rebels pocket I pick and if I ever get back she shall have a relic! We leave here tomorrow and I expect we shall go on with the advance and I expect that the Ball will open now in a few days and then if McClellan gets defeated it will do for his enemys to blow but the men composing his army dont intend to give them that chance for we mean to whip them and I dont believe there is a man but what has perfect confidence in him and is willing to live and die with him. If you could here the swearing that is done here sometimes when they get hold of a paragraph in the papers finding fault with him you would think there was need of more chaplains. I read up what you said you told the Editor of the Journal and the boys said Bully for him and want me to say if he makes any more such remarks to knock him down and they will pay the damage. The fact is the Soldiers have confidence not only in him but in all the leading officers of this wing of the army and they dont want them found fault with untill they have done something that merits it and I think if they cant find any thing else to find fault with they had better wake up and mind there own business if they have got any.

Detail from Letter of May 3, 1862 CFC

The rebels have been banging away all day and they were at it yesterday and last night but one of the Mass 5th battery was down here to day and he said they were throwing 11 inch shell but have done no damage yet. They burst one of there guns yesterday. It was the biggest one they had. It threw a 200 pound ball. We can see the shells burst from here but I expect after we get up on the line we shall see more than we want to but the courage of the boys is good and they say if we have got to fight we will try and do it up brown and I hope we shall come out all right but at any rate I hope we shall do our duty. The talk seems to be that the men in Folletts third Battery showed rather more pluck than the officers at the time of the advance on Yorktown but it dont do to believe all you hear.

You must give my love to all the folks. Tell them my courage is good and if I was as sure of comeing home in July as I am that we shall defeat the Rebels at Yorktown I should feel as though it was dead sure for we are bound to do that as sure as they stand for us to do it. Give my love to Mace. Tell him a little specific would not be bad to take but it is most too much trouble just now to attend to getting out as we are on the move all the time and it would be doubtful about my getting it but I think my back bone will hold out if I dont have any but still I am much oblidged to him for his kind offer and hope I shall have the priveledge of drinking some with him before another winter.

I wrote to Mary down east this week and told her that you would send her a picture.

Give my love to William and his family. Tell him we intend to give the death blow to this Rebellion in this fight and then what there is left of us are comeing home to see the folks. There is some of the Mass first aboard a Steam Boat here. They have made a hospital of it. Some of our boys have been to see them to day. They are in good spirits and doing well. I shall write again soon if nothing prevents so good bye for this time for I must write to the school marm to night sure.

From yours &C
John

PS Winslow sends his respects and says he means to growl as long as he has a leg to stand on but when he gets where that punch and Sardines are he wont growl a mite and he dont care how quick he gets there.

The weather here is delightful. The trees are all in full bloom and there is any quantity of wild flowers.

* * * * * * * * * * *

West Point Va
May 9/62

Dear Brother

When I wrote you last I wrote that we expected to move on but I did not think that we should move as far as this. We hitched up Sunday morning last to go out for inspection and had just got into line when the news came that Yorktown was evacuated. We were ordered back to camp and told to keep the harness on our horses so as to be ready to go aboard as soon as the Steamer could be got ready. We left camp at eight that evening and worked all night and started the next morning at seven and came as far as Yorktown where we stopped that night. I wanted to go ashore there but it was no go for our own officers were not permitted to leave the Schooner but we had a very good view of there defences they had left and all I have to say is they were some but I suppose some of McClellans friends will say there was nothing but a few earth works mounting

Quaker Guns LC

quaker guns. We started again the next morning and arrived at this place the same afternoon but did not unload till the next morning only the infantry but we were at work again all night. We got ashore about nine and had just time to drink a pot of coffee when we were ordered to take our position on the field of battle as they were driving our pickets in. We started out and went into battery and waited for orders but soon we were ordered to shift our position and give them a few pills. We fired a few times then waited about a half an hour when word came that their main body was about two miles off and we were ordered to shell them at that distance. By this time the enemy had got a battery of six pieces to bear on us and they began throwing rotten shot at us but we got the range of the devils and the gunboats opening on them at the same time we soon heard the cheers of the 16th N.Y. and then we knew we were driving them. We drove them from there position and heard no more from them. We drove them back about two miles when night come on and the ball was over. We slept by our guns that night but we have not used them since as our orders were to hold this point if we could but not advance on them any. Yesterday we moved on about a half a mile and here we are camped and our horses unharnessed for the first time since Sunday morning as we never took their harness off coming up the river and they had rather a hard time of it. So you see we have at last had a skirmish but not much of a fight. Our loss in killed and wounded I dont think will reach 150 although some set it higher. The 16th 27th and 31st NY and the Penn Zouaves lost the most. The Zouaves suffered pretty bad. The others engaged had seen such fun before but the Zouaves were under fire for the first time. The rebels were in a thick woods and had their position chosen. It was not the intention of Franklin to have a fight as he was only ordered to hold the point but the Zouaves being anxious to do something went out farther than they were ordered and brought it on and if there was any where near the number of rebels they say there was I think we done well to hold them which we did do and drove them too but I suppose you will see all the particulars in the papers and I will not try to write them. All I have to say is things looked rather billious for us at one time but Mr Rebel dont like these little gun boats and when they can get a chance at them they dont spare them. How long we shall stop here I do not know but I hope not long for now we have got started

Co. F, 114th Pennsylvania Zouaves (detail) LC

with the advance I want to keep in it and where Franklin goes there is where I want to go for in my humble opinion he cant be beat much. Some of our wounded were treated first rate while others were murdered. Some were brought in with there throats cut from ear to ear. There was two of the 16th NY brought in so. One friend of mine was killed from the 16th NY and a noble hearted man he was. Many is the time he has fed me when I was hungry and I was sorry to hear that he was dead but so it is. It seems to me that the best men are bound to be killed first. There was only one Artillery man wounded. He belonged to the Jersey battery. Of our own exploits I have nothing to say. Only that we were highly complimented by the Gen in command. I dont know as I can write any more of interest. My health is good but I must say I am tired for we have had a hard weeks work but thank God for health. If we can have that we are good for them. Give my love to all and send this to Mary after you have read it and oblige.

John

PS Enclosed you will find a few violets that I picked near where my friend Smith fell. I want one of them if I ever come home and you can do what you please with the rest. I went over the field or woods I should say last night and if I ever get back I will try and give you a description of it but I cannot get time to write it. I have not had a letter this week nor seen a paper. The mails are expected to day and I hope to get one and find out what is going on in the world. Strong reinforcements are arriving here now and all we want is to catch the devils in an open field and death is their portion. I have no fears but what we can clean them out but how I shall come out personally is more than I can tell but I have no desire to leave the field. I have seen a little and I want to see more. I must tell one little incident while we were engaged in shelling that battery. One of the 16th was brought in wounded and when he went past us he took off his cap and lifted up his head as far as he could and cried out "give it to them Mass boys". We gave him three cheers and he passed on. He died the same night. There was one Lieut in the 31st was wounded in the arm. He come in had his arm dressed put it in a sling and went out again to his Company but it is of no use. I saw instances of courage that day that you would hardly beleive and this nothing but a skirmish but all I have to say now is I pity the wounded rebel that falls into the hands of the 16th and 31st NY boys after this for they have sworn they will never let one live if they can kill him. Rather savage I suppose you will think but I dont blame them much myself. Write often. Good bye. Direct as before.[1]

John

Three Cheers for the Union and bully for McClellan and Franklin.

* * * * * * * * * *

[1] This letter has penciled editorial marks. This was the letter that was printed in the newspaper referred to in John Chase's letter of June 1, 1862.

White House Virginia
May 18th 1862

Dear Brother

Yours of the 12th reached me last night the first time I have heard from you for a fortnight and in fact I have had but one letter since I left Ship Point and that was from Eliza. I dont feel much like writing to day as I have got a severe cold and feel as though I was about ninety years old but I will try and write a few lines just to let you know I am alive. I suppose you have got my letter about the battle. We left West Point the next day after I wrote you and came as far [as] the farm of William Basset where we stopped untill the next day when we came on about three miles and camped where the rebels had been two days previous. I hunted for relics but all I found was one Secesh postage stamp[2] which I enclose in this. We are now on the farm of Col Lee in a field containing about 500 acres and it is about covered with troops and the trappings of war. We have Signal trains Balloon trains Pontoon trains telegraph trains and most all kind of trains but roast beef trains. We have Sutlers along with us but it costs more than I can afford to pay to live on Sutlers cheese 40 cts a pound butter 50 and other things in proportion. So you see thirteen dollars a month will not buy a great deal of grub at those prices but I make out to live by foraging a little and if my health only holds out I think I can stand it. I expect we have got some thing to do to get into Richmond if the devils only stand and all I ask is to have them for I reckon we are just good for them for I think we can just lick all the rebels they can bring on and we want to get just one chance at them fairly and that will be the last of them in Virginia for I want this thing closed up and if we have got to fight the quicker the better I say. The weather is getting warm here and a good many of the men are sick. We have more sick now than we ever have had before and I hope we shall get through before long. It

CFC

[2] The stamp, a green 5¢ Confederate States of America with a portrait of Jefferson Davis, was enclosed.

is one thing to play Soldier and another thing to be Soldiers but the officers can do a good deal for these men if they are so disposed but I find the most of them think only of there own self I think; I know some men out here that I should like to meet in Boston. If they dont get a peice of my mind then I am a liar. That is all I want to live for now is to get in a place where shoulders bars dont make a man but I will drop this subject for it is not a pleasant one.

You must give my love to all the folks. Tell them I dont feel like comeing home untill the war is over but the sooner it is over the better I shall feel. Winslow sends his love to you and hopes to have the pleasure of meeting you between now and fall. I saw Sam Felton to day. He was at the landing after stores. He looks well but thinks he has got about enough of Soldiering but I must close for my head aches like mad and it is hot enough to melt you.

So good bye for this time and write often.

From John

PS There has 22 Batteries passed our camp to day and that is only part of what there is here.

Monday 19th

Not having a chance to send this yesterday I thought best to open it and write a few lines more. We left Camp at four this morning and now are within 20 miles of Richmond. We have gone into camp on Somebodys farm and a nice place it is and a beautiful spring night. Spring to us. I feel better to day but my eye balls are sore enough and when I look up it is like taking my life but I am in hopes to be better in a day or two. We left four men at the hospital this morning and I expect they will be sent home. There is a good deal of sickness amongst the troops but I dont know as there is more than ought to be expected.

* * * * * * * * * *

Camp near Coal Harbor[3] Va
May 27th 1862

Dear Brother

I received your letter of the 19th to day and you say you have not had a letter from me. I dont understand why as I have written three since we arrived at West Point but things are very uncertain here now. Sometimes we dont get any letters for a week and then we get a bushel at a time. I wrote you the next day after the battle of West Point and put some flowers in it that I gathered on the battle ground. In the last letter I got from you you wished to know the names of the flower that I sent you. It is what they call the sugarberry.[4] It grows in the woods. The trees grow about 10 feet high and they are very handsome when they are in bloom. There is lots of wild flowers here and I often wish that I could send Lizzie and Emily a bunch of them to make into boquets. In my last letter I wrote I sent you a Secesh Postage stamp and will send you a Shinplaster[5] when I get hold of one. We are now right on the line of the rebels and orders was read to us last night from George B and he tells us what he expects us to do. Franklins Division is on the extreme right and they say we shall have the hardest fighting to do. We have had some little skirmishing the last few days. Yesterday we were out and one Regt lost one man and five wounded and we bagged 75 prisoners and hard looking critters they were too. It was a Wisconsin Regt took them. The 16th New York think if they had taken them there would not been so many live ones for they swear they will kill every one they take and I dont blame them for the way they use our wounded is enough to make savages of any body. They killed one of the cavalry belonging to this Division and cut his ears off but I believe they will get paid off yet for I have faith to believe we shall lick them and if we do I think the men of this division will try and get square on them. There is great confidence placed in this division and God grant it may not

---

[3] Cold Harbor.

[4] American Hackberry.

[5] Slang for paper money issued by the U.S. government to replace coins that were being hoarded during the war. In 1862, they were issued in denominations of five, ten, twenty-five, and fifty cent notes.

be misplaced for I should rather die than be defeated. Now I expect the road to Richmond will be a bloody one but I am in hopes we shall get through for if we have got to fight. The sooner we begin the sooner we shall get through and for one I want to see this thing ended. All I ask is to be found doing my duty and I have confidence enough in myself to believe I shall. We shall probably be in Richmond or defeated before you get this but at any rate you may expect to hear a good account from Franklins boys. If you dont I never will guess again. It is raining here to day like the devil and my blankets are wringing wet and I have hard work to get a place dry enough to write in but it begins to grow a little lighter and I hope the sun will come out so we can dry off. We are encamped on the farm of a Surgeon in the rebels service and for a wonder the Artillery got here before the Cavalry and Infantry and the boys found a lot of tobacco a barrel of Cider and a few jugs of Elderberry wine which we were lucky enough to dispose of before they got a guard on. For my part I think this putting a guard on to every rebels house is poor business for God knows we live hard enough and if we could steal a little it would help us out a little but we get a chance once in a while and then we improve it. You must give my love to all the folks and tell them I hope to come back some time and see them but if I never do I hope they will remember the little ones I have left behind and hope if I am called to lie down my life for the cause I may do it willingly and may this war soon be closed and smiling peace once more spread her wings over the whole union is the prayer of your

Brother John

I had a letter from down east last week. All well. I feel very grateful to you for writing when you dont get any from me but rest assured it is not my fault as I have written every week and some times oftener and shall continue so to do.

* * * * * * * * * *

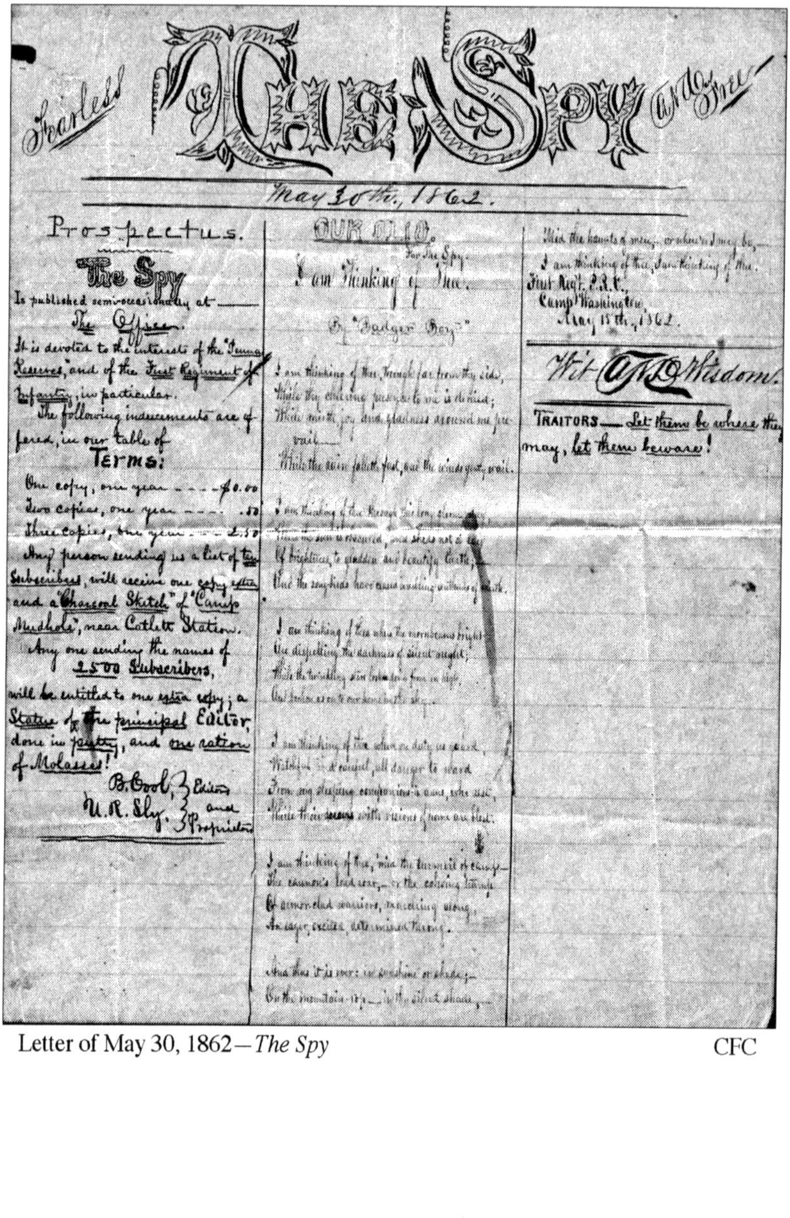

Fearless The Spy and Free

May 30th, 1862.

Prospectus.

The Spy

Is published semi-occasionally at ——

The Office.

It is devoted to the interests of the "Penna Reserves," and of the First Regiment of Infantry, in particular.

The following inducements are offered, in our table of

Terms:

One copy, one year - - - - $0.00
Two copies, one year - - - - .50
Three copies, one year - - - - 2.50

Any person sending us a list of ten Subscribers, will receive one copy extra and a "Charcoal Sketch" of "Camp Mudhole," near Catlett Station.

Any one sending the names of 2500 Subscribers, will be entitled to one extra copy; a Statue of the principal Editor, done in putty, and one ration of Molasses!

B. Cool, } Editors
U. R. Sly, } and Proprietors

OUR OLIO.

For The Spy.

I am Thinking of Thee.

By "Badger Boy."

I am thinking of thee, though far from thy side,
While thy cheering presence to me is denied;
While mirth, joy and gladness around me prevail —
While the [illegible] fast, and the winds [illegible] wail.

I am thinking of thee [illegible]
[illegible]
Of brightness to gladden and beautify Earth, —
[illegible]

I am thinking of thee when the [illegible] bright
Are dispelling the darkness of silent night;
While the twinkling stars [illegible] from on high,
[illegible]

I am thinking of thee when on duty on guard,
Watchful [illegible], all danger to ward
From my sleeping companions [illegible], who rest,
[illegible] with visions of home are blest.

I am thinking of thee, 'mid the turmoil of camp —
The cannon's loud roar, — or the echoing tramp
Of armor-clad warriors, marching along,
An eager, excited, determined throng.

And thus it is ever: in sunshine or shade; —
On the mountain-top, — in the silent shade, —
'Mid the haunts of men, — or where'er I may be, —
I am thinking of thee, I am thinking of thee.

First Reg't. P.R.C.,
Camp Washington,
May 15th, 1862.

Wit and Wisdom.

TRAITORS — Let them be where they may, let them beware!

Letter of May 30, 1862—*The Spy* CFC

[There was no letter enclosed with *The Spy*, which is a mock-up of a newspaper, written on blue lined paper.]

Fearless **THE SPY** and Free

May 30th, 1862

Prospectus.

The Spy
Is published semi occasionally at
The Office
It is devoted to the interests of the
"Penna Reserves," and of the First Regiment
of Infantry, in particular.
The following inducements are offered,
in our table of
Terms:
One copy, one year $0.00
Two copies, one year .50
Three copies, one year 2.50
Any person sending us a list of ten
Subscribers, will receive one copy extra
and a "Charcoal Sketch" of "Camp Mudhole",
near Catlett Station.
Any one sending the names of
2500 Subscribers,
will be entitled to one extra copy; a
Statue of the principal Editor,
done in putty, and one ration of
Molasses!

B Cool } Editors
U.R. Sly } and
Proprietors

OUR OLIO.
for the Spy
I am Thinking of Thee.
By "Badger Boys"

I am thinking of thee, though far from thy side,
While thy cheering presence to me is denied;
While mirth, joy and gladness around me prevail
While the rain falleth fast, and the winds gently wail.

I am thinking to thee through the long gloomy day,
Where the sun is obscured, and sheds not a ray
Of brightness, to gladden and beautify Earth;
And the song-birds have ceased warbling anthems of mirth.

I am thinking of thee when the moonbeams bright
Are dispelling the darkness of silent night;
While the twinkling stars look down from on high,
And beckon us on to our home in the sky.

I am thinking of thee when on duty as guard,
Watchful and careful, all danger to ward
From my sleeping companions-in-arms, who rest,
While their dreams with visions of home are blest.

I am thinking of thee, 'mid the turmoil of camp
The cannon's loud roar, or the echoing tramp
Of armor-clad warriors, marching along,
An eager, excited, determined throng.

And thus it is ever: in sunshine or shade;
On the mountain tops—in the silent shade,
Mid the haunts of men, or where 'er I may be,
I am thinking of thee, I am thinking of thee.

First Reg't. P.R.C.
Camp Washington
May 15th, 1862

Wit and Wisdom.

TRAITORS Let them be where they may, let them beware!

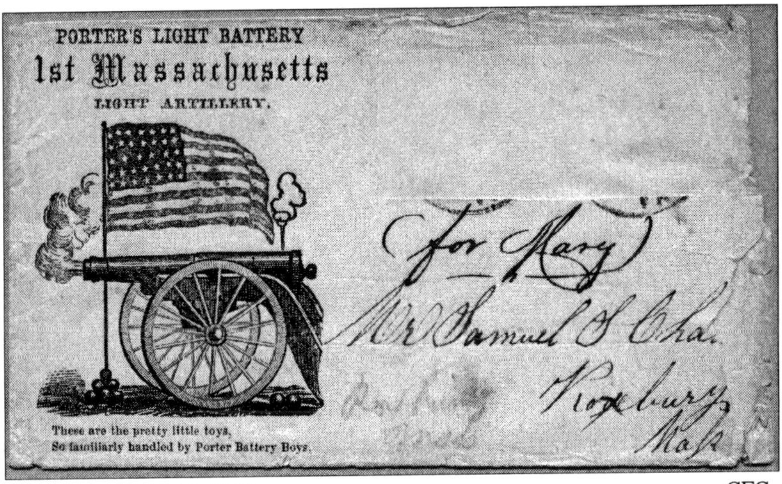

Envelope of May 30, 1862 CFC

* * * * * * * * * * *

Sunday June 1st 1862
In camp on the
Mayfeild Farm

Dear Brother

Yours of the 25th was received to day. I expected the last time I wrote that we should be in Richmond before this but I find the Road to that place is a hard one to travel. Since I wrote last they have been fighting all around us but as yet we have had no hand in the fun but we have harnessed up three times expecting to be ordered out but have been doomed to disappointment.

I suppose you have seen an account of the fight that Porters Division had last week. They brought down 600 Prisoners and a good many of there wounded to this place. The Rebels were mostly North Carolina troops and they talk as if they had got most tired of fighting for the Southern Confederacy and seem to think that Uncle Sam will have a Whole farm or none. The wounded all seem to be glad that they fell into the hands of the enemy for they say they get used better than they would amongst there own folks. Sometimes I think our folks think more of the rebels than they do our own Soldiers. It was a sorry sight to see the poor fellows brought in. There was one of the New York 44th that was shot twice in the head and had his little finger shot off and three holes through his dipper but he said he was going home and be back in a month and join his Regt and the way he hates Secesh is a caution. He told the doctor that before he would ride down here in an ambulance with a wounded rebel he would walk. I have made up my mind that nothing short of a hundred pound Parrott will settle his coffee <u>for him</u>. They commenced fighting on the left of us yesterday about noon and kept it up until night and commenced again this morning at daylight and such vollies of musketry I never heard before. News came here at noon that our forces were driving them like sheep. One of our Batteries have gone out with three reserve Batteries and they are shelling them all along the line. Our Division is anxiously waiting but I think we shall not be called out to day but still I should like to be there and see the fun. I should judge by the Cannonading and the sound of the musket that it must have been a bloody time but you will probably get an account of it before you get this. I am going to take a Sunday afternoon walk after I get this wrote and see our Batteries throw a few shell at them just to see how they do it. I took a ramble in the woods this morning as far as the pickets. I could see the rebels and the last week there has several of theres came over to our lines and concluded not to go back again. I rather think as a general thing they are getting sick of it. Some of them that were brought in here were very much astonished to learn that Manassas was evacuated for they thought they had a large force there now.

I was sorry to hear that Asher had enlisted[6] for I dont think he has any Idea of what he has got to go through but if he has got good officers it will make all the difference in the world for that is what makes a man feel at home is to have officers he can respect and if they are the right kind of men they can do a great deal to add to the mens comfort but I find a good many of them dont think much of a private and perhaps the same privates would not think much of them if they were at home. You must write to him often and that will serve to cheer him up a great deal. Tell him to keep himself clean as he can and not to buy too much stuff to eat and let him have a good rubber coat and leggins and always to keep dry when he can. He can have a good many more clothes in a battery than he could if he was in Infantry because he dont have to lug his knapsacks and he must be careful about the night air. I find I need an overcoat nights now just as much as I did in the winter and I think more on account of the heavy dews and above all the rest he must obey orders cheerfully. No doubt he will think a good many of them foolish but you know it dont do to ask too many questions but all you have got to do is to obey your <u>Superiors</u> and growl to your self in private. I will write to him if you will send me his address and try and give him the best advice I am capable of.

I am very much obliged to you for the papers for reading is a scarce article with us. We get the New York herald but we have to pay 15 cents apeice for them. I think I have read that letter[7] in the Journal before but I never expected to see it in print. If I had I think I should have been more particular but I never was much of a writer and if I only convey the Ideas I want too I am not very particular about the style. You must give my love to all the folks. Tell them I am well as can be expected for it is as hot as the devil and I am sweating at every pore.

---

[6] In the Seventh Massachusetts Battery.

[7] John's letter to Sam of May 9, 1862.

The Magnolias are now in bloom and there are thousands of them in the woods. I wish I could send you one but I have tried to press them and cannot make out the leaves are so tender. Winslow sends his respects and says he cant help growling and thinks you would if you were here. Coye asks me to ask you if you will remember him to Mr Seaverns and let him know he is all right. So good bye for this time.

From your Brother John

[The letter continues on another sheet with an imperfect picture of a flag from which the field is missing. On the back a notation says "Dont like to waste paper so I took this." The message is written crossways on half the sheet and the following list is written at a right angle on the other half.]

First Relief	Second Relief	Third Relief
1 Milliken	1 Hill	1 Russell
2 Daniels	2 Smitherman	2 Harper
3 Slattery	3 Woodbury	3 ~~Heywood~~ Jaques
4 Warren	4 ~~Cheney~~ Rogers	4 Bunker
5 Morse	5 Cheney	5 Sullivan

The boys read Gov Andrews letter to the Secretary of War in regard to more troops and they think if he wants to enlist niggers he had better let the white men come home. God knows it is bad enough to be a Soldier without mixing ourselves up with niggers and if Mass has no white men she had better let the States that have send the troops wanted. I want you to send me a few stamps in your next as I cannot buy one here. Dont send but few for I may not get the letter and when we get to Richmond if I am so lucky I can probably get some as I have a little change left yet. Tell Lizzie not to worry about Asher and not to believe more than half she reads in papers and I hope he will return to you safe and sound. He will probably learn some things that he never knew before and one thing will be to appreciate a good home and a mothers care and one thing he will have to learn and that is to do his own washing.

But I must close for this time. Love to Emily and all the rest of the folks.

I hope the next will be from Richmond.

* * * * * * * * * *

Camp near Chickahominy Va
June 6th 62

Dear Brother

We still remain in the same place but are expecting to move every hour. Smiths Division Crossed yesterday under the fire of the enemy but our guns were too much for them and they finally fell back. Part of our Division have moved to day but where they have gone is more than I can tell for troops are constantly going and comeing but we dont know where they come from or where they are going too. Sometimes one Division is ahead and some times another. The troops are in good health as a general thing. Our Division have been liveing on corn meal a good deal lately and we find the change from hard tack quite agreeable. I dont know as I have anything of Interest to write. Only that we get good news from the other parts of the army but we dare not credit more than half we hear but if half is true we are satisfied. They keep bringing in prisoners and deserters but the information obtained from them is not very reliable I dont think for they are apt to talk a good deal as they feel the troop here are anxious to have a fight here for they think if we give them a good drubbing here it will about close the concern up for they have got to be licked here if they fight although it will no doubt make Virginia the last resting place of a good many union Soldiers. Perhaps I may be amongst them but whether I am or not I dont want to leave the feild now. I want to see the hell hounds punished and I think they will be if they only make a good stand and I think they will.

We were paid off yesterday and enclosed you will find a check for 25 dollars which will be paid the same as before. 10 of it I want you to send up to Andrews folks at Exeter. It belongs to William

Twilight and is for his Mother and if you send it by Express his folks will pay the Expense.

I dont get any letters this week only what I got from you so I dont feel much like writing but feel anxious to hear from Stratham. You must give my love to all the folks and tell them we have had a three days rain here and it is raining now but I like it better than I do the heat for that is awful. I understand the Boston Light [Artillery] were disbanded. Is that so? So with my best love to the folks I will close.

from John W Chase

This peice I cut from a Wisconsin paper but God knows the truths will apply to other States as well. These Doctor Majors are a good deal like Chaplains. A damn humbug. At least thats my opinion.

[Enclosed is a clipping from a Wisconsin paper of a letter from a private complaining about the inadequate care of the wounded of the Fifth Wisconsin Regiment after the battle of Williamsburg.]

* * * * * * * * * *

Mechanicsville Virginia
June 14th 1862

Dear Brother

I received yours of the 8th to day and was very glad to hear from you and to hear that you were all well. We came to this place last Wednsday. It is two miles from our old camp and only five miles from Richmond. We are here doing picket duty and to try and hold the position. There is no other Battery here and only one Brigade of Infantry. We are on a bluff this side of the river and it is a beautiful place naturally. We can see the church spires in the city but whether we shall ever get any nearer to them remains to be proved. The Rebs have three Batteries on the hills the other side and our pickets are only seperated by the river and they exchange papers every day at the Bridge and dont try to shoot one another but they dont favor us that way for the first day we were here they opened on us and we had quite a lively time for about an hour but we came to the conclusion that we got the best of them as they ceased fireing and we could see them lugging some of there men on Stretchers. None of our men were hurt and the most of there shell went beyond us. Some of them came full on near as I want them to me for they are not very musical comeing towards you. Some of them burst in the woods about 50 yards from us to the right and took the limbs off the trees in great style. Some of our boys were in there playing bluff and cooking supper but they came out lively. One a Surgeon came rushing out and he was white as a sheet. When Gen Taylor of the Jersey Brigade came up and ordered us to open on them and blaze away Mac was right in his glory and he had business enough to attend to his two peices.

I have had two spells trying to write this and now I will try again. It is now three in the morning and being Corporal of the guard I have been up since twelve. It is very warm here to night and the Mosquitos and Black aunts are thicker than is anyways agreeable. There was a couple of the Rebel pickets swam the river this Afternoon and came over this side and gave themselves up. They both belong to New York and were pressed into the service. They were in the fort when we shelled it. They say we killed one horse and wounded three men. They say there is all of two hundred thousand men in and around Richmond and think they will make a stout resistance to us but I think when George gets things fixed to his mind they will have to fight harder than they ever have yet to keep this army out of Richmond but there is a heap of them and we are surrounded with enemies both in and out of our lines. They captured 19 of our waggons between here and White House yesterday and our Battery waggons just escaped and that was all. They burnt the waggons right in the road and drove the mules and horses off with them and they also got a regt of our cavalry into a trap and captured and killed the most of them. I think there is some damn poor Generalship shown here sometimes and some of our officers I would not trust any farther than I could see them for I think some of them care more for a nigger than they do of a private Soldier. I think this

Govt better take care of the men that are trying to fight the battles for them and let niggers go to the devil for I believe they have done us more damage in crossing and recrossing our lines than they ever done us good and the best way is to take the food and clothes they give them and give it too the Soldiers for the very ones that have so much symphathy for poor Sambo would rob a Soldier of the last cent he had. Perhaps you will think this is rather hard talk but it is truth and Gods truth at that and there has been times here when a private could not get a pair of pants to cover his nakedness and any quantity of the black devils dressed up in Govt Clothes. It may be all right but for one I cant see it but I dont want to growl but if I ever live to get back I think I can convince you that some of the men in this army have suffered some for there country and some for the nigger but I hope soon it will be over and then if alive we can talk it over together. I could sit here and write a volume if I had time but I must go and call up the men now for it is four o clock. Our horses are all harnessed up. They have been so the most of the time since we have been here and it is not much sleep the boys have had but they stand it Bully and we live like lords. Plenty of green peas and Beet greens out here and Johnny Secesh Gardens and pigs have to suffer. We get our whiskey twice a day when it arrives but if the rebs are going to cut off our supply trains I am afraid we shall come short of whiskey and grub too.

I had a letter from Eliza yesterday and she informs that Mrs Henney has another heir. Rather prolific I think for war times but it is no use. Blood will tell. You must give my love to all the folks. Tell Mace to drink a glass of punch for me the fourth and I hope if I am alive to be where I can get some for myself. Winslow is well but I have not seen him to day as the centre Section is about a half a mile from us and he is with them cooking but I shall probably see him to day and I will ask him about that Punch. If we ever get to Richmond and I am alive and well I shall send for a few things that I want. That is if there is a prospect of getting it but you know Govt takes Possesion of all the rail roads and other means of transportation out here but I believe they allow Adams and Co express to run things.

The weather here has been very hot this week. Last week it was rainy and cold all the week.

At the place we are in now is where the battle was fought on the 24th of May. I think I wrote you an account of it. The houses are riddled with shot and shell and you can pick up any quantity of shell in the woods and feilds. We have been drawn up in line of battle this morning as they expected an attack on our right wing and I have just finished my breakfast at nine o clock but the enemy dont seem disposed to come on. The Ashby Cavalry[8] made two attempts last night to peirce our lines but did not succeed. The boys around here are on the look out and God knows there is need enough of it for we have only three Regt of Infantry and two Batteries and our reserve is three miles back but if they come on to us I think they will not find us napping as they did Caseys Division at fair oaks. If they do I am mistaken but I must draw to a close for the mail is about leaving. I got the papers for which receive my thanks. So hopeing my next will be dated from Richmond I will close.

From your Brother John

I suppose by this time you have got a letter with a check as I sent one a week ago.

Love to all Including Emily.

I will write to Asher the first Chance I get.

* * * * * * * * * * *

Camp at Fair Oaks Virginia
June 24th 1862

Dear Brother

Yours of the 15th did not get here untill to day. I received the papers last Friday and began to fear I was not going to get the letter at all but long looked for came at last and right glad was I to hear from you. I also got one from Mary and find the folks in New

---

[8] The Ashby Cavalry was formerly led by General Turner Ashby, who was killed in May 1862.

Hampshire are all well and busily engaged in the very pleasant business of baby raising for every letter I get from that part of the country gives an account of one or more born or likely to be.

Well you know the knowing ones say there is a soul born when one dies and they have got to raise them fast these times to keep up. The fact when I last wrote we were at Mechanicsville on picket and we were liveing like humans on green peas cherries strawberries and other fixings not omitting whiskey but alas for us Wednsday the order come for us to join our division and cross the Chick &C and here we are on the ever to be remembered battle feild of Fair Oaks. It was an awful hot day and we had to foot it all the way. We started at one o clock and came 14 miles whereas if we could crossed where we were we should not have to come but five But Johnny has possession of the hills and ten pound parrotts are no match for 32s particularly when they count three to one but we got here at dark right in the midst of a thunder shower and we had to turn in the best way we could for it was too dark to pitch ponchos but the worst of it was we could find no water and if ever I suffered with drought I did that night. I would given a dollar for a quart of water fit to drink but when it came light I found a little spring in the woods. The water here is very poor but ours is better than it is farther on the left. There they have to dig holes in the ground and the land being covered with graves and trenches filled with the dead you can form your own opinion of what the water is and what the air smells like for there is dead horses in plenty and some men yet that never have been buried. They are between our pickets and the rebels and neither party dare go out to bury them. The men here are kept busy all the time for when not on picket they are throwing up Breast works and building corduroy roads for the ground is such it is impossible to move an artillery train over it. George keeps us busy with the spade for that seems to be his way of killing rebs. Hookers[9] Division is about a mile and half from us on the left we being on the extreme right this side of the river. I have been to see the boys in the Mass 1st and NH 2nd and

[9] General Joseph Hooker.

I was astonished at the way those two Regts have dwindled down since I saw them last. They have lost a good many and have a good many on the sick list now but what there is left are in good spirits and are anxious for the great battle to come off before Richmond for they think if we give them a good licking there will be a prospect of what there is left getting home some time before there three years are out for they are getting sick of a Soldiers life and want to see this thing played out. The nigger talk of John A Andrews & Co is not relished very well out here. Billy Sutherland says if he is ever lucky enough to get back to Roxbury the first man that mentions nigger to him he will knock him down if he is big enough & Bill is in Command of the Co D as Capt Stones is sick. Horatio Littlefield is in the hospital. He had a tree fall on him but Capt Stone told me he was getting better and he expected him up in a few days.

Governor John A. Andrew NEHGS

Harry Smith Susies husband is quite unwell but he has to stick it out as the Capt of his Co was killed at Williamsburg and the Second Lieut was wounded and is at home on a furlough. He looks miserable. Take it all in all I guess Hookers Division have faired as hard as any other in this army of the Potomac but when they get at the rebels they give them fits. They were out on picket yesterday and the squirrel hunters as the rebels call the NH 2nd went noseing around the woods and stirred them up a little and they had quite a little skirmish but such things happen almost every day now and if we dont have a little shelling to do we get lonesome.

I suppose you all feel anxious to have the fight come off but George is getting ready as fast as he can. He is bringing up some Speakers to talk to them and they will give them argument that they cant get over easy. No man can have an Idea of the work that is done here without he is here to see it and you must be patient but I can tell you one thing. This army or part of it goes to Richmond if they wade there in blood. The men are determined and I think Caseys surprise will be a good thing after all. They have thrown him to the rear and they have troops on the front now they cant catch napping not easy. We are all anxious to have them attack our line but are not quite ready to attack theres but every day brings us nearer and we are all well aware that when it does come it will be the last fight to thousands of us but God grant us the victory and I hope that I may be led safely through but all I can do is to put my trust in him and let him do with me as he sees fit.

I shall write Asher to day if I can get time and it is not too hot. We had an awfull Shower last night and a good many of the boys got drownded out but my hut stood it first rate. I find a little extra pains taken in fair weather helps out in a rain for when it rains here it rains I tell you and the thunder and lightning is some pumkins. Tell Lizzie not to worry about Asher for I guess he will stand it. Some that came out with us that nobody thought could endure it are the toughest boys we have now. It is not so hard in a Battery near as it is in Infantry. There is a good many places to work a man in and make it easy for him. When you write again let me know what part of the play his is and who bought old Woods house. I glad you have got rid of him and the worst wish I wish him is that the old boy had killed him. I reckon he thinks he has paid rather dear for his whistle this time.

Winslow sends his respects to you. He still remains in the cook shop. Covell has gone to the hospital and I hardly think he will come back with us again. He cant seem to stand the pressure and I guess he has got enough of a Soldiers life. My health has been tip top lately and if it will only hold out I shall be glad for I do dread being sick out here. You must give my love to all the folks. Tell Mace that the Whiskey ration has played out. I guess George thought the officers got more than there share. At any rate some of them got awfull drunk and I guess on the whole the men are full as well off without it as they would be with it. Give my love to Williams family and Mrs

Curtis[10] and in fact all that feel interested in the welfare of a common Soldier. Tell them we intend to lick but George must take his time but I must close for this time so good bye.

yours &C
John

PS By the way the boys out here seem to think that Walton is all that the Court Martial made out and more too.

* * * * * * * * * *

City Point Va
July 4th 1862

Dear Brother

For the first time for a week we are haveing a day of comparitive rest as it is just a week ago to day that we commenced the retreat. All I can say is just this. We retreated and fought all the way here and I am still alive but God alone knows how long I shall be as we are drawn up in line of battle now and they keep us busy the most of the time. How this thing is going to end God only knows but I dont think I can stand another such a seige. I thought one day I should give up sure but it was fight or be taken prisoner and I am not quite ready to let them have me yet. You must let the Hampshire folks know that I am alive as it is hard work for me to get time to write this. May we yet conquer is my prayer but I tell you Virginia has drunk rivers of blood the last week and many a hearthstone in New England is left desolate. Hopeing the next time I write things will look better I will close. My love to all.

From John
What there is left of him.

* * * * * * * * * *

[10] Mrs. Curtis was Sam's wife's mother.

Harrisons Landing Virginia
July 6th 1862

Dear Brother

I sent you a few lines yesterday but receiveing a letter from you to day I thought that haveing time I would write again and try and give you some Idea of our retreat to this place. We left Fair Oaks a week ago to day after takeing part in the battle of Woodburys bridge after which we were not engaged but once which was the last fight. We were engaged there three hours and fired 140 rounds of shell. We had one man killed and one wounded. Through the whole thing we had one killed two wounded and two missing. We were in some pretty tight places but through the mercy of God I came out safe but pretty well used up. The last day I thought I should go under sure but I did not want the Rebels to get me but I dont know but what I should be as well off in there hands as I am here. The fact is my patriotism is about played out but still I have sworn for three years and I want to try and do my duty but as to the country I believe the damn Politicians are willing the country and the army may all go to the devil if they can only carry out there party schemes. I used to think I had a country to fight for but I have come to the conclusion that I am fighting to build up a party and a party that believes that niggers must be free if it takes the last drop of the poor white mans blood but still I hope the people of the North may arise in there might and hurl the damn traitors from the halls of congress for I think there has been about blood enough spilled the last week and treasure enough wasted to open the eyes of the people and let them see where the country is going too for let the papers say what they will blood has been poured out like water and men have endured what I never suppose the army could endure and neither do I believe they can go through another such a scene for I think the great majority of them will take the reins in there own hands and then woe betide the men that have caused them to suffer this worse than death. I have seen sights the last week that would draw tears from a stone. What do you think of wounded men paying niggers 25 cts to fill there canteens with water when Govt is paying and feeding them?

Would not such sights as that cause your blood to boil and niggers riding in baggage waggons and our own wounded and sick left to be taken by the rebels. That is what I have seen and a good deal more of the same sort. If such things as those will not cause a man to go back on himself for a damn fool for enlisting in the army he can stand more than I can thats all. But thank God we have a General in which we place our dependence and we believe if he could had his own way this thing never would have been and we believe that yet this army will prove victorious in the end. I believe that this thing must end some time but perhaps I may not live to see it for I find a mans life is not much thought of here and if it was not for my little ones I dont know as I should care how quick I left this world of corruption and robbery but I trust if [I] do not come back that my friends try and take care of them.

I suppose you knew that Lieut Sutherland was wounded and the last time I saw the Regt they did not know where he was as he had not come in but I hope he will come out right yet. Our division has suffered a good deal. We have lost a good many men and any quantity of officers. More than half of our field and line officers have been either killed or wounded and Grovers Brigade in which the Mass first and NH Second are is about all gone. In fact the great army of the Potomac is about played out but they say the President has called for more men and I hope the men will be forthcomeing for I think they are needed bad enough but you know it always is darkest just before day and I hope that day is about to break upon us.

You must give my love to all that want to hear from me. Winslow sends his respects and says he is in hopes to see you again before he goes under but things are mighty uncertain out here but I will close for <u>I am nervous</u> and find I cannot collect my thoughts and if I am spared I will try and do better next time. I have answered all Elizas letters as regularly as I have yours and if she has not gotten them it is not my fault. I received the papers also some last week for which receive my thank so good bye and may God bless you. Remember me to Sarah Fessenden when you write.

John

* * * * * * * * * *

Camp Near Harrisons Landing
James River Va
July 13th 1862

Dear Brother

Yours of the 6th I received yesterday but concluded not to answer untill to day as I was busy building me a house and filling up with ammunition. The farm on which we are encamped belongs to William Ruffin Esq[11] and it is a beautiful farm. The Mansion House is some two miles from here and is described by those that have seen it as being the best looking one they have seen in Virginia. The buildings here are or were nothing but Nigger huts and store houses and those the Soldiers have torn down and used up the lumber in makeing shanties and floors to sleep on. This respecting rebel property is getting played out and the boys go in with a perfect looseness. It looks rather rough to see good buildings torn down in the style they are but I believe it is about the thing after all. Desolate the county and make them suffer from there misdeeds. The only building they have left on this place is a church a neat little brick affair. This they have not touched. You wish me to write the particulars of the fights [we] were engaged. I have written you two letters since the battles and believe I have given you as full an account of it as I can. The only fight in which we were actively engaged was at White Oak Swamp and according to all accounts we were in a tight place. I thought so at the time but did not think we were quite so bad off as it proved we were afterwards. Our guns have all got to be changed as the vent holes are so burnt out that we cannot use them with much effect. That day at one time the tube would explode of itself the gun was so hot. The Infantry say that it was the smartest fireing they ever witnessed and the 16th boys allow that the first Mass cant be beat even by regulars but I dont wish to brag for I think as a general thing that the army of the Potomac done as well as

[11] Evelynton Plantation was the estate of Edmund Ruffin, Jr., whose father, an ardent secessionist, had fired the first shot at Fort Sumter.

any army could under the circumstances and all seem to feel well satisfied with the result but I trust we never shall be called to pass through another such a time for the sufferings on the road were awful to witness but things begin to brighten a little now and I think after the men get rested they will be ready for another whack at them. The Soldiers have the fullest confidence in George and firmly believe there is not another man in the country that could brought them through as he did. He rides around here most every day and if it was not for his well known face we should not know him from a civilian. No Shoulder bars but a common blouse and straw hat on but the boys find him out and the cheers will burst forth where ever he makes his appearance and all feel as though it is no fault of his that we are not in possesion of Richmond to day but there opinion of some of the powers that be in Washington are not quite so high and I think if they could hear of the death of several men that are in high official Station it would be good news to them. The boys feel anxious to hear how recruiting is going on and what the prospect is for filling up the diminished ranks of the army. The Mass 5th Battery is broken up. The men what there is left of them being put in the regular and Martins Battery of that Division. They lost all there guns but two at the battle of Gaines mill and they suffered a good deal in men but you probably get all the Items in the papers. I suppose you have seen that Franklin has been promoted and our division is under the Command of Gen Slocum. He is a Bully man. Cool as a cucumber and one that is not afraid to speak to a private but I suppose that Hooker and Kearney are the fighters of this army and they can just clean the rebs out every time they get at them. I hope the men will be forthcomeing

General Henry W. Slocum AJB

to fill up our ranks and when we once more open on them it may be for the last time. If we are going to put down this rebellion the quicker the better I think for I believe the army suffers more in being Idle than it does in fighting. Let us have an army that will overpower them and then go in while you have the chance. I suppose by the appearance of things that we shall not be called upon right away to do any more fighting without Johnny attacks us here and that I dont think he will do in a hurry for he is afraid of these gun boats but if he comes I think he will meet with warm reception. We have a good position and it will be fight or die here for we cant get any farther. The weather here is some days as hot as the devil the next cool. Fourth of July was the coolest fourth I ever knew. There was not much going on here. The gun Boats and some of the Batteries fired Salutes and the Bands played some and George rode around and looked at us and thus ended the dullest fourth that ever I saw but you know it always is darkest just before day and I hope the day will soon dawn and the Sun burst forth and peace and prosperity once more spread over the whole country for war I think is the greatest scourge that can come upon a nation and may God grant it may soon come to an end. I wrote to Asher but have heard nothing from him and dont know as he received mine as our mails were not very regular for a few days. I have written three letters up to hampshire but all I get in return is what Mary writes me but I suppose they think I have plenty of time and they dont but I think if they were in my place they would see it in another light. Give my love to all inquireing friends and tell them I think I am good for another trip as we are likely to stop here a spell. I want you to send me a box and I will pay for the same and I will try and tell you what I want. I want a peice of cheese a salt fish a box of pepper and a box of ginger two boxes Rochelles powder a half a dozen lemons a bottle of Santa Cruz Rum for myself and a Bottle of Jamacia for Winslow some tea and a pair of cheap slippers no sugar I can get plenty of here as cheap as you can buy it there. We get an order from the officers and buy it if [in] the Commissary. I want you to send a bill of the things as Winslow and myself are in Co and if God spares us we will try and make it right. Any friends wishing to send of course can have the priveledge but my friends have done so much for me that [I] cant have cheek to ask them. By the way Ive forget more [than] half. I want a pound of tobacco and some writing paper and a pencil that will be good to write with. I have got a half a dozen but they are good for nothing and tell Lizzie if she has got a towell she dont know what to do with she may put that in. You can direct the Box to

J W Chase
First Mass Battery
Slocums Division
Franklins army Corps
Harrisons Landing Va
Care of Capt J Porter.

Winslow sends his respects and thinks he should liked a little of that punch. He says he is still in for the union but sometimes feels as though it had about played out when he reads of the wrangles in Congress about nothing. Remember me to Emily and tell her I think if I live to get back I shall take a trip down east and see that School Marm and see if I cant talk some of the nigger out [of] her as she seems to be impressed with Sambo a good deal.

I wish I could be there and have a talk with you to day. I think I could make it a Pleasant Sabbath for myself but with us Sunday is just the same as any other day. The same routine and you never know whether you are going to have time to wash a shirt without being called of [off]. I have not been up to the first Regt since we have been here. They are about a mile from us but I think I shall try and get up in a day or two. If you hear anything about Billy Sutherland just let us know how he is. Remember me to Mace and all the rest of the folks and may the time soon come when I can be with you to thank you for the many favors conferred on me.

From
John

* * * * * * * * * *

Camp Near Harrisons Landing
James River Va
July 21st 1862

Dear Brother

Your ever welcome letter arrived here Friday night but I have had no time to answer untill this morning for Saturday we were kept busy policeing camp and cleaning up our guns and carriages and yesterday forenoon they had us out for an Inspection and gave us a Brigade Battery drill of two hours and in the afternoon I visited the Mass 1st and NH 2nd. The first time I have been out of camp since I arrived at this place. The boys in those two Regt are feeling better than when

Camp of the First Massachusetts Light Artillery on Heron Creek near Harrison's Landing, by Alfred Waud LC

we first arrived here but there is still a good many faces that we once use to see around that we never shall have the pleasure of seeing again. Lieut Sutherland they fear is dead as he was shot in the throat and they have heard nothing from him. The boys in his Regt feel his loss very much as all liked him who knew him and his courage was without a question. He was as much respected as Walton is despised. I saw Harry Smith Susies husband. He is pretty smart but thinks he should like to go home and stop a few weeks. Lieut Perkins of his Co has been home on a furlough. He was wounded at Williamsburg in the hand. He cannot use his hand now but he said he could not rest easy at home and thought he would come back. I find as the stragglers come in that some of the Regt are not so bad off as it seemed at first but still there are a good many that are not fit for service and then there is another class that can eat there rations in good shape but have a holy horror of fighting. They can tell great stories of what they have been through but some how or other nobody sees them engaged in action. Some of this class have been awful sick since we arrived here and some of them have got discharges and I hope too God the rest of them will for I dont think they are any great benefit to the army. They only help eat better mens rations. We buried one man last Sunday. He died with fever. His name was White from Canton. He was one of the best men we had. Always ready and willing to do his duty. In fact I think his disposition to work was one cause of his being sick. We buryied him near the church and had a minister to attend his funeral. We done all we could do for the poor fellow but you know that is not much but it may be some consolation to his friends to know that he received a christian burial. There has been a good many poor fellows died since we arrived here and there is a good many sick now but our hospital arrangements are Improveing I think and God knows there is need enough of it but where there is so many it is almost impossible to take proper care of them. I see by your letters and the papers you sent me that the people are wakeing up again and I hope they will keep at it this time till they raise an army big enough to whip all the rebels and see if this thing cannot be closed up for I tell you this liveing on smoked hog and hard tack and sleeping with toads and bugs and snakes is not pleasant if I know any thing about it. The 32nd Mass Regt has arrived here and the boys think there knapsacks will look smaller by the time they have been out here a year or so for they are pretty well filled out now. You see the boys in the army of the Potomac seem to think they have seen the Elephant and have come to the conclusions that we cannot see any rougher times than we have seen and live. Although we may see more like them I am glad to hear that Georges reputation still holds out and as for Abraham I never felt like going back on him for although not professing to be of his politics I wish all our political men were like [him] for I think he is one of the kind that thinks of country first and party afterwards. He has heaps of friends in this army that never vote for him but if they should ever have a chance there is no knowing what they might do for the President and Gen Mc are tops of the heap I can tell you here. I see the account of Col Cass[12] funeral in the papers you sent me and I think Mass never sent a better Col out here than he was and his loss is deeply felt here both by native and adopted citizens. I tell you these Irishmen can just fight and there is no rubbing it out. Meaghers[13] Brigade I consider is one of the best in the army and that 69 NY Regt are perfect devils and they never have got after the Rebs yet but what Johnny concluded to leave. One of there howls is enough to scare any white man. Speaking of boxes you have probably got my letter before now so you will know that I did not forget to send for one and I think if I get one that the contents will not come in bad for I just feel as though a little of something good would do more towards makeing me feel well than all the quinine & castor oil in the army. I guess 3/4 of our boys have sent home for a box and I expect if we stay here long enough to get them that we shall have a good time generally. Those stamps that Mrs. Curtis sent me I am much oblidged for and you can tell her that there is no danger of my forgetting her for I have things in my knapsack that often make me think of her and other kind friends in Roxbury and my chief desire is that I may prove myself worthy of the many favors they have bestowed on me but one thing I know I have always been at my post so far and I dont feel like turning back untill the war is closed but I dont care how quick that is done that is honorably for I still go in for the whole union and nothing shorter. You must remember me to all friends and God speed the time when I can once more sit down in old New England and if I live I dont think I shall be in a hurry to get out of it again. So good bye for this time.[14]

Yours &C
Jack

[12] Colonel Thomas Cass of the Ninth Massachusetts Regiment.
[13] General Thomas F. Meagher, born in Ireland, raised an Irish brigade in New York City.
[14] An edited version of this letter was published in the *Roxbury City Gazette*, on July 31, 1862.

Roxbury City Gazette.

ROXBURY. MASS., THURSDAY, JULY 31, 1862.

Near Harrison's Landing, James River, Va.,
July 21, 1862.

DEAR BROTHER:—We are kept busy policeing camp and cleaning up our guns, carriages, &c. We were out yesterday morning for inspection and Brigade Battery drill. In the afternoon, I visited the Mass. First and N. H. Second Regiments. It was the first time I had been out of our camp since I arrived at this place. The boys in those two regiments are feeling better than when we first arrived here, but still there are a good many faces that we once used to see around that we never shall have the pleasure of seeing again. Lieut. Wm. Sutherland, the men fear, is dead, as he was shot in the throat, and nothing has been heard from him. The boys feel his loss greatly; they all loved him, and his courage was without a question. He was as much respected as Walton is despised.

I find that the regiment is not so bad off as it seemed at first, but still there are a good many that are not fit for service, and then there is another class that can eat their rations in good shape, but have a holy horror of fighting. They can tell great stories of what they have been through, but somehow or other nobody sees them engaged in action. Some of this class have been awful sick since we arrived here, and others have got discharged, and I hope the rest of them will, for I don't think they are any benefit to the gallant First, or to the army. They only help eat better men's rations.

I learn that the people are waking up again, and I hope they will keep at it, this time, until they raise an army big enough to whip all of the rebels, and see if this thing cannot be closed up.

The 32d Mass. Regiment has arrived here, and the boys think their knapsacks will look smaller by the time they have been here a year or so, for they are pretty well filled out now.

The boys of the army of the Potomac seem to think that they have seen the elephant, and have come to the conclusion that we cannot see any rougher times than we have seen.—Gen. McClellan's reputation still holds out and as for Father Abraham, I never felt like going back on him, for, although not professing to be of his politics, I wish all our political men were like him, for I think he is one of the kind that thinks of the country first, and party afterwards. He has heaps of friends in the army, made up of those who did not vote for him, and if they had a chance, there is no knowing what they might do; for the President and George B. McClellan are on top of the heap, I can tell you.

I regret to hear of the death of Col. Cass. Massachusetts never sent a better Colonel out here than he was, and his loss is deeply felt, both by native and adopted citizens. I tell you THESE IRISHMEN CAN JUST FIGHT, *and there is no rubbing that out*. Meagher's Brigade I consider as one of the best in the field, and the 69 New York are *perfect* devils, and never went after the rebels but what they concluded *to leave*. One of their howls is enough to scare any white man.

Remember us to all friends, and God speed the time when the war shall be over and we shall be among you again.

J. W. C.

John Chase's Letter of July 21, 1862, in the *Roxbury City Gazette* RCG

I had a letter from Eliza last week but the most Information I got out of it was that the weather was damp and hot there and I can say the same of it here decideley.

* * * * * * * * * * *

Dont expect much this time. If you do you will be disappointed.

Camp Near Harrisons Landing
James River Virginia
July 25, 62

Dear Brother

Last night French came in and roused me up out of a sound sleep and told me that I had a dozen letters but the dozen dwindled down to 4 and three papers without I call yours three and it would make three such as I receive from some of my correspondents. I have written to most everybody since I arrived here and I think that it is about time for me to hear from some of them but somehow or other I cannot get much news from Hampshire. I received a letter from Mary but she is young and dont write much but I expect as long as I will write to them I can have it all my own way but I am just going to shut off now and if they want to hear from me they have got to write for I dont believe in this haveing no time without they are more drove than they used to be and as for news I think they could find something to fill up a sheet with. I dont know as it is necessary to write accounts of fires or murders to Interest a person. In fact I know it is not with me for I like to hear of anything that is going on and I like to hear how things look in old New England. When you wrote me how your pear and peach trees looked I felt kind of good. I could Imagine myself seated in your back door smoking my pipe and Elizabeth and Emily a gathering flowers to put on the grave of one that I often think of out here and of the patience with which she[15] bore her sufferings that winter before she was called to a better world

[15] Sam and Elizabeth's daughter, Elizabeth, died in 1859, at the age of 16.

than this and some times I have almost thought I could hear her voice saying keep up your courage uncle John for it is only for a short time at the longest that you have got to stop in this world and I tell you dear Brother it gives me new strength and I feel revived both in body and mind. You know my mind is not very large any way and small things interest me and I think if the folks at home knew how easily they could add to my comfort they would try and write oftener but as I wrote to Father I thank God I have one that has proved himself more than a Brother to me and perhaps you will think I am a fool but I can tell you that tears have actually ran down over my cheeks when I have read your kind letters and thought of the many favors that you and other kind friends have granted for I know it is done without any hope of reward and I hope to live to thank you all in person but if I never do you may rest assured that I never forgot the friends in Roxbury and I know that all I can do to pay you is to do my duty as a Soldier and God grant that I ever may.

I dont know as I can give you much news for with us every thing is quiet. We have gone in to tents again and have got our camp laid out in shape and it is the best camp we have ever had. The Non Commission officers of each section have a tent to themselves and in ours there is only five so you see we have plenty of room as we have the largest size Sibley tent. We have to drill Brigade Battery drills three times a week the whole three Batteries together and I like it much as I think I feel better for the excersise and it is a new thing with us. Capt Porter has gone home on a furlough and Mac is in Command and things have to go straight for he is one of the kind that when he says a thing he means it [The following has been erased, but can be read with difficulty.] Porter is no favorite of mine and between you and I I dont think he is much of a man but you can keep this to yourself . . . [The rest is indecipherable.]

I shall keep an eye out for the box and I guess it will come straight as a number of the boys have got them and if I get it before the Capt gets back I will give his things to his servant and he will take care of them. Tell Elizabeth that Richardson had a box come to day and his stuff was about all spoilt as some of his stuff leaked out and that spoilt most all the rest but if mine comes safe I will not forget him for he never does me and he has had a good deal sent him since he has been with us. His Father is Warden of the Cambridge street jail and Ben is his only son and thinks a good deal of him and he is a good boy and makes a good Soldier. Tell Elizabeth I will try and get her some leaves and would have gone to day if I had time but it is drill day and we have been Policeing the camp and I can hardly find time to write and have to do that by odd jobs. I wish I could send her a magnolia. I have tried several times but if I was lucky enough to get one pressed it would turn all red and spoil but I am going to try and send her one some how. It is a beautiful flower and to see a large tree all covered with them it looks splendid. The last one I sent her is what they call sun dial and it is very pretty. I had to break out the centre in order to press it. I shall send her a four leaved clover with this. It growed at Fair oaks where the battle was fought on the last day of may and first of june. I hunted about all one afternoon for one and could not find one but one of the boys found this and gave it to me and I have had it in my Bible ever since and to day I happened to think of it and thought I would send it to her. You can tell her I dont write any to the School marm now a days. I have promised to write her when I get to Richmond but I am afraid she will have to wait some time according to present appearances. You must give my love to all the folks that want to hear from me and when you write to Sarah I forget the name give her my best respects.

I dont suppose you will be much edified with this letter but I felt as though I wanted to have a familiar chat with you and I feel as though I have had it. I shall write as soon as I get the box if not before and I hope it will get along next week as the rest of them have been about a week comeing. Government sends them up from Fortress Monroe on order from George B. I see some of the northern papers think George is not the man but I dont feel like going back on him yet and I think when the truth is known that he will be found all right. At any rate I shall blow for him untill I see something to condemn. Give my love to Emily and all that want to hear from me and tell them the first Mass Battery dont Bar anything in the service either for drill or fight. Winslow is gaining and sends his respects to all and will have more to say after he tries the punch. So good bye for this time.

Jack

* * * * * * * * * *

Harrisons Landing
James River Va
Aug 5th 1862

Dear Brother

Yours of the 27th I received last Thursday but have delayed answering for several reasons. First I thought to get the Box but it has not arrived but I expect to get it to day as the Commanders of this Division have sent men to Fortress Monroe to look them up and Lieut Mac has sent a special messinger for this Battery. They left last Saturday with a steam boat and two [barges?] and I hope to day they will get along.

Another reason I wrote to Mary and Langdon three weeks ago come tomorrow and wanted them to be sure and write me back as soon as they could but as yet I have received no reply and I dont know what to think for I wrote about something that I wished very much to know about and I dont feel very pleasant in not hearing from them for I am anxious to know how things are with them. When I came into the army I expected to get out of it in a years time if my life was spared but I see no probability of it now and another thing after passing through what I have life looks very uncertain with me and I feel as though I wanted to know if Langdon was satisfied with the arrangement I had made for the Children. If not I wanted to try and fix it some how so that I could leave this world if called upon to do so and not feel as if they were left without a protector. Charley I am satisfied will have one as long as his Grandfather lives and I want to feel as certain about the others and it does seem to me as if Langdon might found time to write by this time but perhaps he thinks I am not anxious to hear but he little knows what I have suffered for the last week and expect too untill I hear from them. Can you blame me and do you think it is asking anything but what is clearly right? If so say so for all I ask is what is right and I want you to let me know when you think of going up to Stratham and I will write to you what I want to know. Sometimes I think you are all the relative I have that cares a damn for me and the reflection is anything but pleasant I assure you. I will not judge too hard for it is possible they may have written and I not received it and I dont want to say or write anything to Injure any one but I cannot help feeling anxious about the welfare of my children for that is all I have to bind me to this world.

But I will drop this subject and talk about some thing else. In the first place in regard to Seargeant Williams the last time I was up to the Regt they had heard nothing from him more than what you saw in the papers but they were more hopeful of him than of Sutherland. As regards Capt Coggswell I never heard much about him as I never saw much of that Regt anyway and about these times it is no easy job to get out of our own camp but my opinion of a man that is well and resigns now is just this. The army is better off without him than with him and there is plenty of good men in the ranks to take there places and I say let such men be set down as Cowards. I see by the papers you sent me that Foster is sick. Mac is also sick and confined to his tent. I guess of the two Mac is the sickest man but I hope he may get well and another thing I hope he may have permanent

Lieutenant William H. McCartney USAMHI

command for things go on here first rate now and some of those that used to curse him are now his firmest friends. He has upset the cooks and made new arrangement in that department. He has visited the hospitals and seen that our men have what belongs to them as far as he has the power and then he has interested himself in trying to get our boxes for us and I think he is just the man to run this Machine Bully I do. Our officers are dwindling down. Capt off and Lieut Lorin is acting Adjutant and stops with the Regulars and to day our orderly Seargeant leaves us to take the position of fourth Lieut in The Jersey Battery. Another loss for us in my opinion that cannot be easily filled for he was the right man for this Concern in my opinion. In regard to our sick I think there has been a decided change for the better. There has been a good deal of stuff sent out here and when there is any one to look out and see that the doctors and stewards dont get it all the sick get theres.

Mayor Fay[16] of Chelsea with a couple of ladies has been out here and they have been to see our sick several times although the Mass first was his headquarters. He is a fine man and the young lady that came with him is thought as much of as it is possible for any one to be. The boys say it seems homelike to have a womans hand to bathe there aching heads and to sing to them the songs they used to hear at home. The boys up there have made her a rustic chair and she is going to take it home with her and I honestley think if it were possible they would not mind making it of Gold.

I should like very much to have you send some things out for our poor fellows that are under the hands of the army Butchers but things are very uncertain with us here now. Hookers division started out on an expedition yesterday and we are under marching orders and have been for a week. Still we may lie here for a month and we may leave before night but I think if some of our good friends in Roxbury would see Mayor Fay he would take charge of anything of that kind for the Boys with pleasure and he comes out here often. He brought out several boxes for men in our Battery this time when he came. He

[16] Mayor Frank B. Fay of Chelsea, Massachusetts.

is just the man to have charge of anything for the sick for all the men who come in constant contact with him like him but if it should look to me as if there was a chance for us to stop here I will let you know for I am willing to do what I can for the benefit of my sick Comrades for I know it is an awful place to be sick here with the best care you can get and I think it is our duty to try and help one another all we can and God knows that is little enough at the most. I see great accounts in the papers of what Halleck[17] is doing and what he is going to do but we dont see it yet. The boys here seem to think that George is our leader yet and for one I dont go back on him yet for although no man was [illegible] if I ever did come to that. McClellan is the man after bringing us through as he did. I call him a great General but if Halleck is any better why let him go in. I go for anybody that can bring this thing to a close let his name be what it will but still I think if some of the defamers of McClellan have got so much military genius they better come out here and show some of it. Here is where we want it and here is where it will be appreciated. I also see that Halleck has ordered the spades to the rear and muskets to the front but I can just go out of my tent and see three hundred men digging and white men too and as for these damn niggers if they would drive them all into the rebel lines I think we should be better off for I dont think they are much account to us only to eat up our grub but some folks will not be satisfied untill they

General Henry W. Halleck LC

[17] General Henry W. Halleck was named general-in-chief by President Lincoln in July 1862.

Horace Greeley LC

Senator Charles Sumner LC

have the whole country overrun with the lazy devils and I wish to God Charles Sumner[18] and Greely and all the abolition crew had them to take care of and feed. Thats so. They are banging away up the river this morning but what is up is more than I can tell but I suppose the papers will enlighten you. They came down the other side of the river last week and opened on our camp but when the gun boats opened on them they left in a hurry. They killed about a dozen niggers for which I dont grieve much. That I guess was the extent of the damage. It is awful hot here to day and the sweat is flowing freely and I guess I will draw to a close. You must give my love to all the folks and I will write again just as soon as the box comes. So hoping this mite find you all well I will close.

Jack

* * * * * * * * * *

[18] Senator Charles Sumner of Massachusetts was an abolitionist leader.

Harrisons Landing
James River Va
Aug 8th 1862

Dear Brother

I am not going to call this a letter but as I wanted to send this check to you I thought just to let you know that I am still alive and in tolerable health but as I expect to get a letter from you tomorrow or to night I will then try and write. I have had company to day from the NH 2nd and then I have been quite busy for the Seargent has gone away to get new guns for us. We are going to have Napoleons Brass 12 pounders.

We have had two or three alarms lateley and I expect every day we shall have to start off somewheres. I hope when we get at the devils next time we may give them all they want of it.

But the mail is about going and I must close. Weather hot as the devil. Love to all the folks. No Box received yet but I live in hope. We were paid off yesterday and I guess I can live for a few days if nothing happens. Good Bye. This check for 15,00 dollars will be paid as the others but probably not for a week or so as the Paymaster has not got through here yet.

Yours &C
John

* * * * * * * * * * *

Harrisons Landing James River Va
Aug 10 1862

Dear Brother

Friday night brought your letter and I was glad to hear from you and to know you had plenty of work. The box has not made its appearance yet. Why I cannot tell. I am satisfied that Mac has done the best he can to get them for us. There is as much as 50 boxes that ought to be here now. Once in a while there will one get here. Yesterday Charles French got one and in it was some tobacco and papers and envelopes postage stamps for me from Father and Pricilla and it works in very handy but I feel anxious about the other one for there is things in it that I want saying nothing about the fluid. I am in hopes to get it yet but the prospect seems to be rather small.

In my last I wrote you about not getting a letter from Langdon. I have got it this week. It was a long time comeing. 11 days. He writes that In case of my death he should like to keep the children and will keep them if I live. I have written him and told him I should like to have him keep them and any money you might have you would pay to him any time the children needed it and more than that if I should die you would collect any money due me and have it go for there benefit. I was glad to know that he was willing to keep them because they will be kept together and I know they will be well used and well brought up. Mary is not very well but the Doctor says it is nothing uncommon for girls of her age. I feel a good deal better about them since I heard from Langdon and think I can rest easy now for I wanted to know that they would have a home in case I was taken away.

I am glad to hear that Roxbury is doing so well in regard to recruits but I hope they will not forget the old Regts. If I was going to enlist I should take an old Regt by all means for a man can learn a good deal in a years Soldiering and the new men can benefit by there experience and another thing I think they ought to look out for them first. Capt Porter has got his furlough extended and is not comeing back untill the first of September. Charles French is acting orderley Seargeant and the care of the detatchment comes on me and it keeps me pretty busy. We have changed our guns. We have got 12 pound Napoleons Brass. They thought we were too smart a crowd to have long range guns so they have given us some that will require more energy to work. I dont admire the change much but it is no use talking. They will do

Napoleon Gun, by Edwin Forbes LC

as they are a mind too with us. We have moved our camp also. They have got some 32 lb Parrotts in the front where we were and have moved us back about 1/4 mile. I dont like it quite so well as I did the old place but it is a good deal better than some we have had. We have 5 Batterys in our division now. Two Maryland Batteries. One of them is Commanded by Capt Wolcott[19] of Roxbury.

We had soft bread for Breakfast this morning and Green told me we were going to have it all this week. That is a half a loaf a day and we get vegatables two or three times a week and I like it much myself and I think the men are a good deal better for it.

The weather here is awful hot and the day we went to the Landing after our guns the glass stood 136 in the sun and 112 in the shade. We have had no rain for ten days and it is awful dusty. In fact it is decideley uncomfortable around these diggings. I would give a dollar just to smell salt water and if I ever get near it again I think I shall stop within smelling distance. You must give my love to all the folks.

As to the Commission of course if I could get one I should just take it for I think I could do as well as some I have seen out here. I hope Elizabeth and Emily will have a good time down East. I wish I could be there and go with them. Give my love to Mace and all the rest of the Boys. Tell them George B will come out all right yet I think. Winslow sends his respects to you. He says he lives in hopes to see the box yet but thinks it is about the same chance that there is to our getting to Richmond but God Grant this thing may soon play out and we once more get North where there is somebody and something. So good bye and good luck.

Yours &C
J W Chase

* * * * * * * * * *

[19] Captain John W. Wolcott of the First Maryland Light Artillery.

Hampton Virginia
Aug 22nd 62

Dear Brother

I suppose you will be looking for a letter from me and I take the first chance to write that I have had since I wrote you last. The next day after I wrote you we struck our tents and turned them in to the quarter master and got every thing ready for a move. We harnessed up Thursday morning at 3 in the morning and kept waiting untill Saturday afternoon when we finally got started. We marched that night as far as Charles City where we camped that night. The next morning we started at 5 o clock and came as far as the Chickahominy. Crossed and camped. The next day we came as far as Williamsburg and camped. The next day arrived at York town and halted about noon. Went about a mile and camped. The next day went as far as Lees mills where you will recollect the vermont brigade had the fight last spring and yesterday we came through Newport News to this place where we are now. To day part of our corps have gone to Fortress Monroe Including the whole of Smiths Division. Where or when we are going is more than I can tell but I expect we shall start somewheres to day or tomorrow. This move seems to be kept very secret and no one seems to know where we are going and I reckon they begin to think it best to keep things to themselves a little more. We had very good weather for our move. The weather was pleasant and not very warm. The roads were very good but awful dusty. We did not march much after noon to day and that gave us time to cook up such stuff as we could pick up on the road for we found some few ducks and chickens that we thought best to levy on

GEN. WM. F. SMITH.

General William F. Smith AJB

for you know that is Popes orders and then we had a chance to look around and see the county. There was some fruit and melons on the road but I reckon there is less now. Some we bought and some we took just as it happened. When we got to Yorktown Asher came out and spotted us and went down where we camped and stayed with me untill night. I gave him some stewed peaches for supper and Introduced him to some bean soup and smoked Hog. Luxuries that he was not acquainted with before and I dont think he will be anxious to continue the acquaintance of the beans and Hog as long as he can get baked beans and pork. He looks first rate only he had a boil on his under lip. I should think he was in a good company but they want a little experience in the field to take the green off. They seem to think it is rather rough this staying at York Town but I think I should like to change off with them a spell. I rather think if they should be put through the course that we have for the last four months they would be willing to do garrison duty in Yorktown without a murmur but it was the same with us when we were at Alexandria and we were always wanting to move but think we could stand it now for a couple of months. I went down with Asher and had a bathe in the York River. The first salt water I have seen for four months as it was four months the 16th of August since we came down the Potomac. I think the bath done me a good deal of good and think I shall repeat the dose today and there is plenty of the element here. Asher was out of Tobacco as he had not received his box. I had some that Father sent me and I gave him a plug and let him have some books that I had read. He seems to think that he can lend all the tobacco and money he wants. I just told him he must learn to look out for himself for a man can have plenty of friends in the army as long as he has anything to give them but I gave him the best advice I could and I think he will learn. If anything will make a boy of a man the army will do it and a man has in self defense to take care of himself first and friends afterwards. We received our mail last night and I got a letter from you dated the 12th of August and I am looking for another to night. I got four. Three from New Hampshire so you must not expect a long letter to day for I must try and get time to write to some of the folks up there. Give my love to all the folks and when I get time I will try and write a good long letter. No box yet and they say the orders are not to deliver any more. How true it is I cannot say but I am in hopes to get it yet. So good bye for this time and Remember me when you drink the punch. Winslow wishes to be remembered to you.

[unsigned]

* * * * * * * * * *

John Chase's Travel Routes in Chapter 3:
August 1862 to October 1862

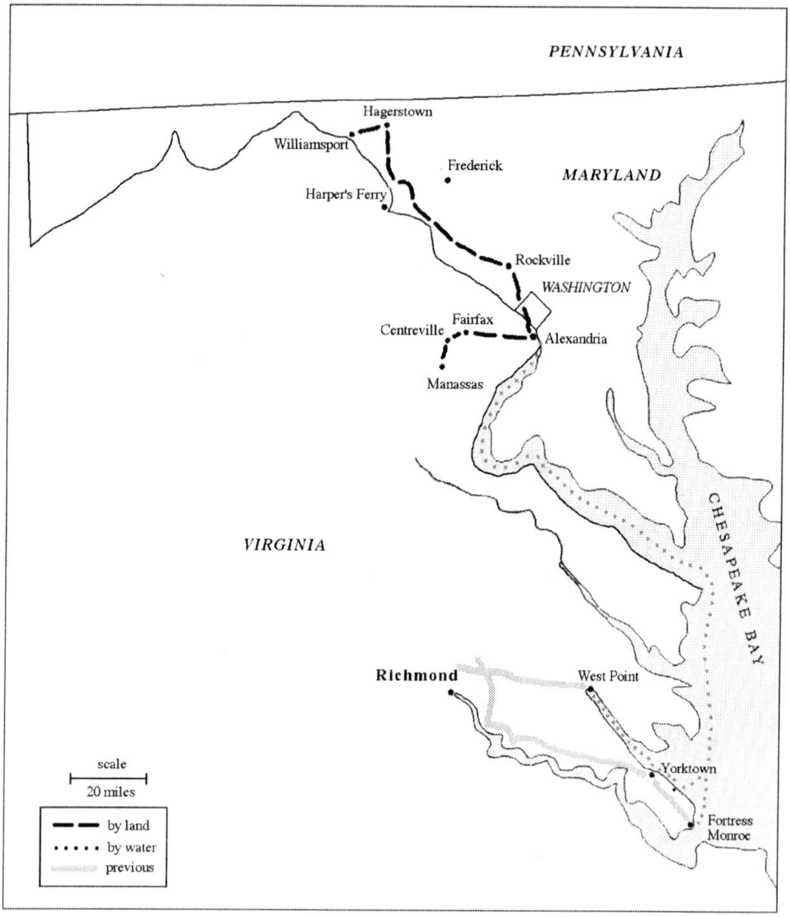

JSC/BBC

CHAPTER 3

Maryland

Returning from the unsuccessful Peninsula Campaign to again be defeated at the Second Battle of Bull Run, the Army of the Potomac moves into Maryland following after Lee's army until the bloody Battle of Antietam. Chase recounts the fights at Bull Run/Second Manassas, at Crampton's Gap on South Mountain in Maryland, and then at Antietam.

Centreville heights
Sept 1st 1862

Dear Brother

I take this chance to just let you know that I am alive and kicking but about played out. I wrote you last at Hampton. We came up to Alexandria and from there here but as yet have had no engagement with the enemy. What the prospect is is more than I can tell but things look very bilious here but I hope they are not so bad as they look. There is a good deal of loud talk about McDowell and I reckon the people of this great country will find out that Gen Pope[1] is not a great sight bigger Gen than McClellan for they can not lay this to George no how. I am not going to say a word at this time for I am too busy. I write this just to let you know I still live. I want you to write to Hampshire and tell them I am well. Did you get my check for the money? I never have heard. I have not got my box yet but still

[1] General John Pope's army, supplemented by virtually all of McClellan's Army of the Potomac, was routed at the Second Battle of Bull Run.

hope. Love to all the folks. When I get time I will write you a good long letter.

Yours &C
J.W Chase

* * * * * * * * * *

Alexandria Va
Sept 3d 62

Dear Brother

I am going to try and write you a letter and if the rebels let me alone and they dont sound Boots and Saddles I think I shall make out. The last letter I wrote was when we were at Hampton. The next day we loaded our Battery on board one of the old Chelsea ferry boats and dropped down as far as fortress Monroe. This was Saturday 23d. We were detained there untill the 26th on account of a severe storm as the old tub we were on had two Batteries on board and about 175 men and the damed old thing was condemed for a ferry boat years ago. The morning of the 26th it was very calm and we made out to get started and arrived at the mouth of the Potomac about nine the same evening when we anchored for the night which was rainy and a very pleasant time we had as we had to sleep wherever we could get a chance but they would not let us occupy the cabins as there was COMMISSIONS in there and <u>of course</u> it would not do to have PRIVATES come near them (<u>oh no</u>) but we lived through it and the next morning we started again as we supposed for Aquia Creek. We arrived at 5 P M when we were ordered to Alexandria. The boys were glad to hear this for we knew nothing about the fighting that was going on in front at the time. We ran that night as far as Mount Vernon 12 miles below the City where we anchored for the night. We arrived at Alexandria about 10 the next day but did not get unloaded till most night. The Battery went off that night about two miles out & camped. I concluded for myself that I would allow myself a furlough that night but could not move around much as the 33d Mass Regt were on guard and they are very particular. I am Inclined to think if this Corps stops around here a great while that they will not be quite so fat but I find these bought men think they are a better class than those that came out first.

Sept 5

I joined the Battery the next Morning when we started for the third time over the Fairfax road going as far as Allendale[2] 7 miles from Alexandria where we stopped that night. Here the reports of the fight were that our folks were getting the best of it and we slept soundly thinking it was so. The next morning we started and went on towards the battle field. We did not hurry and I supposed and our own Co officers supposed that every thing was going on well but on our arrival at Centreville things began to look altogether different and they began to hurry us up. We could now hear the reports of the Musketrey and see any quantity of Stragglers comeing in and we arrived on the field in the midst of a perfect panic. The teams were going in all directions. Gen Newton[3] of our Brigade formed us across the roads and stopped it in a Measure and I think if we had not arrived just as we did Bull Run would have been acted over again only ten times as bad. The panic was finally stopped and our Battery was ordered back to Centreville where we went and tried to sleep but not much sleep that night for the noise of the teams as they were driven to the rear and the Chagrin we felt to think we were defeated was enough to drive away all sleep from our eyes. At least that was my case. The next day we took our position in one of the forts on the heights but no enemy made its appearance and Monday night we left and Tuesday afternoon we arrived at Alexandria and the next day we came over to our old camp where we now are right on the old spot where we lived all last winter. I have nothing to say about the recent battles for I am ashamed to hear anything about them for I think it was a disgrace to us as a nation and begin to think it is about time to stop talking about Conquering the South when we cannot get possesion of one state but I hope to God if we ever make another

[2] Annandale, Virginia.
[3] General John Newton.

move that we shall not have more than a half a dozen leaders and I suppose we shall not as I understand that George is to be Commander in chief. Thank God for that one move in the right direction. I think he is the man for the Army of the Potomac. As for McDowell I dont know what to think of him but the least I can say is he is no General and think he better retire from feild. Pope I have no doubt he is a good Gen but think he advertised rather large on the start and I guess he has found out that Richmond is not so easily taken but I will not find fault for I feel as though every one should try and put there Shoulder to the wheel once more and see if we ever are going to do anything. If not why let the South go and close the thing. That way one thing is sure this thing cannot linger this way much longer. If it does the men of the army will take it upon themselves to close it by going home. They are tired to death of war and if our officers were as good as the men I think this thing would looked different at the present time but the fact is we have too many fourth of July officers. Men who when it comes to fighting Skedaddle & of course the men follow there example.

As for myself I am about played out. I have gone on to the sick list for I have the Piles the worst kind and it about kills me to move and I want you to get me a box of Saville ointment and send it out to me through the mail. That is if it is good for anything. The boys are getting there boxes now. There was 20 came into camp yesterday. I have not got mine yet but expect in a few days. You must give my love to all the folks. Tell them I still live and that is about all. Tell Elizabeth and Mrs Grindell that I have an account of the way they abused the School Marm and I dont think it right for she is a very nice young lady if she did grow down in Maine. Tell Emily that I have come to the conclusion that Vermont men are a little meaner than Maine men. We have a whole brigade of Vermont troops in this Corps and they are the meanest louseiest men I have seen in the army. Dirty and lazy but I dont know how it is with the women.

We had 19 recruits joined us at Hampton. Some of the 300 men and some of them are growing awfull sick of war already and one of them told me he wished they would acknowledge the Southern

Confederacy. I told he was a Damn fool and wanted to earn his money too easy for he had been bought and ought to be willing to do some thing. I think this paying large bounties is wrong altogether for the poor devils that came first had to come without them and it is apt to cause hard feelings. In my opinion we have men enough now if they were only handled right.

Give my love to Mace. Tell him I had a good drink of Brandy that came from Boston yesterday and I dont think it hurt me a bit. Love to William and Mrs Curtis. Tell Mrs C that I Intend to have a good time over that Box yet. That is if the rebs dont drive us all home before I get it. What they are going to do with us now is more than I can tell but probably shall remain here a few days but I am hopes they will go to work soon and close up the concern for I am sick and tired of this way of liveing and I dont find any one but what is.

I have not got any letter from you this week but shall look for one to day but I will close this scrawl by wishing you all the good luck you can get and I hope things will be brighter soon.

So good Bye
Yours &C
John

* * * * * * * * * * *

Some where in Maryland State after Rebels
Sept 11th 1862

Dear Brother

When I last wrote I thought we were going to get a few days rest but it seemed to be otherwise ordered for I had hardly finished writing before we were ordered to pack up and be ready to move which we did the next afternoon and came through the City of Washington as far as Tennylytown where we camped for the rest of the night. Since then we have been on the march till we arrived at this place which is between Poolesville and Boonville.[4] To day we

[4] Barnesville.

have lain still and I reckon it was about time for we were out of forage and a good many of the Regt were out of grub for our waggons were all behind. To night we got a mail and I got a paper and letter from you and in the letter I learn that Mace had come to Washington. I wish he had been a few days sooner for then I should been likely to have seen him which I should liked to have done very much but I suppose he will hardly follow up our Corps as there is no Mass troops in it but our Battery. We have two new Regt in our Division and when they form a line they make as much show as a whole Brigade of the old Regt. I think if they would just take & put them in the old Regt they would do a good deal more service besides saveing a good deal of Cost. The new troops a good many of them think they are a better Class of men than those that came first and a good many of them are Pope[5] men and it leads to a good deal of chin music with the old troops. It is no use for any body to come in to Franklins Corps and talk Pope for they dont see it quite and a good many of them are strongly tinctured with the nigger but I reckon they will get braveley over that by the time they have been out here a year or so. There appears to be good stock in them. All they want is the green taken off and there is lots of it on them in my opinion.

When I last wrote I was about used up but I feel a good deal better now. All but the Piles. They trouble me a good deal. The Country we have come through lateley is a splendid one and there is lots of fruit and I have eaten any quantity of it and I think it has done me a good deal of good. There is a great contrast in the face of the country between this State and Virginia. Maryland resembles our own New England very much and the people are very kind to us. As much so as we can expect but I am sorry to say the Soldiers are not quite so carefull of private property as they ought to be. They seem to forget they are in a loyal State. We are camped about three miles from Sugar loaf Mountain. Day before yesterday the Rebels held it but now old Glory waves in triumph from its top. I am in hopes that it soon shall wave in every state and we believe it will if they will

[5] General John Pope, whom General McClellan and his men disdained.

only let George alone. The weather here has been very hot and the roads awfull dusty and it takes a severe hold of the new men. The last days march there was four dropped dead in one of the new Regts in our Division and quite a number more used up.

You must give my love to all the folks and take this letter as it is as I have to write on the run as we are to start again this morning and everybody is busy getting ready but as we were going to send a mail I thought to write you a few lines just to let you know I still live. My box I learn is down to the City of Alexandria and there I suppose it will stay as there is no getting any thing from there now but perhaps I may some time. Much oblidged for the Post. I shall enclose a peice from the Baltimore Clipper in this that will give you an Idea of what the troops in this Corps think of George B. [No enclosure found.]

Give my love to Mrs. Curtis and Williams folks and Emily.

Good bye for this time.

John

Winslow says he will drink twice to George if he gets a chance. He sends his best wishes.

* * * * * * * * * *

Sharpsburg
Washington County Md
Sept 20th 1862

Dear Brother

The last time I wrote we were in camp near Poolesville which place we left the next morning and kept moveing untill we reached the Blue Ridge Mountains where we ran against a stump in the shape of a few thousand rebels. They were on the mountains but Slocums[6] Division went at them and they left those parts in a hurry. We buried about three hundred of them and wounded a good many more and took 500 prisoners but this victory was not a bloodless one on our

[6] General Henry W. Slocum.

part for a good many of our brave boys were killed and a good many more wounded.[7] We remained on the mountain two days and then started for Sharpsburg where we arrived about three o clock and went directly to the front and went at it again here. They had been fighting since six in the morning and the arrival of our Corps was a very timeley one. I shall attempt no description of the battle for no doubt you have seen that described before now but one thing I will say. It was the hardest fight that has been fought in this war.[8] Our Battery was engaged but not under much fire. Capt Wolcotts Battery was engaged and had one man killed and 13 wounded and lost 11 horses. The men fought like tigers and Wolcott showed himself a brave man. He took hold and helped work the guns himself and at one time there was only himself and three drivers to work one of the guns. The sharp shooters picked his men off at one gun. 10 were disabled. The Rebs have mostly Crossed the river. We are now about two miles from the River and we can hear Stoneman[9] at them with his flying Artillery and the way he is putting it to them is a caution. They have gone and left all the barns and houses full of wounded. I have been around amongst the poor fellows this morning. I made two pots of coffee and carried to them. The most of them say they never expected to get treated all well as they do by our men. The first thing they asked me was where I was from. When I told them Mass they were taken all aback. Some of them were from South Carolina and thought that we were there bitterest enemies. I told them they did not understand the thing as it was but of course that was no time to go into an argument. But let me tell you I have seen all the blood shed I want too and I hope to God there never will be another fight but one thing I think if there is they will get whipped. The army is in the best of spirits for they know they have got a leader that knows his business. God Bless George B McClellan say I.

I got a box of pile ointment from you but have had no letter for

[7] This battle was at Crampton's Gap, on South Mountain.

[8] The war's greatest number of casualties in a single day's fighting occurred on September 17, at the Battle of Antietam.

[9] General George Stoneman.

over a week. We have had but one mail since we started from Washington but expect one to day or tomorrow. There was a load of boxes came to camp last night but mine was not amongst the number but they tell me it is at Georgetown with a number of others. I live in hopes of seeing it yet. My health is first rate. It is enough to do a mans soul and body good to travel through this country. The people are all glad to see us and do all they can for us. At the fight at Cramptons gap the women all turned out and fed our wounded and also our well men but I cannot write what I should like too but if I ever reach home again I will tell you all about it. My love to all the folks Emily Included. Tell them George is at the head and this thing is now to be brought to a close. Enclosed you will find some relics. An Autograph of Fletcher Webster.[10] I picked it up on the Battle field and thought perhaps you might like it.

Yours &C
John

[Enclosed was the envelope shown below, with the following note:]

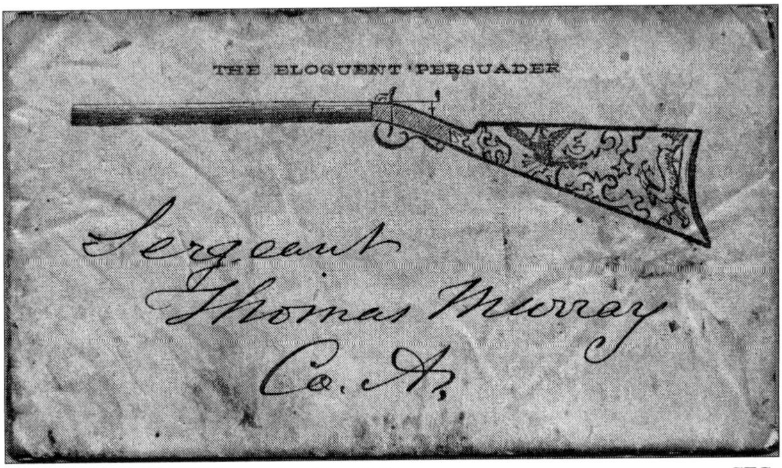

Relic from Letter of September 20, 1862 CFC

[10] Colonel Fletcher Webster of the Twelfth Massachusetts Regiment was the eldest son of statesman Daniel Webster. He was killed at the Second Battle of Bull Run.

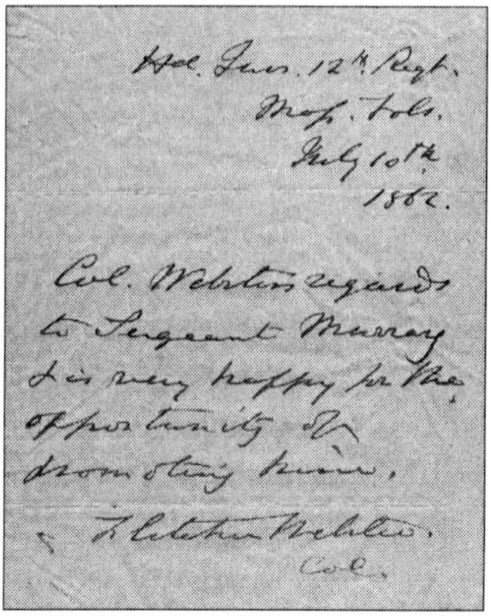

Colonel Webster Relic CFC

Hd. Qurs. 12th Regt.
Mass. Vols.
July 10th
1862.

Col. Websters regards to Sergeant Murray & is very happy for the opportunity of promoting him.

Fletcher Webster
Col.

[Also enclosed was the following poem written in ink in one handwriting, followed by a note written in pencil by John Chase.]

Composed by James Lewis
of Company F 1st PaVC

O pity the fate of a poor
Weary Soldier when hungry
And lame he approaches your door
For he had a home once
With friends to carress him and
No such trials before to endure

But now he is fighting for his
Beloved Country that wicked
Rebellion has tryed to destroy
Alass how he wishes this war
For his country against his own
Brothers forever was ore

But when will sweet peace
Make her dwelling among us and
Rest undesturbed on Colombia's fair shore
Or shall we forever be fighting
Our brothers and force them
By arams our flag to adore

At night when he haults
For to take some refreshments
His bones they are weary and feet they are sore
With no other covering but blue
Heavins ore him he sleeps and
He dreams that his troubles are ore

But alass he's awoke by the sound
of the bugale to arams he is caulled
This country to save and
Here side and side he stands
With his companions manfully
Fighting his country to Save

This poor fellow is buried at Sharpsburg. He died with his face to the enemy. He was a gay Irishman and a sensible fellow.

* * * * * * * * * *

Bakersville Maryland
Sept 26 1862

Dear Brother

I received another of your kind letters last night written the 21st. I expected to get one from Hampshire but I find they dont care much about writeing and I have come to the conclusion to let them have there own way. I have written 6 letters since I wrote you so you see they cannot say but what I write to them but I suppose they dont get time or else paper costs too much. You have asked me in both your last letters if Capt Porter is with us. He is. He joined us at Alexandria when we came up the river and he is with us now but I dont think he is any great help. Anyway my opinion of Capt Porter is very small and there is very little of the article in him that goes to make up a man. He is neither a Gentleman or Soldier and I make no bones in calling him a coward. On the field he stays to his post to be sure but is from no sense of duty for I think I have seen him when he would run away if he could decentley. I tell you Sam if ever I get out of this I shall take a chance to talk with some of the shoulder strap Gentry that have put on there airs out here thats so. Sleeper our first Junior Lieut has left us to take command of the 10 Mass Bat. He is what they call in Boston a damn good fellow because he spends his money free. I dont consider him much of an officer. But one thing he is no Coward I tell you and I hope he may have good success with his command. He always used me well and the boys were sorry to lose him. Mac is still with us and I hope he always will be as long as I am here but still I dont think he has been used right. He should have had the place that Sleeper has got but he is a Democrat and has got no rich friends or Father to help him. Mac has talked to me rather rough sometimes but I can stand it from a man that is smart but to have to take from it a fool is rather rough. One thing Mac spits out what he has got to say and that is the end of it and another thing he can tell the difference betwixt a man and a mouse——.

Captain J. Henry Sleeper LC

In your last letter before this you asked me to send you the receipt for that box. I have lost it. I lost my pocket book the night after the last battle containing the receipt and all my earthley possesions being

Captain Wm. H. McCartney AJB

the sum of one dollar and fifty three cents. I expect it got out of my pocket in the night and we shifted our position before light. I did not see it on the ground but I think the box is all right yet. I wrote to Pricilla yesterday and I wrote her for a pair of shirts and some stockings. I told her to get the shirts made and send them to you and the bill for the cloth and makeing and you would pay her and I shall want you to buy me some drawers and under shirts and when we get to a place where there is a prospect of getting them I will let you know. The weather begins to get quite cool here nights. Last night we had a severe frost and this morning the weather makes us think of under shirts and drawers. Let me know when you write how much money you have got. That is if you have any for I dont know as you have any but I will send you some when we get paid off which will probably be in two or three weeks now.

We are in camp now at a place called Grimes Mills being a part of the town of Bakersville on the Harpers Ferry Road and about 12 miles from that place. We have been here now three days but I expect we shall leave to day for Hagerstown. We have another Division added to our Corps. Couch[11] is a Massachusetts man. It is Composed now of Smiths Couchs and Slocums. If the new one is as good as the old ones I will not find any fault and they appear well but I dont think they can quite come up to Slocums but perhaps I am a little might prejudiced. I am much oblidged to you for the papers. It is the first Boston paper I have seen for most a fortnight. What do you think of the surrender of Harpers Ferry. If you could be here and

[11] General Darius N. Couch.

here the curses bestowed on the commanders at that point I think you would stick out your eyes. What must McClellans feelings have been when he heard of there surrender. That has been the way all the time. While he was whipping them at one point some damn infernal traitor was aiding them at another but still we whipped them and I for one think the more honor is due to McClellan and the noble Gens under him. Thank God for such men as Burnsides Hooker and many others. I think Burnsides has proved himself one of the best Generals amongst us but I tell you Sam it seemed to me that day that every man had made up his mind to win or die. That was the spirit that seemed to press the men on and I shall always think if we had only opened on them the next day we should just cleaned them out but still it is very little we Privates can tell about such things but still we have a right to think. You know one thing is certain. They were pretty well whipped. There is no rubbing that out. I wish I could sit down and talk with you a few hours about the scenes I witnessed that day but I must leave it to abler pens than mine.

General Ambrose E. Burnside LJ

You must give my love to all the folks. Tell them I hope to see them some time and thank them in person for there many favors. Tell

Emily she must not make up faces at the School Marm any more for the Maryland Girls take my eye now. There is some of the prettiest girls out here I ever saw and I dont believe there is a prettier State in the union. I think I could just live here if I only was situated so I could be a free man. The people are very kind to us and do all they can for us but I guess they will be glad to get rid of us for there is a damn pack of loafers around the army that are more to be feared than the rebels I think. But I will Close for this time as I have got to pack up once more. These flowers came from the top of the Mountain where we had the fight.

John

* * * * * * * * * *

Camp Near Bakersville Maryland
Oct 5th 1862

Dear Brother

I have delayed writing this week thinking that our mail would get along and I should get a letter from you but as Sunday has arrived and no mail I concluded to sit down and write. We are still encamped at Bakersville and for the past week everything has been very quiet with us and with the exception of a review Friday by the President & Gens McClellan and Franklin we have had nothing to do but eat and Sleep. Last Wednesday our Capt left us haveing resigned and gone home affairs there requireing his presence. I suppose to look after the affairs <u>of his Father</u>. Lieut McCartney is in command and I expect will be our future commander. We have two vacancies in our Commission Officers to fill and the question seems to be who will they be. I presume we shall find out soon. I hope they will be good ones. Yesterday we buried one of our men. He died with fever and we got news of another that died at Hampton. He being left in the Hospital there when we came away. So you see the boys keep dropping off one by one and we miss a good many from the ranks that were with us one year ago to day. It being just a year ago that we arrived in Washington and a long year it has been to me and I hope before another has rolled around that this thing will be Closed up and what there is left be allowed to return to there homes and see there friends.

I feel kind of homesick to day and wish I could be with you. These pleasant Sundays make a man think of home I tell you and I often think of you and other kind friends in Roxbury who have tried to make life pleasant to me since I have been out here and if it is Gods will that I never come back to see you in person you can take my word that my best wishes have often been bestowed on you and the numerous favors never will be forgotten by Jack. I hear nothing from Stratham only through Mary and I guess they think it dont pay anything to write to me.

The 37th Mass Regt passed our camp to day. They go into Couchs Division which is now attached to Franklins Corps. They look like a good set of men and make as much show as a whole Brigade of our old Regts but some of the old Regt are being filled up with recruits.

You asked me in a former letter about Covell. He has got his discharge and gone home. I dont think he admired a Soldiers life much more particularly the fighting part. We have had quite a number of cases of the Shell and bullet fever. Some of the patients have been carried off and some are still lingering between hope and fear but some how the Doctors cant seem to see it that they are dangerous therefore they cannot get discharged poor fellows.

There has been a great rush of Citizens around these parts from different parts of the country. They come to view the late Battle fields. We had some here from Cambridge and they met with quite a Change while they were here as regards the little Gen and have come to the conclusion that he is about the man to run this Machine and think they shall tell a different Story after there return to Mass. This is the place for men to get Informed. They soon get the minds of the Soldiers about George and that in a very few words.

I have no news to write but I expect that before many days have passed that something will be done for things seem to squint that way.

My health is very good. We get plenty to eat as the farmers around here are willing to sell us most anything they have and at reasonable prices. The boys are looking anxiously for the Pay Master as funds begin to run low.

The weather is pleasant and very dry. We have not had rain enough to lay the dust since we arrived in Maryland. The nights are cool and the days very comfortable.

You must give my love to all the folks. Tell Elizabeth I am glad to hear she has gone back on the niggers and I think if she could see the lazy devils as I have seen them she would not think as much of them as she would of a rebel. Remember me to Mrs Curtis and Williams family and Mace. Tell Mace the next time he comes out here I hope he will hunt us up for I should like to see him very much. My love to Emily and all that wants to hear from me. Tell them I still go in for the union and hope to live to see the old flag waveing over every State. I shall try and send this to day Monday. Our mail has not arrived yet and I dont know but what the Rebels have got the Carrier so good bye for the present.

Yours &C
Jack

* * * * * * * * * *

Hagerstown Maryland
Oct 11th 1862

Dear Brother

You will see by the heading of this that we have left Bakersville and come to Hagerstown. We came here for the purpose of repairing our carriages and painting them and overhauling the Battery generally and at the present our guns are dismounted carriages taken to peices and everything at sixes and sevens. There was quite an excitement here last night. The report was the Rebels had recrossed the river and orders came to us if there was any alarm to hitch up and leave as we are all alone. Very good time we should have had leaveing I reckon for it would take a half a day to get things fixed up.

First Massachusetts Light Artillery Boring New Vents, by Alfred Waud LC

But the troops are moveing up above us this morning and I reckon if there is any Johnnies this side they will get a warming for I think George has got about ready for them but still there is a good deal to do. There is lots of recruits here without arms and some without uniforms and the Batteries all want overhauling for they have done some travelling since last spring.

I received your letter of the 28th last Tuesday with the papers. Much oblidged for the papers for I like to read the Post. I am glad that Capt Kings Co gave so good an account of themselves and I dont think Roxbury has much reason to blush for any of the Co she has sent to the war. Speaking about Capt Wolcott his Battery is some 8 miles from us doing picket and I have seen him but once lateley but when I do I will remember to Introduce myself. That is if the box comes. I have heard again from the Box. It is at Georgetown and Mac has ordered them to this place but the fact is the Govt takes possesion of the roads and it lies with them whether they come or not. I should like to see it about this time being out of funds and to comfort as they tell us we shall not get paid for about 5 weeks. Very consoling for here there is a chance to buy stuff at a reasonable rate for the people are very loyal and they say they dont want to see any of uncle Sams Boys suffer. They are down on rebels I tell you. Speaking about the Presidents Proclamation[12] I suppose you have seen Georges order prohibiting political discussions but that prevent our giveing an opinion and the general opinion is this. That first we catch the hare or in other words that first we better conquer some of

[12] President Lincoln issued his Emancipation Proclamation on September 22, 1862, to take effect on January 1, 1863.

the slave states and then it will be time enough to talk about freeing the Slaves but you see this army think a good deal of the President and of course he must do something to keep the nigger worshippers quiet and this seems to prove a very good sugar tit for them. That is the way it is looked at here generally.

I am glad that Asher continues to like and I hope he will hold out to the end for theres nothing like courage. I shall send this to Roxbury for this a letter to Mary as she writes me she is comeing on there with Father and Mother.[13] You must Give my love to all the folks and excuse the shortness of this for I have the chance to send this down to the Post office and I must close.

So good Bye
From Jack

Winslow still lives and growls as usual. I think it grows on him Sam C.

* * * * * * * * * *

Hagerstown Maryland
October 15th 1862

Dear Brother

I have been looking anxiously for the mail thinking I might hear from old Roxbury but as there are no signs of its comeing and I had got my Box I thought best to write and let you know it. The Box arrived yesterday and when I took it out of the waggon the boys gathered around and we thought we were going to have a good drink all around. I ripped off the cover and my God what a sight met my gaze. The first thing I saw was a broken bottle. I carefully pawed over the saw dust but no punch no rum no whiskey no Wormwood Cordial no nothing in bottles but a bottle of pickels. They were all right. There was the necks of two bottles and the bottoms of three and that was all there was left of the fluid department. Probably there

[13] John is probably referring to his stepmother, Hanna.

was not much swearing about that time. Curses both loud and deep were uttered and if the Hon Gentleman had been there that stole it I dont think he would have been much flattered with the remarks that were made about him. The things in the other end were all right. The pickels mustard fish cheese tamarinds peper ginger and in fact everything but the Rum and the Rochelle Powders. Those had got wet by some means and the contents of the white papers dissolved. There was not so much as the smell of it in the saw dust proveing very conclusively to me that the Stuff was taken out some time ago probably at Fortress Monroe for that place is nothing but a damn den of thieves any way. I found that out the few days we were there. There was no signs of any lemons in the box so I presume they took them also. The Sardines being in the bottom of the box probably escaped there sight or they would have gone too and the other stuff was such as they could get plenty of or else they thought they had got a very good haul and would let me have the rest. Very thoughtfull. Some of the labels were so defaced that I could not make them out but I could see Mrs. Curtis name on quite a number of the articles and I reckon she did not mean that I should suffer for Ginger or pepper but I can distribute around amongst those that are not so lucky as I am. You will return her my sincere thanks for these and other favors and not only mine but those that are associated with me for of course the boys all have to know where the good things come from and when I tell them they want to know what relation she is to me and they cant seem to see it how she takes such an Interest in my welfare. I tell them it is not me it is the cause and they have come to the conclusion that she is one of the right kind of women to have around but seriously how can I ever repay her and my other friends in Roxbury those that are not related to me any way but it dont seem as though they could do any more for me if I was one of there own children and nothing I can write can express my thankfullness. All I can say is I hope they never will have reason to regret there kindness. Tell Elizabeth those matches come in a good time and as I sit and smoke my pipe my thoughts will often go back to Roxbury and I shall feel that I have those there take an Interest in me and it will give me new Strength to try and do my best when called to the battle field. To William for the tobacco which was in good shape and it was a perfect God send being entirely out and out of tin. The fact is there is four of us that quarter together and when one has anything we all have it but we were all in about the same condition as regards funds but a man can get bread in this country when he cant get tobacco. He has the thanks of the Quartette and we calculate we are four just as good men as there is in the Battery. Tell Mace I did not have the pleasure of drinking his health but I shall not go back on him a mite. I feel just as thankfull to him but damn the man that stole the fluid and thats the voice of four of us.

Return my thanks to Mr. Lewis. I shall keep the milk and coffee untill such a time as we go on a march and after trying I will give him my opinion of it. I tried the tea this morning and Winslow tried it last night and we all pronounce it Bully and Winslow returns thanks to friends in Roxbury.

As for the Sardines I dont know who I am in debt to for those but you can tell Mr. Seaver that those he sent to Capt Porter myself and the boys in our detachment will eat and thank God he has resigned and we have the priveledge of eating his Sardines and for one I hope he never will come back to this Battery while I am in it. <u>Thats so</u>. For hankerchiefs paper pencils towels soap &C I am Indebted to somebody and to sum it all up I am thankfull to all and may God bless them. That is all I can say.

Now as regards things with us we are still painting and repairing and probably shall be here for a week. The weather has been very unfavorable for us it being cloudy and wet the most of the time since we were here. The talk seems to be here that Mac is not going to get command of this Battery after all but if J J Andrews dont give him this Battery I say he is a damn rascal. The fact is just here this Battery has got a good name and I say and can prove it that what the Battery is he has made it and no thanks to <u>Capt Porter</u>. There is things in Mac I dont like but when any man undertakes to tell me he is not a good officer I say he is a liar but it is not the men that are fit to Command that gets Commands. I found that out some time ago and I say more is the Shame and it is enough some times to make a man Curse everybody to see the men that are given Commissions to Lord it over better men than they ever dared to be but so it is and so it always will be as long as Political influence is worth more than merit.

But I will drop this subject and go at some thing else. I wrote to Pricilla about some shirts & to have them sent to you and you would send them to me. I want you to get me two pairs of drawers and two under shirts to send with them and direct it to Washington. I would not put them in a box but wrap them in some good strong paper and you may put in some tobacco with them if you are a mind. Direct same as you always did. I expected to have got a letter from you before now but we have had no mail for over a week.

Williamsport Oct 18th 1862

When I commenced this we were at Hagerstown but were ordered up here on Picket. Our carriages were not dry but we had to start with them just as they were. We came here yesterday and last night I got a letter from you speaking about a Commission. Now my opinion about it is just this. There are plenty of men better fitted for it than I am and another thing I could not keep one if I should get it. That is in Artillery for this reason. I can not ride. It would kill me in a month. I have tried it and I know it murders my side so and as for a Commission in Infantry I had rather be a Private in this Battery than an officer in the best Co of Infantry in the service. You may think it strange but I think I can enjoy myself where I am better than I could as an officer in another Co. I have cast my lot with this Battery and I want to stay in it untill I am done Soldiering. I should like the pay well enough but still I feel very well satisfied where I am. I have seen enough of men taking positions they could not fill and I dont wish to add myself to the number. You may think I am foolish but I think if I could talk with you an hour or so you would say I was in the right but I feel grateful to you to know you have Interested yourself and I thank you Sincerely and also Mr. Ritchey and if nothing happens the time may come when I may want both his and your Influence. My determination is with the help of God to do my duty as a Soldier. I did not enlist for honor or pay but to fight for the old Flag and when I see a place that I think I can do more good in than I can here I shall not forget to speak about it. So hopeing this will meet your views I will drop this subject.

My health is not very good and I find these cool nights dont improve it any. I should like to have you send those things as soon as you can and get a receipt and send it to me. I got a letter from Susie Smith yesterday and she informs me that Horatio was taken Prisoner at Bull Run and they are going to send him to fight Indians.[14] Things seem to be very quiet here but they say there is going to be something done soon. Give my love to all the folks and tell them I shall be glad when this war is over and hope I shall be permitted to come back and thank them in person for the favors conferred on me. Give my love to Father and Mother and tell Mary I have not heard from her lately.

So good bye for this time. I shall write again as soon as I get a letter from you.

Yours as ever
Jack

Much obliged for the papers the Post particularly.

* * * * * * * * * * *

Williamsport Maryland
Oct 26th 1862

Dear Brother

I received two letters from you last week. One Tuesday and the other Saturday and thought to day I would try and write a few lines to you and let you know I was still alive but the fact is it is hard work to write for it is as cold as Greenland. Yesterday we had one of our

---

[14] Early in the war, captured soldiers were paroled until they were formally exchanged. While on parole they were not permitted combat roles against the enemy, so Union soldiers were sometimes sent west to fight Indians.

regular Virginia rains and this morning it has cleared off and the winds blow a gale and it comes down off the mountains fluking. I have been wrapped up in an overcoat and blankets all the forenoon but have got a dish of bean soup well peppered and think I can stand it a little while in the middle of the day but without Joking the weather here is decideley cool and this liveing without tents is not very comfortable but I suppose it is no use talking. We have got to take it and do the best we can to make ourselves comfortable.

We are still on Picket with nothing to do but watch the Rebs on the other side of the River. We can see them quite plain from here. Yesterday they came over this side with flag of truce but what is up of course Privates are not suppose to know. The great questions appears to be now are we going into winter quarters on this side of the river? Of course we should as leave go into quarters here as anywheres and a good deal rather but then again it seems to me as if we ought to give the rebs one more damn good licking this fall for I think we can just do it but somehow or other things work very curious and I have about made up my mind to keep perfectly cool and take things as they come. I believe the most of folks think more of who is going to be Governors and Senators from the different States than they do of Settling this war and they will wake up some fine morning and find the Rebs getting the best of them and dictating there terms of peace. It is no use talking. There is a screw loose somewhere and a good many of them in my opinion and it would not surprise me at any time to hear of some exploit the Rebels had done for I believe they are a damn sight smarter than our folks and do more work with a good deal less talk but I hope this will not be the case but I want to see this army move against them and see if we cannot get to Richmond before Winter gets here with its rain & mud. The fact is I want to go home I do for I have been a Soldier just as long as I want to be but still I dont feel like leaving untill the job is finished but I believe it can be finished now just as well as ever it can and I say go in Lemons. If you do get Jammed a little might just as well get shot as to have half of the army in the Hospital sick and that is the way it will be if they go into winter quarters here. Now

Winslow left us yesterday for the Hospital. I dont think he ever will come back with us again. I know he wont if he can help it for he is decidely sick of this business and besides the cold weather uses him all up. My health is kind of decent and I guess when I get my shirts and drawers I can stand it with the most of them. I hope they have started before now. I wrote Mary last week and sent it to Stratham for I thought she would go home with Father. If she has not gone tell her to write. I have not heard from Stratham since I wrote last but had a letter from Eliza. I understand Pricilla has company from Lynn. Just ask Lizzie if she thinks there will be any talking done. I reckon there will a right smart lot of it. I have not seen Capt Wolcott yet. His Battery is in Hagerstown repairing. (Is he the man you repaired the house on Shawmit Avenue for?) Give my love to all the folks that wants to hear from me. Tell Lizzie that Ben Richardsons Mother is here. Came out here to see her boy. He is the one she sent the pie too and we have had quite a number of folks here to see there boys since the last battle. Give my love to Mace and Williams folks and Emily and when you write Asher tell him to write to me. So hopeing this will find you all well I will close.

J W Chase

I should like a hot Whiskey Punch for I am cold.

* * * * * * * * * *

Williamsport Maryland
Oct 29th 1862

Dear Brother

I have been thinking there was one letter from you that I never had got and to day it made its appearance mailed Oct 2nd. I also got the one with the receipt for the bundle also some stamps for which you will receive my thanks. I thought best to write to night for things look as if we should leave here soon. The cavalry will cross here to night. I expect they made a dash across this afternoon and captured six of the Rebel cavalry pickets. Some of the first North Carolina and probably if they cross we shall follow. I hope so for I am tired of this Inactivity. I feel as though we ought to be doing something. Not that I am anxious to get out of Maryland for we have had good times since we came to this state. Tell Emily if she makes up faces at the Maryland girls I shall get mad and when I am mad I am a devil of a fellow. Tell her she is mistaken about there being Secesh for they go in for the Union to a man and without any joking the people of this part of this State are as loyal as any you can find in Mass. It seem as if they could not do enough for the Soldiers or as they call us Yankees. The first Mass Battery they think are some pumkins. They dont think much of the Mass 13th. They were here last winter and used to promanade to church with the nigger wenches and the girls think that men that will go with niggers when there is plenty of white girls around aint no great shakes. I tell you I blow high for the gals in this County. Thats so. But I want to be in active service not that I am so fond of fighting but I know the more there is done now the less there will be to do and I think if we can only give them a few such Victories as they claim to have gained at Sharpsburg that this thing will be likely to come to a head and be very likely to break and I hope the next time I write if I ever am allowed that privilege again it will be to give an account of some victory gained and battle won and that Mac has give them H___.

I have just got that knife and fork and I shall try hard to keep it and If I ever get back I want to bring it with me for I shall prize it highly for the givers sake. May God bless all such women I say. I wish there was more like her. We shall get paid off soon I expect and then I will send you some money. You did not write whether you had enough to pay for those things or not but you can pay yourself then if you did not. I am in hope to get the things before we leave here for I want them badly. Speaking about that tea it is Bully and so is the other thing. The preserved milk I cut on some hasty pudding. I had some meal given me and I can just make a hasty pudding as well as any other woman. The milk made it go first rate and I hope Mr Lewis may live a thousand years. Thats so. I am glad you put some tobacco in for we have to pay 150 per pound for it here and poor at that. I take a good deal of comfort in my pipe for I can lie and smoke and think about the friends I have left behind me and when I get out of tobacco I am all down flat.

I have been to the hospital to day to see Winslow. The doctor says he has the Chronic Dirhorea and if he had not been tough as a bull he would have been dead before now. He looks slim and I dont think he will get back with us again. He wished me to remember him to you for your kindness and returns his thanks for favors conferred on him. I suppose you have seen the account of another Corporal promoted out of this Battery Copr Smith. He goes into the 10th under Sleeper. I know very well what the Capt and one Lieut is and if the other officers are like them God pity the Battery I say. What in the devil Smith is promoted for is more than I can tell. He is no officer. That I know but perhaps he has friends at J J Andrews court but I must dry up for this time. So give my love to all the folks. Tell them if I can only feel as well as I do now I think I can stand it for I have got an appetite like a horse.

(PS This from Jack.)

* * * * * * * * * * *

John Chase's Travel Routes in Chapter 4:
October 1862 to April 1863

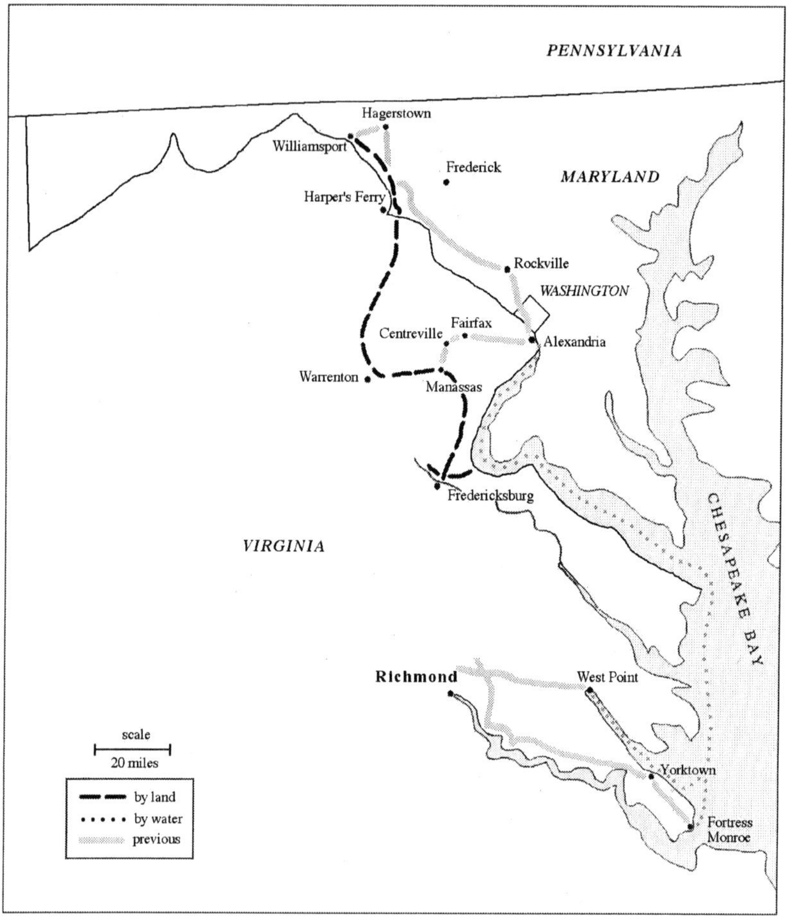

JSC/BBC

CHAPTER 4

Fredericksburg

The Army of the Potomac moves back into Virginia, where, under the command of General Ambrose Burnside, it engages the southern army at the Battle of Fredericksburg, where it again is defeated. The army then settles in for the winter northeast of the city. Chase vents his anger at the generals and the politicians, deals with the day-to-day survival in winter camp, and describes the infamous "Mud March."

New Baltimore Virginia
Nov 13th 1862

Dear Brother

I dont know but what you will begin to think I have forgotten you but <u>thats not so</u> but the fact is we have been on the tramp lately and I have not had much time to write but yesterday we got a mail and the first for a week so I thought best to try and let you know I still live. We left Williamsport the next day after I wrote my last letter but instead of crossing the river there we came down below Harpers Ferry at a place called Berlin[1] where we crossed on a Pontoon bridge. We then came to White Plains[2] where we stopped one day and two nights. We had a snowstorm and had about two inches of snow. The next port we made was this place which is called New Baltimore and is about six miles from Warrenton. We came here last Sunday and

[1] Now Brunswick, Maryland.
[2] The Plains, Virginia.

have been here ever since. What we are waiting for is more than I can tell but there is all sorts of stories a going amongst others that George B is under arrest and that several of the Corps commanders have resigned. All I know about it is that little Mac rode around amongst the troops last Monday and if you could have heard the cheers and shouts of the men and my voice with the rest you would not have thought that the Army Corps of Franklin had gone back on him much particularly Jack. No sir ee. Never. For let the President do what he will with him I shall still believe him one of the best of Generals and what is more in my mind a good man and not untill he turns traitor to his country shall I go one inch back on George B and I think if he has been removed from the command of the Army of the Potomac it is a damn shame and there is thousands here that think the same but they do most anything now I suppose. You have seen in the papers that Gen Slocum has been promoted and given the command of a Corps and Gen Brooks[3] has taken command of our division. I am glad that Slocum is promoted but sorry he has left us for I liked him much and that is more than I can say of Brooks. The first thing Brooks done was to stop our Mail carrier going to Washington. He dont seem to care a copper whether we get any letters or not and then he makes a good deal of fuss about our takeing a little something to eat that we find straying around the country but when he stops our taking things it will be when we are better furnished with grub than we have lately for to tell the truth we have been rather short lately but you know we

General George B. McClellan LC

[3] General William T. H. Brooks.

are in Virginia now and shall have to get along as well as we can. It is no use talking. Somebody is to blame for this army is neither fed or clothed as it ought to be and I might say paid for we have not been paid yet and I dont see any signs of its being and if you can I want you to send me a couple of dollars so I can see what money looks like. I have not got my shirts yet for we cannot get anything from Washington but I am in hopes to get them soon for I am about played out for shirts and this cold weather takes hold. There is lots of our boys had things sent them and we are all in the same fix. You wished to know if I got my slippers. I did. There was nothing gone but the liquor and the lemons. Some of our boys got liquor in there boxes and I am sure it was no commissioners that took mine out but some of the damn theives that hang around fortress Monroe. I dont want you to send me any box at Thanksgiveing without we get settled somewheres for I dont want things sent and I not get them. I am in hopes we shall have a chance to try our guns with the rebels before long for to tell the truth I am getting anxious for a fight for If fighting is to finish this thing I want to be at it and have it over with. I got a lot of papers that you sent me and I got some from Hampshire and three letters from there also but the papers are full of politics now a days and it makes me mad to read some of the stuff in them. I was reading Charles Sumners speech made the night of the election where he says this news will cheer up the Mass troops and all that sort of stuff. I think if he could have heard the swearing when it was known that Andrews was elected he would sing another song. I saw Gen Devens[4] this week and Capt McCartney went and took dinner with him that night. He dont look as if it worried him much. Mac is Capt thank God and according to the talk no thanks to John Brown Andrews but he is Capt and I am pleased. Thats so. Capt Wolcott came to see me the other day and I had a talk with him. I guess he is a good man on the Road. We have been out to day for a general Inspection and Wolcott was rigged up in a new suit and he looked tip top but it takes Mac to take them down on clothes. He is an airy duck

[4] General Charles Devens Jr. of Massachusetts later became attorney general in 1877, for President Rutherford B. Hayes.

and great on his shape.

I shall send a ring in this made of laurel root that was dug at the battle field of Antietam. Mr Coye made it for me and I should like for Mrs Curtis to have it. That is if she would like it not for its value but perhaps she would like to keep it for a relic. I wish it was a diamond. I could give it to her with a free will.

You must give my love to all the folks. Mace William and all the rest of them that want to hear from me. Tell them I feel Bully. Only my side and back trouble me nights a good deal. Probably lieing on the ground but I am in hopes to stand it through for I dont feel a mite like turning back. I dont want to go home untill the first Mass goes the best Battery in the service Sir. How is Lydston? Is he dead or has he enlisted? Give him my respects and ask him to take a drink Medford & Molasses for me and do it quick. But I will wind up for this time.

With my love to you all.
Jack

Rub this ring with a little linseed oil and that will bring the grain out good.

* * * * * * * * * * *

Camp Near Stafford Court House
Stafford County Va
Nov 23d 1862

Dear Brother

Yours of the 9th and 16th I received last night and was very glad to know I was still remembered by you and the rest of the folks. I must plead guilty of neglecting to write for almost a fortnight but I wrote at New Baltimore and you will learn by that the reason. The fact is this has been a hard time with us. It has been cold wet snowy and muddy and for myself I have been both cold and hungry quite a number of times. Then we have not had much spare time for the

Govt is getting so poor they dont give us any candles and we can not buy for they will not give us the tin to buy with but I will try and write every week in future if it is a possible thing if it is only to let you know I am alive. My health is good. Only pains in my back and sides after I lie down at night but it generally passes off in the morning. My appetite is immense. I can eat my ration of Junk and hard tack easy and then look around for more but it is not often I find it. The fact is this is an immense army and it is almost impossible to keep it supplied with forage and grub and to keep it properly clothed. The papers will tell you the troops are well supplied with boots overcoats &C but I happen to know a damn sight better for our own men cannot get what they want to make them comfortable. I have been working to day and I have to handle my shirt with great care or there would not be much of it left. Mac has sent a requisition to Washington for clothes and the officer is going to see if he can hunt up any bundle or boxes for the Battery and try and get them to us. I should like mine very much but have made out to get along so far. We have been here now four days. They are repairing the Roads toward Fredericksburg and I expect when we move again it will be towards that place. Gen Franklin as I suppose you already know is to have the command of the left wing of the army consisting of his old Corps and Burnsides. Bully for him. He can run it I bet. I see the papers have got Richmond all taken now that Burnsides is in command[5] but in my opinion there has got to be one of the biggest fights we have seen yet before Richmond is ours. I dont doubt but what the Hero of Roanoke is a good general and the army of the Potomac will fight just as well under him as under George B but still I had rather have the little Hero. But let who will lead us. I dont feel as much like fighting as I used to for it looks to me as if fighting for the union and Constitution is played out and that now we are fighting for the Abolition of Slavery. Speaking of Abe I have gone clean back on him. He may be a very good rail splitter but rather a poor President I reckon.

---

[5] President Lincoln replaced General McClellan with General Burnside as commander of the Army of the Potomac on November 7, 1862.

Dont send any box at present but I want you to get me a pound of tobacco and send it by mail. There has a number of the boys had it come so and then they get it cheaper than they do here after paying the postage. Get the Navy.[6] Winslow I have not heard from since we left Williamsport. He promised to write me but I have not got any letter. I have heard from Mary every week since she went home but the rest of them keep quiet.

Give my love to all the folks that want to hear from me and I hope soon to have the priveledge of writing some thing else besides complaints but at present there dont seem to be any thing to Inspire a man with a great deal of Courage.

So good bye for this time.
From Jack

Have not had a chew of tobacco for a week. Kind of tough.

* * * * * * * * * *

Camp Near Stafford Court House
Stafford County VA
Dec 1st 1862

Dear Brother

Once more I take my pencil to Inform you that I still live breathe and believe in little Mac. The past week has been one of unusual dullness with me for our mail that was due Thursday was miscarried and we did not receive it untill yesterday and as a good many of the boys were expecting money in there letters as you may judge it caused a good deal of uneaseiness but it made us feel better when we did get it. I got your letter with the stuff and feel much oblidged to you and hope we shall get paid sometime so I can pay you for I should judge by what I can learn that money has become a very usefull article even in Boston & vicinity. We still remain inactive

[6] A brand of tobacco.

General Joseph Hooker NA

and since I last wrote every thing has remained the same with us. Hookers Division passed our camp a few days since on its way to the front and the boys expected the next thing would be a fight as it generally means business when you see fighting Joe Hooker round. I saw some of the boys in the NH 2nd and in the Mass 11th but the first did not come with the others as they stopped behind to guard the baggage train. They have gone to Falmouth which is about 7 miles from here and nearly oppisite Fredericksburg. The talk is now that we have got to fight up there if we wish to proceed farther towards Richmond. Any one would thought to read some of the papers after Burnsides took Command that we were going right strait to Richmond without a struggle but you see I could not see it and it has become a matter of doubt in my mind whether Richmond is ever taken or not. At any rate I believe that if it is taken there has got to be some fighting done that will cause mourning the whole length and breadth of this land. I see the papers begin to talk about the mud and the difficulty of getting supplies to the army as the reason of Gen

Burnsides not moveing there. Things are true enough God knows but then you know they were going mud or no mud. It seems some of the wise ones begin to find out that the army is not properly clothed and shod about this time but they say the reason is that McClellan would not take the damn miserable stuff that was sent him to cheat the Soldiers with but I guess they are not so particular about it now for it is comeing thick and fast and I wish you would see some of the things they call shirts and for which we are charged the price of good ones. My clotheing account for the last year exceeds my allowance by 10,00 and I never have drawn any shirts drawers and but very few stockings. Some of the men are in debt from 25 to 40 dollars so you see how a man is used by the contractors and the damn rascally officers that are willing to accept such miserable stuff.

We had clotheing delivered to us yesterday and we all have got good knit blouses with pockets in them and the boys are strutting around like Peacocks with there hands in there pockets. I suppose I shall have to take some of there damn shoddy shirts and drawers as I have not got mine and it is very uncertain when I shall and perhaps the things may last untill I do get them. That is if I ever am so fortunate.

I received a letter from Winslow yesterday. He is in the hospital at Williamsport but expects to get his discharge in a few days as the Doctor says he dont think he can get well here. I shall write to him and tell him to call and see you when he goes home and get a drink. Ben will relate his experience to you and you can rely on what he tells you as being about the thing. A little radical perhaps in some things but he is a man that dont lie even to please his friends. He has been a good friend to me and I hope to live to meet him when we both shall be free men. If he calls tell him to remember his friends.

I am much oblidged for the Posts and the Boys think with me that some of the talk in it about George is about the cheese and they are always as anxious for my papers to come as I am myself. I received two letters from Mary yesterday. In all I got six letters and 7 papers so you see I had quite a mail.

You must give my love to all the folk. Tell them I can eat my allowance and more too if I could get [it]. My old bones ache nights awfully but I hope to live long enough to see this thing through and the Politicians that have made so much trouble consigned to infamy. I thought of you Thanksgiveing day and (by the way Gov Andrews order to the Mass troops was not read to us or his Proclamation either probably Mc could not see it quite). I had hard tack and coffee and smoked hog for breakfast smoked hog for dinner and coffee and boiled rice for supper. Hows that for a Thanksgiveing dinner? Hardly suit you I reckon but these things are nothing after you get used to them. The trouble is in getting used to it. I am glad Mrs. Curtis liked her ring. Tell Lizzie I will send her one if she would like it.

The leaves enclosed here are Laurel leaves. I have tried quite a number of kinds but they fade in drying. I thought perhaps she would like these they keep so green. So hopeing this will find you all well I will close.

From Jack

Love to Emily.

PS Monday Night Another mail to day and a letter from Pricilla & Levi. Levi seems to think the removal of George is about right & that the Democrat party wishes to run the country. I shall have to give him a dose tomorrow if I have time.

The weather is damp and cool.

* * * * * * * * * * *

Camp Misery
Somewhere in Virginia
Dec 6th, 1862

Dear Brother

Last Thursday morning we were started off before daylight and came to this place. What the name of it is is more than I can tell. All I can say is it is about three miles from Bell Plains which is a kind of bay that makes up from the Potomac and there is where we get our supplies from. The next morning it began to rain and we had to move our camp as we [were] in a hollow and were afraid we should get drowned out. In the afternoon it began to snow and snowed the most of the night and to day it is quite wintrish and the rail fence has to suffer for that is all the way we can keep warm. Build big fires between our tents. Very pleasant this liveing in smoke and mud. We try all kind of expedients to keep warm nights and as a general thing make out very well but it is kind of cold underneath and if it was not for our rubber blankets I dont know what we should do. I dont know how in Gods name the Infantry Stand it for there case is worse than ours for we continue to carry along considerable stuff that they cannot as they have to carry all on there backs and all we had to lug is our haversacks and canteens and our haversacks are not very heavily loaded about these times.

I thought a Summer campaign in Virginia was rough but I find a winter one very much rougher. The roads are in an awfull state although some of the papers talk differently. I will give you a faint description of our last march. The Jersey Battery went ahead. They made out to get to camp with all there carriages. We came next and left our Battery waggon and forge in the road. Capt Wolcott came next. He left Battery waggon forge and one casson behind and the regulars came in with three peices and 4 cassons. The rest struggled along one [or] too [two] [at a] time. My Casson got stuck once and Capt Wolcott helped me out. The Waggon train is not all here yet or were not this afternoon. Only half of the ammunition train haveing arrived and the roads now are a good deal worse than they were that day. Now I think on to Richmond is about played out for this winter. Our horses are about half fed and a good many of them are about played out.

The talk here is that Burnsides is removed but not haveing seen a paper for three days I dont know how true it is. The fact is there is all kind of stories a going and we dont know what is going on so well as you do at home but I expect they will not be satisfied untill Fremont[7]

[7] General John C. Frémont. In 1861, as commander of the Western Department, he had issued a proclamation freeing the slaves in Missouri, stirring up considerable controversy over the war's objectives.

takes command and when he does I think desertions will be plenty I do. I have come to the conclusion that this is a great country but the prospect is that it soon [will] be smaller.

I have not got my clothes yet nor do I know when I shall but I think I should like them about this time. I have made out to get a couple of Govt shirts but could get no drawers but then you know the army is abundantly supplied. I wish to God that some of these letter writers were oblidged to change positions with me for a week or two. I reckon they would sing another song and I dont think I am so bad off as a good many of the poor fellows that have left good comfortable home to come out here and fight for we dont know what. If I could make myself believe that it was for upholding the supremacy of the union and the old Flag I could do it without a murmur but I dont see it. But this fighting for the benefit of niggers and to please a lot of Politicians is something I never enlisted for and I can truly say I take no pleasure in it but I suppose I have got to do it or go back on myself and I dont want to do that. I am much oblidged for the stamps. You wish to know if we use them for change out here. When we were in Maryland some of the boys used to pass them but I never spent any for I knew if we came to this cursed place we could not get them. I never have passed any. The sutlers will not take them and a good many of them will not even take New England money but New York or Baltimore money they take readily if it is poor.

Sunday Morning

I tried to finish this last night but the cold would not admit but I have got in the sun by the side of the fire and will try & close it up. Letter writing is getting to be rather hard work this cold weather. It is awful cold this morning and everything is covered with frost. Last night I laid under three blankets and an overcoat & then I was cold. I tell you Sam it is damn rough this Soldiering but I feel first rate all but nights. My old bones ache nights some I tell you. I am going to make one more trial to get my clothes. I told the mail carrier if he would get them I would pay him when we got paid off and he says he will try.

You must give my love to all the folks that want to hear from me and excuse this writing for I am all of a shiver. I wish I was seated in your old kitchen. I should like to talk to you about a couple of hours on matters and things in general.

So good Bye for this time.

Yours &C
Jack

Five crackers to a man to day as the supply train has not got in. Beautiful Prospect for hungry men.

* * * * * * * * * *

Battlefield Near Fredericksburg
Dec 15th 62

Dear Brother

I received yours of the 7th with the stamps. I have also received the others with the money also the Tobacco. We crossed the river last friday. How things are going on is more than I tell. All I know is the fight is going on. We have had two men wounded so far. One has lost his leg. The other wounded in the arm. Mac is a hero with the boys and they say or the most of them damn John Andrews and Porter too. If I live through the struggle I will give you the particulars about Macs Commission.

There has been some tough fighting but I anticipate nothing to what we have got to see.

My love to all and if I never write again may God Bless you and all your family.

From Jack

Direct Brooks Division. That will be right.

Good Bye.

I wish George B was here. But Burnsides I hope will give <u>them</u>

hell. The shells are Bursting all over the field and my time is rather limited.

Love to Mace. I wish I had some of his Whis.

Fredericksburg, by Alfred Waud LC

* * * * * * * * * * *

On the road in Virginia
Near White Oak church
Dec 19 1862

Dear Brother

Yours of the 14th I have just read and you say you received mine of the 7th. I suppose by this time you have got one I wrote on the battle field. When I wrote that I did not know how it would turn. I have found out and know that we were pretty well whipped. With shame I say it but it is no use talking. So it is we recrossed the river

Monday night and to be honest I felt decideley better after we got across than I did when we were comeing. I shall not write any particulars as I suppose the papers give you all the details. As for our own Battery we received the aprobation of our Division Gen that is Gen Brooks. The old fellow gave us a great name. The best Volunteer Battery in the service—but Sam I think it was a shame for our men to be murdered as they were on that field. They stood no show at all for the enemy had every advantage in position and we might just as well have given it up at first as after losing some 10,000 men more or less. What our loss was is more than I can tell but I know it must be great. We think that we were very lucky in only haveing two men wounded for we were under a severe fire of the enemys shell. The Rebels charged on our Battery once but the Yorkers were too much for them and drove them back. Gen Brooks cried swore and done most every thing but it was no use. We had more than we could handle and I think if the Rebels had tried they could made it worse for us than it was but I guess they thought they had murdered about enough of us. There was some of our men that were left on the other side. There was two of the Mass 37th Regt they stayed behind on purpose to be taken prisoners and when the Rebs found them they called them cowards and all kind of hard names and made them swim the river. The last I heard of them they were under arrest. Hope they will get what they ought to have. That in my opinion would be hanging.

We moved to day from the river and now are about 6 miles from it. What is up now I cannot guess. Whether it is winter quarters or another move towards Richmond. But for one I dont think this army ever will see that place. They have got there tails down and I think have done better fighting than they ever will again. But I may be wrong and I hope I am.

Speaking about Porter we saw in the papers that he was not comeing out and to day we started a petition for Boston asking for Mac for a Captain. There was 115 signed it and we only number 125 and there was more that would signed it. I dont know only two in the whole Co that would not do so. There is a long story connected with the command of this Co. If I ever home I will tell you all about it but as it is we are not afraid but what we shall have Mac for a Capt. I have not received my clotheing yet neither have we been paid. I got the tobacco and I have got everything you have sent me with the exception of the clothes and I still live in hopes of getting that. I should like it pretty well for to tell the truth I have been kind of cold sometimes but I hope this thing will play out before long for to tell the truth I am sick and tired of this way of liveing or staying for I dont call it liveing but still I want to see it settled honorably if there is any such thing but I think if there is no more honor in this world than there is with those that have control of this Army it must be a damn scarce article. I dont want to say anything harsh or wicked but I begin to think that this Soldiering is a damn big humbug or to say the least there is a good deal of humbug connected with it.

I had a letter from Mary to day. The children are all well and I wish I was with them. I think I should stay there and let somebody else do the fighting but then you know it is to late to repent when the devil get you and a man might as well keep his courage up.

Give my love to all the folks Emily with the rest. I should like to be seated in your old kitchen and spin a few yarns and live in hopes of being able to do so some day but if I never do receive my thanks for many favors conferred and believe me still your Brother.

Jack

Excuse this writeing for the candle is a poor light to write by when the wind blows.

John W Chase
First Mass Battery
Brooks Division
Franklins Army Corps
Washington D C

Thats the ticket.
Hurrah for George B.
Thank you for the Stamps.

* * * * * * * * * * *

Camp Near White Oak Church Virginia
Dec 27th 1862

Dear Brother

I have not received any letter from you this week but thought I would write & let you know we were still alive as I wanted to send this receipt which you will find enclosed to be paid same as the others. They paid us four months pay keeping back two as I suppose they thought it would not do to give us all that belonged to us. The weather here is nice and warm and I hope it may continue. The army remains about the same as when I last wrote and the boys begin to think it looks like winter quarters but we cant always tell. I see by the papers there is a little something doing down in North Carolina but I dont think these small skirmishes pay much. I see Gen Wilson says the morale of this army is excellent and they are eager for another advance but I dont see it. No doubt they will fight if they get into it but they are not anxious I tell you and a good many of them wont fight if they can help it and if they were where they could get off there would be plenty of desertions and there is some as it is. I suppose you have seen the testimony of Gens Hooker Sumner[8] Franklin and others as to the cause of the late defeat and have drawn your own conclusions in regard to it. I think next time Burnsides will look a little sharper before he goes in quite so strong but still I suppose he thought he was doing right but then it is only ten thousand. That aint much. We had a good time Christmas. Beef steak and POTATOES the first since last September. Quite a rarity and then we had a little Whisky just to work it down. This morn I had baked beans and they were Bully. I tell you my health is tip top. Never better. I have not got my bundle yet but my faith is good. Perhaps fourth of July will fetch it up. Lucky for me the weather is so mild. You must give my love to all the folks that want to hear from me and tell them I hope to live to see John A Andrews hung for

[8] General Edwin V. Sumner.

I think he deserves it as much as anybody ever did. Remember me to Emily and everybody else. So good bye untill I hear from you.

Jack

This ring for Elizabeth.

* * * * * * * * * * *

Camp Near White Oak Church
Stafford County Virginia
January 1st 1863

Dear Brother

I have been thinking it strange that I got no letter from you last week but last night the mystery was cleared up on the arrival of the mail as it brought a letter from you and two from Mary. I presume they got stuck on the road as one of them had been 22 days in comeing. I wrote you a few days ago sending a receipt for thirty dollars also a ring for Elizabeth which I suppose you have got before this time. I hardly know what to do about those clothes. I have tried all the means that I could to get them but have not made out. The mail carrier would have got them for me but they have made new arrangements and he dont go to Washington now. Some of the boys have been haveing them sent by mail but it costs a good deal but I think on the whole I will send you the receipt and if you can get them to me I should like them for I have suffered for them and no mistake I did set out to buy me a pair of under shirts at the Sutlers but they were so devilish mean I would not humor them to give two dollars a peice for them for you could shoot peas through them and I thought it was about the same as throwing money away and after sending home 30 and paying up for my extra clotheing I did not have a very fat wallet and I like to have a little in case of a drought and I cannot get what I want from the Govt although the papers say the army is abundantly supplied.

I expect we shall leave here soon as we have order to have three days rations cooked and the Infantry the same with 60 rounds of

Harnden's Express Receipt CFC

Ammunition so I suppose that they Intend to give us another fight somewhere but I hope it will not be another such affair as the last for I am getting sick of war anyway but when it comes to wholesale Slaughter I think it is rather rough and I dont consider that affair anything but that and I think if Lee had known that night what we were doing it would have been a good deal worse than it was. I dont know who is to blame or dont care but one thing I do know Gen Franklin was not and he is my man next to little Mac. You never would caught George that way. I heard men say the day we crossed and men of rank too that they did not like the appearance of things. The Rebels were altogether to quiet to please them and the sequel proves that they were right. Lee well knew if he only got us where he wanted too he had us and nothing short of a miracle ever could have saved the army of the Potomac. That the affair has had a depressing effect upon this army there is no mistake. Newspapers may say what they please. I know for I have travelled around amongst the Soldiers some since we have been lieing here and I find the same feeling amongst the whole of them. They have no faith in Burnsides and they all say give us McClellan the man who knows when to fight. I dread another battle for I believe that there is plenty of men that will not fight if they can help it. In fact I know there is for they make no secret of telling of it. The papers say the army is not demoralized and is eager for an advance. They be but they want to advance towards home. They begin to think they have been fooled about enough and I think if the powers that be could hear the remarks passed on them that I hear they would try and do better than they do now but what do they care. Some body is makeing money out of this thing and what do they care how many widows and orphans are made as long as they dont have to take care of them. I tell you Sam this thing will take a turn before long or this once noble army will go to the devil. I may not live to see it for I dont hold life of much account now a days but remember what I tell you if I should step out that six months more such works as we have had the last two and this army is a goner and as for the new Regts they are worse as a general thing than the old ones and some of them in the last fight proved themselves Cowards. Now I dont like fighting no better than anybody else but I hate a coward. After a man has sold himself I say let him do what he is paid for doing. Thats my motto. What do you say? As for me I am glad that being in for it that I am in the first Mass Battery for I think they have proved themselves and Gen Franklin in an order complimented us very highly also Gen Brooks. If Mac can only get the command or keep the command of us we are all right but I expect John A Andrews will keep him out of it if he can. Capt Wolcott left here this morning. They say he has resigned and gone home but I dont know how true it is but he has gone somewhere bag and baggage. Some say he is going to try for this Battery but I hope not for I dont like the way he talks to his men and I think he is rather rough on them. That he is a brave man there is no question but I think a Private has rights as well as those who are placed over them and if your own officers dont look out for you who is going too? Thats the question. It is bad enough to be a Soldier at the best but I think that those in command can do a good deal towards making things pleasant or if they are disposed they can keep a man in trouble all the time. We are haveing very easy times of it at present. Nothing to do and plenty to eat. The boys haveing money our officers give us orders on the Commissary and we buy beans flour potatoes &C and we are liveing high. I have had baked beans now for four days at breakfast and intend to have some for dinner to day if nothing happens for I can just eat baked beans regular every day. I am bound to live as long as I can for I kind of like good liveing. It is a failing you know with the family. Yesterday I had fried turnovers of my own make and they were Bully I tell you. I am a great cook and more than that I can just eat too. My health never was better all but the Rheaumitis that kind of takes hold sometimes but as long as it dont affect my appetite I can stand it I guess.

I am glad you are going up to Stratham but I suppose you will be back before you get this. I wish I could be there to go with you. I think if I could come home and see the folks I should be willing to come back again for with all our hardships I can truly say I dont feel so low spirited since I have been in the army as I used to when I was at home but I want to see the thing settled for the benefit of the country but I must say the Prospect looks poor enough at present but let us hope for the best put our trust in God and not in Politicians particularly Blacks— —.

I hope you will see George when he comes to Boston and I want Lizzie to see him too and if she dont like his looks I will agree to make her a New Years present. I am no man worshipper but I do like that man for I believe he is a Patriot and a Man and that means a good deal now a days and I think he has been used shamefully but history will do him justice if his country fails too.

I hope you will succeed in getting Asher a Commission. He is a young man and it might be a benefit to him more ways than one but as for myself I am contented where I be although the pay would be very acceptable but still I had rather be where I am than to take a Commission in some of the Batterys that have come from Mass. Thats so for here I know my duty and so far I believe I have done it acceptably to my superiors. I believe I have written about all thats on my mind. Probably a good deal more than you will find Interesting but I got a writeing fit on and want to work it off somehow as I keep a account of the letters I write and receive. I have been looking over to day and find I have written 160 the past year and 55 of them to you so you see I have writen more than one a week. I feel very much oblidged to you for writeing to me as regular as you have and for takeing the interest in my welfare. Also to my other friends in Roxbury and I hope this will find you all enjoying a happy new year and I hope before another year has passed away that this war will have come to an end and Peace once more spread her wings over us all.

You must give my love to all the folks that want to hear from me and be sure and let me know what Lizzie thinks of the little Gen. Love to Mace. Tell him to take a new years drink and charge it to me. Also remember me to Emily. So with my thanks for the papers and stamps I will close hopeing this will find you all in good health.

Yours &C
Jack

PS It is a beautiful day here. Clear as a bell and just a shade cold but I expect it is a weather breeder.

Friday morn

PS No 2 Yours of the 28th I received last night but I will not write any more now.

Let me know how the ring suits.

[Enclosed in this letter is a receipt from Harnden's Express.]

* * * * * * * * * *

Camp Near White Oak Church
January 3d 186[3]

[Dear Brother]

I dont suppose you will be looking for a letter from me but I write this just to tell you not to do anything about that bundle untill you hear from me again for the Capt is sick with the Reheaumitis and expects to go to Washington and if he does he is going to try to get our things to us. The other Regt are getting boxes and if our Brigade quartermaster was worth a copper he could get ours but the fact is he is one of these useless appendages to the army that dont get waked up untill the next day. He is one of these clever kind of men but when you come to the smart it is not in him. I think if I succeed in getting this bundle I shall not try again for it is most too much trouble to get them. It would amuse you to see some of the articles that come out here in the mail boots shirts drawers tobacco and most everything that you can think of. We are haveing beautiful weather here now and I hope it will last. Everything is quiet.

They are busy building Corduroy roads but I dont see any Contrabands at work on them but they are all white Soldiers. We have all kind of stories afloat but it is more than I can guess what the next move will be but one thing I think they will have to do something before long. If they dont the Johnnys will be doing something with us for they have got so now they ride all around us when they want to. I had a letter from Hagerstown Md last night and they told me we had about 25,000 troops there. What in Gods name they are doing there is more than I can tell. It appears to me that the union army is scattered all over Gods creation and part of some other country. I should think it was about time to concentrate it somewhere but its no use talking. There is damn queer works in this war and I think by the time it is through this country will be about played out. For my part I wish the Rebs would get to Washington and take Abe and all his allies Prisoners and carry them off to Richmond. I think it would be a blessing to the country at large. We are liveing very quiet. Nothing to do but eat and sleep and do our ordinary camp work. We have got 40 new horses and to day we expect 16 mules. Mac is the Boy to keep a Battery in order. The Commissary furnishes us good grub and with what extra we buy we are liveing Bully. My health is tip top. I never felt better and in the words of Artemus I am a gay and festive Cuss. I find a man may as well keep up good courage and do the best he can under the Circumstances. Like Mark

Tapley I have made up my mind to be jolly when I can. Give my love to all the folks. I dont hear anything from Stratham but I suppose they dont get time to write. They are generally awful busy in the winter time. Well they must do as they please. My day may come yet. You know Mark Roberts used to say every Dog would have his day and every female Dog his afternoon. My respects to Mace and all the rest of the folks and believe me.

yours &C
Jack

* * * * * * * * * *

Camp Near White Oak Church
Stafford County Virginia
Jan 11th 1863

Dear Brother

I have been looking ever since the night of Thursday for my weekly letter and last night brought it and I was very happy to learn that you still live. I am glad to hear that you had a good time up to Stratham and I wish I could have been with you. I think I could enjoy myself if I was up there. I have not heard anything from that part of the town for some time. Not since I wrote Levi. I suppose he did not like what I wrote but there is one thing I am not very particular whether he likes it or not. Its no use for a man to talk nigger to me for I dont believe in it. As to what I have wrote I never have wrote a word that favored Secession. I am a strong union man. That is what I enlisted for was to restore the union but I am not willing to shed one drop of blood to fight Slavery up or down. Let the niggers go to hell for all [of] me and if a man wants to preach Abolition Emancipation or any other ism he must find somebody besides me to preach it too. As for being sick of the war I am tired of being robbed and cheated by a set of damn unprincepled contractors and know if the Govt done there duty they could not do it and then I am sick of going cold for want of Clothes for God knows I have tried hard enough to get them both from Govt and from home but as yet have not made out. I never have known whether they were at the office or not and I am tired of trying and if you can do anything I should admire to have you for they would be very acceptable about this time for the weather although not very cold is not much like summer. If we only had any one to look out for us we might get things. The Mass Regt and the other Batterys get theres and they also have clothing given them. The third Battery all had new knit blouses given them and they have had things given them several times but we never have had so much as a pair of stockings given us by anybody except our personal friends. I expect there is too much hard shell Democracy amongst us for I tell you Black Republicans has not many friends in this Battery. Well let them go it if we can only get what belongs to us we can stand it I reckon. If they will only give us George back we will try and put her through the best we can. You did not say whether you got my receipt for the money or the one for the box but as you got the letters I suppose you got them. Tell Lizzie that ring is made of the same kind of wood but it did not grow in the same place. That came from Maryland at Sharpsburg and hers came from Virginia near Fredericksburg. Tell Hitty I will remember her if nothing happens for I have not forgotten the Box last winter. I had a letter from Langdon and he wrote that he wanted some money to make up what he had paid to clothe the children and I have written him to call on you for I supposed you had some that belongen to me. How much I could not tell but I guessed enough to satisfy the claim. If not he must wait untill we were paid again for what little I have I want for I dont mean to starve if I can help it and my pocket book is not very fat. Let me know if you got the receipt and how much money there is on hand if any for I never have kept any account of the matter.

I was sorry to hear that James was sick but I suppose if they all were dead they would not write to me. I had a letter from Winslow and he writes that he is at home sick. Been home a fortnight but has not been out of the house. Says he will call and see you when he gets able. Capt McCartney has gone home. I should like to have you call and see him if you would like to. He lives at No 2 Indiana Place. I dont doubt he would receive you. I dont think Asher likes to get letters as well as I do. If he did he would write oftener. I think as much of a letter as I do of a good dinner and that is saying a good deal out here.

We have moved our camp this week and the boys are fixing up there tents for winter quarters. I expect by the time we get comfortable we shall have to leave again. I have got a shanty built of logs and a canvass roof. Quite a good place. Wood is scarce with us. Nothing but green Pine and that is poor stuff to burn green. I believe I must close for this time. I dont know as you will find anything interesting but the fact is I have got Company and it is hard work to write and talk too. My love to all the folks and receive this with the best Wishes of

Jack

Take this note and buy me some postage stamps. I had plenty but I have lent them around and find it hard work to get them back and then I have several that will not stick. If you have any wafers in the house put in a few in your next.

Tell anybody that says I am Secesh that it is a damn lie. I am a union man to the core and for that I am willing to fight as long as I have a leg to stand on.

Did Lizzies ring fit and ask Hitty whether that one is right size for her.

Quit.

* * * * * * * * * *

Camp Near White Oak Church
Stafford County Virginia
Jan 15th 1863

Dear Brother

I have just finished reading yours of the 11th and as the night is warm and not feeling sleepy I thought I would write tonight not knowing how soon we may have to march as they keep telling us we are going to do soon. We like yourselves are blessed with very pleasant weather the last few days. We have had a Southerly wind and it is so warm that a fire makes our HOUSES uncomfortably warm but I reckon we can stand all such weather like this and I hope the same may be continued to us. I am sorry that Mrs Curtis should think I am Influenced by any outside pressure but you can tell her that I have fought under George and I have fought under some other Gens and I ask no mans opinion of there merits and if she will come out here and go through the Army of the Potomac she will find a good many thousand that think just as I do but I shall not quarrel with her for her opinion but I think a person of good common sense out here can tell most as well about an officer as those at home. I know and could call by name men who the papers say are very Brave efficient officers but I knows and others knows them to be damn cowards and let a shell burst over there heads they will turn pale with fear. What I knows I knows and no man Knows some things I does knows but as you say let the squirrel set. Time proves all things.

In regard to the money I wrote you that Langdon would make a requisition on you and the balance I think you better keep by you for there is no knowing when we shall get paid again and I may want some of it and it would be a bother to you to get it. I am glad Asher has had a chance to hear the Music of the balls and I hope if ever called to go into battle again he may come out all right. I dont know how he felt being under fire but the first time I was I felt something like the other man I wa wa wa want scart but I was k k k kind of cold and I take notice I felt decideley more comfortable when the sun went down and the shooting stopped. That was at Gaines Farm but there we were under fire and doing nothing ourselves. If a man is only busy attending to his own Gun he dont mind it half as much as he does to be doing nothing for he has something to take his attention. At least thats my experience. I hope you will call and see Capt McCartney. If you do ask him about that affair at Gaines Farm. I think I wrote you in my last he lives at No 2 Indiana Place.

Its not much use to talk about a furlough at the present time and as for going home with sick and wounded there is always enough to take all such chances. I should like a furlough first rate but I dont want one bad enough to act as damn mean as a good many I know have to get one. I am good for three years if I can feel as well as I have lately and only lucky enough not to get killed or wounded for I feel just as willing to fight for old glory now as ever I did but nary a drop of my blood for niggers. Thats me and if anybody dont like my style they no need to have it. Let the Champions of emancipation come out. There is plenty of good Regt that want men to fill there ranks and then we shall have a chance to see how much blood they are willing to spill for the great and holy cause. We had some of that kind amongst our recruits last fall and the same men are now willing so they say, to let the South go but as much Secesh as I am I am willing to fight a little longer first. Only give us a fair shake. Thats what we want.

We have the same rumors here about this Command as you do but I dont see us anything different has taken place yet. Gen Franklin would be my choice if we cannot have George but I suppose that the wisdom at Washington will do as they please without consulting PRIVATES.

I received a letter from Eliza a few days since and she informed me that Sewall was in the Nahant[9] and that was about all the Information I did get. I have heard nothing from the Ridge yet therefore I Infer that they are afraid of being arrested for corresponding with Rebels if they write to me but however I got a couple of letters from others there and I understand that Stratham is still alive doing something towards raising recruits as they give an account of several babies born in town lately. You tell Lizzie that I expect she put you up to ask after the girls at Hagerstown and you can tell her they were all well at the last accounts and were almost wishing the Rebels would come over there again so that we should have to come and drive them out. That Maryland is a great country I tell you. I wish we were there in winter quarters. I wish you could afford to come out here. I would give a good deal to have you and I

[9] The USS *Nahant* was a Union ironclad ship that participated in the blockade of Southern ports. It also was one of nine ironclads that attacked Fort Sumter in April 1863.

think as we are now situated I could get you up a dinner that you would not despise for we are liveing first rate about this time. It is either a feast or a fast with us in the Army and we have to make the most of a good thing when we can get it. I had some roast chicken for dinner yesterday. It came in a box from old Boston for there is now and then one that gets through but it is no sure thing about them. I think if you should come here and see for yourself you would find some things different from what you think for now for you know old Weller told Samuel that after he was married he would know a good many things he did not then. But whether it was worth a while to go through so much to find out a little was a matter of opinion but he rather thought not and it is about so with the Army.

But I think I have written enough but I had no news to write and felt just like writing and had to say something if it was not very bright.

You must give my love to all Inquireing friends and tell them I am gay and happy. So hopeing this will find you all well I will halt.

Jack

I have read the papers very carefully the last few days trying to find a victory somewhere but I dont see it. Was Col Burrill killed at Galveston? I cannot seem to find out by the New York Herald whether he was or not.[10]

If I think of any thing more I will write it in the morning.

Friday Morning

I dont think of any thing else. We had a real old Virginia rain last night but it is clearing up fine now so good bye for this time.

Yours &C

Jack

* * * * * * * * * *

[10] Colonel Isaac Burrill of the Forty-second Massachusetts Regiment, who was from Roxbury, was captured at Galveston, Texas, and was held captive for almost two years.

Camp Near White Oak Church
Stafford County Va
Jan 27 /63

Dear Brother

I suppose you begin to think it is about time to get a letter from me but then you see we have been performing one of Burnsides Stragetic movements.[11] We left camp last Tuesday and started up the river. The first day we had good roads and good weather but that night it commenced raining and has continued to do so the most of the time. Since the 2nd day we made about 3 miles and of all the travelling I ever saw that beat it. My Casson was the only one that got through the rest being left a mile behind. Thursday the order

A Stormy March, by Edwin Forbes LC

came for us to try and get back to our old camp. We started and got about a half a mile and found it impossible so we hauled up in peice of woods and camped and the next day tried it again and Sunday we reached here pretty well used up. We found the camp cleaned out of everything in the shape of shanties & now we shall have to go to work and fix up again that is if we stay here. We had a ration of

[11] Known hereafter as Burnside's Mud March.

whiskey Sunday and another Monday morning Lieut Green thinking it would do the boys good and I dont think it hurt them any. It is raining here to day and I am on the sick list suffering from a head ache and pains in my limbs generally but I guess its nothing but a slight cold. I suppose the papers will give you all the particulars of the late movement and I will not remark on it. The talk here now is that Burnsides has resigned and Hooker is in command but I dont know how true it is. But if it is so I am glad of it for I think Burnsides is Played out.[12]

I received yours of the 18th with the stamps and I am in hopes to see Hiram with the stockings for I think I can find a use for them. Its no use talking about my selling anything for I never did sell anything to a brother Soldier yet and I never shall unless I am starveing for there is a party of us in this Battery that when we have more than we want we give to one another. I have seen enough of this damn meaness in the army one to another and I dont believe in it. I think instead of trying to make money out of one another we all ought to try and help and thank God there is boys in this Battery that are willing to do it and as long as I have any thing they can have part of it for I know they would do the same with me.

I hope I shall get those shirts but my faith is rather small for the way things are conducted out here is enough to disgust anybody.

I had a letter from Pricilla this last week. Been on the road 26 days thats all. Seems to be a spell put on her letters.

You must excuse this letter for I dont feel much like writing but thought I would just let you know that I still live. Remember me to all my friends and tell Mace I wish he would get mad and come out here again for I should like to see him very much. So hopeing this will find you all well I will close and will try and do better next time so receive this with the best wishes of

Jack

[12] President Lincoln replaced General Burnside with General Hooker on January 26, 1863.

I shall enclose a letter I cut from a Hampshire paper. One of the $200 men. I call it a damn silly concern and I should like to kick him whos to blame for his being lousy but his lazy self. [No enclosure found.]

* * * * * * * * * * *

Camp Near White Oak Church
Stafford County Virginia
Feb 3 [1863]

Dear Brother

I have been anxiously looking for a letter from you as I have got so now that if I dont get one every week I think you have gone back on me as you are the only Brother I have who considers me worth writeing too and if it was not for your kind letters I dont know but what I should think that none of my Relations except my children cared a copper for me but when I get one of your letters I think there is some that there Friendship consists in something besides words for let me tell you it looks like a simple thing but it makes a man feel a good deal better if he can get a few letters every week for he kind of thinks that somebody cares for him. I dont write this as applying to you by no means for God knows about all the comfort and symphathy I have had has come from you and my other friends in Roxbury and God bless them say I for the favors they have conferred on me and I find

From Envelope of February 3, 1863 CFC

its no fault of yours that I got no letter last week as it arrived to night and I find it was by some ill luck misent but I have finally got it and glad was I.

I suppose you have got my letter before this giveing an account of the last Stragetic movement and of its being knocked in the head by the rain and mud which I suppose will now learn folks that a Winter Campaign in Virginia is no easy job.

Since I wrote last we have been visited with an old fashioned snowstorm but it has now mostly disapeared and the latter part of last week was very pleasant but to day it is as cold as ever I saw it in Virginia and to night it is awful and if you cannot read this letter you can lay part of it to the cold for I am decidely shakey. We have been at work since we came back fixing up a place for our horses building chimneys for the officers and trying to make ourselves a little comfortable but then you see wood is getting kind of played out around here and in a very cold night its hard keeping up steam but I am in hopes we shall not have a great deal of such weather as we are having to night. I expect to send this by Seargt French as he is going home on a Furlough if he ever gets it. His name with others haveing gone in for one and I expect he will start tomorrow or next day. I did not send my name in for I did not think it would pay to go home for 10 days. It would cost me between 30 and 40 dollars at the least and I concluded the money would do the children more good than my visit would and then my next pay I get I have promised Mary she should have to pay for some grave stones for her Mothers grave which to my shame be it said I have so long neglected to

Sarah F. (Marston) Chase, John's wife, who died in 1857 CFC

have done and I thought take every thing into account it would hardly pay not but what I should like well to come even for a short time but then you know we cannot always do as we would like particularly poor folks and as nigh as I can learn money is none to plenty with folks at home these times.

Thursday Forenoon

I will now resume my writeing for the cold the night I commence was such that I could not finish. I think I suffered more that night than I ever did a night before in my life for I could not sleep or keep warm and the way the cramps took hold was a caution to sinners and to crown all my side which has been no trouble to me this winter hardly commenced again since the last march but I have been giveing it the Camphor treatment and I think it is getting better. Yesterday was quite a cold day here. I went off in the morning and was gone all day visiting some of the NH and Mass Regt and amongst the rest was the NH 9th and if you could hear them fellows groan you would think nobody ever suffered as they have and they are decidely sick. Some of them allow they never will go into a fight but I hope Hooker will shoot a few of the damn loafers just to teach the others what to expect. For one I am ashamed of some two or three of the last Regt that State sent out here and think if such men as those are worth $200 that some of them in the 2nd Hampshire are worth a thousand. I was at the 2nd saw Marys husband and took supper with him had a little whiskey and Frank gave me a dozen cigars. He is cooking for the Adjutant. He looks well and is pretty well contented. I called on Mr Wright and obtained my stockings &C and return my thanks to Elizabeth and Mrs Robins and as the saying is may there shadow never be less and if there is more pleasure in giveing than in Receiving there pleasure must be great for of all things that I was in want of Stockings was what I wanted most for I had my last pair on my feet. Tell Elizabeth she just pleased me in sending that hankerchief for although I have several yet white ones are not just the thing for a Soldier although a good deal better than none and now if I could only get those shirts I should be all right.

Speaking of a box I should like one but I dont see any way of getting one. At least there is no sure way that I know of and I dont want my friends to send me things and I not get them but if I see any chance to get one I will let you know. Some of the boys have sent and if theres get through safe I will see what luck I can have but I want you to send me a couple of pounds of tobacco by Charley French when he comes back and let me know what it costs for one pound of it is for a friend of mine and he will pay me for it. I have not heard anything from Langdon since I wrote him and if he dont want money bad enough to write for it he can wait for he certainly must know that I have none to send him or ought to at least. I will write Mary as you request. Do I direct to South Brooks? I have forgotten. I reckon you did not see Capt Mac. He got back here a week ago last Tuesday. Speaking of Sawin[13] he is on detached service and dont stop with us at all. He is a good fellow but not what you would call a smart man. It is snowing here to day and is cold as the devil but I will stop for I am about froze but if I get warmed up I will write more as Charley has not gone yet and will not now before tomorrow and if he dont start then I shall send this by mail.

Lieutenant Robert L. Sawin USAMHI

(The Same Continued)

I see by the papers that Ashers Battery has been haveing quite a little fight down on the Blackwater[14] and that they were pretty roughly handled losing two men and having 8 wounded and the other Battery with then haveing 12 killed and wounded. I rather think the Johnnys "got range of them." One of our recruits by the name of

[13] Lieutenant Robert L. Sawin of the First Massachusetts Light Artillery.

[14] Near Franklin, Virginia, west of Suffolk, on the Blackwater River.

Manning belonging in West Roxbury has been commissioned Senior Second Lieut in this Battery thus jumping Lieut Green. I suppose John A Andrews thought he must do something to offset Mac [McCartney's] apointment and I think he has just gone and done it this time for the fellow dont know how to take a post on the Gun or how to march from front to rear but then he is a good Republican and I suppose has got Influential friends at Court but such appointments dont do much towards increaseing Andrews popularity in the Battery and I think a majority of the boys would like to hear of his death if it was only Gods will. I see hes been authorized to raise some nigger Regt. I think he will have a good time doing it. I dont see niggers enlisting in a hurry. They aint the kind that does it for they dont like war I reckon But I will try and close up. I have received all letters up to date stamps &C but I am in hopes to have the pleasure of perusing one from you to night.

My love to all the folks of course Including Emily and I hope the weather will soon grow warmer as it is decidely hard work to be Gay and happy such weather as this But Good Bye.

Yours &C
Jack

Friday Forenoon

No mail last night consequently no letter. It is raining great Guns here to day and I am rolled up in my blankets and my joints feel as if somebody was trying to pull me apart but I live in hopes of seeing better weather before long. Some of our boys were up to the first Regt yesterday and found them gone. They started with nothing but blankets and five days ration probably to reconnoitre. Sumners Grand Division is on the move some say to North Carolina but of course we dont know where they have gone and can only guess. All is I hope they will not move us untill better weather but then you know Hooker is a worker and I dont expect he will let us rest if it is possible to move us.

As I see no prospect of French getting off I shall send this to day by mail for I expect you will be looking for a letter long before you get this so give my love to all the folks and believe me Still for George B and the union.

Jack

I see by the paper George is haveing a great time at Boston and the Gun Boats have got into trouble down at Charleston.

Give my love to Mace and tell him I wish I had a rum punch to day. I think it would help this Rheaumitis Slightly.

* * * * * * * * * *

[Feb 6, 1863]

Dear Brother

I wrote and sent you a letter to day but as Seargt French has obtained his furlough I thought I would send a few lines not knowing which you might get first. I want you to send me a couple of pounds of tobacco by him and send the price as part of it is for another man. Send the Navy brand. This miniature is one that was taken from the body of a Reb Seargent at Antietam. I suppose it must be his lady love that is with him. [No miniature found.]

Give my love to all the folks and I will not write any more as I suppose you will get the other about as soon as you do this.

Yours &C
Jack

PS Send me some black thread if you please.

* * * * * * * * * *

Camp Near White Oak Church
Stafford County Virginia
Feb 8th 1863

Dear Brother

Yours of February first I received to night with some half a dozen others. I expect they have been keeping them untill they got a pile together as they were mailed all the way from Jan 26 to Feb 3d. Last night I went to bed mad with everybody and everything but to night I feel gay as a peach only a little tired for I am trying to fix up a better place to live in than I have had since we got back to camp And to day we have had a horse back ride in the mud. We took horses and went to the Bell Plain Landing after grain bringing up a four bushel bag on each horse. We had 42 horses and brought 42 bags to camp as it is some four miles down there and the d___dest road you ever saw. You can judge it is no pleasant job but we must have forage you know and it is more than three six mule teams can do to keep us supplied the roads are in such condition. I wrote you yesterday and sent a note by Charley French and I meant to tell you if you had one of those pipes on hand you spoke of a while ago you might send it to me by him but if you get the tobacco I guess I can find a pipe for I can make a cob one if can not do any better for you know they used to say old Hickory used to smoke one.

Tell Elizabeth that leaf was one that was sent me in a letter and they called it a fig leaf. It struck me as being a very pretty one and I thought perhaps she would like it. I shall not tell who sent it for fear Emily will be put out and want to make up faces at them. "Oh no maam." I have received the papers you spoke. I am glad that the people do honor to the General. I wish to God he was in command here but I reckon I have seen most as many people assembled to cheer him as there was there and I guess if he could come here now that there would be a little noise made. When we were on the last march I saw in a number of places written with charcoal Burnsides stuck in the Mud give us little Mac and the Soldiers did not fear to say so right out in meeting. I dont wonder Burnsides gave up for he knew well enough this Army had no Confidence in him. I think they have more in Hooker. I am sorry Franklin has left us and I think that is the feeling through this Grand Division. He told us in his farewell that it was not voluntary. Gen Smith is now in command of the Left Grand Division but the talk is Reynolds[15] is to take it but you can

[15] General John F. Reynolds was commander of the First Army Corps.

Direct same as you always did at present as Franklins name will not die right away. Harry Smith has not got back or had not the day I was up there but they were expecting him every day. The last letter I wrote Susie I told him he better resign but I guess he did not like it very well but when I see him I am going to tell him why. I tell you Sam I dont think I am quite a fool if I am nothing but an humble Corporal I can tell him things that I reckon he dont think I know. Thats so. Shoulder straps dont always give a man sense if it does authority. In a former letter you said that Levi said I must got somebody else letter but Eliza wrote he went to hear Wendell Phillips[16] lecture and was very much pleased with him but if he can sit and hear George B abused as Eliza says he was by Phillips I think he must be a great McClellan man but the fact is Levi is under keepers and has some nigger loving friends to think for him. I dont want to hear any thing about his love for George for he is one of them that talk war and desolation to the South but is damn careful to keep his own body out of the way. I dont want any nigger lovers to write me for I am none of theres. Never. That man you speak of as belonging to the NH sixth left a good Regt thats none of your Bounty Regts. I suppose you used to know Benny Brooks who is in this Battery. He has told me several times to remember him to you and now I will try and do so. Benny is a gay boy and now and then favors us with a little singing. He is expecting a Bundle when Mr Stewart comes so I suppose he intends to visit us. I should like to see Some body from Roxbury first rate but I believe I have written all you will want to read and I will close hopeing this will find you all in good health. I am quite smart now. Sunshine and letters works wonders with a Soldier. This peice of Box I got out of a garden at Sickles[17] head quarters. Give my love to all and tell Emily she must not do it. We have soft bread tomorrow for the first time. Hurrah.

Yours &C
Jack

---

[16] Wendell Phillips was an abolitionist orator from Boston.
[17] General Daniel E. Sickles.

N B No yaller gals here. Played out. Nothing but a few Clay eaters and they are no ways fascinating I tell you but Golly cant they swear (WHEW) I reckon.

If you have a chance send me a piece of Sponge to wash with.

* * * * * * * * * * *

Camp Near White Oak Church
Stafford Va
Feb 17th 1863

Dear Brother

I will now try and answer yours of the 16th which I received last Sunday Night informing me of your sending me a box by Stewart and Porter. Messers Marston and Morse were at our camp last Friday and told me they expected the boxes would be there Saturday but I did not go after mine untill yesterday. I got the box but did not hear any thing about any Whiskey. Stuart & Morse were gone to Falmouth and had not got back when I came away So I did not see them. The contents of the box were in good order and I am much oblidged to you and Lizzie for the contents. Also to William for the tobacco. He has a good Idea of what a Soldiers want. I opened the box up there and Horatio Littlefield and myself made it lighter to lug but I found it enough before I got back to camp although Ben Brooks was with me and helped bring it. It is about two miles up there and not the best of travelling and I guess it was about as well as if you had sent more but I suppose I should got it to camp some how if it

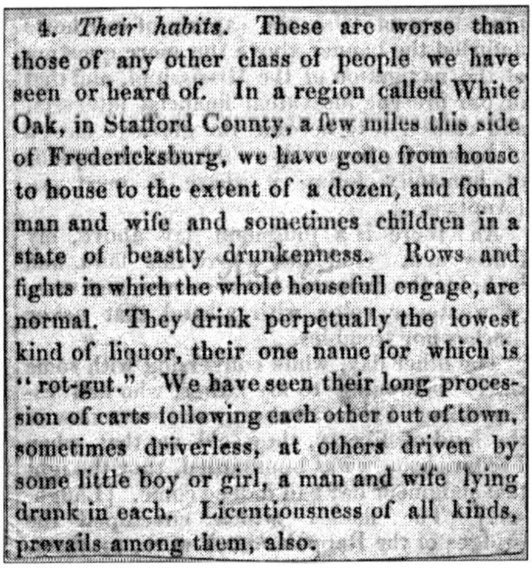
4. *Their habits.* These are worse than those of any other class of people we have seen or heard of. In a region called White Oak, in Stafford County, a few miles this side of Fredericksburg, we have gone from house to house to the extent of a dozen, and found man and wife and sometimes children in a state of beastly drunkenness. Rows and fights in which the whole housefull engage, are normal. They drink perpetually the lowest kind of liquor, their one name for which is "rot-gut." We have seen their long procession of carts following each other out of town, sometimes driverless, at others driven by some little boy or girl, a man and wife lying drunk in each. Licentiousness of all kinds, prevails among them, also.

Clipping in Letter of Feb. 17, 1863 CFC

had been as large as the one you sent to Harrisons Landing. I am glad you thought of the Fish for now I can have some Hash fish and that will be a great treat to me. I called and saw Frank Hays yesterday and eat off crockery as he had Genl Marston[18] there too breakfast and I also got some good whiskey (not Busthead). Frank has a box on the road which weighs 200 lbs and I feel kind of anxious to have it get along before we move for I think I shall try and ring in for some of the Contents as Frank has given me a polite invitation to call and see it opened. Harry Smith has not got back yet but he is now Capt Smith. Soft thing. Been home six months and now promoted. Thats about the way the thing goes. Merit is a damn poor recomendation to a man for a commission these times and as the boy wrote to his Father "some mighty mean men get office out here" and some times I think there is not much inducement for a man to try & do his duty as the dead beats seem to get the best of it but then there is one thing. If a poor devil lives to get out of it he will have the satisfaction of knowing he done his duty and that will be worth some thing to himself but I tell you Sam there is a good many that call themselves men that have come out here and are nothing but dead beats drawing pay and doing no duty. You will find any quantity of them in all the Regt and most all the Cos and so it goes. I shall not write much to day but will write again as soon as French gets back or I hear from you. I was sorry to hear of Nappys death but all I can say is I hope we all shall be as well prepared to go as I think she was.

My love to all the folks.

JWC

[Newspaper clipping enclosed.]

* * * * * * * * * *

[18] General Gilman Marston had been a congressman from New Hampshire.

Camp Near White Oak Church
Stafford County Va
Feb 23d 1863

Dear Brother

Charley French arrived at Camp last Saturday night and I received a letter from you and to day he went to Falmouth and got his valise and I received my bundle. Tell Mrs Curtis I am much oblidged to her for the pipe. It suits me exactly. I have had several offers for it but you know they cant have that pipe no how. The hankerchief too I am very thankful for and the tobacco is just what I wanted. I believe I am all right now for a forward movement. I received a bundle from Stratham containing three pairs stockings so you see I am now pretty well supplied with them.

Mr Stewart was down to see me last week and he informed me that the bottle of whiskey you sent me got broke. I was sorry but such is the fortune of war but I suppose he will tell you all about it. That peach preserve was just high. We made an apple pudding and used that for sauce. Benny Brooks came up to dine with me and we concluded we would be willing to lug down another just such a box. I was very agreeably surprise when I opened the can marked Green Corn for I found it contained apple sauce which was very much more acceptable but you ought to seen it fly when I first started to open. I began to think it would all fly out but I put a pan under and let it go it with a perfect looseness.

I am glad you did not send that Abolition sheet of Nigger Sumners out. I have got a friend that works in that office from who I get papers but I have barred that and told them never to send it to me. The old Post is my style for Politics for I think they talk like Christians. Charley says your dinner suited him first rate and I think I could destroy about a Point of that kind of feed if I had it <u>that is</u> if I <u>was hungry</u>. I dont know as I can write any news. Part of this army has gone somewhere. The 9th Corps Burnsides old Corps has gone and Siegels[19] too so I expect somethings up. Hooker is kind of

[19] General Franz Sigel.

stirring things up a little. He has adopted the old McClellan style of dividing the Army. No Grand Divisions now. Couch commands our Corps today but who will tomorrow is more than I can tell for they seem to keep Changing every week. I hope Hooker will have a fair shake just to see what he can do. I think he will do well enough if they only let him alone "but will they do it?"

We have about a foot of snow on the ground but I am in hopes it will not last long. I think we are getting more than our share of winter weather here. At any rate more than we like.

Give my love to all the folks. Tell them I am well and in as good spirits as a man can be under the circumstances. Tell Mr Stewart I forget to thank him for his kindness but you can do it for me. Remember me to Emily and tell Mrs Curtis I had a glass but gave that one to one of my boarders for you see they call me the Landlord just because I am grey headed. Good bye for this time.

From your Brother
Jack

Ask Mr Marston[20] what he thinks of Virginia mud and White Oak Church. I am Posted on Stratham for Charley brought me a letter from Pricilla. Tell Elizabeth instead of fig I meant pineapple plant. Not much difference.

* * * * * * * * * *

Camp Near White Oak Church
Stafford County Va
March 1st 63

Dear Brother

Yours of the 22nd was received and although I have not much to write I thought I must just let you know that I am still alive and as Elder Piper used to say blessed with a measure of health although to day I have a fit of the blues. The fact is the weather is such that its

[20] John's late wife's father, Thomas Marston.

enough to make any poor devil blue. First its snow and then its rain and as to mud we have that all the time. I went up to see Frank this last week hopeing to find that box had arrived but instead I found the Regt gone and I suppose by this time they are amongst the hills of the Granite State as the talk seemed to be that they were going home to recruit. It makes the boys of the first Mass Regt feel kind of blue because they could not go too for those two Regt always blow high for each other and I think myself they are two hard ones to beat in this army. I felt bad when I found them gone although I am glad for there sake but I used to take a good deal of comfort in going to see them. I hardly care to go amongst any other Regts except them and the first out of our own brigade for I dont allow that they can beat that you know but ours are two years men the most of them and there time is most out so I expect the next thing will be a brigade of niggers to take there place. The rumour here now is that we are going to Newbern or somewheres down that way but how much truth there is in the report is more than I can tell. All I know is that a large part of this army has gone somewhere and they are fortifying here down towards the river therefore I think somethings up. For one I dont much care where we go if we can only stop this war for I am getting decideley tired of this doing nothing and I think fighting is better than this lieing still and rotting in camp. People seem to think Hooker is going to do something wonderful and I hope they may not be disapointed and I dont think they will for I believe he will hurt somebody or get hurt himself when he does get at them for he is a hard fighter and no mistake I am in hopes that before another fourth of July this thing will be pretty well cleared up and I think if things are handled right it will be but all we can do is wait for the Waggon.

You must give my love to all the folks. Tell Mace I am sorry that bottle got broke but I had a canteen full to celebrate Washingtons birthday that a friend got for me out of the Commissary but it was not equal to that he used to keep in his. I have not heard anything from Hampshire since French got back but shall expect a letter to night. Last night we got no mail.

I wish they would send us down where Asher is. I think I should visit him often but there is not much danger of there sending us anywheres except where they think there is something to do but I will close hopeing this will find you all well and in better spirits than it leaves me.

Yours &C
Jack

* * * * * * * * * *

Sunday Evening March 8th 63

Dear Brother

Yours of the 1st of March came duly to hand and as Sunday has once more rolled around I thought I must write although I have nothing of any importance to write more than that I am well and in very good health. To day I have been down to Bell Plain Landing after grain and it makes me feel rather stiff for this riding bare back is rather hard business for an oldster like me. The roads continue decideley muddy and the weather is rather inclined to be moist but I am in hopes now Congress has <u>risen</u> that they will improve.

They are sending along the boxes now from Washington and some of them are boxes that were sent when we were at Harrisons Landing and I <u>may</u> get those undershirts and drawers by the time the hot weather gets here when I dont want them. They open all the boxes not so much to see if there is liquor in them as to find citizens clothes. In a lot that came last week they found 30 suits which they confiscated with the other contents. Sometimes they take liquor out and some they dont. Just how they happen to feel. If they feel dry I suppose they take it. Two of the boys that live with me have sent for boxes and if they get theres safe I shall send for one but I dont care about risking it yet a while. Those pies were in good order broke up some but we had no trouble in finding the peices. That box was a God send because it was unexpected. Tell Mace I felt bad myself about that <u>busthead</u> but I dont think that Stewart could help it for I dont think he is any such man. As for Marston I will not give an opinion. Franks box did not get here before he went away and Eliza wrote me they were going to have it fetched back to Exeter. Speaking about Capt Smith I reckon he is a kind of a dead beat but this is private you know for it would not do for me to say anything about my Superiors. You know all I have to say is he may be a damn smart man but for one I dont see it in that light but there is a good many just such men in this army and the more shame for those who have the apointing of them but I hope such critters are about played out at least if Hooker carries out his orders and I bet he will for he generally does when he starts. He has published an order that all the Regts and Batteries that are up to the mark can have three men to every hundred go on a furlough at a time and our Battery is the only one in this Division that is allowed the priviledge so you see we stand A No 1 at Head Quarters. Big thing. I expect a man by the name of Hall will go this comeing week and if he does he says he will call out and see you. If he does I want you to send me two pounds more tobacco and a box of Rochelle Powders and a 1/4 pound black pepper for the pepper we buy here is like so much ashes and it is some thing I like to have in the House. And I want to lay in a stock of tobacco to last if I can untill the war is over. He is a first rate man and anything he agrees to take for me you can just bet your life he will bring to me and if you ask him to take a drink he will do that also. He is an old Chum of Winslow and by the way I have not heard a word from Winslow since last Dec and I am afraid the old fellow has gone through as he was sick when he wrote me but if Hall goes home he will go to Bridgewater and see him if he is alive.

Speaking about Shooting deserters I think myself it is about time to do some thing with them for they are getting altogether to plenty and as far as I am concerned I could see them shot with a good relish but if it was not for the mean cowardly officers there would not be so many in my opinion. I always said and I say now that the Rebel Army is better lead than ours for there if an officer dont do his duty he catches H___ and thats the way it ought to be. We are not troubled with desertions in this Battery and I dont think we shall be as long as Capt McCartney commands us. He is now in Washington. His wife is there and I expect he is enjoying himself hugeley. All I am afraid of is he will leave us for something higher for he is highly spoken of by the Genls in this Corps. I should like to see him promoted but should hate to lose him. Do you ever hear anything of Capt Porter? Now a days such a valuable officer I should think would want to be in active service and I guess he would if he did not have to do any fighting. He is what I call a coward and I should have no trouble in makeing you believe it I reckon if I could see you but let the poor devil slide as long as he dont come here.

I have had six letters this last week and amongst them one from Jim.[21] What do you think is going to happen but seems he thinks I am all right now although he began to think I was going back on the union once. Hah hah. Makes me laugh. I wish some of these great big Patriots would show it in some other way than Words. Dont you tell Lizzie I am just of her opinion about George B. I wish everyones record was as clean as I think his is but I must draw to a close. When I commenced this I thought I had nothing to write but I find I have filled up both sheets but perhaps if I had stopped with the first you would have been better satisfied but take it for what it is worth and let it go at that. So give my love to all the folks and tell them we get soft bread 5 times a week now. Good Bye.

From yours &C
Jack

PS Love to Emily.
What did you think of that Rebel and his Lady I sent you?

Monday Morning [Mar 9, 1863]

Sam

It is a fine morning here and the birds are singing gayley and I have just finished hanging out my clothes and had a good wash and I feel quite smart. Harry Hall thinks there is no doubt but what he will go home and I wish you would have those things ready so he will not have to wait for them as his time will be short and he wants to go up

[21] John had an older brother, named James.

country. I have been reading the New York Herald of Saturday. I find we have lost another battle out West because the Genl who [was sent] out to did not reinforce Col Coburn. I wish some one would shoot the rascal. I think it is about time to shoot a few officers as well as Privates for I think it would have a good effect.

I also read an account of the great War Demonstration at the Cooper Institute and I like the speeches first rate. Such talk as that after reading NH papers is like the Sun after a storm for with them you would think that the Democrats were all traitors and the Republicans something worse. For my part I dont believe in any party that dont go for putting down this damn infernal Rebellion. "no Sir ee" I dont. Put me in a couple of packages of envelopes if you please.

Thats all.
Jack

* * * * * * * * * *

Monday March 16th 1863
In Camp Near White Oak Church

Dear Brother

Yours of the 9th I received last Thursday and it found me laid up with the Rheaumitis but I am happy to say that Whiskey and Quinine has once more given me the use of my limbs. I dont admire my Whiskey that way but still I have take it so or not at all. I suppose you think it is about time for Mr Hall to make his appearance but you see one man that had a furlough has not come back and that has stopped the game and I dont know as any more will go but if you have got those things you can keep and perhaps you may get a chance to send them some time. If I knew when Copeland was comeing (He is the man that is there now) I would let you carry them to him. If you should happen around Cambridge Street and would call at his house you might find out. I will get the number and give it you in this. We are now under marching orders and ordered to keep eight days rations on hand so I suppose that Joseph soon intends to find us something to do. We are to have a review of the whole Corps this week and the Infantry are at work cleaning up the ground for it. I suppose we shall have to wash and scour up to keep up our reputation. It makes the other Batteries mad as the devil to think they have to drill twice a day and as yet we have had nary a drill. I am sorry for them but dont see how they are going to help themselves for Gen Brooks Says so.

Yesterday we buried one of our members. He was our Blacksmith and a first rate man 26 years old and belonged in Canton Mass. He has a sister resides in Rox but I have forgotten who with. To show how much the Capt thought of him he went to Gen Brooks and asked the priveledge of fireing a Gun over his grave but the Gen thought it was not necessary for a private. Well the Capt says if I could have my way I would fire a case for he was a good deal more deserving of it than one half of the officers but then red tape will rule.

Blacksmith—First Massachusetts Light Artillery, by Alfred Waud LC

The weather here dont improve much. Yesterday we had snow and rain and last night a thunder shower of hail and to day there is about an inch of snow on the ground and the weather is decideley drizzly and I might add dreary.

Speaking about Copper heads[22] I see by the New York Herald that there is no choice of Gov in Hampshire and the legislature is decideley dark so I suppose the long agony is over and that now the people can rest in there beds without fear of sold to the South. I tell you Sam I wish they were half as much in earnest about this war as they are to elect some particular man to be Governor. I think that things would take a new turn. I dont care whether a man is a Copper head or a Copper tail as long as he supports the Govt in prosecuting this war and from what I read I think the Democrats are most as if not more friendly to the Govt than the so called Republicans. That great man Charles Sumner I see did not wish the soldiers to be furnished with tobacco. I wish to God he was here a private and all the rest of the damn nigger loving crew. How is J A Andrews getting along with his Nig Regts? Do the streets swarm with them or has there patriotism kind of faded? Verily this is a great country and requires a great deal of looking after. Well I am willing if they can make Niggers useful but I am afraid it wont pay much. Speaking about Asher I should think he might write once a week if he wanted too. I write a letter most every day some wheres but perhaps he dont like to get letters as well as I do. I wrote to him twice but I never heard from him. You must give my love to all the folks that want to hear from me. I had a letter from Susie Smith and she told me she saw William up to Concord. He is not around making Stump Speeches is he?

But I must close and I hope this will find you all in good health.

Yours for the Country.
Jack

John Copeland
202 Cambridge Street
Boston Mass

* * * * * * * * * * *

[22] Copperheads, who called themselves Peace Democrats, supported restoring the Union through negotiation rather than by total victory, while War Democrats supported military victory. Both factions opposed the abolition of slavery.

Sunday March 22nd 63

Dear Brother

We are still at the same place and by the looks of the weather are like to be for it has rained or snowed here now every day for most a week and still keeps on. I received yours Thursday and was sorry to hear that my letter caused such a commotion and it seems the swearing is not all confined to the Army but then you know I am no Box Soldier and I guess I can live without it. You say you have not seen Harry Hall yet. I am afraid you will not for Copelands not comeing back has spoilt all of our furloughs. I hope to God he will be Shot for a deserter. But those things you have for me I want you to put in a small box and send it by Express and Direct to John W Chase First Mass Battery in Care of N. P. Kemp 343 Penn Avenue Washington DC and he will forward it to me. He belongs to the Christian Commission[23] and visits us now and then and said he would take charge of small parcels but the best way would be to put it in a small box and I think I shall get it. You had ought to see some of the Boxes that have come here lately. Every thing taken out that was any good. Tobacco cigars and Shirts &C. The Capt has complained to head quarters but I suppose it will not amount to much. I have given mine up for good but I hope to God the man that wears them will get the 7 years itch and lice too. I should like first rate to have your photograph and in your next I want you to send me a dollar. I want it to buy bread with for I am getting up an awful appetite since I was sick. We get fresh bread now every morning and one loaf wont last me through. We draw flour and have it baked at the Regimental bakery. I see by the papers that Ashers Battery has been in another fight but I did not learn the particulars.

I dont know as I can write any thing more for news is scarce here. I expect we soon shall leave here and then perhaps I may pick up an item now and then.

Give my love to all the folks. Tell them Jack goes in for War to the Hilt and damn the peace man without it is an honorable one. I see

[23] The U.S. Christian Commission was organized by the YMCA to provide physical and spiritual comfort to the soldiers.

Gen Naglee[24] is not good enough for Gen Hunter.[25] He is a good general and I hope Hunter may prove himself as good but this Nigger seems to cause a good deal of trouble but I hope we may get some good out of them to make it up. Good Bye for this time.

From your Aff Brother
Jack

Dont forget the Photograph.

* * * * * * * * * * *

Camp Near White Oak Church
Stafford County Virginia
March 26th 1863

Dear Brother

Sunday night has once more rolled around and I thought I would occupy a few moments in writing you a little to let you know that I am still alive and in very good health. In fact I am getting so that I can eat my rations and all the extra I can get hold of and that has been considerable for we have had two boxes in my shanty this last week. They came through in good shape being only six days on the road but some of the boys had some that had been robbed. They took out of one box a pair of boots that cost the owner 10 dollars in Boston two shirts 2 pounds of tobacco 5 pair of stockings all of his envelopes and the most of his paper leaveing him a little writeing paper one lead pencil and a half a dozen fried sausages. Warren thinks the damn rascal left the paper and pencil so he could write home the result. There has been several came that had been gone through the same way. I did think of sending for one but I concluded if I should get one that had been served that way I should have to do a good deal of swearing therefore I would not run the risk. The Capt has tried all he can to help us but then it is hard to prove who the

[24] General Henry M. Naglee.

[25] General David Hunter.

guilty devils are but then Soldiers are considered fair game for anybody to steal from and I think take them as a nation they are pretty damn well robbed. I dont know as I can write any news. We have been out for inspection to day and were kept out four hours. A Col who is Corps Inspector was the man and he done it up brown and had a good many questions to ask but I guess he found the Non Coms pretty well posted but they do say he stuck Lieut Manning John A Andrews pet lamb (he is a hell of a man). One of our Corporals is going home to recruit for the Battery and he told me he would come out and see you. I expect he will start tomorrow. If you know any good fellows that want to show there Patriotism tell them the First Mass is just the place for them for it is a BIG THING to belong to but we dont want any Dead Beats. We got enough of them with our bought men last fall. We had one recruit come a fortnight ago. He is a son of Professor Longfellow of Cambridge and he appears to be a first rate chap but I guess he is a little wild when at home but I guess he will get tamed here.

I had a letter from Susie Smith this week and she wrote me that Judge Scammon[26] was dead. I felt quite bad to hear it for I always liked the Judge very much but then we all must die sometime and death will find us at home as well as on the battle field. Susie talks as though she was haveing great times at Concord. So much for having a Capt for a husband.

Judge John Scammon CFC

We are haveing awful bad weather here. We have had but few pleasant days this Month and to night it is awful cold and I am on guard but I have got a good fire a going. Went and lugged wood on my back about a half a

[26] Judge John Scammon's granddaughter, Mary Parker Smith, later married John Chase's son, George.

mile this forenoon. Rather hard work but then it is better than being cold and then I have a good nipper of Busthead to take about 12 o clock so you see I am all right. But I guess I have wrote more than you will find of any interest and I will cork up. Give my love to all the folks and tell them I go in for Crushing this damn Rebellion if it takes 10 years to do it. Go in lemons is what I say. Joseph advertises big and I hope he will succeed in carrying out what he says he is going too. He has got the tools I believe if he only knows how to use them.

So good bye for this time.

Yours &C
Jack

Corporal Pettingill is the man that is comeing home and if he calls dont ask him to drink thinking he will refuse for he is no such a man.

I received yours of the 20th all right.

* * * * * * * * * * *

In Camp White Oak Church
April 2nd 1863

Dear Brother

I received yours last Monday with the receipt photograph and dollar greenback and came to the conclusion that it was quite a letter take it all together. I think the photograph a first rate one and so does all that has seen it that ever knew you but they seem to think you are a better looking man than your brother but then you know I cant see that. I sent a picture to you this morning by Copr Pettingill. It is for Pricilla but I thought she could get it from there. I dont think it a great picture. Only the feet. Those are immense but Pricilla said the children were anxious to have one and I thought that would suit them because it was all painted up in big shape. I received a notice from Brother Kemp that my box was there waiting my order. I supposed when I had it sent there that he would bring it here himself but it seems he only forwards them at the owners risk. I think I shall let it stay where it is at present for if it comes here I shall be likely to lose the preserve and just as likely as not all the rest of the stuff and I may have a chance to get it some other way. At any rate I shall not order it at present for I suppose there is nothing in it that will spoil. The preserves I know will not. Neither will the tobacco. I have no news to write. We keep liveing along day after day the same old story and I tell you I am getting anxious for a move or something to break this monotony of camp life. We dont drill much. Only when the officers dont know what else to do. Then they take us out and drill a little but the other three Batteries have to drill every day when it is so they can but then you see they are not No 1. We are great fellows we are. The recruit Longfellow I wrote you about took his farewell of us to day. He has a Lieut Commission in the first Mass Cavalry. So you see there is another promotion from the first Battery. This is a great country and there is nothing like nigger antecedents with the great John A &C but he is a good little fellow and I am glad he is in such good luck but still I had rather see some poor fellow have it that has done his duty as a common soldier but then it is no use talking. This promotion in the army is a damn humbug. Thats so. I never have had a letter from Asher and I guess they took the wrong road. I had one from Pricilla this week and I am pretty well posted as to births and deaths. I find the Chase family is in no danger of dieing out at present according to her report. She tells me that Mrs Henry informed her that she did call on Lizzie when she was in Roxbury and then proceeds to inform me that she dont think that she can worry Lizzie much. I hope not but as I dont know anything about the matter of course I cannot say anything. Speaking about news I expect you will get enough of it soon. Be patient. That is all I can say. Thats the way we have to do here. Never say die while there is a shot in the locker. Thats what the First Mass says Sir. You must give my love to all the folks and tell Emily not to talk to hard about those Maryland girls for they are good ones and no mistake State of Maine aint a circumstance. Cant begin even there Schoolmarms. No sir ee. French has been quite sick but is better now. He sends his respects to you. Also does Brooks.

So hopeing this will find you all gay and happy I will Close.

Your Brother

Jack

Tell Mace he is a brick but if I lose this whisky it will cause a heap of swearing.

* * * * * * * * * *

Camp First Mass Battery
White Oak Church
Apr 8th [1863]

Dear Brother

I received a letter from you this week mailed Feb 12th. It had been to the 7th & 9th Batterys. It seems you directed it to the 7th and I suppose nobody would have it and they finally sent it to me and I was very glad to get it if it was old for there was three sheets of it and I liked it first rate and found a good deal to interest me for there was truth in it as I well know myself.

But to business. I set down to write this to tell you that you may start a box for me as soon as you please but only dont put any liquor in it. They come now pretty strait and we of the house here all concluded to send each for a box and see if we can be as lucky as our neighbors. I dont care what there is in it but all I have to say is put in a little butter and the rest you can put up what you think best for you have sent enough to know what Soldiers like. I would not send a very large one or put in any thing very nice for I am afraid that it will make me sick but I feel this morning as if I could eat about four pounds of corned beef and not hurt me a mite and I have just finished a half a loaf of bread and quite a peice of Army butter which folks at home call fat pork.

The Infantry are all on the Move here this Morning for Abraham is here and they are going to have a Grand Review to day and the Artillery tomorrow. At least that is the talk.

I cannot stop to write much for I am going off on a pass to day just to take a peep around the Country. Benny Brooks sends his

Respects to you and says he should like to be in old Roxbury once more. I had a letter from Sewall a few days since and I am going to send it to you and see how you like his style. I admire it and I think he is about the cheese. I shall also enclose an extract from the Ballot so you can see they have finally settled it that Chase is not a Rebel. I have had only 14 letters the past week but I have not had any from Asher. I believe every body else has written me.

But I must close for I want to be off.

From your Brother Jack

Direct the Box thus
John W Chase
First Mass Battery
Brooks Division
White Oak Church Virginia
Care of Capt William H McCartney

We have news in the New York Herald that Charleston is taken but dare not believe it yet. I hope it is so.

Give my love to all the folks and tell I feel Bully this morning.

* * * * * * * * * *

Camp of First Mass Battery
Near White Oak Church
April 10th 1863

Dear Brother

Yours of the 5th I received last night and was very glad to hear from you and to know that you were well &C. I received my box yesterday and found everything all right. One of the Brethren was over to Washington and brought it to me and gave me a few treats at the same time. I think I shall speak a good word for the Christian Commission for I am indebted to them for the safety of my whiskey and tobacco. You must give my warmest thanks to Mace and the other Contributors. Tell Mace that Benny Brooks and myself drank to old Roxbury Friends and hope some day to have the pleasure of

U.S. Christian Commission LC

thanking them in person. The Whiskey was good and I took a good drink and it made me feel good all over. My Boarders concluded that it was a much better kind than the Busthead we get here sometimes. Tell Lizzie I think she dont mean that I shall go dirty for want of a towel to wipe on for I have about a half a dozen on hand and we have about twice that number in the tent but I will try and take good care of them bccause I may conclude to settle out this way and they will be very handy to have in the house particularly where there is Children— —. I suppose you have received the letter I sent you about the Box. I went to see the big review that day. For a wonder we did not have to turn out as they only reviewed the reserve Artillery and I had the pleasure of being a spectator for once. There was three Corps reviewed and they looked first rate but they do say that the 6th did rather take them down and Brook.s Division was a little mite ahead of any of them. The Jersey Brigade in our Division looked splendid. They all had on white gloves and collars and looked as they always do as neat as a pin. I dont hesitate to say they cant be beat in the Army of the Potomac. The Mass first and 16th looked well but the Bloody 11th was the dirtiest and meanest looking Regt there and that is what everybody says that saw them. There was not two men dressed alike and both officers and men looked like some of the

Militia Regts of ye olden time. Its no use talking Sam. They cant no more compare with the first Regt than nothing at all and all a man has to do is to visit there camp and he will be satisfied of that fact. We calculate here that the First Battery and First Regt can just knock spots out of anything that has come from the old Bay State yet. Thats So. I take a good deal of pleasure in going up to the first for I see a good many old friends and always receive a hearty welcome. There is hardly a day passes but what some of our boys are up there or some of them down here. I was there to dinner the day of the Review and had some baked peas and they were quite a luxury. Horatio is fat as a pig and in the best of spirits and in fact is all the boys. This Army I dont think was ever in a better condition than at present and I hope when we move that it will be to some purpose and I just think it will. I never felt in better spirits in my life than I have lately and I am getting kind of anxious to Start but I am willing to wait and let Joseph say the word. The Gen looked finely the day of the Review but the President looks very care worn. Much more so than when I saw him last which was Shortly after the Battle of Antietam and I think he will be glad when he gets to be a citizen again. At least I think I should not want the load on me even if I was capable of taking it. I also Saw the Celebrated Mrs. Sickels[27] and she is a fine looking woman and a Splendid rider. The President and his wife passed our camp last night. The boys turned out and gave him three cheers which

President Lincoln NA

[27] Mrs. Sickles was the wife of General Daniel E. Sickles, a former congressman from New York. In 1859, he shot and killed his wife's lover, Philip Barton Key, who was the son of Francis Scott Key. Sickles was acquitted of the crime because he was defending his home and family.

seemed to please Abraham very much. He asked the guard in the park what Battery it was and of course was informed it was the Mass First. But I dont know but what I have done bragging enough for once and will drop the subject. Harry Hall started for home yesterday and said if he had a chance he would call and see you but as I had received my stuff all right of course I did not urge him although I should like to have you see him but ten days is a short time for a man to do much visiting in. Lieut Manning starts for home to day and I suppose will be received with all by his friend J A &C. I dont know but what you will think strange of my sending for a box but we put our heads together and all concluded to send and thought not to have anything in it of much account if we did not get it. So I hope you will not make much of an outlay on it but then I am decidely hungry these days. Not but what we get enough to eat but then you know a man gets tired of the same thing over and over again and even an indian cake would be a rarity for you cannot buy even meal in this God forsaken country. I shall enclose another leaf with this. I received it from the same source I did the other. Tell Lizzie not to lose this one and I shall not claim it even if [I] should come back for all such things I intend for her. When I want anything saved for myself I shall mention it. Tell her I dont see myself writing on those small sheets not to Maryland for I have to say a good deal when I write there which is seldom for you know I want to keep on the right side of the people in that State.

Jack

* * * * * * * * * *

Camp of First Mass Battery
Near White Oak Church
Stafford County Va
April 14th 63

Dear Brother

As we are under marching orders I thought I would write and let you know that the long expected time has come when Gen Hooker has commenced his great movement. The Cavalry passed up by our camp yesterday some 6000 of them and to day orders came to us to turn in all our stuff we could not take with us and we have turned in all our clothes but one suit & a change of under clotheing and we have to put 5 days rations in our knapsacks and when we march to take three in our haversacks. Our clothes we have boxed up but I dont imagine we ever shall see them again if we live but then if they pay us for them I suppose it will be all the same as they take an account of all we turn in. There was quite an overhauling of knapsacks and books &C will be plenty in this camp after we leave but as yet I have thrown nothing away nor do I intend to untill it comes to carrying our knapsacks on our backs and then I think I shall not carry many superfluities. I have often looked at a drinking tube that I was foolish enough to invest the sum of 50 cents in before I came out here and thought what a devilish fool I was for it was about as much use as a cigar holder would be for. As for drinking out of it a man would choke to death before he could draw enough through it to satisfy his thirst but I was green then and did not see Soldiering in just the same light I do now for I have found out that a man must accomodate himself to circumstances very much. So I expect that Hooker is calculating to give us a hard march as we take eight days grain on our Cassons and off horse and dont intend to take any waggons. We some expect to start Tomorrow but then you know things are very uncertain these times but then the Pontoons went up to day and that looks rather suspicious.

Well we have had a good long rest this winter and I think the boys as a general thing are ready and willing to try there hands once more with the Johnnys. All I hope is that we may have good luck and not have to fall back again but we must leave that for the future.

We dont seem to get much to encourage us from the South and the report here to night is that Gen Foster has surrendered to the Rebels. We hope it is not so but are rather inclined to fear it is to true but then I think we are not always going to meet with reverses and God speed the time when the scale may turn and Victory once more crown our efforts and the old Stars and Stripes once more wave in

Triumph. I want to see this thing pushed through and every enemy of the Glorious union Crushed (yes thats the word) Crushed out whether they live North or South. Them is my sentiments and that is what I go in for and thats what I think will be done. I may not live to see it but if I dont perhaps you will and you will have the Satisfaction of knowing that Jack with all his faults loved the old Flag and was willing to lay down his life to maintain the Liberties that our Fathers fought to establish. But still I hope to live it through but then it is best to be prepared for the worst and I hope I may always be found where duty calls.

I was in hopes that we should get paid before we marched so that I could sent Mary the money to pay for those Stones but I have written her to day and told her if she wanted it before we got paid off to send to you and I thought you would send it to her. I am sorry now that I sent for that box but then I thought we should not move in a hurry and we may not now but then it would be my usual luck. You must give my love to all the folks and tell them that Jack still lives and remembers his Roxbury friends who have done so much and tried to do more to make his time pass agreeably while away from home and friends. There is one thing Sam. I have found out who my friends are since I have been here and if I ever do come back I hope I never shall forget them.

Enclosed with this is a ring for Hittie. I should sent it before but could not get it made. All the corps have a mark to distinguish them one from the other and wear it on the top of there cap. I shall enclose ours. Sickels is a diamond shape but I dont know what the others are as I have not seen them. I think it will be a good thing. Write often as you can and I will do the same.

Yours for the Cause
Jack

Love to Emily.

Thursday Afternoon [Apr 16, 1863]

No Marching yet. It began to rain this morn about 2 o clock and we are having a regular North Easter and it is raining as it never rained before anywheres out of Virginia and all we can do is to lie in our bunks and take all the comfort we can under the circumstances but there is a small pond under mine but I am in hopes it will not flood me out. All I can say is we are lucky not to have got started for it would have been decidely rough marching. I think I see by the Herald that the Nahant was struck 500 times at Charleston. I think there must have been some music round about there and I guess Sewall would rather been in a tin shop. I also see the Mr Shed has Skedaddled and gone off with another female. Who was his wife and was she a Roxbury woman? You must give my respects to Mace and all the other natives and believe me ever true to the cause &C.

Jack

I have had a letter from Mary Littlefield and wrote her again as she said you did not write to her nowadays. I did not ask any questions why for I supposed you considered you had good reasons for not doing so. She wrote me a good letter and I thought a very feeling one and I thought I would let her know that I was not quite so depraved as some of my Relatives try to make me out to be or at least used to for I happen to know one of dearly beloved Sisters has given me an awful name in days gone by and I suppose is constantly hopeing to hear now that I have been Court Martialled for some Enormous crime but I dont mean that she shall be gratified if I knows myself and I think I does verry intimately but thank God those things dont worry me a mite for I am willing to trust myself and my Character in the hands of those that know me best and let them sit in judgement on me. The day may come when she will see things in another light. But Good Bye and My Love to all the folks that want to hear anything from Jack.

Put a quarters worth of stamps in your next and charge to his Nibs JWC.

I think you will have to call this a long letter but perhaps if it had been shorter it would been more sensible but it is to late now therefore you will have to take it as it is.

We are having regular Marching winds. Cold and drying.

[Enclosed in the letter is a Sixth Corps cross of red cotton flannel that is about 1 1/2 inches square.]

* * * * * * * * * *

Camp of First Mass Battery
Near White Oak Church
Stafford County Virginia
Apr 27th [1863]

Dear Brother

I received yours of the 17 and 20th last Thursday but have been putting off writeing for we have been expecting every day to get paid off as the Pay Master is here and has paid part of our Brigade but as yet he dont make his appearance in our camp so I thought I would begin a letter and then after he does come I will finish. It is all quiet with us as yet. To day we have been out and had an Inspection by Col Tomkins Chief of Artillery on Hookers staff and my opinion of the critter is that Gen Barry who was with Gen McClellan has forgot more than the whole family of Tomkins,s ever knew. Of all the damn foolish questions a man ever asked he beats the lot. For Instance enquireing how many fellows there is in a wheel and how many dowells there is &C just as if a man could not be a Soldier and fight without he could calculate an eclipse. I have got sick and tired of the damn foolishness and want a little active operations. Thats the place to try men and officers to find whether they are worth a damn or not. We dont get but few fair days here and I think its lucky for us for it is either an Inspection or a Review when we do have one And I am tired of it and then I want fighting Joe to go ahead and show his great Generalship. There has been a good deal said of what he was going to do and its most time to commence I reckon but then what the devil has a Private to do about it. His life is worth nothing and is no account compared with Shoulder Straps but thank God there is a day comeing when a man will be a man and a damn pack of drunken officers that now flourish will find there own level and that will be with the loafers and gutter drunkards. It is really quite amusing to see some of them put on airs particularly when well charged with Busthead for you know its no hurt for Officers to get drunk. Only keep it away from the poor miserable Privates but enough of this. Its all right I guess. If not we will make it right after the war is over.

I shall be a looking for my box this week but dont much expect to get it right away. Pettingill comes out again tell him the claw hammer is safe and all right and I should like to be where it came from for a little while. I think I would enjoy myself for a few days I do myself.

I think as you do about the potato trade and supposed it was something of that kind that had caused the trouble but concluded it was none of my business therefore kept mum. Tell Lizzie I will take good care of the towels for I expect dry goods are very high and by the looks of some of the Virginia damsels I should think scarce. I have finally found out what a Copper head is. That is in the eyes of the NH Nigger Worshippers and I will enclose a peice from the Ballot and you can see for yourself. According to my english it means a man that has the audacity to vote any thing but the Black Ticket and I think if I had the priviledge of exercising my right of suffrage I should have to be Classed with them for I have no faith in Abraham or his advisers. That is Played Out Long Ago. I happen to know this Wm F Laighton and I wish we had no worse men in the Country. I think we should have less Croakers and more business done but then Nigger is King with some folks and there kinds are so full of it they cannot see anything else.

My health continues good and I try to keep my courage up to the sticking point but sometimes it is awfull hard work for here we are doing nothing and have altogether to much time to think but I hope we shall soon get where we shall find something to take our attention and have a chance to try our luck and see what the Army of the Potomac can do with its new Commander and I hope for the good of the Country we may make an Impression.

You must remember me to all the folks Including Emily and Asher and I hope soon to be able to write something that We have done towards crushing this Rebellion but I must dry up now for the bugle is blowing and I must away to attend to my arduous duty. That is call the roll.

As the order has come to march in the morning I send this without waiting for the Pay Master. I suppose we shall get it some time if we live and if we dont some body will get it for us.

I hope that we soon shall meet the enemy and if we do and I am spared I will give you the particulars.

From your Brother
J W Chase

Good Bye and God Bless you and yours.

This ring is one Mr Coye asked me to put in and request you to give it to Mr Seaverns as he had not time to write to night.

[Included in this letter is a newspaper clipping of a letter to the editor condemning the government's employment of a man in the navy yard who came to Portsmouth, New Hampshire, to vote "the copperhead ticket [while he was] under the pay of the government that he was trying by his vote to overthrow." The writer expressed his dismay at the employment of "rebels, to the exclusion of true and loyal men," to which John Chase penciled in, "poor fellow."]

* * * * * * * * * *

John Chase's Travel Routes in Chapter 5: April 1863 to August 1863

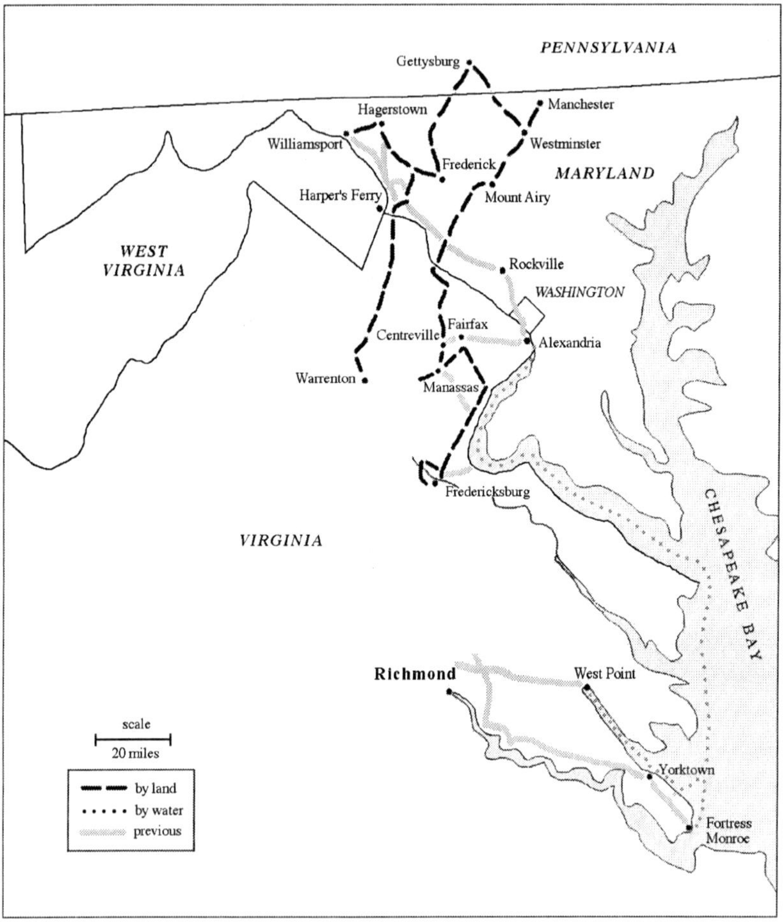

JSC/BBC

CHAPTER 5

Chancellorsville to Gettysburg

General Joseph Hooker, having replaced General Burnside as commander, engages the Confederate army at Chancellorsville, just west of Fredericksburg, with no success. General Lee, pressing his advantage, moves across Maryland to Pennsylvania where the Union army, now under the command of General George Meade, defeats the Southerners at Gettysburg. Chase describes the battles and complains about not engaging the retreating Confederate army.

Tuesday Noon [April 28th 1863]
Raining like the Devil

Dear Brother

The Pay Master rounded us up at one o clock this morning and paid us off but as we are ordered to march at 2 o clock we had no time to make out checks therefore I risque 20 dollars in a letter hopeing it may reach in safety. Also a picture of the Celebrated White Oak Church to give you an Idea of the public buildings of Virginia. The sign over the Door is United States Christian Commission. I am glad to start but I dont admire rain to commence in but its all in a life time.

My respects to all the folks and let me know as soon as you get this if you do get it.

Yours &C
Jack

White Oak Church LC

* * * * * * * * * *

May 6th [1863]

Brother Sam

Jack still lives but things looked very mixed but I hope to live it through but that is all. If Hookers gains any glory this time it is yet to come. Thats so.[1]

From yours &C
John W Chase

PS Home is gold.

* * * * * * * * * *

[1] Despite being severely outnumbered, Lee's daring counterattack against Hooker's army won the battle of Chancellorsville for the Confederate army.

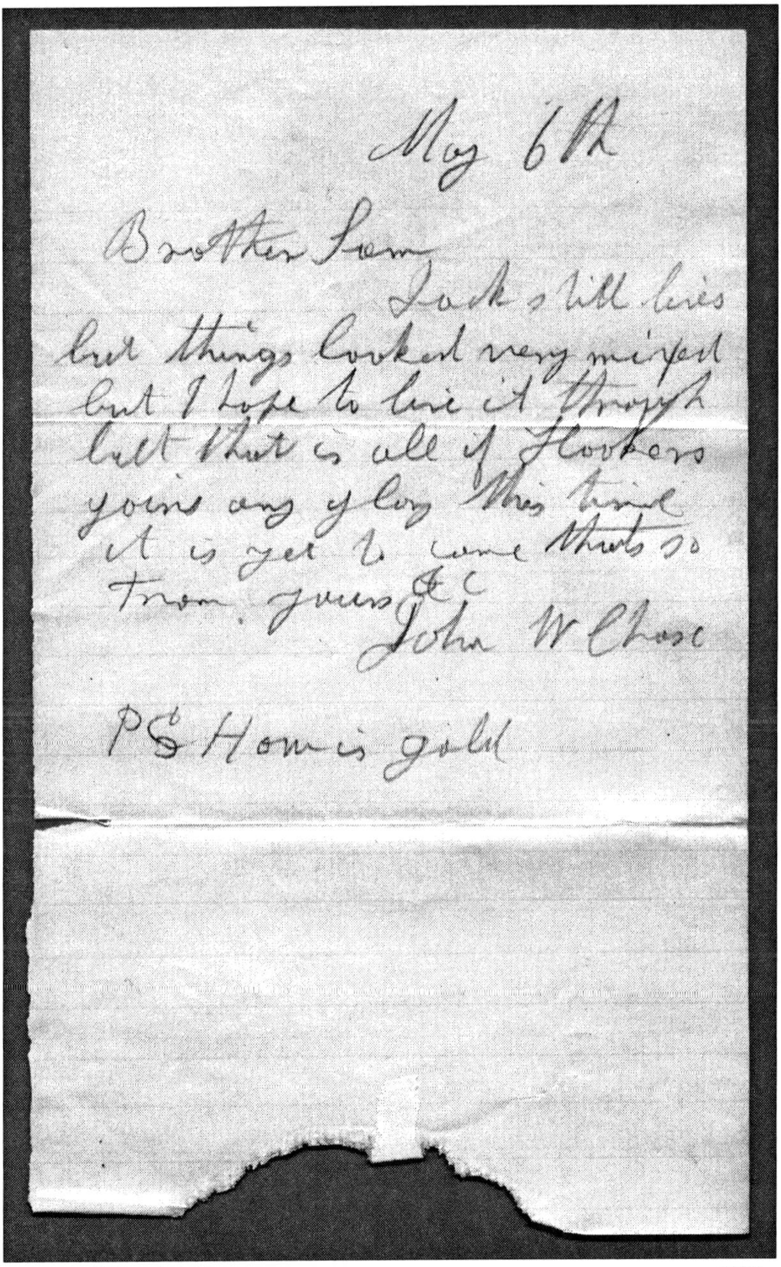

May 6th

Brother Sam
Jack still lives
but things looked very mixed
but I hope to live it through
but that is all of Hookers
going any glory this time
it is yet to come thats so
from yours &c
John W Chase

PS How is gold

Letter of May 6, 1863 CFC

Camp Near Kellys Ford
May the 7th [1863]

Dear Brother

I received yours of the 3d to day and was glad to hear from you and to know that you were well and had received the money for I felt a little worried about it as things were so kind of mixed up here. I suppose the papers have given you all the particulars of the fighting but I will just say that we never saw any fighting before that was a patch to this. Our Battery was charged upon twice and we had to use cannister and drive them back. Sunday we had the 15 Jersey to support us and the damn cowards run and left us and at one time we could not fire there was so many of them in the way but the Col finally got them out of the way and we managed to get off with a whole Battery but at one time it looked rather doubtful. We hear all kind of stories here as to what the other Corps have done but of course can tell nothing about the truth of them. All I can say is I feel thankfull to God that I am once more permitted to write to you for in more than one Instance the past week I began to think that Jack had wrote his last letter but here I am again.

Our Battery behaved finely and I dont hesitate to say now that it cant be beat. We had one killed and one wounded. Both Boston Boys. The one that was wounded was young Richardson that Lizzie sent the pies too. He was shot through the thigh with a musket ball. The others name was Daniels. He was struck by a shell which killed three horses at the same time. We have lost some of our best officers amongst which was Col Town of the 95 Penn.

I am much oblidged for that Photograph and you will give Mrs. Curtis my warmest thanks. If I get time I will write more minute about the fight but every thing is confusion here and the talk is we are to try it again which I hope is true for I want to fight it out now we have commenced. So with love to all I remain yours &C.

Jack

Bully for the Union God and our Native Land.

These flowers came from the heights of Fredericksburg. I could not press them very well for I had no chance.

* * * * * * * * * *

Camp of First Mass Battery
Near White Oak Church
Stafford County VA
May 10th [1863]

Dear Brother

I thought perhaps you might like to have an account of our last march and to day haveing leisure I thought I would try and give you some of the Items. We left camp on the Afternoon of April the 28th and marched within a half a mile of the river and halted there for the night. The next morning we went to the bank of the river and the regular Battery crossed with the Infantry of Brooks Division the rest of the Batterys going into position on this side and Howes and Newtons[2] Division of Infantry also remaining on this side. There was not much opposition to our crossing as the enemy only fired one volley and then took for the woods. Things remained this way untill Saturday afternoon when our lines were advanced and the rebel pickets drove in and that night the rest of the Corps crossed and Sunday Morn at four oclock the fight commenced in earnest. Our Battery was on the extreme left and had a warm time of it. The Rebs advanced on us and our Infantry which was the 15th Jersey or about 200 of them fell back and left us to fight it out. We fired every round of Ammunition we had and then left on the double quick but our folks were getting the best of them on the right and the rebs did not advance any farther. We carried the hills about noon and we marched through the city and advanced about three miles when we had another fight and a severe one as the enemy had been strongly reinforced and the next morning found us completely flanked on the left and our forces falling back and all day we worked hard to

[2] Generals Albion Howe and John Newton.

preserve ourselves from Destruction which at one time I thought must come. But thank God the 6th Corps still lives and I think if all the Corps had fought as well as ours the result would have been different but its no use finding fault now. All I have to say is there was a Blunder some where. But of course the fault is not Gen Hookers because that is out of the question for him too make any mistake.

We came back to this place Friday and are reforming up ready for another move. What it will be is more than I can guess. I am about used up to day. My head aches and teeth and I feel sick all over and last night when I tried to turn over I felt as if I was breaking in two but I hope to feel better soon. I enclose ten dollars with this for I did not like to trust too much in one letter. You must excuse this letter for its as much as I can do to hold my head up.

So I will bid you good bye for this time. My love to all the folks.

Yours &C
Jack

Much oblidged for the posts. I guess George is about as good as those that talk about him but Humbug is the order of the day in this Army. (Thats So.)

* * * * * * * * * *

Camp of First Mass Battery
Near White Oak Church
Stafford County Va
May 15th 1863

Dear Brother

Yours of the 11th I received last night and as I have nothing else to do I thought I would sit down and write a few lines just to let you know that things are quiet in Hookers army. We still remain in camp near the church but some changes have taken place with us. The Battery belonging to the Corps are now all camped together and we are under the charge of a Col Tompkins. They have taken two

Batteries out of the Corps and sent them to the reserve. One is the First Maryland the one that Capt Wolcott used to command and the other a regular Battery leaving us six in the Corps. I think this will be a better arrangement for us and hope now we shall have a Brigade Commissary of our own So that we can get what belongs to us in the way of rations which is more than we ever have got. The 16th and 27th New York Regt have gone and left us they being two years troops and there is three more Regt to go out of this Div. The 16th passed our camp Yesterday morning and the boys turned out and gave them three cheers. They say they never shall forget the first Mass. We have 27 men from there Regt in our Battery. They came out as recruits expecting to go home with the Regt but got done out of it and they came into the Battery rather than go in a Regt of Infantry. There was about 140 of them and they would all come if we could have taken them. They are good boys and I think we were very fortunate to get filled up so easy. The 16th time was out and the day we had our fight on the hills but never a man of them backed out. They lost about a dozen killed and quite a number wounded. They were good stuff and we hated to part with them but then when all the Regts in the field have done as much as they have it will be about time for them to go home. There was about 250 left to go back to York. I never have seen much about the last battles in the papers as all the papers that are allowed to come into the army is the Washington paper and some other nigger concerns. Hooker has all the N York Herald destroyed but people will talk papers or no papers. They cannot make me believe that we gained a great victory across the river for I was there myself and I think we got damn well <u>whipped</u> and think we were lucky to get off as well as we did. Not but what I think Johnny got punished as bad as we did but then when a party backs out and leaves the field I consider that party is whipped. I do. But still I think the army is feeling good and think as a general thing they will pitch in the first chance they have with a good will. The fact is the old army of the Potomac have about made up there mind that they are bound to be used up in this war and they might as well go in and take there chance and have the show over with and they try to think we shall get the best of the Rebels one of these days and keep our courage up a good deal as I used to sometimes when I was a boy in passing a grave yard at night. Keep up a good whistle and look straight ahead and I hope things will come out right yet. I do myself.

My health is very good at present. I have got rid of the Neuraligia mostly but I expect it will trouble me a good deal as my teeth are rotting very bad and hard tack is death to all grinders without they are better than mine. I suppose you have received another letter from me before now with ten dollars in it and I shall send five in this. You need not send that money until Mary sends for it for I wrote her to that effect. I have sent her seven dollars which I think will keep her in spending money and I should like to get a few dollars ahead if I can for if I should happen to get out of this alive I think it would be very handy to have in the house. Particularly if I should take a notion to make some poor unsuspecting female miserable by persuading her become Mrs. Chase but still as I always said if they need it let them have it but I guess you had better keep it untill such a time arrives.

As to the Box there is a lot of Boxes at Aquia Creek and one of the Christian Commission was down there and tried to get them for us but the Provost Marshall would not sign a permit to have them landed so I suppose we shall have to wait untill such a time as red tape can condescend to do so and probably by that time the box will have gone where my shirts &C went. I think it is the last time I shall ever send for anything of that kind but I want you if you see a chance to send me a half a pound of ginger. Perhaps Pettingill will bring it for me when he comes.

I dont think of anything else to write at this time. You must give my love to all the folks that want to hear from me and tell them the First Mass still leads the column and believe they have done more fighting than all the rest of the Mass Batteries put together for there is the 3d & 5th in this army and neither have fired a gun since the malvern hill fight on the Peninsula last summer and they keep the 10th 11th around Washington to look at. Well thats the way this thing goes. Some contrive to get a soft thing and they hang to it and I wouldnt mind if they would give us a little of it just to see how it would seem but I dont expect they will be able to see it.

Remember me to Mace. Tell him to take a drink for me and Benny Brooks who is well and wishes to be remembered to Sam and all his Roxbury friends. But I will bid you good bye hopeing the weather is cooler there than it has been here for it has been hot as h___ here but we had some heavy showers last night and the air feels quite cool to day. I have been engaged in raising up my bedstead for the water came under me last night several inches deep and I dont admire that way of taking a bath. So with love to Emily and all the rest of the women I will bid you good Bye for the present.

Yours &C
Jack

If Mrs Curtis would like this picture let her have it. If not give it to Mace.

* * * * * * * * * *

Camp of First Mass Battery
May 19th 1863

Dear Brother

I now sit down to let you know that I have received my box. It came last Saturday and everything was in first rate shape. The Inspectors punched a hole in the can of peaches but as good luck would have it there was not much leaked out and what did done no damage. The Col of this Brigade of Batteries interested himself in getting them and that looks as if we should have someone to look out for us now. The contents of the box suit me tip top. You could not improved it if you had tried & I am much oblidged for the same and then it comes in a good time for here we are doing nothing and have plenty of time to enjoy ourselves in eating. I had some of the peas for breakfast this morning and they were immense.

There has three of our boys gone on a furlough this morning and one of them told me he would bring me a small bundle and I want you to get me a hat. One that you can do up snug and a pound of tobacco and carry it to 196 Cambridge Street to Mr. Francis E Longley and Frank will take it any time between now and the 26th of the month. I dont want a very wide brim hat. You know about what my style used to be and one that will fit you will be about right. Give my love to all the folks and I shall write again as soon as I hear from you.

All is quiet here. The Regt are moveing into new camps and nothing seems to indicate another move right away.

But enough for this time.

Yours &C
Jack

* * * * * * * * * *

Camp of First Mass Battery
Near White Oak Church
Stafford County Va May 30th /63

Dear Brother

I suppose you will begin to think it about time to hear from me but the fact is there has been so much work a going on here and the weather has been so hot that writeing was a job that I dreaded. But to day the weather is cooler and there dont seem to be quite so much business going on but I expect that our Dear Friend Col Tomkins will get up something for us before night. We have I believe at last got our Camp so that they cannot find any fault with it. Got our ovens built and shades erected over all the niggers and horses belonging to the Col and Staff. We have a nice camp of our own with the exception that it is very dusty as the ground is sandy and no grass on it and the weather is so awful dry that it is like an ash heap.

Every thing remains quiet here as yet with the exception that the first Corps is under Marching Orders but where or when they are going is more than I can tell. We have all kinds of rumors and amongst others that we are to try the Peninsula route again but I hope that is not true for God knows the Rappahanock is bad enough but I think altogether better than that God forsaken country. But however if that is the way we can defeat them all right. I am willing to go any way if it only results in a victory for I think this Army has been fooled about long enough. We call it here the Military School to make officers in for as soon as we get a good one he is either relieved of his command or sent off somewheres else. We have got a new Division Gen a General Wright.[3] Who he is I dont know nor do I care much but one thing I dont believe he is any better than Brooks for he was an old fighter and no mistake Brooks was relieved at his own request for what cause I know not but I think the last fight had some thing to do with the matter for I know he was disgusted with some of the moves at that time. He was one of the kind that believed in trying to do something and not playing Soldier in camp and fooling away time in Reviews and Inspections and drinking Whiskey. That seems to be the order of the day now but the devil of it is the officers get all the Whiskey and the rank and file all the labor although I have fared pretty well for both lately. I find that a poor devil must try and look out for himself in this country and not depend altogether on his Rations and I have made a few friends in the Commissary and find it Pays a good Interest. Hiram Wright sent me an Invitation to visit him and I think Sunday if nothing happens I shall give him a call.

I read your letter about Col Cowdin[4] to the Boys and they seem to think about as you do in regard to the case. One of our detachment says he must See Sam if he ever lives to get back for he thinks he is a good sound Democrat. He use to live a neighbor to the Col and thinks a good deal of him and in fact all the Privates that ever knew him speak well of him and think it a <u>damn</u> shame for him to be used the way he has. But kissing goes by favor and so does Army apointments. I have not forgotten John A Andrews in our own Capt Comission yet nor do I think Mac has or will in a hurry but I have seen so much of the damn humbuging in the army that I have got used to it and dont let such things trouble me much for it runs from

[3] General Horatio G. Wright.

[4] Colonel Robert Cowdin.

the President down to the meanest Private. Thats so. But I want to see this Rebellion put down and then we will try and see what we can do with those who have fooled us all along. Longley arrived last night and I am much oblidged for the things you sent me. The hat is just the thing and the ginger very aceptable and tell Lizzie she is mistaken about my wishing to wear it to Maryland but I can say this much. If I ever get out of this alive and well I shall pay Hagerstown a visit and see some of those Maryland women for I believe there is some just as good ones there as ever was. Much oblidged for the Posts and the book for truth is a scarce article in the army of the Potomac.

I wrote Asher this week and if I dont get a letter from him I shall give up in disgust for I cannot see why I dont get his letters. I also had a letter from Sewall and guess he has got all the glory he wants at present. Perhaps he will go into the recruiting business. My Mary seems to think that it will be a good plan for them to go to keeping house as she can work off some of her superfluous fat but I am thinking she will be getting some on. Tell Lydston that John Doherty and William Keenan was at our camp this week and John said he should like to have him out here just to see how he would like it and to hear him relate his adventures on picket. I see by the papers that Grant[5] is doing well at Vicksburg and I hope his good fortune may hold out for I think it will be a great blow to the rebs to lose Vicksburg and Grant is a good Democrat. I cannot imagine why we are lieing still here without Hooker is planning another Flank movement. I hope if he does he will try and fight some of the army that laid still on the other one and let the 6th rest if any.

It is trying to rain here to day and I hope it will make out for we need it bad enough. My health is very good. My teeth trouble me a good deal and I have had one out and dont know but what I shall have to lose more but dont like to spare them for this gumming hard tack I think must be slow work.

You must remember me to all the folks. Tell them I hope to see

[5] General Ulysses S. Grant. Vicksburg was the key to taking control of the Mississippi River.

her out yet and be able to come back and thank them for there many favors. Remember me to Mace and Emily.

My picture of Mrs Curtis I sent to Sis to keep for me. Mary thinks there is no trouble telling who it was taken for and I think so too.

But they are sounding the drill call and I must close.

So with my love to you all I will dry up.

From your Aff Brother
Jack

Direct like this
John W Chase
First Mass Battery
First Division
6th Corps
Washington D C

Benny Brooks is well and send his respects to all friends.

* * * * * * * * * *

Camp Battery A
First Mass Artillery
June 2nd 1863

Dear Brother

I am not a going to inflict a letter on you but we were paid two months pay yesterday and I thought I better invest a part of it in the hands of my banker. You will find a check for $20,00 payable the same as the others I have sent you. I sent $5,00 to Mary in a letter thinking she might want some for the Glorious Fourth. I think 25 out of 28 is much as I can go but thought if I should happen to want a dollar some time I could send for it and if I kept it might spend it foolish as a good many others do.

The Weather here is awfull dry and we are troubled with dust. All is quiet with this Corps. The 5th has moved about 15 miles up the river guarding the different fords. All eyes are now turned towards Vicksburg and I hope Grant may give them fits before he gets through with. Love to all the folks and tell them all is quiet on the Rap.

From your Brother
Jack

Col Tomkins says have your letters directed like this.

J W Chase
First Mass Battery
Artillery Brigade
6th Corps
Washington DC

So I suppose we must have them done so for Tompkins is a great Critter.

[Enclosed with this letter is a clipping from a New Hampshire newspaper of a letter from a private of the Tenth New Hampshire Regiment written after the crossing of the Rappahannock. It speaks merrily of the vandalism in Fredericksburg and then of the success of the Union troops the next day, followed by severe reverses. He concludes with a most pessimistic assessment of the state of the troops and their chances to defeat the South. John Chase's penciled comments are as follows:]

The truth is bad enough God knows but then you know the new Regts are a better class of men. At least that,s what they said. I dont see it.

Probably measured the distance those bullets run. [to the assertion that ". . . bullets did not average 10 inches above our heads. . . ."]

Poor fellow. Did he expect to have a bed to sleep on? [to the sentence, "We are laying now on the cold ground."]

* * * * * * * * * *

Across the river
Sunday Noon June 7 [1863]

Dear Brother

Here we are once more. Came across Friday night. No fighting yet of any amount but I am expecting every hour it will commence. If it does I think we shall have a hard one. We shelled the rebs out of there rifle pits to protect the bridge builders taking about 100 prisoners but since we crossed there has been nothing but skirmishing but enough of that to help a few of our fellows out of the service. I sent you a picture yesterday and if I live through this I want you to have some Photographs taken from it for me as there is several of the boys that want one as they say it is a Bully picture of the old veteran.

But I will close. My love to all and may God give us Victory this time. I had a letter from Asher this week. He appears to be gay and festive.

Yours &C Jack

If permitted will write again as soon as this thing comes to a head. The skirmishes have commenced again and expect we shall get at it before night. Good Bye.

* * * * * * * * * * *

Plains before Fredericksburg
Friday Morning June 12 [1863]

Dear Brother

I received yours of the 7th last evening and thought I would write a few lines just to let you know that we are still Here. Since I wrote last we have built breastworks and Forts and fortified our position here. As yet we have had no general engagement but the sharp Shooters have been busy on both sides and they throw the bullets in and around our Battery with a perfect looseness. They have wounded several of the Infantry but as yet none of our boys. I am back with the Cassons about an eighth of a mile right on the banks of the river

John W. Chase—"The Old Veteran" CFC

and there is neither tree or shrub to make a shade and the ground is a dead sand and you can judge our position is not very pleasant as the weather is both hot and dry. What we are here for or what is going on with the rest of the army is as well known to you as me for we are

Envelope of June 12, 1863 CFC

shut off from any communication with them as there is no getting back after you once get here except you are an officer or a nigger. There has been any quantity of women here the past week. They come across and ride out to our skirmish line. What the devil they are here for is more than I know but I suppose they think it is a kind of Military Parade. Gen Hooker visited us last night and the boys kept shouting oh Joe Spades is trumps yet and many other remarks anything but Complimentary. I reckon Joseph dont find it quite as easy to run this machine as he had an Idea of but however I hope it will be all right. Digging seems to be the order of the day now. Grant is at it and Banks and we are digging here. But if we only succeed in digging the grave of this Rebellion why then Glory to God say I. Anything to get rid of it. I see the 11th Battery had a great reception when it came home. Big thing for them who never saw a rebel except he was a prisoner but I suppose they can talk war just as well as if they had been through the whole of it and probably feel just as well satisfied. Give my love to all the folks and excuse this letter but I know you will not expect much under the Circumstances. I received those stamps all right and you may send me some more when you write again.

Yours &C
Jack

* * * * * * * * * *

Fairfax Court House
June 19 [1863]

Dear Brother

I received yours of the 14th last night in which you say I have not wrote whether I received your last letters or not. I will now say I have received them all and you must excuse my not saying so before but the story is letter writeing is done under difficulties these times for we are constantly on the move on watch and all the time we get we have to take out of our resting time when we feel more like sleeping than writeing. I will try and give you a faint Idea of what we have been doing since I wrote last which was on Friday the 12th.

The next day we had some shelling from both sides but no one hurt with us but we made out to silence one of the rebel guns by dismounting it. That night we recrossed about midnight and took position on the bank of the river in case the bridge builders were attacked but everything was quiet and we got everything off without a fight and about daylight took up the march and came as far as Stafford Court House and it was one of the hottest days I ever knew and the dust ye Gods. It was a perfect cloud. That night we were sent on picket which the boys thought was rather rough after being on picket ten days on the other side but that,s what a Battery gets by haveing a good name. Only get your name up and they will find work enough for you to do but we went and lived through it and the next morning started off without a thing to eat and that day we marched to Dumfries where we halted until 1/2 past one in the morning when we were started again and came to Fairfax Station. There we remained one day on a burning plain and not allowed to even put up a shelter tent for we were expecting orders every moment. Yesterday we came here and here we are now but how long we shall be allowed to stop is more than I can tell. We hear all kinds of stories but dont believe anything. All we know is the rebs are somewhere and Gen Lee is busy and I think Hooker will have to keep a bright look out or he will get severed as some of our other great men have. This last move has been the toughest and roughest we ever have had for the weather has been awfull hot and the dust ancle deep. It has been hard on the Infantry. There was a good many of them dropped dead and any quantity sun struck. There was 35 in one Regt and a good many of them never will get over it. I think I suffered more than I ever did before although I was mounted for I suppose I must tell you that I have been promoted to Seargent[6] but I dont think I shall retain the berth a great while for I dont think it pays. There is too much work for the pay for you have everything to see to and have to take more meaning than is agreeable to me. I did not want it any way but the Capt wanted me to take it and the Boys in this detachment urged me and I thought I would try it and see if I could bare it but I dont admire the position. In fact I am getting damn sick of any part of this Army for I consider it a damn big humbug and growing worse every day. The latest order Hooker has promulgated is to turn in our knapsacks and lose all the little property we have got for no one expects to ever see any thing after it is turned over to those who have the managing of things here. The Clothes that we turned in this spring have all gone to hell and I suppose they want the rest to go with them. For one I have lost all hope but will try and do my duty untill my time is out but as for ever expecting to see this Rebellion crushed or the union restored that,s played out decidely. Perhaps you will think I am getting my tail down but thats not so but I have seen enough on this last march to convince me that there is no head or tail to anything. All our officers

[6] John Chase was promoted to sergeant on June 9, 1863.

care about is there own baggage. Every thing and every body else can go to the devil if they can only secure there own comfort. There is some exceptions to this rule but that is the way generally.

But I must close as the mail is just leaving. Give my love to all and send me a few stamps. About a quarters worth.

Yours as ever
Jack

As the mail carrier got off before I could catch him I will fill my sheet by saying I have written to Pricilla about some shirts and told her to send them to you and I want you to pay her for them and keep them untill I send for them for I dont want them at present if we are to have no knapsacks to carry them in. I suppose Joe wants us to get lousy and sick by wearing dirty clothes &C. The boys here damn Hooker and wish for little Mac and any one that says Hooker is as popular as Mac is a damn liar and I can prove it. I am sorry to hear Lizzie is sick but I hope this will find her better for if it is as hot there as it is here it must be awfull to be shut up in a sick chamber. They say the Rebels are in Maryland. If thats so perhaps I may get to Hagerstown again. That would be very pleasant to me I assure you for then I could see some of those girls that Emily thinks so little of. Have me a dozen of those Photogs taken and send them to me in your letters. You can put two or three in at a time you know. Give my love to all. Tell them I am not tired or sick of fighting for the union but I am tired of the damn humbugging there is carried on here by a pack of damn loafing Whisky drinking officers. Thats whats the matter.

But I will shut down for I am getting mad and I cannot write when I am mad. Remember me to Asher when you write. Tell him I will write as soon as I can but at present I only write to you and Mary and one Particular Friend.

So good Bye and I hope things will work for good yet.

Yours &C
Jack

* * * * * * * * * * *

Camp of First Mass Battery
Near Manchester Md
July 1st 1863

Dear Brother

I take the first chance I have had since I received your last letter to try and answer as we have been kept on the go both night and day lateley. The last time I wrote we were at Fairfax. The next day we started and went to Bristows Station on the Orange & Alexandria RR on picket. There we remained until the 25th being there 5 days and a nice time we had for we could get all the cherries milk butter &C we wanted by going outside the pickets which we could do very easy as the Vermont Brigade was doing picket and the First Mass Boys are all right with them. But this thing was a little too soft for us and Thursday night in the midst of a drenching Shower we were ordered to hitch up and March which we did and came to Centreville arriveing there at 1/2 past one in the morning. After one of the darkest and worst nights that we ever did march turned in and were ordered up again at 1/2 past three and that day came to Drainsville 26 miles raining all day and the mud was delightful and slippery. That day we got a mail the first since we left Fairfax and I got quite a bundle of letters and papers yours with the rest. That night we turned in about 10 and turned out at 1/2 past one AM and Marched to Edwards Ferry where we crossed the Potomac & found ourselves once more in good old Maryland and the Boys began to cheer and feel better as soon as we crossed and got out of the God Forsaken State of Virginia. Here we got turned in about nine or at least the men did but your humble servant did not for being Seargeant of the guard was oblidged to stay up untill midnight and all hands were called out at 2 AM and hitched up and started marching through Barnsville where we halted and fed our weary horses at noon. Then through Bardstown to French,s Mills where we went into camp. Here we got turned in about ten and were roused up at 2 AM when we started again and marched through Newmarket and Mount Airy to

Sims Creek or as the natives call it Jensburg and camped. Yesterday we arrived at this place which is about two miles from Manchester which is close on to the Penn line and according to appearances we are going to stop here to day or at least a part of it as it now is nine o clock and no orders yet and I guess it is most time for both horses and men are about played out for we have Marched the last 5 days over a 100 miles with not one full nights sleep and no time to even stop and have a talk with the Maryland girls but we have the pleasure of seeing them as they all turn out to see the Soldiers pass. Yesterday we passed through the town of Westminster which is a lovely little town as ever I saw although I must say the people have a decidely Secesh look with them and one nice young lady who lives outside the town told me they were rather inclined to favor the Rebels in there moves. The Rebel Cavalry were in the place in the Morning. Came the night before and she said the folks a good many of them turned out and received them with open arms displaying Secesh Flags &C. But then there is some good union folks there and it is easy enough telling at such times who they are for they turn out and greet the boys with Something to eat and drink. But the Cavalry get the best of it for being on the lead they generally eat everything up before the rest of the troops get along. But let the poor devils have it for they have done something lately and the cavalry arm of the service is getting to be some thing besides a laughing stock these times and they have kept them pretty busy lately and I think Gen Lee will keep them at work a spell longer for <u>we</u> think that he has rather more to do with this army now than our own Gen. At any rate Gen Hooker will not fight him on his own ground right away. I reckon we have all kinds of stories a going here as to who is in Command of us[7] and where we are going too &C. Once we were going to Baltimore sure and we got within 28 miles of it but now they say we are going to Penn. All we know is we are going that way but then this Corps turns some very short corners sometimes and we may be back in Va in a week. We have not seen any other part of the Army since we

[7] General Hooker, denied requested reinforcements, asked to be relieved of his command. He was replaced on June 28, 1863, by General George G. Meade.

went across the river and the 6th seems to be going on its own hook somewhere. But I guess as long as uncle John Sedgwick[8] leads them they will be all right and give a good account of themselves. At any rate I am willing to bet my pile they have done more duty and more marching the last month than any other Corps in this little army and if we have not done any fighting it is because we could not find any thing to fight. But the Boys stand it pretty well but they all say give us the little Mac and fighting Joe take his old Division thinking that Machine is about large enough for him to undertake to run. He cannot hold a hand big enough to Call Lee no how and he might just as well pass out. At least that is the Private opinion of not one but many thousands of Privates in this Army of the Potomac. But I suppose it dont make any difference with those in Power who the men want to lead them but they will have there own way if we all go to hell together but I am inclined to think that this Campaign is going to end this show either one way or the other for if Lee gets the best of us now we are gone up and its no use talking and I think if we get the best of him he is gone the same way. So let the fight come soon as it will. We will try and do our best and leave the event with God hopeing it may prove a good thing for us and there let the War rest.

I am much oblidged for the stamps and papers although as yet I have had no chance to read much but have just looked them over and keep them against I get time.

Speaking about some folks you know the least said the soonest mended therefore I shall not say anything. But If I ever live to get back I may possibly do some talking and will let it rest there. I am glad that Lizzie is getting better and I hope this will find her entirely recovered. Tell her I hope the Battery will be ordered to Hagerstown again and then wont I live. Tell Emily the girls look more beautiful than ever and anybody wanting to see the prettiest girls and best country in this Union ought to come to Maryland. If I was pleased with it before I am more so now and say for richness of scenery it cant be beat. Give my love to all the folks that want to hear from me.

---

[8] General John Sedgwick was given command of the Sixth Corps after the Battle of Fredericksburg.

Tell them I still live but my Patriotism has played out and I am a Soldier now because I am oblidged to be for I have lost all faith in seeing the Rebellion Crushed or this union restored but Still I am in hopes to live her through 14 months more and then J Chase will Resign. I reckon Benny Brooks is almost demoralized but I guess a little rest with a drink of Whis will make him all right. At any rate if we stop here I am going to try and raise a little and try him. That is if I can get Mac to sign an order on the Commissary. Remember me to Mace and all the other natives and take a big drink of punch for us on the Fourth. I expect we shall have a fight on or before that time all is [here]. If we do I hope to get through safe and get a large ration of Rebs for my share of the Glory.

We have just been called out to be mustered for two months pay which I suppose we shall get some time if the Rebels dont take Washington.

But I will close thinking I have written more now than you will find interesting So Good Bye for this time and may this find you all Gay and festive.

Yours &C
Jack

Excuse all errors for I have written this in an awfull hurry.

* * * * * * * * * *

Camp of First Mass Battery
Near Middletown Md
July 9th 1863

Dear Brother

I just seat myself to inform you that Jack still lives and received your letter with the Photo this Morning. For the last 4 days we have been on the Road night and day but this forenoon are compelled to stop for the shoes are about all off of our horses and both they and the men are about played out. I have no time to go into the

Particulars of our late engagement[9] but will just say that Gen Lee caught H___ this time and found that the old Potomac Army was not quite so demoralized as some of its dear friends try to make it out and that it can fight if Hooker is not with them. I begin to think we have got the right man at last. At any rate I know this Army never was put through so before by any Gen we ever had. The boys bear it like Martyrs saying if we can only get at them again before they get out of Maryland and get as good a Ration of Rebs as we did at Gettysburg that Lees army will look rather small although our own loss was no trifle but theres was much larger than ours. I suppose you Remember Tom Barri who used to live in Rox. He was killed. He was a Capt in the 11th Regular Infantry. He has a Brother in this Battery. He was wounded on the Skirmish line in the foot and as his men were bringing him in after dark he received three more balls. One in his breast one in his leg and one in his arm. Another good fellow gone to swell the list of brave men who have lain down there lives for there country.

But I must close for we are as busy as bees cleaning and drying our clothes for we have been wet the last week. As Soon as I get a chance if I am suffered to live I will give you all the Items.

So with much love to you all I remain yours &C.

Jack

You must not find fault with this letter for I have been without sleep now for three [days] except now and then a nap when we halted.

So Good Bye and I hope you may hear Good news soon. We hear that Vicksburg has gone. If so Bully for Grant but will not the Nigger lovers want to remove him.

The Pictures are tip top but I would not have you think my shirt is as white or my whiskers as black as represented. Not by a damn sight for I have not changed my shirt for a fortnight.

Good Bye.

---

9 The Battle of Gettysburg.

Love to Emily.
Maryland Girls as lovely as ever. Thats So.

* * * * * * * * * * *

Maryland July 17th 63
Camp First Mass Battery
Raining like the devil

Dear Brother

I received yours of the 12th to day makeing two I have had from you since I wrote. When I last wrote you I supposed we were going to have another fight with Lees army here in Md but you see we are not therefore we are once more moveing towards that land of plenty (<u>of lice</u>) Virginia. Why in H___ we did not fight him here is more than I can tell and I think it a damn shame that we did not for I honestly believe we could just cleaned them from the word go and give them the worst whipping they ever did get. The rank and file of this Army are badly disapointed for after we had made up our minds to fight they keep us drawn up in line of battle three days and let Lee make his escape. It may be all right but I dont see it. I believe we could just about settled the thing right here but I suppose that is the last thing a good many of our damn poor apolagys for officers want to see is this war ended for then there occupation gone and they will have to retire to there former obscurity. So this army must be marched back to Va and I think one more Campaign there will about finish it up or at least the old part of it for a good many of the Regt dont muster a hundred men now and will muster less after they cross for I think a good many will desert and a good many have done so already. We have lost 5 and one regular Battery in this Brigade has lost 32 and probably from the eight Batteries there has a hundred gone. There was 1200 marched to head quarters yesterday and a great part of them were dressed in citizens clothes but they did not succeed in getting off. I dont believe in desertion but sometimes I think I hardly blame them for a man here has no show for anything without is to be kicked about by a pack of damn loafers. I am growing sick of the show every day and if I had no friends or children think I would leave myself for I am tired of eating pork and hard tack. We had fresh beef to day the first time for a month. Our bill of fare has been Salt pork coffee hard tack. That is just what we have had served to us the last six weeks and not a thing else. Only fresh meat once. Now you know we are allowed other things and Govt pays for them too so who is making the money out of. That,s whats the Matter.

But I hope that the thing is about played out and by what we hear can but think so. I see they have got to fighting in New York and Boston and I think that such things look as if the Rebellion was in its death struggles thinking they must make one more effort for life but I hope to God this Govt will put them down and enforce the laws. I dont think but damn little of the Conscript law but I want to see this Govt enforce all there laws and let the Ballot Box be the place to resist them. Its no worse for one man to come out here than it is another and let them all have a sight I say. But I will not preach any more for I have not time as I hear we are to move again to night. We are now camped about 4 miles from Berlin where the bridge is and where I suppose we shall cross. There is the 5th 2nd 6th 12th 11th Corps here all in camp but some of them are now moveing. 5 PM and of course the 6th will not be the last. I would like to give you a history of our exploits the past two months but have not time and to day I have been sick all day. My food hurts me and I have been troubled a good deal lately with cramps &C. Sometimes I think It dont matter much whether I ever get out of this or not for I dont expect I ever shall be worth much for I find I am growing old fast and perhaps shall only be a burden to my friends but I mean to try and keep up if I can and try and believe all is for the best and that it all will come out right in the End. But I now will drop this and answer your questions. That Man was right about flying Artillery. They are intended to go with Cavalry and act with them altogether. They all go mounted and only have two boxes on there Cassons. There was only two Batteries of this kind when we first came out here but now there is quite a number and two Batteries have left this

Corps lately to Report to Col Hunt for flying Batteries. They are what is called the 3 inch gun being a rifled peice and light only weighing about 700 lbs. Our Cavalry you know is some thing to talk about now and the question of who ever saw a dead Cavalryman is no longer asked here. They have done nobly in this last Campaign and have earned a good name for themselves. They have proved themselves a match for any Rebel cavalry. They can start and I hope they will keep up there reputation. Hooker Is entitled to the Credit of makeing the Cavalry of use instead of ornament and is entitled to all the credit of it. So you see he done some good while he was in command.

I received a letter from Mary and she wanted me to ask you to send that money but I suppose you had done so therefore I said nothing about it to you. In her last she said nothing about it therefore I am in the dark about it. Will you let me know how it is. I want you to send me out a box of pills. Something that is good for biliousness for I am troubled a good deal with it and my food dont digest well at all and I suffer a good deal in consequence and I dont like to go to the Doctors here for I dont think much of them and dont want anything to do with them if I can help it.

I would give you an account of the Gettysburg fight if I had time and felt able but I am pretty well used up to day any way and it is a wet nasty day and I feel decidely old. You know we have been marched round some lately. They marched us to Williamsport then back through Hagerstown and other places where we were last year but we did not stop in those places at all so I could not call and see any of my Maryland friends but I had the pleasure of shakeing hands with some of them and the gals were as blooming as ever and strong for union. I wish we could stopped in Hagerstown a few days but onward seems to be the word.

You must give my love to all the folks. Tell Emily Maryland Girls are all right as far as heard from but damn Penn. I dont want any thing to do with the natives of Cumberland valley for I dont like there style. I hope this will find you all well and enjoying yourselves and hope you will kill all the Rioters[10] there is in Boston and teach them there is still a Govt in this Country. I dont suppose you will find this a very interesting letter but you must excuse it and I will try and do better some other time so receive it for what it is worth and I remain yours &C.

Jack

* * * * * * * * * * *

Camp of First Mass Battery
Near Warrentown Virginia
July 27th 1863

Dear Brother

I dont know but what you will begin to think that Jack has given up and that you will hear from him no more but the fact is we have neither received or sent a mail since the 18th of this month but I thought to day as we were lieing here Idle that I would write a few lines just for the fun of the thing thinking perhaps I might get a chance to send it some time or other and to amuse myself for the time being. We are camped just outside the city of Warrenton. Came here night before last so you see we have had one days rest and we did not get it before we needed it for both men and horses are about played out particularly horses. We have not horses enough to mount all the men that generally ride. My horse is lame and if we have to march to day I shall have to walk and two other Seargents are in the same fix. When we started for Maryland we had the best teams we ever had and they were noticed by most every one on the road but travelling over the mountains and rocky roads and the hard long marches has about used them up. We have left 25 since we started from the Rappahanock on the road and have several now that can hardly crawl but I am in hopes that we shall get some before we have to start out again. Since I last wrote you we have done some hard marching but as yet no fighting. We are now what they call a

[10] Rioters complained that the draft put an unfair burden on the poor; the soldiers complained that unwilling conscripts made poor soldiers.

Flanking Corps and they keep us going from one place to another. We went up towards Manassas Gap and just got unharnessed when we were ordered off again as everything was all right there. We came here and now they say the Rebels are at Culpepper and I suppose we shall have to go in that direction next. I have seen no other Corps since we left Gettysburg untill last night when I saw a part of the 3d and have not seen a paper so I dont know much what is going on the world. The country we have marched through lately is very much like Maryland but now it begins to look like Virginia again. We have had any quantity of blackberries on the road. I think I have seen more of them the last few days than ever I saw before in my whole life and I know I never eat so many in any one year. When we would make a halt it was an easy job to pick a pint dipper full and it was quite a number of pints that I have eaten on the road and they have done me a good deal of good. My bowels now are as regular as a clock and I reckon its the berries that has done it for I am very sure it was not my rations for it has been pork and hard tack and not much of that for we have been on short rations for three days before we got here and the berries gave me an appetite and I think if I had one of Lizzies apple puddings I could made a large hole in it. I never knew what it was to go to bed hungry untill I came into the army but I have quite a number of times since but I am hopes in the course of 13 months to get where I can once more get filled up. But I dont like this going hungry. I dont. I should like to hear from the folks and also to see a paper and hope if we remain here to day that we shall get a mail as the cars run to this place and it seems to me we ought too. I received a letter from Pricilla that was mailed the 26th of June. Been about three weeks on the road. Rather a long passage I think but then better late than never you know. But I must hold up for there is something up.

Tuesday Morning 28th

I will now try and finish up my letter. I found out what was up yesterday. We had to wash our Carriages and oil Harness and clean up generally and to day I am Seargeant of the Guard and there seems to be no signs of a move. We received a mail yesterday and I received a letter from you and one from my Mary and one from Eliza and several bundles of papers from you and a Harpers Magazine from a friend in Boston. So you see I am all right for something to read for a few days at least. Benny Brooks got a printed list from Rox of the victims of the draft. I am glad that my friend Head[11] is one of them but I have no Idea he will come out for I think he is too big a Coward but you know if I ever get back to Roxbury alive and well and that Gent is in the same condition I am going to give him a damn licking for he has wagged his tongue a little too much about me since I have been out here. Perhaps he thought I should not know it but as it happens I have and he has got to pay for it sometime but let the damn fool go at present. I can afford to wait. I suppose you knew that George O. Manning had resigned his position in this Battery and returned to his friends in West Roxbury where I hope he will have sense enough to stay or at least keep out of the army for he is not fit for a private much more an officer. I am in hopes Charley French will get the chance and the Capt has written to Lord John and recommended him but I suppose some other nigger loving friend has some weak headed Son who thinks he would like to be a Lieut in the best Battery from the State of Mass. If you can do anything to help Charley I hope you will do so as I think he is the one that should have it. I was up to the 3d Corps last night. A part of them are on picket towards the Celebrated Sulphur Springs[12] which are only about four miles from here but then you see it is not very safe visiting there

Lieutenant Charles French USAMHI

[11] George Head was the husband of John's late sister, Susan, who died in 1860.

[12] Now named Fauquier White Sulphur Springs.

at present as Mr John Henry is there and he dont admire visitors dressed in blue. Speaking about the Commanders of this army I dont know now who commands us and dont know as it makes much odds for I think the Govt at Washington does more towards managing it than the Gen Commanding. For one I have no faith in any of them and only look to the end of my enlistment to get out of it and then I shall be free again. If I ever live to see that time I will a tale unfold to you that you will hardly believe but then it will be none the less true. But I will draw to a close for I think I have written more now than you will want to read. You must remember me to all the folks and tell them Chase still lives but his Patriotism is Played Out. The 2nd 5th 12th New Hampshire Regiments left this army yesterday and have gone to Point Lookout at the mouth of Potomac under the Command of Gen Marston to Guard Rebel Prisoners. Safe thing for it is one of the Pleasantest places in the country. That leaves this army without a single Regt from NH. Big thing to have a Member of Congress to care for you but it dont look to me as hardly a fair thing but perhaps it may be.

Good Bye
Yours &C
Jack

Tell Lydston I hope he will get drafted.

Benny Brooks has just come to my quarters and tells me to send his respects to all the folks. Benny felt bad to hear of George Everetts death as he was quite intimate with him. He tells me he has been reading yesterdays paper and that our folks have captured John Morgan.[13] Bully for them. Hope the Good news will continue to come in. It is very pleasant to hear. Kill all the Rioters you can and send us out the Conscripts and down goes the Southern Confed Right Smart. We can hear heavy fireing to day but know nothing of what is going on but I hope its all right.

---

[13] General John H. Morgan was a legendary Confederate cavalry commander in Tennessee and Kentucky.

* * * * * * * * * * *

Camp of First Mass Battery
Warrenton Va
Aug 5th /63

Dear Brother

Yours of the 26th came all right pills and all. I also received another today and it worried me that I had not written since I received the Pills. In yours of the 26th you request me to give you a report of the Battle of Gettysburg. I wrote you one letter giveing a description of it but I dont think you ever got it as I sent one to another person the same time and they complain that I have not written to them. This describeing a battle so as to make a person understand it is a hard job as they cannot see how the lines run or the position of either party.

Now the Battle of Gettysburg was mostly fought before we were ordered to the Front but I will try and give you a faint Idea of it after we arrived on the ground. We left our camp near Manchester on the night of July first at ten o clock and marched all night and arrived near Gettysburg the Afternoon of the 2nd about three PM neither stopping to eat or feed our horses on the road. The distance was 38 miles. The longest march we ever made and you can judge we were pretty well played. We expected to go to the front that night but after keeping us hanging around until midnight told the Capt he might go into park and unharness which order it did not take us long to obey and your Brother Jack was soon rolled up in his blanket and paying very particular attention to Sleep. The fighting had now been going on two days and this day our folks had lost ground untill we arrived when our Infantry went in and the Rebs fell back thinking that the Cross on the Cap meant something besides Penn Militia. There was all kinds of stories flying around in the rear as usual. Some telling us that we were whipped to death and any Gods quantity of our Artillery captured and I began to think that Lee was haveing it all his own way for we could see parts of Batteries going to the rear and Skedaddlers coming in with long faces and one Capt begged a peice

Detail from Gettysburg Cyclorama NA

of bread from me for his supper told a very pitifull story and I began to fear that things were very much Mixed. But about 10 PM I ran across an orderly of Gen Meades and he told me that at Head Quarters they thought we had done very well. The stories of our loseing any guns were all false although the Rebs did uncover quite a number but the timely arrival of the 6th Corps and there not being able to carry them off or even spike them left them all right with us. So I concluded that Mr Capt was a damn Skulker and Coward and I retired to rest feeling that all was right and we would give them H___ the next day. I slept untill about three AM when the cry was heard hitch up and be ready to move and about four Johnny opened and kept up a slow fire untill about sun rise when he opened in earnest and now began one of the toughest fights that ever was fought by this Army. All the forenoon the Artillery fire was the heaviest I ever heard but we were in the rear untill noon When we were ordered to the front and now we had a chance to see what had been going on. The wounded were comeing in and they told us Go in boys you will find it one of the hottest places you ever got into but said they We are giveing them H___. One Col was going to the rear with a bad wound in his arm. Says he Boys we are just warming them and giving them the damndest whipping they ever got. We were ordered to trot and we rushed along with the shell flying around about as thick as ever I saw them and I began to think that somebody was going to be hurt. There was plenty of dead men and horses strewing the ground. Guns and cassons knocked into a cocked hat. Wounded horses flying hither and thither and in fact things looked as if there had been one of the largest kinds of rows but we gained the hill and went into position relieving a Ohio Bat who to get out of it had hid some of there Ammunition under a hole that was in the rear of them and whose only aim seemed to be to get off the field. Gen Meade rode up and asked the Capt what he was leaving for. He told him he was out of Ammunition. The Gen told him that was no reason as there was plenty in the Train and all he had to do was to send his cassons and have them filled but however he let him go after giveing him some little advice and giving him to understand he would look into his case another time. We took there position which was just at the left of the Cemetary (of which I suppose you have read).

I supposed now we had to go at it in earnest but our orders were not to notice the Rebel Batteries nor to fire a shot without we saw the Rebs advancing towards and then to use nothing but Cannister which we had lieing by the side of the gun. Therefore we quietly laid ourselves down by the side of our peices and watched the motions. We had a fine view of the field and could see the Infantry popping away but Johnny made no advance towards the first Mass but amused himself by directing his shell towards us but the most of them went over and beyond. One Gun a Whitworth would send over one about every 15 minutes but as good luck would have it hurt none of our boys but did some damage to the rear and left of us. They are a saucy thing when well directed and the music of their Shot is not quite as agreeable to me as Lizzies Bob used to be. The Rebs kept up there fire until Sun Set and made one charge to the left of us but met with rather a warm reception and we took the most of them prisoners. That is what was not killed and wounded. They charged the hill we were on just before we went up there and finding the Yankees too much for them concluded they would stop on that side of the field and come in and gave themselves up. Some 500 of them with 4 stands of colors. They charged[14] in three lines and one Rebel

[14] Pickett's Charge.

officer remarked that the fire from our side took the first line off there feet and said he A million men never could take those heights and I guess he was about right for we had guns in position as thick as they could be placed and it was death to all insects if the men only stood at their guns. So here we remained all the rest of the day only fireing one gun and that merely to get the range. The loss on both sides this day was very heavy and the field that night presented a sight that even the most blood thirsty might shudder at. Dead and wounded Rebs and Yanks piled up together. Dead horses and dismounted peices &C presented a sight that I never care to witness again and the groans of the wounded and shrieks of the dieing was enough to make the most hardened weep to hear. I thought Antietam was awfull but it was not a circumstance to this one although to realize it a person had to travel over it as the wheat and grass was so high that it hid the dead from sight. That night about ten the Rebs made an attack on our extreme right in the midst of a heavy shower thinking I suppose that our Boys was asleep but found there mistake for they were expecting as they supposed the Rebs would try and break them there so as to gain the Turnpike but it was no go. For about an hour there was the most incessant fire of musketry I ever heard and then all was quiet untill about 2 AM when they made another effort with a like result. Those that saw that part of the field told me the Rebs were fairly piled up winrows as our boys were behind a breast work and the rebs came snug up to them and our folks fairly Slaughtered them and this ended the night of the 3d. On the 4th we laid in position all day but there was nothing going on but Skirmishing. Only a few Shells. This day was spent in taking care of the wounded and burying the dead and the next morning our folks made a dash and drove the Johnnys out of Gettysburg and this ended the fight at Gettysburg. This morning we were relieved went to the rear and after feeding and cleaning our horses were ordered to start again with the whole Corps after the Rebs. Crossed the field leaving Gettysburg on our right and came up with Johnnys rear guard about night and Some of the leading Batteries shelled them. This day we passed a great many fine large barns all filled with Rebel wounded.

The next day we were oblidged to halt being hitched up ready to start but the Rebs had blockaded the roads so that we did not get started untill four in the Afternoon when we marched all night arriving at Emmetsburg about three AM haulted and started again about 5 AM. But here I will close and resume some other time thinking this will be all you will want to read at once. I have now tried to give you a faint Idea of the battle but if I could sit down and describe it to you think I could make you understand it better my descriptive powers not being as good as I wish they were.

The End.

I had a letter from Langdon last Sunday and learned that Mary was quite sick but they thought improveing. I also had a letter from Winslow and have wrote him. I expect we shall get paid this week when if we do you may expect to hear from me again. I want you to send me some stamps and a rubber headed pencil. Give my love to all the folks and tell them Chase still lives so no more at present and I guess you are glad of it.

Jack

Speaking of warm weather it is hot as H___ here but being all right with Mac get an order for a Canteen of Busthead now and then and make out to live.

If you think it worth while send this to Pricilla after you read it. Perhaps she would like to read it.

* * * * * * * * * *

Camp of First Mass Battery
Warrenton Va
Aug 7th 1863

Dear Brother

As it is a rainy evening and haveing nothing to amuse myself about I concluded to write to you and give you an account of our travels after we arrived at Emmetsburg as I believe there is where my last letter left off. We arrived here about three AM of the 7th of July and started again at 7 AM. So you see we did not get much rest that time but however the word was go and of course all we had to do was to travel and we moved on passing through the village of Mechanicstown & Catoctin where there is a furnace for Smelting Iron ore and moved on up into the Catoctin mountain and about 4 PM found we were into the Mountain as far as the Devil went. That is as far as we could get for stones or in other words were on the wrong road oweing to the Blundering of our Col Tomkins who may be a very smart officer but I dont see it myself but however here we were and we could get no farther and being the leading Battery and the Waggon Train behind us we were in rather a bad fix. So all we had to do was to unlimber our carriages and turn them round the best way we could as the road was very narrow and it was impossible to turn any other way. We got turned about and then the train being in the way we could not move consequently we remained in the road all night and as it was raining right smart and had been all day we felt very gay and happy as you may well suppose. However we made the best of it and there being a Solitary House and an old Sawmill there what could got into them persuading the women to bake us all the flour they had which was a very small lot and passed the night as best we could. Your Brother Jack laid down by the side of the road about dark and went to sleep but awoke about 10 and found himself decidely moist and very cold therefore he made tracks for the mill and found a small space there to stow his bones in and took quiet possesion not paying very particular attention to those he was treading on as long as he got laid down. I laid untill about Sunrise when we once more got started and went back about two miles and took another road that wound around the mountain and after some of the toughest pulling that our horses ever done we arrived at the top just at sunset haveing to double our teams up and haul a part of our Battery at a time and now we had to go down and as it was getting dark there was a very pleasant prospect before us but we got down without killing any body and arrived at Middletown about 2 o clock in the morning of the 9th and turned in with the comforting order be ready to start early in the morning. We were turned out at 1/2 past four but as a good many of our horses wanted shoeing and we were out of rations and forage did not get on the road again untill noon about 1/2 past 12 when we started and marched through the town of Middletown to Turners Gap in the South Mountains through the Gap to Near Boonsboro where we went into Park and had a good nights rest. This was a fine march through a fine country and a nice Turn Pike all the way and it was a beautiful day and here we met the Cavalry comeing in haveing amongst other Prisoners the Rebel Genl Jenkins.[15] The next morning we hitched up at 6 AM Marched through Boonsboro and about 4 miles beyond and halted remained there untill about Sunset when we went into Position on the hills near the road and by the side of Antietam Creek four miles from the old Battle field and all being quiet after haveing a ration of Whiskey served out to us we turned in thinking the Country was safe. We remained here all the next day and night in position but saw nothing of the Johnnys. On Saturday we started about noon and marched through Funkstown on the Pike towards Hagerstown and arrived at the Battle line about night. It was very rainy and we went into park and I supposed we should go into position that night but we did not. Just at night the Jersey Brigade made a charge and drove the Rebels. When they drove them and took about 40 prisoners one of the Vermont Brigade who was sitting on the fence seeing the fun looks up and says to another one I say Jim them Jersey fellows fight well and I would give a half a dollar to be there with them and help drive them greybacks. But for some reason that I cannot see into they did not force the fighting and there we remained all that night and the next day expecting certain to go in and drive the rebs to the river and give them a high old basteing and we could just done it too for I never saw the army before when I thought they wanted to fight but I do think they did that day and I believe it was one of the greatest mistakes of the war that we did not fight them but I presume our Gens had good reasons for not doing so therefore I am willing to

[15] Probably an erroneous rumor that General Albert G. Jenkins, the leader of a Confederate cavalry brigade at Gettysburg, had been captured.

abide by there judgement. On the Forenoon of the 14th we started again and went to Williamsport passing the Rebel Earthworks and rifle pits they had thrown up but I saw nothing so very formidable to frighten an army nor do I think it would if they had been allowed to try them. We arrived at W about 4 PM to find Gen Lee and his Army all across the river. The next day we take the back track passing through Hagerstown Funkstown to Boonsboro where we camp the next morning start at 3 AM Cross the South Mountain through Bolivar Middletown Petersville to the left of Burketsville and Cramptons Gap where we had the fight last year and arrived near Berlin about Sunset when it commenced to rain and continued all night. Had a Ration of Whiskey served to us and being Seargeant of the guard got no sleep that night. We remain here the next day still raining and very muddy and we passed not a very pleasant day. The next day the Sun made a strong effort to shine but hardly made out. This day we had Whiskey and new Clotheing Issued to us and George O. Manning took his departure and no tears shed. In the Afternoon it clears up and we are ordered to march tomorrow but I will now close and if this prove of any interest to you I will resume it again at some future day.

We have not seen the Pay Master yet although they do say he is round. Things remain quiet here with us Col Tomkins being home on a Furlough. We as yet have had none of his foolish Inspections but as he is expected back to day I suppose we shall get one tomorrow when he will be around in all his Glory. Give my love to all the folks. I have heard nothing from Stratham since I wrote you last but then I suppose they think I am not anxious to know whether the children are dead or alive or else they think it costs too much to write and pay postage but then there is a better day a comeing. Wait a little twelve months and then I shall once more if alive be your happy Brother.

Jack

Tell Lizzie she better come out and see the Boy. She never will have a better chance and I think she would like and then she can come to Warrenton and see me.

This Letter may not be very interesting to you but then it keeps me out of mischief and from haveing the blues so you see I get good out of it and you must bear the infliction thinking it is a benefit to a weary Warrior.

It is Hot as Home here. Very melting. Thats So.

* * * * * * * * * *

Camp of First Mass Battery
Warrenton Va
Sunday Eve Aug 9th/63

Dear Brother

It is awful hot here. How is it there? Or rather it has been all day but as it is now about Sunset it is a trifle cooler but is plenty warm now. I am not going to write you a letter but thought I would write just a few lines as I wanted to send you this check. We were paid this morning and then went out and had a Battery drill and the glass up to a hundred in the Shade. Delightful very but then I have had a Canteen of Whiskey to keep my blood in order therefore feel as if the Country is still safe. I have heard nothing from Stratham this week only by a letter I had from a friend of mine up there who I think thinks more of me than my relatives do for he does write me and that is more than some of them will do but then it shows what they are made of. I think they would write me damn quick if there was 5 dollars oweing them and they thought I should send it to them but then you know the difference betwixt tweedle dee and tweedle dum is great particularly at this time of year. I have just been to supper. Blackberries and fried heart. Not human but oxes and I feel very much refreshed as it was the first I have eaten since 5 o clock this morning. We Warriors dont get our meals very regular for we generally eat when we can get it and that is not always when we want it.

There has been quite a display of crinoline around the camp to day. Black white and yellow but the fair damsels of Warrenton dont take much notice of a poor private thinking I suppose that there pockets are not quite so well supplied with green backs as the Officers for I am very sure it is not because they are not as likeley and know as much but then you know money makes the mare go &C. I will tell you a little incident that happened to me the other evening. As I was takeing a quiet walk through the Streets of the City I saw a young FFV[16] sitting by the window and she was singing the particular melody John Brown and I began to think I had ran across a young lady of union sentiments but when she arrived at the verse which runs we will hang Jeff Davis to a sour apple tree she happened to look up and discover your venerable brother looking at her and she substituted our worthy friend Abe for Jeff. I being a little inquisitive asked the young lady how she proposed doing it but she did not see fit to inform me but turned up her nose and proceeded with her song and I passed on thinking how easy it was for a innocent man like me to be mistaken in a Woman. Particularly in her political Sentiments in war time. But I will wind up by wishing I was there with you this evening and we had pitcher of Punch for I feel as if a little with Ice in it would suit me to a T. The boys are all well and in good spirits. As for health we have not a man on the sick list. Quite a difference betwixt this and last year at this time when we used to have about 15 on an average. Love to all and receive this from

Jack

I want you to send me out a dozen cards two by three inches. I suppose you will want to know what I want them for but I will send you one after I get it marked and then you will know. Get some that are not Enamelled because they will have to be marked with a pencill. The Storekeepers will tell you what I want. The Sunday Chronicle from Washington has just arrived in camp and the boys are reading the news. The news from Charleston seems to be encouraging. Hope soon to hear of its fall. This Army is Somewhere

[16] First Family of Virginia.

I cannot tell where as all there is here is the 6th Corps and not all of them but I will not trouble you with any more to night but will Halt.

Love to Emily.

Send me this in Stamps. That is this 50 cent Shin [Shinplaster].

Yours &C

Jack

A Fifty Cent "Shinplaster" JSC/BBC

* * * * * * * * * *

John Chase's Travel Routes in Chapter 6: August 1863 to April 1864

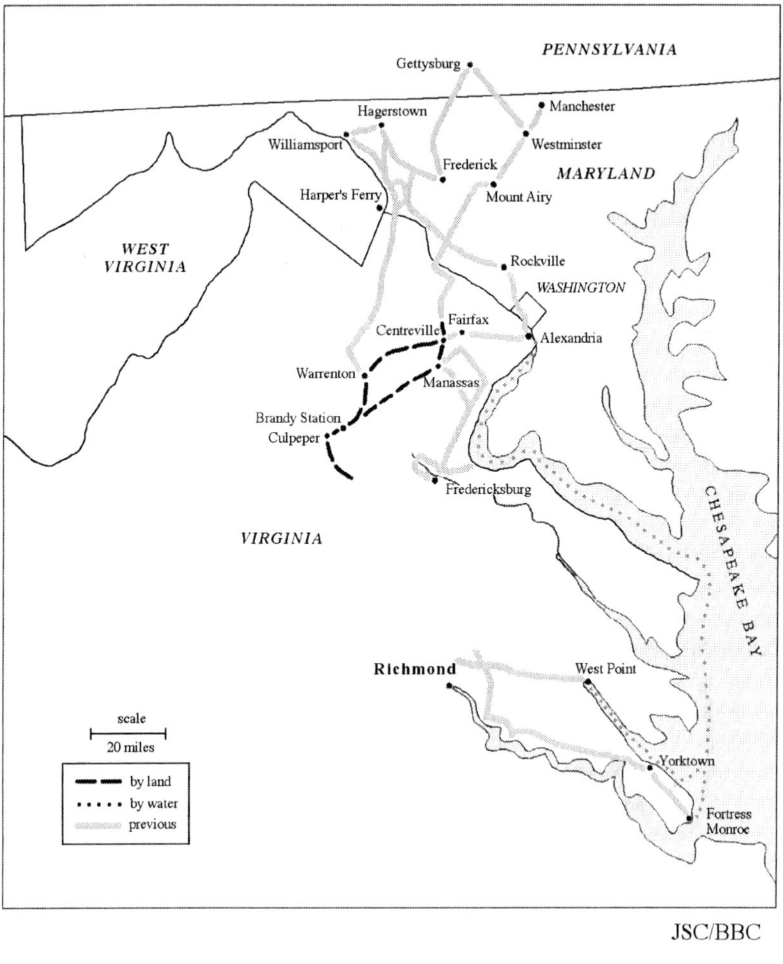

JSC/BBC

CHAPTER 6

Warrenton and Brandy Station

Following the Battle of Gettysburg, the two armies maneuver in the area around Warrenton and Culpeper, Virginia, with an engagement at Rappahannock Station in November. The Army of the Potomac spends the winter of 1863–1864 near Brandy Station. Chase deals with problems at home, but he also chooses to reenlist.

On Picket
Near Sulphur Springs Va
Aug 17th 1863

Dear Brother

I received yours last night and was very glad to hear that you were still in the land of the liveing for I began to think you were sick or else had gone to the war but it seems you are all right. Speaking about Asher and the heat all I have to say is if it is any hotter than we have had it here I pity him for it has been awfull here. A leetle warmer I think than I ever experienced before although I hardly think we suffer as much with it as we did last year at Harrisons Landing for the reason that here we are on a high range of hills and do get the air when there is any stirring and then we have a Chesnut Grove to flee to where we can get in the shade. But some of our officers it seems to me try to keep us out in the sun all they can particularly our wooden headed Lieut Federhen.[1] But we have to console ourselves

[1] Lieutenant Jacob Federhen.

with thinking the poor devil dont know any better but for one I cannot help wishing some times that he might get sunstruck but I think it would take a right smart sun to affect such a wooden head as he is. As a specimen of his hellish works one of the hottest days we have had he took us out grooming our horses no less than three times while when Green is officer of the day we never go but once and that is about the difference there is between them all round. But I will drop him thinking it is only a year more and then all such critters as he is will have to keep there mouth shut to me or they may get a bust in the nose. I have got about sick of being ordered about by a damn fool but then you know it dont do to let your angry passions rise too high to Shoulder bars. We are now on Picket about 6 miles from Warrenton and near the North Branch of the Rappahannock. All this Brigade of Batteries are here scattered around. Some guarding the fords while others are covering the Pike to Culpepper. We have a nice place to bathe in the river which is about 3/4 of a mile from us. Our pickets are on the banks of the river but we dont see anything in the shape of rebels although they do say there is some on the other side. The rest of the army what there is left here are scattered all the way from here to Falmouth but a good part of them have gone from here. All the Regulars have gone and last week the Vermont Brigade left here. Gone to New York they say to enforce the draft and God pity the crowd of Rioters that ever comes in front of them for you never will catch them fireing any blank cartridges for they want to see the game drop when they fire and I dont think they will have any more scruples about fireing at a lot of rioters than they would at a Brigade of rebels. I dont think there will be much a row in York but if there is you can just bet there will be a warm time for this army however much they may dislike the Conscript law still believe it is the law and consequently believe in enforceing it. I received from a Friend of mine in Stratham the list of drafted there and I see amongst others they have got the Orthodox minister. Bully for him. I have not heard from Pricilla since last June. Dont know whether she is dead or alive. I got a few lines from Mary this last week informing me that she was better and that there was a Doctors bill to pay but she did not say how much but I suppose will let me know as I asked her too. Let me know how much money you have and if you have not enough I will raise it for I am bound it shall be paid. I can always hear from there quick enough when there is any money to be paid out but at any other time they are in no hurry to write but I suppose it is all right but I cant help thinking some times if I only had what Govt pays me to support my Children on they would come most damn short. I suppose they cannot hurt a poor devil for thinking can they? I hear from a friend of mine that George Head has got exempted on the ground of haveing a Motherless Child under 12 years of age but it strikes me that Ella is older than that but I cannot seem to remember when she was born but I have no doubt the damn loafer would swear to a lie any time to safe $300.[2] But I hope if he has he will get fetched up to the mark I do. I dont think of any more to write at present. The stamps pencil and papers came all right and receive my thanks for the same but as to a Box I dont think there would be any sure thing about my getting it and therefore I dont want you to send it for at the depot there is no one that thinks about anything but himself and there was not some one there to take it as soon as it got there some loafer would have it and go through it and then I should have to do a heap of swearing.

You must remember me to all the folks that want to hear from me and tell them all is quiet on the Rap and the only thing that troubles us is the fact that Blackberries are Played out. So hopeing to hear from you again soon I remain

your Brother Jack

* * * * * * * * * *

[2] The commutation fee to avoid the draft was $300.

Camp of First Mass Battery
Near Sulphur Springs Va
Aug 29th 1863

Dear Brother

Yours of the 23d came all right. I had been looking for a letter as I supposed you would write from York but I suppose you was so much engaged in looking at the Sogers &C you could not get time. Well I see by the papers that the draft passed off quietly. Guess they thought it want just the time to kick up a muss. Most too many blue jackets round. Glad they had so much sense although if the only injury done would be to kill off about eight or ten thousand of there chaps that make all this trouble think it would be a good thing but the trouble is the innocent have to suffer with the guilty

Had a letter from one of the Vermont Brigade which is in York and he seems [to] think that the troops there are going to be sent off to Charleston or some other place as they are loading transports with Rations Forage &C. All I can say is they have taken away a good part of this Army and carried them somewhere and as a general thing have taken our best fighting Regt and are putting conscripts in there places which may be all right but I dont hardly see it. That is if we are going to do any fighting for I am not one of the kind that believes that Lees Army is all gone yet but think if we do get at them that they will fight just as hard as ever. Its no use

General Robert E. Lee LC

talking. Lee has got the best Soldiers there is in the Rebel States and they fight Like H___eroes they do.

There is not much doing here. The weather now is quite comfortable days and nights it is quite cold. So much so that an overcoat is quite a comfort and it makes us think of whats comeing and to day we are haveing an Easterly Storm and it is quite cold. Yesterday we celebrated our Second anniversary and Mac had a lot of Whiskey Punch made up for us and some of the boys retired last night feeling quite gay and happy but everything passed off in good shape and no trouble. As the cold weather draws near it makes me think of those shirts and I want you on the receipt of this to do one of them up and send it to me by mail as I can see no other way of getting it and then after I get that you can send the other. It is rather a costly way of sending them but I guess it is a good deal the surest. I got a Letter from Pricilla a few days ago. I had written to Father day before and I suppose they will think I talked rather hard to my Bretheran and Sisteren but I cant help it. I have got about tired of this writeing to folks and they not takeing notice enough of it to write me and have come to the conclusion that they can just go to Hell. I dont want anything from them and probably they dont from me so its all right I suppose. But however I have stood it out here two years and hope by the help of God to get through the next one if we have to stay as long but I am in hopes the thing will be closed up by spring and think if the people do there duty it will be. The Boys here are growling because we are lieing still and some of them wishing they could be down to Charleston but I dont see it. I have had all the fighting I want and think the Potomac Army has done about its share but however if it comes all right. Chase never did show the white feather yet but he has seen the time when he would just as quick last a half a day as not (he has).

I received a letter from Mary yesterday but she did not write the amount of the Doctors Bill but when she does I will let you know. I want it paid that is if you have money enough in your hands of mine to pay it for I want to keep square with my childrens accounts if possible. As for my own I can do as I damn please about them. I have an Idea that I am looked upon as a person would look upon a good Cow (that is by some people) as long as I furnish a good mess all right but when the feed grows scarce and the mess small rather a poor critter. But I am in hopes if God Spares my life to sail my own ship once more before I die and think I shall try at least but then its no use makeing a fuss about what you cannot help.

Tell Lizzie I wish she had come out here. We would got up a fight with the Rebs just for her benefit and shown her what kind of a sight a battle is. I am glad you had such a good chance to see Asher and think he must have been highly delighted.

But I must draw to a close. I suppose you will not derive much information from this letter but then you see it is dull as Sunday here and a poor devil cannot get up steam to write much. The Boys are all well. We had one leave us last week to take a Commission in a New York Regt. He was one of our 16th Boys and a d____d good fellow. His Reg is down to South Carolina. Remember me to all the folks and dont forget to send me those cards.

So good Bye
Yours &C
Jack

Seems to be the impression here that Gilmore[3] is about the cheese for Charleston. Dont fool away his time teaching niggers to read.

I got the paper you sent from York.

* * * * * * * * * *

Camp of First Mass Battery
Near Sulphur Springs Va
Saturday Night Sept 5th [1863]

Dear Brother

I have delayed answering your last letter which I received last Thursday for I have been waiting to hear from Mary thinking she

[3] General Quincy A. Gillmore led the shelling of Charleston, South Carolina.

would send me the amount of that Doctors bill but I got a letter to night and she writes me that the Dr has not made it out yet so I guess Kittredge is not much worried about it consequently shall not make myself anyways uneasy about it but as we say here let it go untill next Pay Day. All remains quiet here with us. They get up an alarm once in a while but as yet there has been nothing serious come out of it. They keep the Cavalry moveing and you have probably read of Kilpatricks[4] last exploit which was retakeing the Gun Boats (or rather sinking them) that the rebs got from us. I think it was a damn smart operation on the part of the Rebels getting them but just a leetle smarter in the Gen sinking them and I think going into Naval expeditions with Cavalry is something new under the sun but if you can find anything old Kil will not do I would like to know what it is and if all our Gens had been like him I think Gen Lee would have got a damn good warming when he was in Md for Kilpatrick was strong for going at him there but then its too late to talk about that now and we are left to say what <u>might have been</u>. The Regts around here are haveing great times celebrating there Anniversaries. Some there first and some the 2nd. The 139 Penn which is here supporting our Battery had one this week. There first one and if they did not have a good time then shoot me. They had a foot race for $5,00 two greased poles 25 feet high with a 5 00 green back on the top of each a sack race greased pig sparring Match jumping match &C. The boys got both the notes off the poles after a great deal of labor. One of our boys took the prize for being the best Boxer and another for makeing the best jump beating the privates 2 feet and the officers 16 inches. Big thing for the first Mass. There was any quantity of Stars eagles and any quantity of bars present. Generals Birney Howe Shaler Wheaton Bartlett[5] and others being present with there Staffs besides a few Ladies but they only stopped a short time. You better believe

[4] General Hugh J. Kilpatrick was known as "Kill Cavalry" for his recklessness in battle. His cavalry sank two gunboats at Port Conway on the Rappahannock, south of Fredericksburg.

[5] Generals David B. Birney, Albion Howe, Alexander Shaler, Frank Wheaton, and Joseph J. Bartlett were all in the Sixth Corps.

there was some Whiskey punished particularly by the Shoulder Strap gentry. Of course it would not do for privates to do so but then they did make out to get just a little and take it all together it was a damn good time and I think if the Rebs had crossed about nine o clock that night they would found about as gay a set of Boys as you could start I do. But then you see we must improve such chances when we get one for I can sware they dont happen very often (bet your life that,s so). Speaking about Conscripts I have seen none of them yet as we have had none come to this brigade yet but I learn there has been a good many come but being out on the front we dont have much chance to see what is going on. By what Mary writes me from Stratham I think it will take a long while to recruit the Army by the draft for only 5 from Stratham passed and I think they are a damn site more particular than they were with the Volunteers for of all the damn pretences they get up to get clear it takes me down and I rather think the Draft is a DEAD BEAT I do myself. Its all very fine you know for some to go and be shot at but when it takes me or my children its a horse of another color and these same folks will prate about Gen McClellan and Porter and others being traitors and be as Patriotic as H___ themselves as far as talk goes but I am damned if I see it and I wish to God the Rebs would just make them one of there Maryland visits. I think they would see things then as they were and would be willing to do something but prate about putting down the Rebellion and I say to H_ll with these Patriots that are afraid of there own children,s going to fight for I dont believe in them and think there Patriotism extends just as far as there own safety and safety of there pockets goes. But I must close for to night for I find I am getting excited and think I should like to kick some of these self same Patriots if I could reach them. So I will drop the subject and try and get a ration of sleep.

Sunday Noon [Sept. 6]

Have just come in from a Review and Inspection and Prayer by the Rev Dr Burkhart of Philadelphia. It was very warm out this morning and I am afraid that the Lords name was taken rather oftener than was consistent for a good Christian. Its a new dodge they have got here. Go out and have a Review Sunday Morning and then prayers but I dont think it has a very good effect this hot weather. Charley[6] has been mustered in a Lieutenant. Commenced his duty this morning. Wished me to remember him to you when I wrote you. He and the Capt have gone to a horse race down to Warrenton to day. I tell you this army is a great place for fun about this time. Saw a lot of Conscripts in the Regts this morning and it makes a regiment look as large as a Brigade used to.

I think Asher has rather hard luck but you must tell him I always found the best way was to look out for your own deeds and not trust to Corporals. Great wonder here now to know is going to be our orderly Seagt. Charley wants me to take it but I dont see it. Too much riding for me and this horse back riding dont agree with my constitution. I went down to Warrenton last week and felt the next morning as if I had been drawed through a knot hole.

I have just had a ration of Baked Beans and they were immense you better believe. We are liveing Bully these times. Plenty of soft bread and a very good share of vegetables and we find them very toothsome. When you write Sarah F give her my best respects and tell her if she has a boy baby she may call it John but I should advise her to carry it out of Maine to have it Christened. I have heard nothing from the Ridge and I dont expect they will write to me again for I suppose they will think I talked hard to them. Cant help it. Would talk worse if I could see them for I dont see the point of there Sympathy I dont myself. It dont show itself as I think it might but then Jack is a tough cuss and hard to kill and if they dont like my style they can just sell out they can.

Give my love to all the folks that want to hear from me and tell them everything is lovely with the First Mass. But I will draw to a close thinking this will be all you will want without it is better.

So good Bye
Yours &C
Jack

---

[6] Charley French was promoted from first sergeant to lieutenant.

PS I dont know as you can read my writeing. If you cannot say so and I will try and do better for I think I can by being a little more carefull. Benny Brooks is well and sends his respects to all friends.

* * * * * * * * * *

Camp of First Mass Bat
Sept 11th 1863

Dear Brother

Yours of Sunday reached me last night and I was glad to hear that you were all well. The Shirt came through all right and you may send the other as soon as you please. I also want you to put me a pair of Suspenders in the bundle also some pant stripes to put on the leg of my pants. They want to be 1 1/2 inches wide. I suppose you will think I am getting rather dressy but you see I am Orderley[7] and must fix up a little. Charley has got his nig and he is the best looking Cuss we have got. I thought I would take the berth as there is some priveledges connected with it but still as you very well know it is not the easiest place in the Co for a person to get along in but I think I can run the Machine with Macs help. The Capt has gone to Washington to day and I expect French will go tomorrow. All is quiet here. You seem to think strange that Meade dont do anything but if you knew what a small force was here you would not wonder at it. I dont think myself that it is intended for Meade to attack Lee but to let the squirrel set here in Va and give the other parts of the Army reap a little glory but still I may be Mistaken. My health is good and the weather here is very comfortable.

Remember me to all Friends and excuse this short letter. I will do better next time.

Yours &C
Jack

---

[7] John Chase was promoted to first sergeant on September 7, 1863.

Tell Mrs. Curtis I am very much oblidged to her for the Box. I find it very handy. (The cards were just right.)

Jack

* * * * * * * * * *

First Mass Battery
Near Culpeper
Sept 19th 1863

Dear Brother

I have not much time or much of interest to write but thought I would just let you know that I still live. I suppose you are aware that the Army is once more in motion. We left our camp last Tuesday Afternoon and marched as far as the Springs where we halted for the night only moveing about three miles. The next morning we started and marched to this place which is about four miles from Culpeper makeing a march of 18 miles and it was a hard road to travel as we came over the mountains so as to move on the Flank and keep the Johnnys from troubling our rear.

General George G. Meade LC

We have lain here ever since and what the next move will be I suppose the papers will tell you. I have no Idea of what the Programme is to be but I hope whatever it is that all will be right and I think Gen Meade is the Lad to keep his eye open for Lee. Dont think he will get much the start of him. We are haveing a cold storm which I think if it keeps on will pass for the Line Gale for the wind has blew some and it was lucky for us that we got across the streams and mountains before it came on. Yesterday there was 11 men shot in the 3d Corps for desertion. They are about two miles from us. There was quite a number of this Corps went up to see them shot but I had no disposition to see it although I fully approve of it and I think if they had done the same thing in the first of the war that desertions would have played out before now but its better late than never. They put it to the conscripts here on a march. Rather rough that is the substitutes and they are a damn hard lot of citizens take them as a nation but I reckon they will get tired of kicking up rough before this Cruel War is over.

I had a letter from Pricilla this week. She thinks I am rather hard in my language as she had been sick and could not write but I did not intend to blame her any for I have an Idea of how she is situated but I shall not change my mind any as to the others. I have come to the conclusion that they dont care but damn little about me and I dont think I shall trouble them with letters in future. I calculate I am just as good as any other Chase that travels I do. I may be mistaken but thats my impression. As to that Bed Mary wrote me she wanted it and I told her to get it. The one she laid on belonged to Henry and as his family is on the increase he needs more beds. I suppose you have sent the shirt at least I hope so for my old ones are about Played. I have the one you sent on and I like it first rate. Have to stick up a little now you know just for appearances. I like my new position first rate so far as we have a Clerk and he is a first rate fellow and he and myself and the Quartermaster Seargt have a wall tent all to ourselves. But my sheet is full and I must close.

Love to all the folks.

Yours &C
Jack

I got your letter and papers this week. Please send me stamps in your next. I expect the Pay Master here every day as he is here in the Corps somewhere.

* * * * * * * * * *

Camp Battery A, Mass Volunteers
Near Culpepper
Sept 25 1863

Dear Brother

Another week has passed and here we are in the same place where I wrote you last Although they tell us every night we shall move the next day. Last night I thought we were going sure as we got all ready but about ten PM orders came to turn in and go to sleep so I dont know now when we shall move. I have come to the conclusion that We shall not see much more fighting here this fall but still I dont see why for it seems to me if the Rebels have gone to reinforce Bragg[8] that it would be a good time for this Army to try there hand but then you know a Private is not supposed to know anything and if he does he must keep it to himself. We were paid two months pay this week and the boys are haveing a merry time as the Capt gives them orders for Whisky to the extent of 10 Canteens full a day and thus far everything has passed off pleasantly. I have not sent any money home this time and dont think I shall for I had to buy me a watch and then we have been getting up a badge which costs us $5,50 apeice and that dont leave me a great surplus on hand. I suppose some of my friends will think I had ought to send home all my pay but I dont "see it" for I think what I get from the State and what I have sent you ought to take care of the Children. What,s your opinion? If you should happen in Boston drop in to Newall Hardings Jewellers in Court Square Avenue and see the badge and let me know what you think of it. We think it rather the best thing out. We had one sent out for a Sample and the most of the boys are going to have one. We have also Presented or going too Seargeant Reynolds who lost his leg at Fredericksburg with a gold headed cane that costs us 90 dollars. I dont know but what you will think it rather extravagant but I tell you the Boys would have given him three times that sum for he is a man that they all liked. In fact he was a Whole Man and that embraces a good deal more than the most of folks have

[8] General Braxton Bragg led the Confederate victory against General William S. Rosecrans at the Battle of Chickamauga in Georgia, near Chattanooga, Tennessee.

an Idea of. He has got his discharge and is at work at his trade which is a Gold Beater. He works in Concord Mass. Pettingill has got back. Says he should have called out and seen you but was ordered off so soon that he had not time. He tells me you did treat him rather too strong when he was out there and allows he was pretty well filled up when he left but Pett says Sams a Brick. I have not heard from Ben Winslow and I am afraid the old fellow is sick again. I had a letter from Horatio last night. The Regt is still in New York. The Shirt and the other things arrived last night. Please give my love to Mrs Curtis with my thanks for the Present and also for the many favors I have received at her hands since I have been in the service. Such things may look small with folks at home but they are big things with a Soldier I assure you. At any rate it goes to prove they are not forgotten. I have not received the amount of that Doctors Bill yet but will let you know when I do. The Boys here seem to think that Charleston is a high old place to take but all have faith that Gilmore will do it if anybody can. They also have faith Rosy and think Mr Bragg will yet have to Cave in. In fact We believe that the Rebs have seen there Best days and this army is going to be top of the heap. The Vermont Brigade has got back and the boys are feeling bully although some of them are rather lame—but will probably will get over it with care. This Cane of Reynolds is makeing at Henry Haddocks and Co corner of Court and Washington Street. Call in and see it.

But I must close up. Give my love to all the folks and tell them Chase still lives.

I hope Mr. G Head will get put through for I think he ought to be damn a liar. In answer to your question we Enlisted for three years. Benny Brooks and French wish to be remembered to you.

Good Bye for this time.
Yours &C
Jack

PS If you receive a picture of three Sogers take it down to John Peirson and ask him if he knows the boys on the right and left. The one in the Centre I dont expect he will know. Remember me to Asher when you write.

(Love to Emily.)

* * * * * * * * * *

Camp Battery "A" First Mass Vol
Near Culpepper Virginia
Oct 1st /63

Dear Brother

Your Letter of the 27th reached me this evening and I was very happy to hear once more from old Roxbury and to learn that all was well with you.

We still remain at the same place although constantly expecting to move but I am of the opinion that when we do move it will be towards Washington instead of on to Richmond but it is rumored that we shall go to help Rosy out of his trouble. I presume you are aware that the 11th and 12th Corps have already gone and that leaves this Army rather small but I think it can hold its own with Lees yet.

The last excitement here was caused by the proposed testimonial to McClellan which I suppose the papers have given you an account of but I will state it to you. It was Proposed to make a testimonial to the Gen. Such Men as Gen Meade Sedgwick and others going in for it. The subscription was limited Major Generals giveing 20,00 and so down to Capts who were to pay 150 Lieut 100 Seargeants 25 cts and Privates 10 cents. In our Battery and in every Regt in this corps the men all signed and had paid there money when some damn fools got troubled and began to cry out Politics and the Washington Chronicle was in a hell of a way about it and began to cry out in loud tones against it. At last it was deemed best by those who were the leaders to give it up as our Great Big Men said it was in violation of the articles of War so the money was sent back. So you see the Black Hell Hounds have not left off scenting anything that smells of McClellan and he is the Ghost that troubles there slumbers. I have Nothing more to say for I suppose you will see it all in the papers.

All I have to say is the men of this Army never thought of Politics in connexion with the thing more than the subscribers to the Washington Monument did but they supposed it a mark of respect to one and I dont hesitate to say the best Gen this Army ever had. And I say Bully for George and Damn the Washington Chronicle and all the Black Hearted crew that support it. Thats me to a damn But I will drop this and take another text. They are offering inducements here for the Soldiers that came out in 61 to reenlist. Perhaps you will be surprised to hear that the Idea has entered my head to do so but such is the fact. I look at it in this light. I have nothing now to live for but for the good of my children and it runs in my mind that I can do as much or more for there support where I am than I could to come home when my three years were out and go to work at my trade for to tell the truth I always did despise the business and never was contented when I worked at it and I cannot bear the Idea of ever going at it again. And another thing when I am there as you very well know I am not any too steady nor ever was although perhaps I ought to be ashamed to own it but I often think of what our departed Mother used to say. It is one half in owning up to the truth and I think you know me well enough to know that Hypocrisy was never one of my besetting sins for I always thought I was too honest in some things for my own good. Now I want a little advice on the subject for without wishing to flatter you any I must say that I think more of what you and Lizzie may say than I do for any one else. In fact I look upon you as a kind of a guardian for me. As to my other relatives setting aside my parents and children I dont think they trouble themselves much about what becomes of me consequently I shall not trouble myself to try to find out what there opinion of the matter may be. There is many things in Soldiers life that I dont like and we have to put up with privations and hardships that we should get rid of in civil life but then again there are things in it I do like and if it was not for the distinction there is made between a Private and a lunk head of an officer I should like it better than I do but then you know there is a no rose without its thorn in this world. At least if there is I have never found the bush it grows on and I think I have hunted the Garden some I do myself. I would like you to write me just as soon as you can and give me your opinion of the matter. About the picture I sent you I hardly think I should know myself who the chap in the middle was. The others are Ben Brooks and a fellow by the name of Conway who used to work in the Market and came out when Ben did but if it pleases Mrs Curtis let her have it and I will send you another one that perhaps you will like better. The Stamps came in good time. I was in no hurry for them but dont like to be out of such things although I have cut my correspondence down some and think I shall more before long. I received a letter from Mary and she writes me that Doctors Bill will be about 25,00 but I guess we will let it rest untill next Pay Day for I dont know how much funds you have on hand and I dont think that Kittridge will have any hard feelings if he does have to wait a couple of months for his pay but if there is any great hurry I will inform you.

As to my new position I like it thus far but a Non Commissioned officer berth in this army is a verry uncertain affair as he is likely to be broke at any moment but I shall try and do my duty and not give them any reason so to do although we often see it done without any reason but then you know its worth something to have the approval of your own conscience.

My health has not been very good the past week. I have got the dysentery on to me. I wish I had some of that Brandy you used to get in to Dunbars but that is a thing that does not visit the army. I can get Whisky enough but that is not just the thing for Sickness.

But I will draw this long letter to a close for I fear you will get tired of it before you get through reading it therefore with my love to you all I will wind up for this time.

Yours as ever
Jack

Was it not Edwin Swain that Emily used to be rather sweet upon? Keep this letter a secret from the Hampshire folks. Dont let them know I think of entering the service for another term.

A Virginia Butterfly for Lizzie.

Benny Brooks, John Chase, and Francis Conway CFC

* * * * * * * * * * *

Saturday Oct 3d [1863]

Brother Sam

According to promise I send you another picture. The Boys call it a good one of me but not so good of Conway and Brooks as the other. You will see the Corps badge on my breast. You can let Mrs Curtis have the other one and keep this yourself if you wish too. The 3d division of this Corps have gone from here and gone to Bristows Station on the Railroad between here and Alexandria and I think we shall all go back before long but I may be misstaken and hope I shall be for I never want to be any nearer Washington than we are now. Yesterday we had a hard old storm but to day it is nice and Pleasant.

Sixth Corps Cross AJB

Enough said.
Yours &C
Jack

Love to all the folks.

* * * * * * * * * * *

Camp Battery "A" Mass Vol
Near Raccoon Ford on the Rapidan
Oct 9th 1863

Dear Brother

I received two letters from you to day and was very glad to hear that you were all well and that you had a plenty of work and I hope you may a good thing out of it. We came here last Monday and I expected we should had a fight before now as the Rebels threw there shell over here the day before with a perfect looseness but as yet all remains quiet. We are Camped on what is called the Slaughter Farm and near the celebrated Slaughter Mountains where you will remember that Banks had a muss with Old Stonewall and where the Great Gen Pope commenced his movements towards Washington and which ended in his being damn well licked &C &C. But as all these events must be fresh in your memory I will not stop to rehearse them here. We are camped about two miles from the river the Infantry doing picket on the Banks. Our Pickets and the Rebels are within talking distance but they do not fire on each other but sometimes when they can catch a sight of an officer they let blim at him. It is a flat country where we are and the frost strikes down here hard and the nights and mornings are very cold but as there is plenty of rails for fuel. We make out to live and the Farm we are on abounds in squash cabbage tomatoes &C and the boys make frequent requisitions on them which makes quite an addition to our bill of fare. I dont think we shall stop here long as our Co Waggons with all superfluous baggage have been sent to Culpepper which is about six miles to the rear therefore I think we shall go out of this a flying some fine night and dont think we shall stop much this side of Fairfax County but still I may be wrong in my conjectures.

Now as regards my reenlisting I will when I get time and opportunity give you all the particulars but at present I have not time for a part of the Battery is off to the rear and the Quarter Master Seargt with it consequently I have both Rations and forage to see to besides the other duties. But then you see I am in no hurry for I have talked with what I consider a Good Man and he tells me to keep Cool. Time enough yet to Enlist therefore think I shall keep quiet at present. I received a letter from Mary to day and she is strong against it. Seems to think it rather degrading to a Man to be a Common Soldier but you know I dont see it. I think it a damn sight more degrading to stop at home and makeing a damn ass of yourself and trying to get others to go but then if God spares my life I shall have the priveledge of telling some folks what I think of them I Shall.

As to the Doctors Bill the Dr adress is this.

George W Kittredge

Newmarket N H

I have nothing to say as to what I think about the children as I am not so situated now that I can alter anything but of this I shall perhaps have more to say hereafter. As to Mr Head I am glad he had to come down with his little 300. I think it will make an impression on him but I think it a damn shame to make a difference between him and the others but this is a great Country and Nigger is King. Give my love to all the folks that want to hear from me and tell Lizzie When I get to be a Lieut I am going to write on a Sheet as big as a Newspaper.

Good Bye
Yours &C
Jack

Benny and the rest of the Boys all wish to be remembered to Sam.

Thanks for the Papers. This ring is for Sam S Chase particularly.

* * * * * * * * * *

Camp of First Mass Battery
Chantilly Virginia
Oct 17th 1863

Dear Brother

Yours of the 11th reached me last night and I was very glad to hear from old Roxbury and more. I also received three bundles of papers which I was very glad to see for I must have a little good democratic reading once in a while to keep me in humor for after reading the Washington Chronicle the Post is a god Send. I suppose the Papers have informed you that the Army has once more got in motion and what we have been doing but I will give you a report of our travels for the last week. We left the Rapidan on Saturday night the 10th and marched towards Culpeper and halted for about two hours. Starting again at Daylight marched to the Rappahanock where we crossed and halted reaching there about 4 P M. The next morning we were roused up long before daylight and remained harnessed all day starting about three P M and going back about 5 miles to Brandy Station where we expected to have a fight but the Cavalry had drove the Rebs back. Consequently we went into camp but only to be routed out again about 11 at night and take the road again toward the River which we crossed just before Day light and then Marched to near Bristows Station where we camped for the night. The next day we Marched to Centreville and camped. There had been fighting in the rear of us all day but we did not get into it. Thursday we came here as it was expected the Rebs would make an attack here but thus far all is quiet. We have earthworks thrown up the whole length of our Front and have a fine position. We are on the same field where Gen Kearney was killed last year. What this move amounts too is more than I can tell for I have not seen a paper nor heard a word about the fighting but I suppose the papers have given you all the particulars. All I know is here we are within 20 miles of Washington and where I have been expecting we should be for some time back. My health has been very poor all through this March but I am now feeling better. I have had the Piles very bad and think I never suffered as much before since I have been out here but I hope to weather it and come out bright yet. At any rate I shall try it and go in lemons— —.

I had a letter from my Mary last night. She writes that Sarah[9] has been and is very sick but hope she is out of danger and I hope the next time I hear from there she will be better. The rest of the folks were as well as common. I understand that George Head has been takeing things that belonged to other people and came near getting into trouble by the means. Perhaps you will think it strange that I hear so much about the damn skunk but I tell you I have a little bird that flies over and tells me things sometimes that I should not hear of any other way but let him go to H___ his own way for I think he will

[9] John's daughter Sarah, age 6.

get there quick enough. You must give my respects to all the folks and excuse this letter and sometime I will try and do better. Brooks French and all the Boys are Gay and Festive and the Report here now is the Rebs are in My Maryland once more. If thats so I hope we shall spend the Winter there for I think I can recover my health there.

So good Bye for this time.

Yours &C
Jack

They say we start for Maryland to night. I hope it is so I do myself I do.

* * * * * * * * * *

Warrenton Va
Oct 28th [1863]

Brother Sam

I sit down this morning just to let you know that I "still live" for I cannot get time to write a letter for we are danceing around from one place to another but what in H___ we are trying to do is more than I can tell. Yesterday I pitched my tent and took it down three times and the day before twice moveing not more than two miles both days but then you see it is enough to keep a fellow busy all the time and that has been the way ever since I wrote you last but when we get settled (if we ever do) I will Write you a good long letter. The weather here is quite cold and last night we had Ice a quarter of an inch in thickness. I had a letter from Mary Sunday and she writes me that Sarah was very low when she wrote but I suppose they will not write again under a week whether she dies or lives. My health is better than it has been but I am not feeling particularly Bully now. Give my love to all the folks and try and make this do for a letter until I get time to write a better one.

Good Bye
Yours &C
Jack

* * * * * * * * * *

Camp Battery "A" Mass Vol Artillery
Warrenton Virginia
November 2nd 1863

Dear Brother

I have just finished reading a letter from you mailed the 28th of Oct. It is the first mail we have had for two days but as they have got the Cars running here now I suppose we shall get our mail regular. That is without we move again of which there seems to be very strong talk around Camp to day but whether onward or upward is more than I can tell. It seems to me as if the two Armies here in Virginia were playing a very Big game of Tag about this time and I suppose it will be our turn to run next judging from the past. They say you know that Abraham told Gen Meade to find Lees Army and fight them when we were at Chantilly. Well I think he had no trouble in finding them but as to the other part of the job he dont seem inclined to do that. Now the question seems to be whats to be done. When little Mac disobeyed orders (<u>In a horn</u>) he was removed. Will Meade be? I reckon not. Why you know or can guess and so can I hey Sir. Rosencrans[10] I see has been shoved. That I suppose was for doing as he was told to do so whats a poor devil of a Gen going to do to please Halleck Stanton and Co.[11] I reckon its damn hard work to tell. Well this is a great country and this War is a big thing for some one particularly Contractors and Recruiting Officers. All I have to say is I hope if we dont attack Lee that he will us for then we shall have to either fight or run and either is preferable to remaining stuck in the Mud here all winter for I dont think it will hardly pay to go into Winter Quarters yet. I see by the Papers this Morning that they have commenced throwing Greek Fire[12] into Charleston again and I

---

[10] General William S. Rosecrans was relieved of his command after the Battle of Chickamauga.

[11] General Henry W. Halleck was still general-in-chief and Edwin M. Stanton was secretary of war.

[12] Incendiary cannon or mortar shells.

hope to God that Gilmore will keep it up untill he burns the whole Place up and after he gets through there I think he better come to Washington and throw a few in there just to stir them up a little. But without any joking I dont see when or where this War is going to end for it looks darker and darker to me every day and I think it about time that some one should take hold of it besides the Pack of imbeciles who are at the Head of it now. This kind of talk I know is not allowed by the Articles of War but I hope you will not enter a complaint against me to the Provost Marshall.

I got a letter from Mary to day and she writes that Sarah is better and thinks now that she will get well. She also informs me that George wants a new coat and seems to be in trouble as to how he is to get it. I told her I thought you would be willing to buy one for him and wait untill I was paid off the next time for the Pay as I intended to send you some money then. If you will do so I will be much oblidged. I dont know whether Langdon is afraid to trust me that amount or not but it looks so to me. Any way I had 20,00 I was going to send you this week but Lieut French haveing a good chance to buy him a horse and being a little short I lent it to him thinking I might want to be accomodated sometime and that they were not suffering for the money at home. I wish I could find out something how I stand with Langdon as I hear nothing. Only what Mary writes me but if the State Allowance dont take care of them I have told him several times to call upon you for all the money you might have belonging to me but somehow they either dont or will not understand it. I go in for fair and open dealings and think I should have it. There seems to me to be something behind that I am not allowed to know but I cannot help thinking I have a right too but I dont see how I can help myself as I am situated at present but any way I want the children to be Clothed and think I can afford to pay for it. At least I will try too. I hate to trouble you with so much of my own affairs but I dont seem to have any [one] else to look too as they all seem to be afraid to write to me or take much notice of me. Any way if it was not for my children they might go to Halifax the whole of them but as it is I suppose I must stand it. But I will not say any more about it at present.

I received the Papers for which you will receive my thanks. I like Sleepers Speech much and it has been read by a good many of the boys with pleasure. That ring of yours was made from wood that came from Antietam. One of the boys was going to make a pipe of it but it checked and spoilt and he gave me that peice. But I must close as the mail is about to leave. Give my love to all the folks and remember me to Emily and tell Mace to take a hot Whisky for me &C. Brooks and French are well and send there respects to Sam.

Yours as ever
Jack

* * * * * * * * * *

On Picket Near Brandy Station Va
Nov 9th [1863]

Dear Brother

As I suppose you are well aware before this we are once more on the git but this time towards Richmond instead of Washington. We left our camp at Warrenton last Saturday morning and marched towards the Rappahannock Station when within about 2 miles from the river we discovered the Rebs Pickets. Our men soon were in line of battle and we drove them to there riflepits and forts on the banks of the river and now the old 6th had a chance to show themselves once more to get them out and either drive them across or take them prisoners. The ground our boys had to cross was a level plain rising as you neared the river and the rebs held a very strong position but the boys went at them and at dark we held the forts and all the rebels on that side were prisoners. We captured 4 guns with the Cassons and took 800 Prisoners but it was not an easy victory for us for the rebs fought like devils and many a brave boy of the old Maine 5th and 6th shed there blood and left there bodies on the banks of that stream which has already cost thousands of good mens lifes to get the army across but for once we can claim a Victory bloody though it

Sleeper's Battery at Kelly's Ford, by Alfred Waud LC

be and thank God the whole of it belongs to the 6th Corps. The 3d crossed at Kellys Ford which is below. Our loss I dont know but then it is enough. I saw one trench in which were put 32 of the 5th Maine and about all of there officers were either killed or wounded. Bartletts Brigade of the First Div had the worst of it as they had to charge on the Forts.

Yesterday we crossed the river and came as far as Brandy Station which is 5 miles from the river and here we are to day in line of battle. The 6th corps on the right and the 3d on the left of the Rail Road. What we are waiting for is more than I can tell without it is for the Rebels to get well fortified on the Rapidan but then I am willing to leave it with Gen Meade for I think he knows more about it than I do and I think he rather caught Gen Lee napping this time for the Rebs were affixing up here in great shape for winter quarters and Lees Head Quarters was within a gun shot from where the Battery is in position to day and by the looks of things they left here in a hurry and I hope we shall be allowed to hurry after for I think we can whip them I do.

I have been prowling around through the huts they had got all built but could not find many relics but I found this Reb Song which I enclose with this. [No enclosure found.] The weather here is clear and cold and to day a little squally. Spitting snow some but I am in hopes that we shall not get a storm. My health is good and so is my courage and I believe the 6th Corps can lick H out all the Rebs they can bring on with a fair show.

My love to all the folks and I will try and write again as soon as possible. Good Bye for this time.

Yours as ever
Jack

* * * * * * * * * *

Camp Near Culpepper Va
[Nov. 1863]

Sam

I will write when I get time. Enclosed find a check for 40 dollars. Your last letter was received and I know you will excuse my not writing a longer letter for I have been hard at work all day and have had no supper yet and it is now after dark.

Yours &C
Jack

Every thing is lovely.

* * * * * * * * * *

Camp Battery "A" Mass Vol Arty
Near Culpeper Va
Nov 17th 1863

Dear Brother

As I have got over my hurry somewhat I concluded I would try and write you a short letter just to let you know that Jack still lives.

I suppose you have received my letter written after the Fight at the Station. Also received the check. We came to this place last Tuesday and both Men and officers have fixed themselves up quite comfortable quarters although we expect every day to move. We are camped on the Estate of John Minor Botts[13] and are about 3 1/2 miles

[13] John Minor Botts was a congressman from Virginia who had opposed secession and who was, in early 1863, imprisoned for supporting the Union.

from Culpepper and 7 miles from the River. We are on the extreme right and there seems to be nothing front of us so I suppose the Rebs are occupying there old position on the Rapidan and whether Gen Meade intends trying to drive them from it or not is the talk of the Army about now. I was in hopes that Lee would have given us battle on the ground we are now on but true to his own interest he takes to his Stronghold and you can rest assured he never will leave it without he is oblidged too for it is a perfect Gibralter and if Meade ever tries to drive him from it there will have to be a good many lifes lost but I hope something will transpire to help us and that some other movement may serve to draw him from it but I am done with hopeing anything from any other quarter for this Potomac Army always has to take care of itself and I guess always will But I have no fears but what it can do so. At any rate if we always do as well as we did at the Station I think we are all right. They have got the Cars running across the river once more and I suppose the next thing will be to March on to the Rapidan——.

I am glad you sent the Money for the Veterans coat for I guess he needed one and I want to keep the children comfortable if I can and I shall try and send all the money home I can and I always have done so for if I had had no children you can <u>just bet</u> that I should have spent rather more on my belly and back than I have done. But I have tried my best and deprived myself of things that would have added much to my own comfort knowing as I did that it must cost more to take care of them than it did when I was at home and then I thought it would be very handy to have a dollar or so after I got out of the service but I dont care for that. If the Children need it let them have it and I will try and take care of myself for it is very little money a man can save in the army. At least I have found it so. I shall continue to send my money to you as I always have done and if they want it they will have to send for it. <u>Thats so</u>. Tell Lizzie that I hardly see Richmond yet but I wish we might. We have tried for it so many times.

Remember me to all the folks and give my respects to Asher. When you write and tell him I should like some of his butter as the last I eat I paid 60 cents a pound for and I cannot afford much at that price.

This song I send you relates to the Rebel Raid on Gen Bartletts Head Quarters in which they captured the Brigade Flag. The Battery spoken of is ours of course as that is the Brigade we always have had to support us in our different fights.

Good Bye
Jack

* * * * * * * * * *

Camp Battery "A" Mass Vol Artillery
Near Culpeper Virginia
Nov 20th 1863

Brother Samuel

Nothing haveing occured since I last wrote to disturb us we still remain Here and to day we have had a reveiw of the "Sixth Corps" by Gen Sedgwick. Also several Roosian or Hessian Officer I am not certain which nor do I care for reviews are about Played Out. I have been expecting every day that we should move as we are getting rather too comfortable here to have it last but as yet we get no orders and I see the New York Herald is in a H___ of a way for fear that Meade is going to settle down in winter quarters but I reckon if the Gent what wrote that peice had been chasing rebels and haveing rebels chase him all summer he would be willing to wait for the Wagon and the Motions of Gen Meade. For my part I have no desire to settle down. Neither have I any particular desire to be one that will sacrifice themselfs in driveing Lee from his Strong Hold on the Rapidan and I hope something will turn up so that we can catch him on a more equal footing for I am one that believes that this Potomac Army can whip the rebs if they only have a fair show but to have to drive them from one fortified place to another is rather too much for Humans.

But if Meade says go in then we go in and if he says wait we wait and the Herald can Howl and be d__ned. Thats whats the matter. But as I have no news I will write you a list of wants. In the first place I want you to see that Dr bill settled if you will for I dont like to owe any thing in the shape of a Dr and I should like to have him paid between now and the First of January. 2nd I want you to send me by Mail another box of Savills Pile Ointment. Also what you pay for it as it is for another Man and he will pay me for it. 3d I want you to send me by mail two memorandums for 1864. I want them with a whole page to each day of the month. Not very particular about the style but want a good durable article. I also want you to send me the price as one of them is for the Quarter Master Seargeant. Now I will give you a list of the Battles we have been engaged in since we have been out here. The First was at West Point the second Gaines Farm Charles City Cross Roads Antietam three times across the river at Fredericksburg & Gettysburg. These are all except Mechanicsvilles where we have been actually engaged but at Malvern Hill and Rappahannock Station we were in position but did not fire a Gun but then for choice I should rather be engaged than to be waiting and looking on with Shells flying around and no chance to return the compliment. Thats all this time. Perhaps you think its enough without its better.

love to all &C
Yours as ever
Jack

* * * * * * * * * *

Camp Battery "A" Mass Vol Arty
Near Brandy Station
Culpeper Co Virginia
December 5th 1863

Dear Brother

Although I am not feeling very well either in body or mind I thought I must try and write and let you know that I was still alive and had not forgotten you. I suppose you are well aware that this Army has been on the move and been across the Rapidan. We were ordered to Start on Tuesday the 24th and at Daylight we were all pitched in and packed up ready to go and after waiting in rain untill noon orders come to unhitch and pitch our tents which order we very quick obeyed. The next day we remained in camp but Thursday we moved at Sunrise and that night the Battery crossed the river but I being stuck in the Mud with the Co Waggon did not. Consequently I spent my Thanksgiveing Evening in the Mud about half way to the river and that night I had a mince pie and some coffee for supper and remained up all night watching the waggon and you better believe I thought of those who at home were enjoying the comforts of a good house and fire saying nothing about the good things to eat. The next night I reached the river and crossed about 2 o clock in the morning and found the Battery about noon on Saturday and I was very warmly welcomed for both Men and Horses were about out of Rations. There had been Some fighting by the 3d Corps the night before and they drove the rebs with the half of one Brigade of the 6th. Saturday was spent in putting our troops into position and that day and Sunday was spent without much fighting except some skirmishing. Monday we were ordered to the extreme right of the line with three more of our Brigade of Batteries and two of the Reserve with the 5th and 6th Corps the 3d being in the Centre and the 1st and 2nd on the Left. Sedgwick had command on the right and Warren[14] on the Left. We were ordered to commence on the right at 8 o clock and as soon as the Batteries got into position they opened and you better believe the Rebs opened on us. I think I never saw so many shot strike in and around our Battery and nobody hurt and no damage done. But the music did not last long for orders came from Gen Meade to cease fireing for Warren had tried them on the left and found them too strong for him and for one I can say I was not sorry when we stopped for as soon as we ceased the rebs did the same and thus ended the fighting on our part although on the left of the line it was kept up most all day. The next day we were in position in the centre and not a gun fired all day and that night we started back

[14] General Gouverneur K. Warren.

Marching all night and all day and one of the coldest nights I ever marched in my life. Yesterday we arrived here which is near our old Camp. How long we shall stop is a matter of doubt as we are under Marching orders again to day.

Thus ended our great move and I suppose that some folks will condemn Meade because he did not charge the Rebels works But I dont although I think if we had we could took them but at a sacrifice of 15 or 20,000 men and then Lee would have fell right back to another position which those who know say is just as good and I consider this one much worse for us than even Fredericksburg heights were and you know what it cost Burnsides to try and get them. Again we were about out of Rations and the weather was extremely cold. So much so that men in the 5th Corps who were on picket and could have no fires were froze with there guns in there hands.

Therefore I pretend to Say Meade done just right and thousands of Women and Children can thank God and Gen Meade that they are not Widows and Orphans to day. But I will not say anything more about this for of course you see it all discussed in the Papers.

Yesterday we got a mail the first we have had for over a week. I received your letter with the Books and Ointment for which you will receive my thanks. I also had three letters from Mary and Langdon one of which informed me that my dear little Sarah had gone to join her Mother in another land.[15] It was hard news to me but I have long since given up the Idea that death is the worst thing to happen to mortals. But you well know what it is to lose a child you love[16] and you can judge how much worse it is to be away from them and to hear they are gone and you never to see them more. But I have no doubt but what all was done that could be to save her for I think Langdon thought just as much of her as he could if she had been his own child.

You must give my love to all the folks and excuse my writeing for it is so cold that I am all of a shake. In fact I have not been fairly

[15] John's daughter, Sarah, died November 30, 1863, at age 6.
[16] Sam and Lizzie's daughter, Elizabeth, died in 1859, at age 16.

warm except when rolled up in my blankets for a week but I will not find much fault as long as it dont rain for cold is better than Mud.

But I must bid you good Night for I am tired Sleepy and about played out. So Good Bye for this time.

Yours as ever
Jack

Please send me some Postage Stamps. I sent to Washington for some but dont see as I am likely to get them.

Brooks and French are well and wish to be remembered to Sam &C.

* * * * * * * * * *

Camp Battery "A" Mass Vol Artillery
Near Brandy Station
Culpepeper County Virginia
Dec 8th 1863

Dear Brother

As Christmas is comeing and the prospect is that active operations are over with this Army for this Winter I have concluded to send to you for a Box as there is a few things that I should like which if I can get them I think I can make out a Christmas Dinner As I have a Cook that can just get it up if he can only get the fixins And I thought if I could get them from you it would cost less than it would of our Army robbers or Sutlers. In the first place I want about 5 lbs of butter some raisins nutmegs allspice and about 6 cans of milk and I believe thats all as Flour Sugar apples meat &C we can procure here but I must have a box of yeast powders. Thats Certain.

As to any thing else you put in I shall leave it to you but you can put in some Cayenne pepper and a box of Rochelle Powders. Dont put anything in that will spoil for I may not get it right away although the Boxes are comeing through now with a Rush.

And tell Lizzie to send me two Hankerchiefs like those she sent me last Winter. The Weather here is very cold nights but pleasant day times and the boys are busy building up huts and Chimneys. My health is good and I am feeling Bully. All ready to Reenlist when they say 30 days Furlough and not before.

Direct the Box to

Lieut C W French
First Mass Battery "A"
Artillery Brigade
6th Corps

and put from S S C on one corner.

Yours as ever
Jack

PS If you put any thing strong in it put it in a can and let it be S C Rum. Please Pay for the articles and send me the bill as I think you have done enough for me already and I think I can afford to pay for them.

Have it directed in Large Letters &C.

* * * * * * * * * *

Camp Battery "A" Mass Vol Arty
Near Brandy Station Va
December 27th 1863

Dear Brother

Once more I find myself at my old business of writeing letters &C. I Arrived at Camp on the night of the 23d and I can truly say I was glad to get back for I was about caved in.[17] I found that recruiting had been going on since I had been gone and 19 of the old boys had gone in for another three years and the next day I was mustered in with them so you see I am Sold again. I expect the children will take it rather hard but I have looked the thing all over and feel satisfied that I have done right. There has about 5,000 enlisted in this Corps and uncle John is about crazy.

---

[17] John Chase had gone home on furlough to bury his daughter, Sarah.

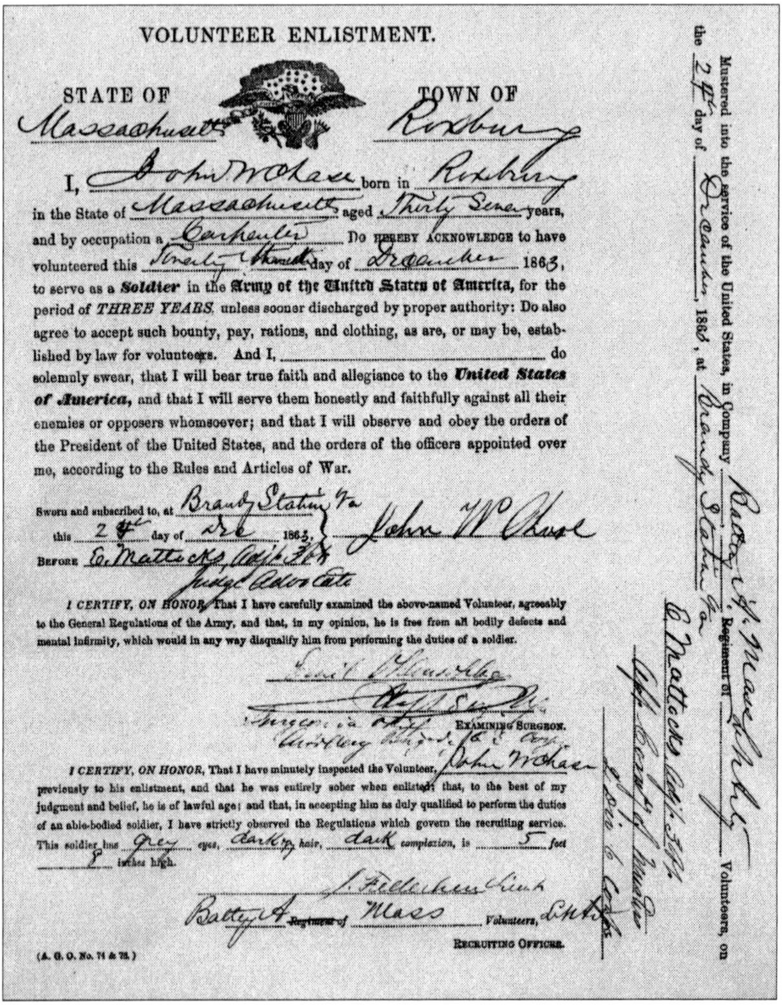

VOLUNTEER ENLISTMENT.

STATE OF Massachusetts TOWN OF Roxbury

I, John W. Chase born in Roxbury in the State of Massachusetts aged Thirty Seven years, and by occupation a Carpenter Do HEREBY ACKNOWLEDGE to have volunteered this Twenty Fourth day of December 1863, to serve as a **Soldier** in the **Army of the United States of America**, for the period of *THREE YEARS*, unless sooner discharged by proper authority: Do also agree to accept such bounty, pay, rations, and clothing, as are, or may be, established by law for volunteers. And I, ________ do solemnly swear, that I will bear true faith and allegiance to the **United States of America**, and that I will serve them honestly and faithfully against all their enemies or opposers whomsoever; and that I will observe and obey the orders of the President of the United States, and the orders of the officers appointed over me, according to the Rules and Articles of War.

Sworn and subscribed to, at Brandy Station Va this 24 day of Dec 1863, John W. Chase
BEFORE E. Mattocks Asst. Judge Advocate

I CERTIFY, ON HONOR, That I have carefully examined the above-named Volunteer, agreeably to the General Regulations of the Army, and that, in my opinion, he is free from all bodily defects and mental infirmity, which would in any way disqualify him from performing the duties of a soldier.

EXAMINING SURGEON.

I CERTIFY, ON HONOR, That I have minutely inspected the Volunteer, John W. Chase previously to his enlistment, and that he was entirely sober when enlisted; that, to the best of my judgment and belief, he is of lawful age; and that, in accepting him as duly qualified to perform the duties of an able-bodied soldier, I have strictly observed the Regulations which govern the recruiting service. This soldier has grey eyes, dark hair, dark complexion, is 5 feet 8 inches high.

J. Fillebrown Lieut
Batty A Mass Volunteers,
RECRUITING OFFICER.

(A. G. O. No. 74 & 75.)

Mustered into the service of the United States, in Company Batty A, Mass. Lt. Arty Regiment of ____ Volunteers, on the 24th day of December, 1863, at Brandy Station Va
E. Mattocks Asst. Judge Advocate

John Chase's Reenlistment Form, December 23, 1863 NA

I want you to see what course I have got to take to get my State Bounty. The other Boys have all gone home on a 35 days Furlough but I thought it was best for me to wait a little while before takeing mine. In regard to the State Bounty give me your opinion as to which is the best way for me to take it for I should like a little advice on the subject. I had a good time comeing back. I took the moon train from New York and that gave me 6 hours in Philadelphia and I had a first rate time and I Say Bully for Philadelphia. It is almost equal to Maryland for good things. I expect French will start for home in a few days and if he does I shall send some money to you by him and I guess If I have my health that I shall be able to keep the Children from the Poor House the next three years. I wish you would put that Lamp in a small box and send it to me. Also let me know the cost of doing it as Russell intends to pay the bill. I want you if you have not done so before you get this to write and let me know how Asher is and I hope he is better before this. Remember me to Mr Fergurson and all the rest of the Folks that wish to hear from me and tell them the Veteran is OK and had just as Merry a Christmas as the next Man. Plenty to eat and drink both. Tell Lizzie the Cake and Cranberry sauce paid well for takeing along but it was a hard job to lug the bag to camp.

Yours as ever
Jack

Remember me to Emily and that little critter that was with her that evening.

* * * * * * * * * *

Camp Battery "A" Mass Vol Arty
Near Brandy Station Virginia
Feb 14th 186[4]

Dear Brother

After much delay &C I found myself in the old camp Saturday night about dark and think if ever I was glad to get to any place it was this for after leaving New York it was nothing but stop and wait untill I began to think we never should get here but we did![18] There was 10 of us came from Washington together and when we got here found all the Veterans had arrived but some of them were 10 days behind but there was nothing said. Some of the boys are a little home sick but are working it off by degrees and probably in a few days will feel at home once more. They have been fixing up the camp in great shape since I went away and I hardly knew the place and now they are building a log house for the officers. Yesterday we were out

Winter Quarters Headquarters at Brandy Station LC

for a Review and to day have been out on Inspection and drill. 22 of our recruits have arrived and take them together I think they are a good lot but there is a few of them that I think are beats on the Goverment. All is quiet here at present and we hear nothing about

[18] John Chase had gone home again on furlough as a bonus for reenlisting.

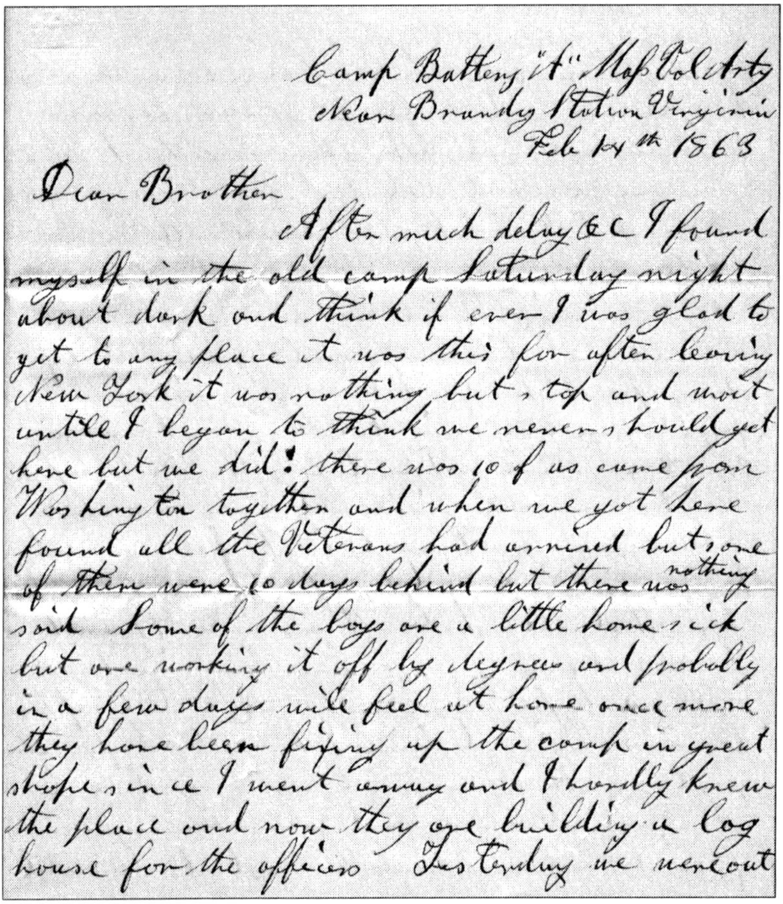

Camp Battery "A" Mass Vol Arty
Near Brandy Station Virginia
Feb 14th 1863

Dear Brother

After much delay &c I found myself in the old camp Saturday night about dark and think if ever I was glad to get to any place it was this for after leaving New York it was nothing but stop and wait untill I began to think we never should get here but we did! there was 10 of us came from Washington together and when we got here found all the Veterans had arrived but one of them were 10 days behind but there was nothing said Some of the boys are a little home sick but are working it off by degrees and probably in a few days will feel at home once more they have been fixing up the camp in great shape since I went away and I hardly knew the place and now they are building a log house for the officers Yesterday we were out

Letter of February 14, 186[4] CFC

this Corps moveing but would not be surprised if we did before long for I hardly believe there will be much more fighting in Virginia but then you know we cant always tell. The box with the lamp & Matches came all right and it works to a charm. Tell Lizzie that I went to Barnums[19] when I was in York and I perfectly agree with her

[19] P. T. Barnum's Museum of sensational exhibits.

that the whole thing is a Humbug. I dont know of any news to write. I am well. As happy as can be expected after leaving the good times I have had for the past month. You must give my love to Mr and Mrs Joe and all other inquireing friends and as Elizabeth said she would not do so to Emily I suppose she will have to go without it but I hope the dear critter will find a Man soon for I think if she dont she will be insane if she is not so already. Sometime when you are in Boston I want you to go into Hamiltons and have me a dozen more pictures taken as the Boys want them Bad.

Write as soon as you get this and let me know if you have heard from Asher and all the rest of the news.

So hopeing this will find you all well.

I remain yours as ever
Jack the Vet

* * * * * * * * * *

[Brandy Station Va]
Sunday Feb 28th 1864

Dear Brother

Yours of the 23d I received last Friday and I was much pleased to hear from the old Bay State once more. I was glad to hear such good accounts from Asher and I hope they will have a good time down in the Southern Department and that he may live to come back to you and relate his experience in the Army of Abraham. The first Mass Bat has gone off some where leaving Chase in charge of the Camp with about 15 Sick men and the like number of horses. I am very comfortably situated in the officers quarters and all I am praying for is that this Army will not move in a body for its too much like work for all the camp and garrison equipage is left behind. There is three Batteries gone from this Brigade and one Division of Infantry. What is up is more than I can tell But the whole Army is under marching orders. The Weather is fine and the roads in good condition and if it is On to Richmond I hope that it may prove a success I do. I expect you had a great time there the 22nd. They had a Ball here in the 2nd

Corps but in the 6th there was not so much as a Gun fired and the day passed off without any demonstration at all. I want you to tell Lizzie that I did not call to see Ben but I have heard from him and I guess that he is done for in this world.[20] All that kept me from seeing him was Women and that was always a Dead Beat on me and I expect will be as long as I have the use of my limbs but still I am willing to bet a trifle that Emily cannot Beat me much for I Dont See It for she is not my Style not much. As to that picture if she thinks she is any ahead for Godsake let her think so for where "Ignorance is bliss its folly to be wise" and its no use to take any comfort from the poor critter if she can take any. I think it a pity the poor gal cannot find some Young Man to help her out of her trouble for I dont feel myself equal to the task for I have lived on Hard Tack too long——. You say Levi has come to enlist and wants to go in a Battery. If he had told me so I would got him in here but I suppose there is a chance now in Capt Wrights 14th Battery and if he wants to try a Soldiers life there is plenty of room. But I think he is a damn Fool and I guess he will after a while. Give my love to all who take pains to enquire for and tell Mrs Joe that I pity her muchly but think I can beat her at a small game of all fours. I will write again in a few days if nothing happens and let you know what is going on. Remember me to Mr and Mrs Fergurson and Emily. In a hurry.

Yours as ever
Jack

* * * * * * * * * * *

Camp First Mass Battery
Brandy Station Va
March 4th 64

Dear Brother

Yours of the 29th of Feb reached me last night and I thought I would sit down this evening and write you a short epistle and let you

[20] Ben Winslow died of chronic diarrhea and consumption on April 4, 1864.

know that the Battery still lives. They got back to camp Thursday night after an absence of 5 days. What they accomplished is more than I know but I suppose that time will tell. They were not engaged at all but the last two days they had it rather rough for we had a storm of rain & Snow but the boys say they had a good time as there was plenty of wood and yaller gals— —. All is quiet here now and tomorrow we shall try and do a little painting and I suppose by the time we get fairly at work that they will get up another tramp for it does seem as if this Battery always had to go on all such scrapes but so much for haveing a Reputation. As to the Morgans[21] I have not met with any lodge here. There is one however in the 2nd Corps but none in this that I know of but I have met with some Morgans.

I would like to know what gave rise to the story about my being married. They had the same story here while I was at home but if I was married it must have been while I was asleep or else drunk as I have no knowledge of it and I would like to know where Lizzie got her information. I would like to know what possessed Levi to enlist[22] and what Father is going to do. I hope it may be a good thing for him but as old Jim Winkly used to say I cant See into it I cant myself. I have not heard anything from Mary this week but the last time I heard from her she thought she was better.

I expected to have some money to send you this week but Lieut Federhen wanted it and I let him keep it but if Ben wants his pay take some of the other for I dont want him to wait for it and I think we shall get paid again before long but of course that is very uncertain.

About those cards I never have had them marked yet as my friend has been off on detached duty but he says I shall have them soon if he can get time to mark them.

You ask Lizzie to look in Harpers for March and see if in that picture when Lily is handing the inkstand to Bell and see if Bell dont look like Emily somehow. I thought so but perhaps it was because I

[21] Morgans is a facetious reference to Masons, because Morgans were actually members of an anti-Masonic movement.

[22] John Chase's brother, Levi, enlisted in the Sixteenth Massachusetts Light Artillery on February 29, 1864.

was thinking so much of her &C. I am invited out to night to Brigade Head Quarters as a friend of mine leaves there tomorrow to take a Commission in a Nigger Regt and he gives an Oyster supper to night and as it is now eight o clock I think I must start. You must give my respects to all inquireing friends. Tell them Jack is hearty and ready for another campaign and thinks he is good for it. Remember me to Asher when you write him and thus I remain yours &C.

Jack

How could Levi enlist from Roxbury?

[Enclosed is a note on fine white stationery with spidery writing:]

West Andover, Jany 31st /64

Mr. Carroll Sir

In glancing over the captions of "special notices" in the Waverly my eye fell on your invitation. If your motive be honest please address,

Miss Louise Carpenter
West Andover
Ashtabula County
Ohio

[A penciled note at the bottom by John Chase reads, "Very pretty writeing dont you think so?"]

* * * * * * * * * * *

Camp Battery "A" Mass Vol Arty
Brandy Station Virginia
March 12th 1864

Dear Brother

Yours of the 6th I received and was very glad to hear from you and to know that you were all well. I wish I could say the same of myself but cannot for I have been quite unwell this past week. I have had a bad pain in my side and sharp pains in my breast and every thing I eat distressed me very much but as yet I have kept on duty and have not been to the Dr but think I shall soon if I dont get better. And with my own troubles I have bad news from Stratham as my Mary is down sick again and under the Doctors care and some how I fear she never will be well again but hope I may be mistaken. I have written to Langdon to not let her want for anything and if he wants money to send for it. I was in hopes she would get well again for she seemed to be gaining when I was at home and was quite smart after I came back but I suppose I must leave it in the hands of God and hope for the best. There is nothing new with us here. The same old rumor is going around (that is) the 6th Corps is going off somewhere and I hope it may prove true for I think most any kind of a change will be for the better. Gen Grant[23] is here with Gen Meade but I have not seen the Hero yet but hope I shall get a sight at him before he leaves. I see by the papers that Gen Meade is to be Court Martialed on account of the Gettysburg affair. I think it would have been about as well to have done it before now if he deserved it but I suppose there is someone anxious to take this Army therefore they must get rid of Meade somehow. Well let them go it. Its a long lane that has no turn and I believe that some of our Generals will come out right in the end. Tell Lizzie that I dont think it was Women altogether that kept me from going to see Winslow but I am willing to confess that had something to do with it but then you know it is hard resisting the Dear Creatures after being away from them two years. It takes a Man a little while to get rid of his tender feelings.

General Ulysses S. Grant LC

[23] General Grant was named general-in-chief of the army in March 1864, replacing General Halleck, who was made chief of staff.

Thats so. But I dont believe she would pull my ears very hard if she knew all that I know but I have no time to explain now. I think I showed considerable Moral Courage in resisting one angelic creature and think that should go to extenuate my fault in a measure.

You must remember me to all the folks. Tell them I hope to see this thing through but you cant always tell.

Give my Love to Mrs and Mr Joe and all that wish to hear from me. Has Joe got over his Exeter fever yet? I see by the papers that the country is safe as far as New Hampshire Election goes. But I will close now hopeing this will find you all well.

Yours as ever
Jack

How do you get along with the house? Most ready for the Exeter folks to come down and have a House Warming? The first of April draws near very.

Send me some stamps if you please.

* * * * * * * * * *

Camp Battery "A" Mass Vol Artillery
Brandy Station Virginia
March 24th 1864

Dear Brother

I have not written you lately for several reasons. One was I have been rather unwell and another because I did not feel sprawl enough to write But thought to night I would try and pluck up courage and go in Lemons. Yours of the 20th I received yesterday with the stamps and Photographs all right. I dont care about any more of them at present. When I do I will let you know. I have had a letter from Mary and she is better and I hope she may continue to grow better now warm weather is comeing on. She is very anxious to go off somewhere to school and I have given my consent but she has not made choice of any particular school as yet but is going to write me when she does. I have also had a letter from Pricilla with the latest news from Stratham and full particulars of Levi,s enlisting and I think she bears it like a Christian and I hope that Levi will try and behave himself now and I think if he does all will go well with him for as far as money goes his family will be better off and if he lives through it he will have a chance to learn some things that may be of some benefit to him.

We were expecting to have a Grand Review here this week but we have had a severe Snow Storm and yesterday morning there was about a foot of Snow on the Ground but it is most all gone now. The 6th Corps were makeing great preparations for it and every man was to appear on Parade with white gloves on but I dont know whether we shall have one now or not. Gen useless Grant came to the Front to day and I suppose now he will run this Machine a Spell. Long enough probably to kill him off out of the way. But I hope he may succeed and show himself what the papers try to make him out to be the greatest Gen in the Country. <u>I dont see it</u> <u>I dont</u>. But I am willing to let him try Gen Lee and if he dont find him a tough Cuss I am mistaken. Speaking of Little Mac,s Report we have it here and lots of Copies of his life and we find them very interesting for a good many of the scenes we figured in slightly and think we know something about them. <u>We Do</u>.

I want you to send me out a box of pills. Something that is good for Indigestion for I am troubled a good deal as Ward Mason,s Wife used to be when she was first married. I cant keep my breakfast down and I begin to think that I must have been married when I was there and not been sensible of the fact. At any rate I feel like a new married does some times. We have been expecting our Pay Master here but have got word that he is sick and if some other one dont pay us I suppose we shall have to wait a while longer. The other troops are all being paid in this Corps but this Artillery Brigade.

Two peices of this Battery with two from three other Batteries was out to fire at target last Monday and Mac made the two best shots that were fired but there was no Tampion[24] in the Gun. Elijah

[24] A tampion was a muzzle plug to keep out rain, etc.

Wood was down to see me and I think he never looked half as well before in his life and I think it has made a decided improvement in his looks going for a Soldier.

Lieut Federhen of this Battery tried to get the command of the one that Levi,s in but John A couldn,t see it but Fed was well reccomend but I suppose his heel wont [be] long enough quite.

I would like to have been down to Mr Hick,s with you for I think Mrs H and myself could beat any other two Playing and think I could done a little justice to the cheese and other fixins. I am glad to hear that Joes fever has abated for I think he is better off where he is.

Give my respects to all inquireing friends and dont forget the Pills. Remember me to Asher when you write and to Levi when you see him. Not knowing what else to write I will hold up for this time.

Yours as ever
Jack

PS I wonder if I cant get an invitation to that House Warming.

This picture is Seargt Frank Longleys. He is on old Ben Winslow a horse I used to ride. [No enclosure found.]

* * * * * * * * * *

Camp Battery "A" Mass Vol Artillery
Near Brandy Station Va
March 31st 1864

Dear Brother

Yours of the 28th came to hand to night and also the pills but as I am feeling to night I shall not take any for I have felt better to day than I have before for some time. I have been expecting to get paid but think our Paymaster has gone back on us as he dont seem to make his appearance. I thought when we got paid I would send for a box but have made up my mind to send for it before and will tell you what I want Which is 2 lb tobacco for I have not had a decent chaw for a week as mine that I brought with me has all disappeared. A few raisins a peice of cheese and some nutmegs and I want you to get a couple of cans that will hold about 2 qts apeice and fill one with Santa Cruz Rum and the other with Medford. The Medford is for a friend of mine that cannot drink anything strong. If you can start a box to me by next Wednsdy I shall get it the next week Thursday as all the boxes for this Corps come up to the Station Thursdays and the 6th Corps is the only one that Boxes come into without being opened. Uncle John [Sedgwick] wont have them opened after they get here no how and it makes the boys in the other Corps rather think that he is about the Man and so say we all of us. Direct the box just the same as you do my letters and I think there will be no trouble about my getting it. I had a call to day from a Man who is going to Reenlist himself with about ten others. He called to ask me what quota he better go on and I told him Rox and if they go there I shall give him a letter to you so that he can get his Bounty. Tell Berry that the Boy he enlisted for bugler is getting along first rate and he appears like a fine little fellow. He is as neat as a pin and I think will make a good Soldier. I am glad to hear that Asher is in such good spirits and hope he will get through safe and sound. I have no news to write. They seem to be busy here getting the Army in order and have made quite a change in the different Corps but I suppose you see all that in the papers. Gen Grant is here but I have [not] Seen him yet but expect shall soon for we are to have an Army Review if it only holds fair long enough. Benny Brooks got hurt to day quite bad by a horse running against him and knocking him down but he is more comfortable to night. He and French send there best respects to you &C.

Remember me to all who inquire for me and tell them I am all right I think. Tell Mr Hicks I shall call when I come that way sure. But it is Bed time and I must close so with love to you all I remain

Yours &C
Jack

* * * * * * * * * *

Camp Battery A Mass Vol
Near Brandy Station Va
April 7th 64

Dear Brother

I received your letter Wednesday night and it found me sick abed and I have done no duty since but have taken about half a box of pills and think I shall be better or worse soon. I went over to see the Dr this morning and he thinks he can help me. I dont know what the devil has got into but begin to think I must be in Love. It is either that or Dyspepsia I aint certain which. As to liveing on light food I have been liveing on bread and oysters but as the Pay Master dont see fit to call around I have given up the oysters for my funds are getting low but not quite broke yet and dont want to be.

A Sutler's "Fruit & Oyster House" LC

Speaking of storms we have had some here. Hardly a fair day lately and now the Mountains are covered with snow and things dont look much like a Forward Movement. Ned Head was down to see me Sunday. He is in the 16th Regt. Been out here about six weeks and likes very well considering. Very glad to hear of Lieut Williams good fortune and the Gen Arnold[25] he is with use to be our chief of Artillery and a bully old brick he is. We always called him Dick and he was not afraid to speak to a private or to hear there story if any thing was wrong but he was some on his rum I tell you but he was much liked here but was only Captain then in the Regular Army. There is quite a change going here with the different commands. We lose our Quarter Master tomorrow and have one from the third Corps for which I am very sorry for we have a tip top officer and I dont believe we shall make anything by the change. The Boys went over and seranaded him the other night and he put them through Big and I am afraid they were not all perfectly sober when they came back. He thinks a good deal of our boys and says Battery "A" can get up anything even to a Glee Club.

I hope you may succeed and get Asher promoted but then it seems to be the policy of John A to give all the Infantry the first chance. At least it looks like it I think. I have not much news to write for there is none here of any importance that I hear of. I will let you know when the Box gets along and shall look for it next week.

I would like to have you send Mary that money if it is convenient for I know she wants and should have sent it myself if we had been paid. Remember me to all the folks and I hope that the next time I write I shall feel better than I do at present. Brooks and French wish to be remembered to you and Ben is getting along finely.

So good Night.

Yours as ever
Jack

[Enclosed is a clipping titled "Gen. Hooker and the Cavalry" that says that the efficiency of the federal cavalry dates from the speech in which he says he has never seen or heard of a dead cavalry man.]

* * * * * * * * * *

[25] General Richard Arnold had been chief of artillery for General Franklin's division in the spring of 1862.

Camp Battery A Mass Vol Art
Near Brandy Station Va
Apr 16th 64

Dear Brother

I have been waiting all the week to get a letter from you but as none has made its appearance I concluded to write a few lines to and let you know that I have got my box. Got it Thursday and found it all right Rum and all and I want you to send me a bill of the Rum as there is several interested in it and are very anxious to pay there part of the Cost and I have no objections to there doing so.

We were to have a Corps Review to day but instead of that we are haveing a beautiful Rain Storm so I suppose the Army will not move just yet. All the Sutlers and camp followers have gone and left us. They took there departure this morning. They have had a good harvest this last winter and can afford to lie still for a spell.

We were paid off this week and you will find enclosed a Check for $45,00. We did not get our $50,00 Bounty that we should have had but we have got a new Pay Master a New Hampshire man and a d____d fool. He makes more trouble about the Rolls than his neck is worth and I would,nt give old Major Jones for a Army like him but then I suppose we shall get it next time.

My health is much better and I think the Fluid helped me muchly I do. I have no news to write therefore I will hold up.

Give my love to all the folks that want to hear from me and

I remain yours
Jack

* * * * * * * * * * *

Camp Battery A Mass Vol Artillery
Near Brandy Station Va
April 23d 1864

Dear Brother

Yours of the 17th I received in due course of mail and I was very glad to hear once more from the old Bay State. I did not think you had forgotten me for I had three letters delayed a few days and I concluded yours was in the same fix For I have got so that I expect a letter every week and dont feel satisfied without I do get one. My health is I believe now fully restored. I have been troubled with a sore throat but have got rid of it and at present feel first rate and eat half a mince pie for supper besides other articles too numerous to mention.

It is rumored here that we move the first of next week but then you cant always tell. We have turned in our wall tent and I have got to come down to a Shelter tent this summer but think I can stand it. There has been a great time sending stuff to Alexandria this last week and things look as if we should move soon. The roads are in good shape now and we have had four fine days right off and that is something to speak of these times. Well I am all ready. Got my knapsack all packed and a stock of tobacco on hand and I hope when Grant does move it will be to some effect and I think if he does half what the papers say he is going to that there will be H___ to pay somewhere. We have had a Horse race to day for $50,00 a side. Lieut French and the captains horses run and French got beat. We have quite a number of races here this spring and I begin to think that the Army is more for sporting than fighting but rather think we shall get enough of the latter article before we get to Richmond. I want you to tell Mrs Wiggins I am much oblidged to her for her good intentions as regards the smoked beef and give her my thanks for the doughnuts &C and tell her that doughnuts with good St Croix to wash them down is big feed for a Soger. Thats so. I meant to have told you to put some salt fish in that box but I suppose did not as there was none in it. The Sutlers kept it to sell this last winter but now we have none with us but I have the promise of some from Washington by a man that furnishes our officers mess. Benny Brooks is well and thinks he would like to drink your health often if he could get the right kind of Stuff to do so with. I received a letter from Pricilla this week. She informed me she had the whole family with her and I have an Idea there has been some talking done the past fortnight. Happy to hear of Ashers good luck and ask him when you write if it is the Gen Grover[26] that used to be in this Army for I would like to know. He used to command the brigade that the first Mass was in. Give my love to all the folks and I will try and keep you posted if we move if I have my health and dont get hurt.

So good bye for this time and I remain

Yours
Jack

I suppose you have received the recept I sent you.

* * * * * * * * * *

[26] General Curvier Grover.

John Chase's Travel Routes in Chapter 7: May 1864 to July 1864

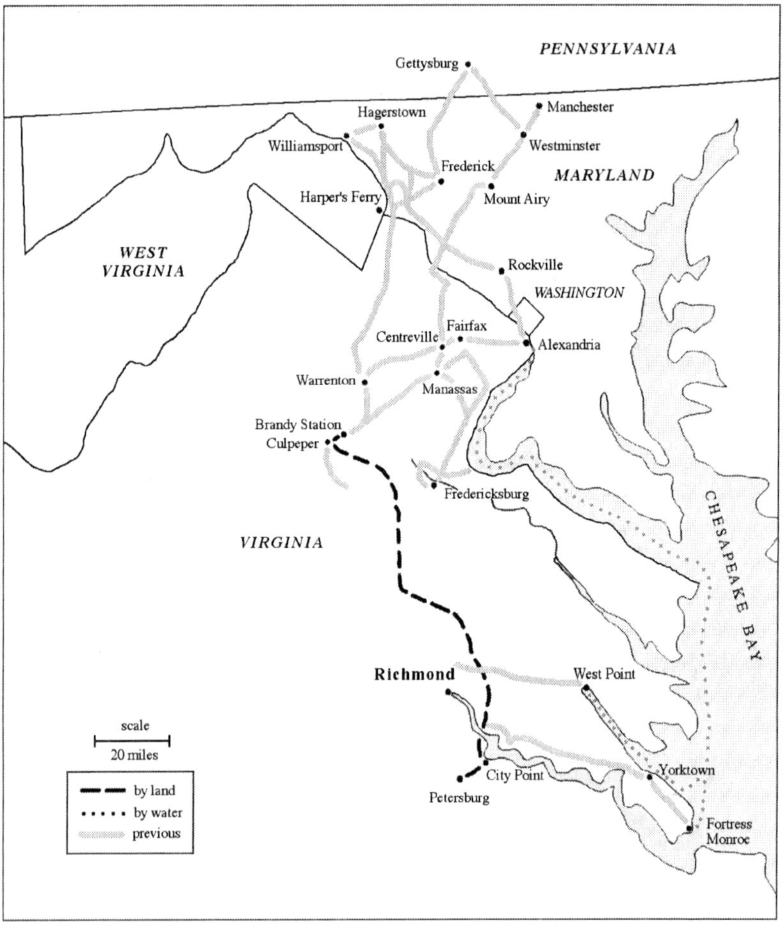

JSC/BBC

CHAPTER 7

The Overland Campaign

Spring of 1864, with General Ulysses S. Grant now in overall command of the Union army, brings the beginning of the Overland Campaign, a war of attrition against General Lee's smaller army. Chase describes the losses after the Battle of Spotsylvania Court House, and is slightly wounded at Cold Harbor.

Camp Battery A Mass Vol Arty
Near Brandy Station Va
May 3d 1864

Dear Brother

I received your letter of the 24th of April but have delayed answering for I have been pretty busy as we have been turning in Camp and Garrison property &C and reduceing baggage generally prepareing for the comeing campaign but we have finally got rid of all extras and are now down to fighting regulations. I expect we shall start to night or tomorrow but every thing is kept very quiet and no one seems to have any Idea of what is going on but all seem to think that Grant is going to make one grand effort. He has a large force gathered here of at least 125,000 our Corps numbering 30,000 and is the smallest of the three Potomac Army Corps and then Burnsides is here with I dont know how many but I know he has 9 Batteries for Capt Wright who commands the 14th Mass Battery was here Sunday and he told me that much but said he did not know how much Infantry and cavalry there was. The newspapers seem to talk as if

Lee would fall back on Richmond as soon as we advance but I dont see it and if we dont have the biggest fight before we get many miles across the Rapidan river then set me down for a false prophet thats all. It is reported here that Lee has 80,000 men 22,000 Cavalry and if thats so he will make a desperate fight. I have made up my mind to see the biggest fight of the War in the comeing campaign and I hope we may whip them but I have left off counting chickens before they are hatched and dont mean to brag untill I see something to crow for I think the Rebs are haveing things pretty much as they want them so far this spring for as to our victory on the Red River I dont see it and think Gen Banks better Resign I do but I suppose its all right for Banks but how would it have been if Franklin Porter or some of that school of Generals had been in command. I reckon you would heard some howling from the Nigger Worshipers. We have lost one man by disease lately and have two more in the hospital now and last week John Moyers little Brother died. He was Captain Mac,s Boy. Had been out here about three months.

We Contributed $115,00 in the Co and sent the body home which cost us 45,00 and sent the rest to his Mother. He was a first rate smart little fellow and everybody liked him. He died very sudden only being sick 4 days. I suppose Ashers Battery was not in that fight at Red River as I could see no account of it in the papers. Our Clerk had a brother in the Mass Cavalry and he was wounded in the shoulder. I have not heard anything from Levi but Capt Wright told me his Battery was at Camp Barry but had no guns or horses so I guess he will have to stay there a spell. I suppose Pricilla is down to Lynn enjoying a Ration of talk with the natives. What a quiet time it must be there with all the Boys. You can tell Mrs Joe those dough nuts were tip top and I am much oblidged to her for the same. I have been liveing on Ham and greens lately. There is any quantity of dandelions here and I bought a couple of Hams and are liveing high but get a very short ration of Whisky for our new Commissary is a Temperance man and says if he could do as he would like he would not have any at all and for my part I wish he could have his way for I dont think it is any great benefit to the army myself. I like the new

Commissary very much for he supplys us liberally with vegetables which he thinks is much better than Busthead.

You must give my love to all who inquire for me and If I dont get knocked out of time and they dont stop the mails you will hear from again soon.

Tell Lizzie I think I am getting over my love sickness. I think Greens helped me But I think you might just let a fellow know how Emily is getting along and whether she has Seduced Enos yet.

But good bye.

Yours Bully
Jack

Enclosed you will find $5,00. I had no particular use for it and thought if I should get popped over somebody else might get it and I have enough left to keep me in money untill next pay day.

* * * * * * * * * * *

Artillery by the Rapidan, by Alfred Waud LC

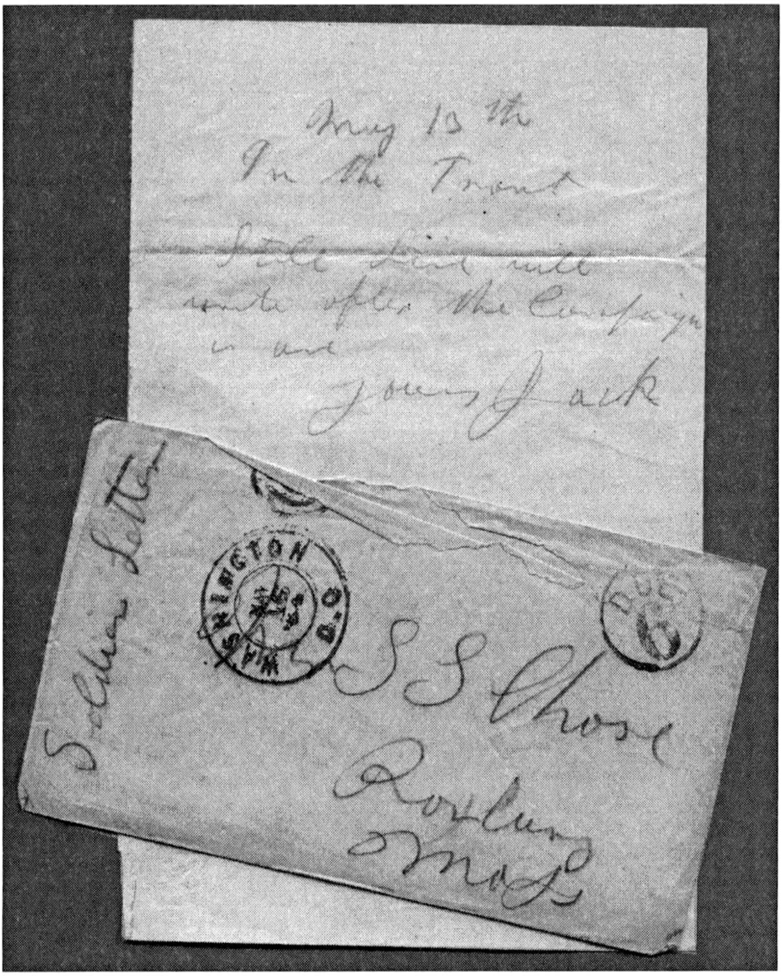

Letter of May 13, 1864 (Battle of Spotsylvania Court House) CFC

May 13th [1864]
In the Front

Still Live. Will write after the Campaign is over.

Yours
Jack

* * * * * * * * * * *

In the field Near
Spottsylvania Court House
May 20th 64

Dear Brother

The first mail since we left camp arrived this morning and haveing a few leisure moments I thought I would write you a few lines and let you know I Still Live. The papers we received by the mail seem to think that we are giveing Lee H___ but I am not able to say whether such is the case or not. All I have to say is there has been some hard fighting and we expect more before the Campaign is over. It is hard telling sometimes whether we are advancing or retreating but I think thus far we have rather got the best of them. We have been backing and filling for the last week. Sometimes we are on the right and then on the left and the boys begin to think it is a damn poor thing for a Battery to have a good name but they hang out well. We have plenty of Rations but our horses have been on half rations for the past week and it rather tells on them. All of Meads Batteries have turned in 2 Guns and are now four gun Batteries keeping the 6 Cassons. This is on account of want of horses and forage. We have lost a good many horses thus far our own Battery haveing lost 10 killed. The Rebel Sharp Shooters have troubled us a good deal. It was them that killed uncle John[1] and wounded Lieut Federhen. The Gen was Standing near our Battery when he was struck and I saw him when he was carried off the field but they would not tell us he was dead

General John Sedgwick AJB

[1] General John Sedgwick, commander of Sixth Corps.

and tried to keep it from the troops. Gen Morris was wounded the same day and near the same spot. Also one of our Seargt. It was as much as a mans life was worth to show his head. We have lost heavy in officers so far. This Corps has lost its head and a good part of its tail. Gen Wright was slightly wounded but still keeps the field. Gens Seymour Shaler Morris Upton and Sedgwick[2] have been taken from us besides others who I can not think of now. Our Battery has been very lucky thus far but God only knows how soon we may catch it for it is fight now every day and some times a good part of the night. After the campaign is over I will try and give you the particulars of the different days fighting but have not time at present. Neither am I going to say whether we have whipped Lee or not for I think that remains to be proved. All I can say is I hope we shall get Richmond this time but I tell you it is a damn hard road to travel and we are paveing our way with good men. There has lots of Heavy Artillery arrived here the last few days and they seem to be pushing all and everything to the front and I cannot help thinking that if Gen McClellan had been reinforced as Grant has been that we should have been in Richmond two years ago but however I am glad that Abe has learnt wisdom at last. Gens Grant and Meade have been busy. I have seen them most every day and I am one of the kind that believes as much praise is due Meade as there is to Grant but damn the Odds if we only succeed. Capt Martin did not lose any of his own guns. It was a New York Battery but Gen Griffin[3] took all the blame for he shoved it down on to the Skirmish line and the rebs killed all there horses and the guns remained there for two days and neither party could get them but when they drove our right wing in they took them off. There has been no fighting to day up to this 12 noon but the Battery is in position and I am some 2 miles from them with the waggons but expect orders every moment to go and join them.

You must give my love to all the folks and remember me to Emily.

---

[2] Generals Truman Seymour, Alexander Shaler, William Morris, Emory Upton, and John Sedgwick.

[3] General Simon G. Griffin.

This picture is of Lieut French and his Dog and I want you to send it to Mary when you get a chance. [No enclosure found.] I tried to beg another one but he could not spare it. If Lieut Federhen comes to Boston Call and See him for me. I will Send you word where he lives as Soon as I can hear from him.

I got three letters from you in the mail for which you will please receive my thanks.

So Good Bye for this time.

Yours
Jack

A ration of Whisky to be served out to night.

Will write again Soon.

* * * * * * * * * *

In the field
Near Mechanicsville Va
May 31st 1864

Dear Brother

We received a mail last night but I got no letter from you but thought as there was a chance to send a letter to night I would try and write a few lines and let you know that Jack still lives. We are somewheres near Mechanicsville and about 14 miles from Richmond and our Corps the Infantry part of it is banging away like good ones in front of us but for a wonder the First Mass is lieing back in the shade but I expect every moment when we shall be ordered out. We can hear the rebs howling like devils and now and then a round shot comes whistling through the woods where we are but dont reach us. We cannot see anything for there is a thick woods between us and our line of battle. I expect they will get up quite a warm time here before night as it keeps getting hotter and it is now only 12 noon. The report is that Lee has concentrated his forces here and in the neighborhood of Gaines Farm and if such is the case we may have a chance to try our luck on the battlefield which proved so disastrous to us in 62. So you see that after all the talk about the Rapidan route we have finally got back on to McClellans old ground but I have nothing to say and think Comment is needless. I never did believe we should go to Richmond by the Rapidan road after we tried it last winter and think I told you so when I was at home last winter. I dont know as we shall this way but I am satisfied that if we dont go this way we shall never go there. The report here is that Butler[4] has been whipped down to Petersburg but as we dont get the papers [all] we have to go by is Stories. I hope it is not so bad as represented but think if it is so he better take his force and come up here and I think Grant and Meade will give them a chance to win glory for themselves. This is a rich county we are now going through. There is plenty of chickens meal and flour and the article of salt of which the papers have so much chat about seems to be very plenty for we find any amount of it in the houses as we pass along. There is plenty of corn. We went to a barn night before last and took 20 bushels and there was more than 1000 left. It worked in very handy for us for our horses have been liveing on half rations the past fortnight and the corn was a perfect God send. I have enjoyed my chicken soup most every day for the last week and if Grant would only allow me a regular ration sleep I would be all right but he keeps us hopping right and when we aint fighting we are marching. I never knew so much night fighting as there has been in this campaign for when the rebs dont go at us we open on them and so you see sleep is a luxury about this time. No further disasters since I last wrote. Only the loss of several horses and I losing my corkscrew with a small amount of silver change amounting to the sum of 63 cents.

Give my love to all and write when you can.

Yours as ever
Jack

* * * * * * * * * * *

[4] General Benjamin F. Butler's Army of the James failed to cut off Richmond from Petersburg.

At the Front Near
Coal Harbor Va
June 4th 64

Dear Brother

We received a mail to night and with my batch I received a letter from you and although it is now near ten o clock I thought I would try and write a few lines and let you know that Jack Still lives and Grant is still after Lees army. We have been banging away here now 4 days and have been engaged every day and I might add nights for Lee is H___ on night attacks but thus far he has failed of makeing a point and on the whole I rather think he loses by the operation.

Since we have been engaged here my horse has been shot under me and a peice of shell struck me in the side of the neck but thank God it only made it stiff for a while and thus far I am all right but God only knows how soon my turn may come for a mans life is worth but little here although our Battery as usual we have had but few casualities. One man badly wounded in the arm and 4 very slightly. To give you some Idea of things I will relate this evenings experience. We had a bit of a picnic in front of us just after dark but things got quiet and we unharnessed and I went over to see Frank Henry who is with Gen Marston about a mile to our right. I had been there about 20 minutes when the rebs attacked our line in front of them and as the Gen is one of the kind that keeps his Head Quarters to the front the bullets began to come in Splendid with now and then a Shell and I thought best to leave for the Battery not careing to be shot quite so far away from the Battery as no one knew I was away. This is about the way it has been for the past month and it may be very pleasant to some folks but I cannot say I admire it much. But I must draw to a close for I have to turn out at 2 o clock in the morning if the Johnnys will let us alone to that time and I dont know as you can read what I have wrote as I have to use my knee for a writeing desk and the wind is blowing the small peice of candle in all directions.

Write as often as you can and remember me to all inquireing

friends and tell the Croakers that I begin to think that Grant is going to get the best of Lee if his wind only holds out.

So good bye.

Yours
Jack

PS The candle is about gone.

PS 2nd It is raining here and I have got to sleep with a wet blanket as my stuff is all back in the waggon.

Sue Smiths husband is wounded in both legs. Very good evidence that he has been in one fight sure.[5]

* * * * * * * * * *

Battery A Mass Vol Artillery
Coal Harbor Virginia
June 11th 1864

Dear Brother

Yours of the 5th came all right and I was very glad to hear from you once more and to know you had heard from Asher. I saw a letter from an officer that was in that affair and he rather seems to think that Banks is not just the man for that kind of Business but perhaps he is not so much to blame after all. Speaking about Levi I rather think if he was with us he would have some travelling to do for we have dismounted all our duty Seargeants not haveing horses for them but we expect to get more in a few days. Since I last wrote we have remained in position but have not been engaged any. We have had one man killed by the Sharp Shooters. They are throwing up breast works here in all directions but I dont think we shall proceed any farther toward Richmond this way. A part of the Army have left here and gone somewhere but I have no means of knowing where but I think Grant will break out somewhere before long. I think he can run

[5] Captain William H. "Harry" Smith, Co. E, Second New Hampshire Infantry, died June 7, 1864, at Ft. Monroe, of wounds received at Cold Harbor four days earlier.

this Machine. He seems to be useing up all the stock we have. Whole Regts of dismounted Cavalry here and they have to frog it and are armed with Muskets. How are you dismounted Cavalry? Kind of rough aint it.

I had a letter from Langdon a week ago to day and they thought then Mary was a little better. I am anxiously looking for a letter and hope I shall get one to day. I wrote to Mary if she wanted any money to send to you for it as I have but little and dont know when we shall get paid again And I like to have a little by me. I also wrote to Pricilla to make me a pair of shirts and send them to you and I will write you when I want them sent. I wish if you could send me a Hat by mail you would do so as I have none and have burnt my nose most off now. If you get one get it a black one with a pretty wide rim and about 7 3/4 in size. I spoke to French about the picture and he said would give me one sometime. He send his best respects to you and Mrs Chase. That one I sent you is one I picked up on the battle field. It is a Lieut Col of an Illinois Regt. I have forgotten the name. Speaking about Mocking Birds I have not seen one untill to day but this morning I saw two beauties but the trouble is to catch them. The Infantry here call the Rebs Shell Mocking Birds but I dont suppose you care for that kind. The rebs have got a Mortar at work and they use it nights throwing a Shell every half hour but as yet they have not done much damage. They burst one over our Cassons night before last but done no damage. I suppose they do it to keep us awake. They threw a Shell into a Casson that was near ours a few days ago and blew it up killing one man and wounding another. I happened to be looking right at it and the way things flew around for a while was a caution and it was a miracle that it done no more damage. We are haveing very hot weather here and in this Sandy Barren country you can judge it is decidely dusty but I rather have that than mud. There is quite a number of 100 day men at Whitehouse and Burnsides Niggers are guarding the rebel Prisoners. Rather rough on the Chivalry I think. But I will draw to close hopeing this will find you all gay and festive. Write often as you can and send me some stamps in your next.

I have been thinking of writeing to Emily but dont know as it will have a good effect.

My love to all inquireing friends.

So good bye.
Yours &C
Jack

6 o clock PM

Our mail has just come and I had a letter from Mary. She is better. She sent me a Photograph of Sarah and one of Sadie that she had copied from those miniatures but I dont think much of the style of them. We had an Artillery duel here this afternoon. One man in our Brigade was wounded. I rather think we shall leave here to night as things seem to squint that way. But I will keep you posted as to our Whereabouts if nothing happens to me.

Good Bye
John

I dont send this Magnolia for its beauty for that like mine has departed but you can get some Idea of the scent of them. I think it very nice.

Benny Brooks is all right.

* * * * * * * * * *

June 16th 1864

Brother Sam

We are on the South Side of the James River. When I get a chance I will write but have not time to day. I thought I would just write a few lines and send this Photograph as the mail carrier said that there would be a chance to send it to night.

Weather is very hot and dry but Bully for a Campaign. Hopeing soon to have a Victory to write about I will close.

Yours &C
Jack

* * * * * * * * * * *

Battery A Mass Vol. Arty
In position front of Petersburg Va
Monday Eve June 20th 64

Dear Brother

I dropped you a line a day or so ago but to night I thought I would try to write a few lines and let you know that I had found out where we are. We left Coal Harbor on the night of the 12th and after Crossing the Chickahominy and James River arrived here the night of the 17th and are now on the front line in a Breastwork that the Rebs throwed up [but] we [are] filling up the ditch. The boys have worked all night now for three nights and as yet we have only fired 6 rounds. They dont open any Batteries that we can reach. We are in a hot place as the rebs have a Parrott Battery that fires Completely across us but as yet have done no damage.

Wednsday Afternoon

Have been trying to get a chance to finish up my letter but what with fighting & marching my time has been pretty well occupied. We Spent all last night on the road and a part of to day and a fair prospect of another night spent the same way. Our Corps is fighting in front of us but with what result is more than I know. We still keep moveing to the left and if Grant says as the papers say he did that he was going [to] Fight it out on this line I think his line a very long one to say the least. I hope he will do something soon for I am about Played out and I think if he keeps this Campaign up much longer that this whole Army will be in the same state.

I begin to think that if I get no punch untill We get to Richmond that I shall go dry sometime yet But I am no croaker. I am willing to wait and see the Glory of the Lord but it is rather fatigueing I tell you. I was glad to hear that Asher is so well off and I hope he may keep his situation untill his time is out. I had a letter from Levi a few days ago and one from Pricilla so you see I am well posted. I think Levi has reason to thank God that he is where he is for it is tough on the new men. I have never heard of Johnny Dohertys death. The last I heard from him he was guard on the Train. Benny Brooks is all right although under a heavy fire. He is apt to get somewhat demoralized but none to hurt.

The weather here is hot and dry and we eat drink and Sleep in dust.

But I must close for they begin to move the Column. I am expecting a big fight tomorrow but may be mistaken but the papers will inform you for you know more about what is going on then we do.

So Good Bye for this time.

Yours &C
Jack

Write when you can.

* * * * * * * * * *

Camp Battery A Mass Vol Artillery
Near Petersburg Virginia
June 26th 1864

Dear Brother

Yours of the 19th I recieved last Wednesday night and was very happy to hear once more from you And to night I thought I would try and write and let you know that I still live. We are now to the left of Petersburg but are not in position nor is any of our Brigade of Batteries. We were relieved Friday night by the 2nd Corps Batteries. We came here from the front of the city where we amused ourselves by throwing up Breast Works and tossing a few shell into the town. The 18th Corps relieved us there and I was no ways sorry to leave for the Sharp Shooters were rather to thick to suit me and the Rebs had a Battery that could rake us fore and aft. They threw a few shot over us just to show us what they could do but we got out of it without any loss except two horses. I cannot tell what is going on here. We are about 4 miles to the left of Petersburg and they keep up a continual fireing to the right of us but what is going on is more than we know but I suppose it is skirmishing as they dont call anything a battle now without the whole army is engaged and a loss of some 8 or 10 thousands. But in my humble opinion we have not gained much glory this past week take all things into consideration for I know the rebs have got the most of one Brigade of infantry and 3 Peices of Artillery from the 2nd Corps and Handcock[6] has done nothing but swear ever since he is not able to be in the field himself but I hope he soon may be for his Corps has done too much good work to lose there reputation now. I cannot help thinking at times of the difference between this and George Bs Campaign before Richmond for then they would not even let McDowell come to help him while now everything that Grant wants is done. We have Iron Clads and any quantity of reinforcements but I rather think we shall need them all before we get to Richmond but I suppose it wont do to speak your mind on this subject. If you do they will say you are a Copperhead and perhaps a poor cuss like me might get shot. But this much I say and every day I am more convinced of the fact and that is if Gen McClellan had been fairly dealt with that Richmond would have been in our possesion a couple of years ago for I am just of the same mind now I always was and that is that he is the greatest General in the Country if he dont smoke. But however I am in hopes that after all the blood that has been spilt this summer that something good may come out of it but things look decidely mixed to me at times.

The weather here is decidely hot. We have not had a half hours rain now for over 30 days and the heat and dust is fearful and water is about as scarce as whisky. We have to go a mile to water our horses. We Water them in Blackwater Creek and I suppose we are somewhere near that part of the country that Asher made his Campaign in. I dont know what will become of us if this kind of weather holds on much longer for it dont seem as if men could stand it but this army has been through so much that I dont know as you

[6] General Winfield Scott Hancock.

can kill them off now but I am afraid that sickness must follow such severe hot weather. One thing I will give them credit for and that is we are well fed. Never better even when we were in camp. We are supplied with all that any army ever was and plenty of it and that which is good But the boys begin to think that it is most time for Mr Chase to come down with a few Photographs of Abraham for our Stock of extras is most played out and I think you will think so by the look of this paper but I have to be Saveing and this the last run and I dont know when I shall have a chance to get any more. That was Simsons boy that was killed in the first heavy [Artillery]. They have suffered severely. When they came here they numbered 1,400. Now they number less than 700. The heavy Regts have done some good fighting and I think they are paying for the good times they have had around Washington. We have not heard from Federhen lately but I expect he is still in Washington as he was unable to move when we heard from him last.

Tell Lizzie that I dont think I shall take up any new Correspondents at present for I dont hardly get time to write to my old ones but I shall keep my eye peeled for some heiress so if I do live through this show that I can retire with a Fortune to help me out.

The last letter I had from Mary she was getting along nicely and the doctor had advised horse back riding for her. She has given up the Idea of going to school this summer altogether.

I suppose the house is all ready by this time and the House Warming over with. I would like to be there just to see the movements of things.

Monday morning

French and Brooks are gay and festive and send there respects to all who inquire for them. You must remember me to all inquireing friends and tell Mr Fergurson to take a big drink of Punch for me Fourth of July and I hope he may have some good news to make it go good. There was heavy fighting all night on the right both Cannonading and musketry but you will probably know what it was all about before we do as we have to take the papers to find out what is going on around us. I am looking for my hat as I suppose you have sent it before this. The stamps I received all right But I must bid you good Bye as it is getting to warm to write and it is not 6 o clock yet. So good by for the present.

Yours &C
Jack

Tell Lizzie if she was here I think she would want as many as four niggers to [too] for her.

PS If you have any of those Photographs of mine please send me two.

[On the back of the envelope:]
Battery A Mass Vol Artillery
Near Petersburg Virginia
June 27th 1864
Where it is decidely hot.
[On the front:]
From the Army of the Potomac

* * * * * * * * * *

Battery A Mass Vol Artillery
Near Petersburg Va
July 5th 1864

Dear Brother

Yours of the 26th came safe to hand and I was very glad to hear from you and to know that Note was settled and I think if my brother Ben waits for the balance untill I order you to pay him he will wait untill this Cruel War is over. Not but what the money was his due after I gave him the note but I was a damn fool for ever giveing him the note and I think if you knew all the circumstances you would think so too. But let him have it and go on his way rejoiceing. I believe I can take care of my little flock without it. If not I will call on someone besides him. Its not the first mean thing he ever done for his soul never was bigger than a ten cent peice and marrying never improved him any. That hat I guess I shall never see for it has not made its appearance and I guess some sugar eater has made love to it although I still have a hope but its a very small one. Glad to hear that Asher still remains at Head Quarters[7] and guess you need not fret any more about him for good clerks are not quite so plenty now as they were when the first troops came out for its not that kind that enlists now. For a sample take our Battery. When it came out there was two men who could not write there names. In the recruits we got last winter there is eight and I dont know of only one man that will be left that we can make a Company Clerk of and I calculate ours are more than an average lot for intelligence. I hope the Boy will be permitted to come home and enjoy his chamber with his Grand Mother. Yesterday was the Glorious Fourth and for the first time in the army I had some Punch. Not quite equal to your manufacture but thanks to the Sanitary Commission[8] and Capt Mac it was very good. The Sanitary furnished the Lemons and Ice and the Commissary the Whisky. We have had several small lots of stuff from the Sanitary through the Brigade Surgeons but it was generally so small that it was more trouble to divide it than it was worth. Consequently Capt Mac thought he would try what he could do So he sent his team down to City Point and we got 2 barrels of pickeld cucumbers 2 of pickled onions 1 of dried apples 12 gallon cans of tomatoes and a dozen bottles of Lemon Syrup and if we had been a day sooner we could have got more but the boat was about cleaned out. The Agent gave us an invitation to come again for he said it gave him more satisfaction to give it out so than it did to have it go to Brigade Head Quarters first for it has to pass through too many hands then for the privates to get much. So you see we have obtained some benefit from the Sanitary. Then we got some articles from the Christian Commission amongst which was some paper and envelopes which

[7] Asher transferred from the Seventh Massachusetts Battery to the Second Division Headquarters of the Nineteenth Corps.

[8] The U.S. Sanitary Commission provided care to sick and wounded soldiers.

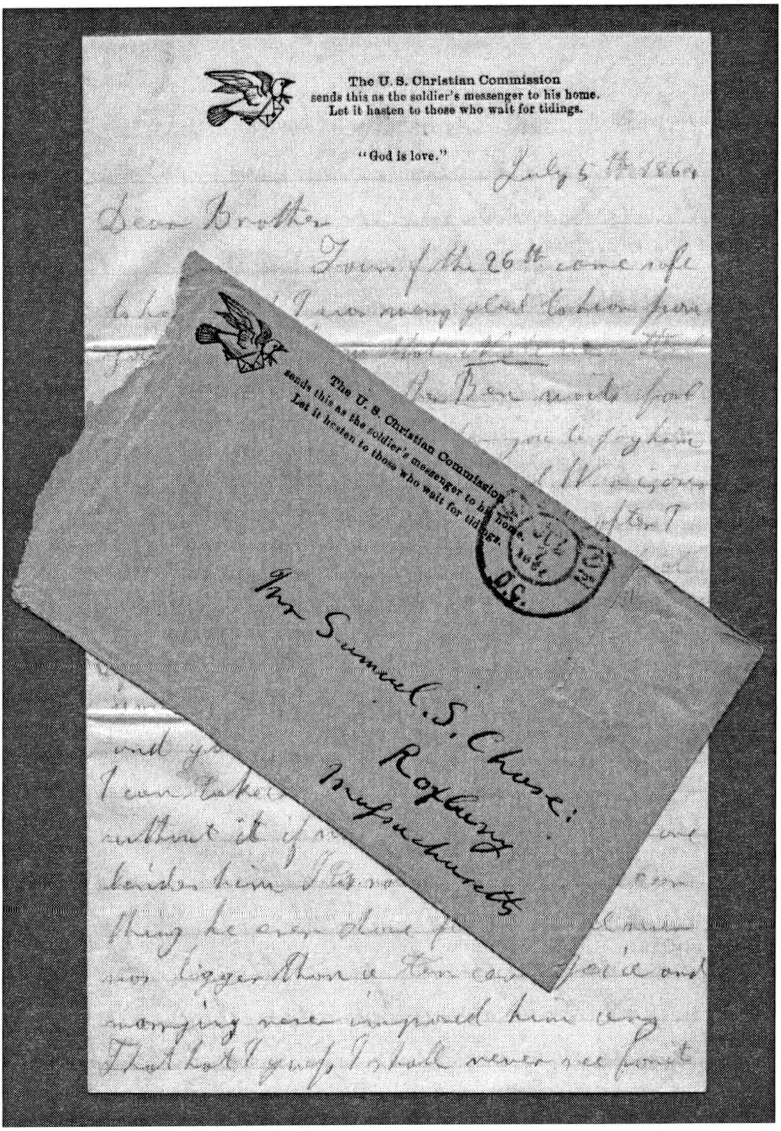

Letter of July 5, 1864 CFC

was very much needed as the boys are out of money and no prospect of getting paid take it all together and it would amount to more than we ever received before put it all together and the Boys say Bully for the Christian Commission and Sanitary. There is no mistake it has been a Big thing for the Soldiers on this Campaign not but what there is a good deal of Humbug about it but we must expect that from so large a concern and I think the officers try hard to manage it fairly and would if they could.

Since I last wrote you we have been off on a Raid and destroyed the Weldon and Petersburg Rail Road. The Cavalry went up there and got hung up and we had to go the rescue and of course it must be the little 6th if there was any marching to do. We had no fight except a little skirmishing but we obtained a few chickens some flour &C of the <u>starveing inhabitants</u>. The Cavalry got pretty roughly used but I never have seen any official report. We are now about four miles to the left of the City on the Flank but thus far all is quiet in our front and if it was not for the hot weather and the dust we should be very well situated but it is awful hot and ye Gods the dust. We have to eat and drink it for it is a perfect cloud all the time. No rain now for 40 days. On the right towards Petersburg they keep up a continual Shelling and every night we can hear the musketry but the Boys seem to think its all right and that Grant will be the winner in the end but I think it will be a long seige I do. But I will cork up. You must give my respects to all the folks that wish to hear from me. Tell them Jack still lives and gets his Whisky quite regular but Commissary prices are on the rise and dont think I can stand the press much longer. I want you to send me $5,00 as I am about out of change and I see no prospect of getting paid. They are going to pay the General and Staff officers but I suppose they think Privates and line officers dont need any money. French and Brooks are well and send there respects to Sam.

Yours as ever
Jack

The mail has come and still no hat. I guess its a goner.

Ned Head was down to see me this week. Ned makes a good Soldier and looks first rate.

I received two papers from you last week and to day I got two more with the initials S E C marked on the wrapper and I cannot make out who it is and I feel worried.

* * * * * * * * * * *

John Chase's Travel Routes in Chapter 8: July 1864 to February 1865

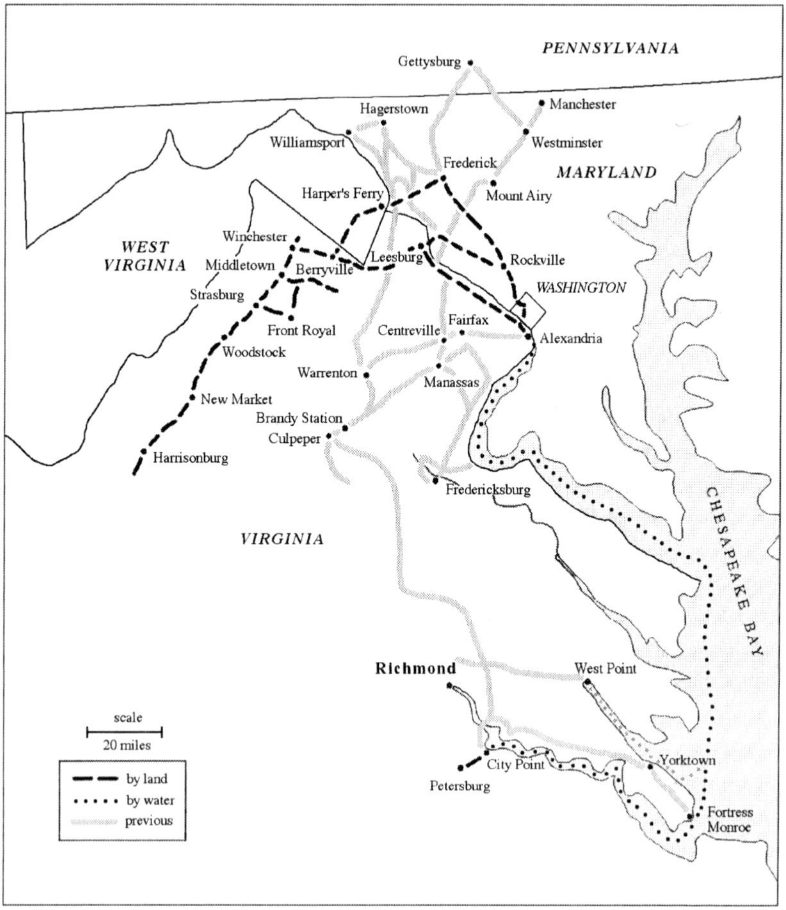

JSC/BBC

CHAPTER 8

The Shenandoah Valley

In response to Confederate General Jubal Early's advance on Washington in July, General Grant sends the Sixth Corps to reinforce the capital's defenses. Then, becoming part of General Philip Sheridan's Army of the Shenandoah, Chase moves up and down the Shenandoah valley. The First Massachusetts Battery is dissolved when most of the men's three-year enlistments run out. Now attached to the Fifth Maine Battery, Chase describes the chaos of the Battle of Cedar Creek.

Tuesday Evening July 12th [1864]
Aboard the Steamer Hero of Jersey
Sailing up the Potomac

Dear Brother

I dont know but what you will be surprised when you see my letter comeing from this place but so it is here. The First Mass Battery is on board a large Steamer heading towards Washington. We left the Front Sunday and remained at City Point untill yesterday afternoon when we embarked and Started at Sunset came down the James then across the Chespeak bay and are now at 9 P M about 30 miles from Washington. The Boat is a large one used generally as a Hospital boat and as there is only our Battery on board we have plenty of room and are enjoying ourselves hugely and the boys to night are singing and amusing themselves with the colored ladies of which there is about a dozen on board. But not being fond of Female

Society I thought I would amuse myself in writeing a letter to you. It has been a very hot day on the water and God only knows what it has been on the land for I thought I should cave yesterday for we laid on the wharf untill most night before we could load and it was just as warm as ever I want to see it and the dust ye Gods. I thought it was as bad as could be at the front but marching 12 miles to the Point through it and after we got there it seemed as if it grew worse all the time. We had just got things fixed up had a good position and Bully Breast Works and all the Rebs in Virginia could not drove us out of them and then we had the horses in the woods and had dug wells so that we could water them and not take them off the picket rope and were haveing a good soft thing of it. But then Lee must start for Maryland and of course the 6th Corps must be the ones to Start after him. In the first place the orders was for the Artillery not to go But Gen Wright begged for them and they let him take 6 Batteries. So of course McCartney,s Battery must be one of them because it Is a good one Although the Captain is not a rich mans Son and never had his portrait in Harpers Weekly like what the Captain of the Saucy Battery did. For further particulars see Harpers of July the 8th.[1] I was in hopes we were going to get a little rest for I have been about Played out for I took cold and began to think that Chase was a victim but Ayers Pills helped me and since we got on the river I feel a great deal better. I have kept on duty all the time but if I had been at home money could not hired me to done anything but lie in Bed. You can bet on that and win. And now I expect we shall get put through again for according to the last paper I saw the Rebs are in force and raising merry H___ generally and I suppose we must fight them. Sometimes when I think this Campaign over I get about discouraged to think of the lives that have been lost and What have we gained. I fail to see what damn great things Grant has done more than George B done before him and he was cursed and reviled by the very men that now pretend to say that Grant is working wonders. But I am like the boy that dirtied the bed. Nothing to say but I think very loud sometimes

[1] Captain J. Henry Sleeper of the Tenth Massachusetts Battery was featured. He was formerly a first lieutenant in the First Massachusetts Battery.

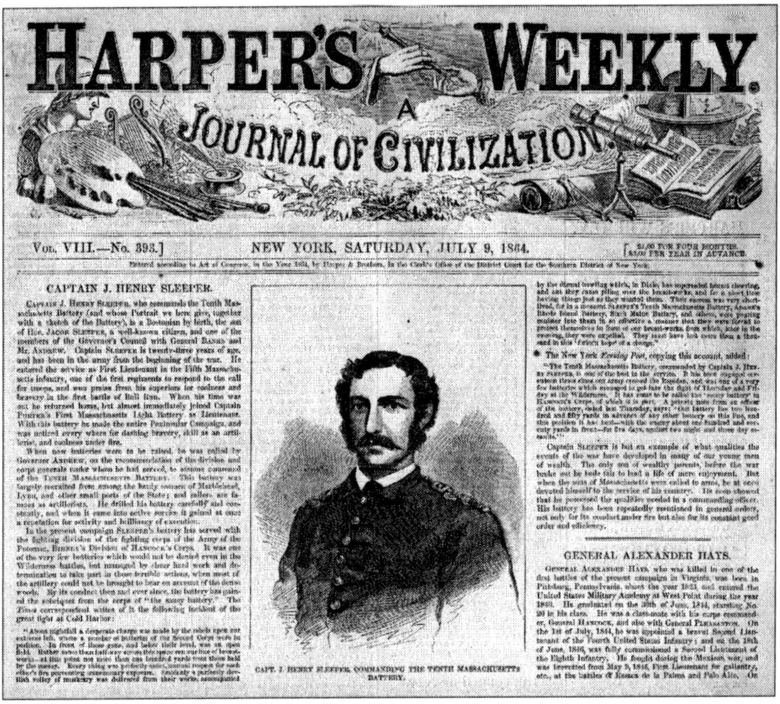

HARPER'S WEEKLY.
A JOURNAL OF CIVILIZATION.

Vol. VIII.—No. 393.] NEW YORK, SATURDAY, JULY 9, 1864. [$1.00 FOR FOUR MONTHS. $4.00 PER YEAR IN ADVANCE.

CAPTAIN J. HENRY SLEEPER.

Captain J. Henry Sleeper, who commands the Tenth Massachusetts Battery (and whose Portrait we here give, together with a sketch of the Battery), is a Bostonian by birth, the son of Hon. Jacob Sleeper, a well-known citizen, and one of the members of the Governor's Council with General Banks and Mr. Andrew. Captain Sleeper is twenty-three years of age, and has been in the army from the beginning of the war. He entered the service as First Lieutenant in the Fifth Massachusetts infantry, one of the first regiments to respond to the call for troops, and won praise from his superiors for coolness and bravery in the first battle of Bull Run. When his time was out he returned home, but almost immediately joined Captain Porter's First Massachusetts Light Battery as Lieutenant. With this battery he made the entire Peninsular Campaign, and was noticed every where for dashing bravery, skill as an artillerist, and coolness under fire.

When new batteries were to be raised, he was called by Governor Andrew, on the recommendation of the division and corps generals under whom he had served, to assume command of the Tenth Massachusetts Battery. This battery was largely recruited from among the hardy seamen of Marblehead, Lynn, and other small ports of the State; and sailors are famous as artillerists. He drilled his battery carefully and constantly, and when it came into active service it gained at once a reputation for activity and brilliancy of execution.

In the present campaign Sleeper's battery has served with the fighting division of the fighting corps of the Army of the Potomac, Birney's Division of Hancock's Corps. It was one of the very few batteries which would not be denied even in the Wilderness battles, but managed by sheer hard work and determination to take part in those terrible actions, when most of the artillery could not be brought to bear on account of the dense woods. By its conduct then and ever since, the battery has gained the sobriquet from the corps of "the saucy battery." The *Times* correspondent writes of it the following incident of the great fight at Cold Harbor:

"About nightfall a desperate charge was made by the rebels upon our extreme left, where a number of batteries of the Second Corps were in position. In front of these guns, and below their level, was an open field. [illegible]

CAPT. J. HENRY SLEEPER, COMMANDING THE TENTH MASSACHUSETTS BATTERY.

[illegible] Sleeper's Tenth Massachusetts Battery, [illegible] Rhode Island Battery, Sixth Maine Battery, and others, were pouring canister into them in so effective a manner that they were forced to protect themselves in front of our breast-works, from which, later in the evening, they were expelled. They must have lost more than a thousand in this 'forlorn hope' of a charge."

The New York *Evening Post*, copying this account, added:

"The Tenth Massachusetts Battery, commanded by Captain J. Henry Sleeper, is one of the best in the service. It has been engaged [illegible] since our army crossed the Rapidan, and was one of a very few batteries which managed to get into the fight of Thursday and Friday at the Wilderness. It has come to be called the 'saucy battery' in Hancock's Corps, of which it is part. [illegible]"

Captain Sleeper is but an example of what qualities the events of the war have developed in many of our young men of wealth. The only son of wealthy parents, before the war broke out he bade fair to lead a life of mere enjoyment. But when the sons of Massachusetts were called to arms, he at once devoted himself to the service of his country. He soon showed that he possessed the qualities needed in a commanding officer. His battery has been repeatedly mentioned in general orders, not only for its conduct under fire but also for its constant good order and efficiency.

GENERAL ALEXANDER HAYS.

General Alexander Hays, who was killed in one of the first battles of the present campaign in Virginia, was born in Pittsburg, Pennsylvania, about the year 1823, and entered the United States Military Academy at West Point during the year [illegible]. He graduated on the [illegible] of June, 1844, standing No. 20 in his class. He was a class-mate with his corps commander, General Hancock, and also with General Pleasanton. On the 1st of July, 1844, he was appointed a brevet Second Lieutenant of the Fourth United States Infantry; and on the 18th of June, 1846, was fully commissioned a Second Lieutenant of the Eighth Infantry. He fought during the Mexican war, and was brevetted from May 9, 1846, First Lieutenant for gallantry, etc., at the battles of Resaca de la Palma and Palo Alto. On

Captain Sleeper in *Harper's Weekly*, July 9, 1864 HW

and I expect if Some of the Blacks knew what I thought they would say he is a McClellan man and a Copperhead. But I claim to be a George B admirer and a Patriot and one who is willing to fight for his country and not to carry out the Ideas of a pack of men that dont care a damn for any thing but there own hobbies. But what,s the use talking. The people wont see it but perhaps they may sometime. <u>Let her rip</u>.

I received your letter of the 5th and was glad to hear that Lizzie continued faithful to George and I also got the papers for which please receive my thanks. Happy to hear of the prosperity of the Morgans and want you to pay my dues. Thought I told you before I left as I meant too. I would like to be there and meet with you and wouldn,t mind takeing a few of those Strawberries &C. Please remember me to such of the Bretheren as I know and to all inquireing friends. I saw James Monroe at City Point. I did not know before that he had been promoted. Was glad to hear of it. He looks first rate but his wound had broke out and he was on his way to the Hospital.

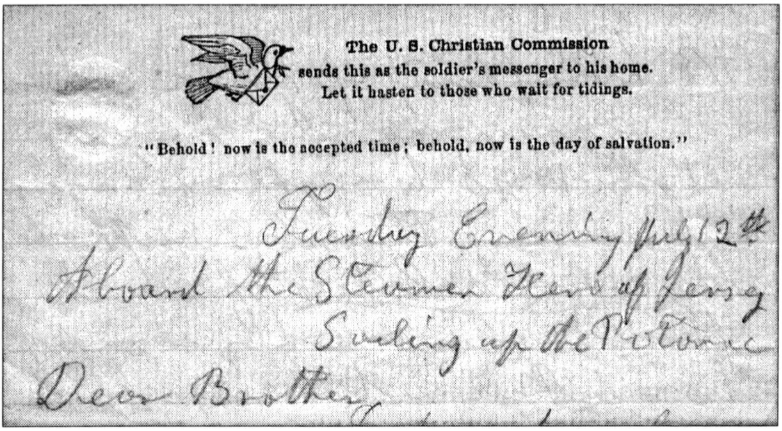

The U. S. Christian Commission
sends this as the soldier's messenger to his home.
Let it hasten to those who wait for tidings.

"Behold! now is the accepted time; behold, now is the day of salvation."

Tuesday Evening July 12th
Aboard the Steamer Hero of Jersey
Sailing up the Potomac
Dear Brother

Detail from Letter of July 12, 1864 CFC

My hat I have not seen and guess its a goner but I am in hopes to get that 5,00 for I see no prospect of getting paid off and I think a little money in Maryland will be very acceptable if I dont get popped. But I guess I have written more now than you can make out for my candle is a very poor light and I am a very poor writer.

So Good Night and I will try and get a nap.

Yours &C
Jack

Please send me a few stamps.

Tenlytown Near Washington

I have had no chance to send this letter for we have had no mail since we left City Point. I will write as soon as I hear from you and give you the particulars of our Campaign of the past fortnight but I feel most to much Played out to attempt writeing to day. We got here last night and they tell us we have to move to City Point to night or in the morning.

Good Bye at present
Jack

* * * * * * * * * *

Monacy[2] Mills Maryland
Aug 5th 64

Dear Brother

We received our back mail to day and I thought to night I would try and do some writeing but orders have come to move and I must postpone it. It is nothing but march and Countermarch with us now. No peace day or night. The 5,00 came all right.

I will write just as soon as I can.

Good Bye.
Yours &C
Jack

[This letter on The U.S. Christian Commission stationery is captioned:]

"God is love."

* * * * * * * * * *

Camp Battery A Mass Vol Ar,ty
Near Harpers Ferry Virginia
Aug 9th 1864

Dear Brother

Although I have had no letter from you since I wrote I thought as I had time I would try and write and let you know how we were getting along and what we were doing. I believe I have not written what could be called a letter since we started from Georgetown and I

[2] Monocacy.

will try and give you a faint Idea of where we have been since. We left there the 26th of July at noon and marched to Rockville getting into camp at midnight. Started at 3 the next morn and marched to Hyatstown. Halted a few hours then to Monacy Junction on the Baltimore and Ohio Rail Road within three miles of Frederick City but not being ready to let us rest as yet we Marched all night and

Harpers Ferry in 1865 NA

arrived at Jefferson at 2 o clock in the morn. Started again at 5 and marched to Harpers Ferry near where we are now. Here they told us the Rebs were about 5 miles off but we laid quiet the next day untill dark when we took the back track and kept it untill we came to Near Frederick once more. Here they let us rest one day & then at night we were on the road and morning found us at Monacy Mills where we remained two days and then marched back to this place arriveing here the night of Aug 6th. So you see for the past 10 days we have been kept on the road the most of the time and nary reb have I seen except a few prisoners they have dragged us around. Part of the time we have been under Gen Wright and then Hunter But now I hear that Sheridan[3] has command of this Army and I think if such is the fact we shall soon find out whether there is any rebs in the valley or whether Moseby[4] is causing all this travel. The Inhabitants I find dont think much of Hunter or his forces either & they tell funny stories about them and I rather think there is a good deal of truth in them. I never had any opinion of Hunter since he kept the nigger schools down to Beaufort and think he is better qualified for that than Leading an army. In fact I have come to the conclusion that this War is a damn Humbug any way. But I suppose I have got to stand 2 years and a few longer But I see no bright spot ahead and begin to think that we must look to some one besides Abraham and his friends to finish up the job. I have talked with some of the People who live where the rebs passed through in there raid and they say the rebs express the wish that A peace candidate may be elected this fall and the thing closed up and for one I say Amen. For I begin to think that it is not for principle but Party we are fighting for and I am d____d if I see it But suppose I must do it. Now I wish they would let George B take this Department. I rather think that the people of Maryland would rest easier nights than they have lately but that would be asking too much I suppose. I have been down to the Ferry several times since we came here and I think that the man who would give up such a place as that must be a damn traitor or a larger Coward.[5] The natural fortifications of the place are enough to keep it against a large army. I think it must have been a very pretty place before the war but there is not much left to admire now except the Scenery around it.

I believe I wrote you that I got my 5,00 but the Hat I never have seen but I have one however. I received two letters from Langdon when we got our back mail and he spoke very despondingly of Mary

[3] General Philip H. Sheridan was put in command of the Army of the Shenandoah to destroy the farms that were supplying food to the Confederate army under siege at Petersburg.

[4] General John S. Moseby led an effective band of Confederate rangers.

[5] Colonel Dixon S. Miles had surrendered his 12,000 Federal troops at Harpers Ferry, just before the Battle of Antietam, in 1862.

and seemed to think she ought to have some one with her. I wish if you can you would go up and see her and let me know what you think of her care and what can be done for her. I will pay your expenses willingly for Langdon never writes more than 6 lines and I dont feel satisfied. I will spend all I can make if I can help her any for I believe I love that girl better than I do myself and I think that is saying a good deal. If she must die I dont care how quick I go for although it may be wrong she seems dearer to me than both of the Boys. You know it would be impossible for me to try and get home and if you will do this favor for me I will do anything in my power to pay you. See her and let me know the truth. If she must die I want to know it and if to the Contrary I want to know that also. The last letter I received from her she said Aunt Sophia told her to tell me she was sick but Mary wrote me not to worry about her for she thought I had troubles enough of my own but then she was always in good spirits as long as she could hold her head up.

But I must close as I [have] to go and see after forage for our horses. I shall take this to town and mail it as our mail is played out. There is no regularity about it. Give my love to all the folks and write when you can.

Yours &C
Jack

Thank you for the papers. Although some of them were old when I got them the truth was there.

* * * * * * * * * * *

Camp Battery "A" Mass Vol Artillery
Halltown Va Aug 23 [1864]

Dear Brother

For about the 20th time I will now make one more effort to write to you and let you know that I am yet alive and enjoying tolerable health with the exception of a bad head ache caused I suppose by going without Sleep for the past two nights as we have been either trying to fight or keep out of one and I dont know which. Since I wrote you last we have been up the valley as far as Strasburg. Here we found the rebs ready for us but instead of fighting we laid there a day or two and looked at them and then fell back to Charlestown And here the rebs found us and showed fight and then we fell back to this place which is about two miles from Harpers Ferry. We are in Battle line and there is some sharp skirmishing going on but whether we get into a fight or not remains to be seen but I dont think Sheridan will Surrender as Miles did without rather more of a Struggle.

But I am done forming any opinions about War matters but try and do what they tell me and enjoy myself the best way I can. I enjoyed the trip up the valley much for we took any thing we could get hold of to eat and I have dressed a good nice sheep this morning and have a couple of good turkies tied by the leg ready to be offered up when I get turkey hungry. I never lived better in my life and the people say the 6th Corps beat all the Soldiers that ever visited the valley yet for Stealing. I just told them we should not starve as Hunters force did as long as we could find anything in the country. The Capt has gone home on Furlough of 15 days. Lieut Federhen has got back and the Boys are in trouble to know when they shall go home as it seems to be a question whether there time is out the 28th of August or the 3d of October that being the day we left Boston. I dont know how it will end and as I am not interested of course it dont trouble me much but I cannot help thinking that they ought to go the 28th. But you know its no use to Contend with "Sam" for he will get the best of it in some shape.

As you remark I suppose there will be a change of officers here soon. I have had some vague hints thrown out to me that perhaps I might stand a Show but I am not over anxious for if it was not for a few priveledges that you cannot have as a Private I would prefer to remain where I am But suppose if the place opens I shall take it. Drop in and see the Capt if you get a chance but dont let him know that I told you to. French is in trouble for fear they will keep him three years from his Muster as a commission officer. If they do his time will be out 4 months before mine but he will go out of it if he can.

I received your letter giveing an account of your visit to Stratham and was glad to hear you left them some money. I did not say any thing about it thinking you would be likely to do so if they needed it. I wrote Mary last night and hinted that I thought a change of treatment would be a good thing if she does not improve in health and I should like to have you consult Mrs Freeman in regard to her case and then perhaps I could understand it better.

I would like to see her well once more if it could be.

Our Batteries have opened and I must close for there is rather too much going on to write any more.

Brooks and the rest of the Boys are all right.

Yours as ever
Jack

* * * * * * * * * *

Camp Battery A Mass Vol Arty
Near Berryville Virginia
Sept 15th 1864

Dear Brother

As they tell me there will be a mail leave in the morning I concluded that I would write and let you know that I am still alive and in tolerable health although I have not been very smart the past 3 weeks. We are still in the valley but dont seem to do much in the fighting line but rather act on the defensive although we do have little skirmishing now and then just for amusement. The Capt has returned from his furlough and according as things look now the First Mass will cease to be after the 3d of October next and what will be done with the Veterans and recruits remains to be seen. Quite a number of the Vets have sent to his excelency John A for a Commission but I have not As I have the Capt at work for me in another way and if I prove successful it will please me better than it would to have a Brig Gen Berth. Part of our men have already gone.

Gen Wright took it upon him to have them mustered out but found he was wrong and Mac was right. Consequently the rest of them stop untill the 3d of next month and I am in hopes by that time to be all right. At any rate I shall wait patiently and look for the Glory of the Lord. Asher has been to see me twice the past week. He looks first rate and has got a good soft thing and is all right untill his time is out I guess. Your letter of the 29th came safe to hand and you must excuse my not writeing before but I had nothing of any importance to write and have not felt just like doing as I have been on the anxious seat and when I see you if I ever do I will give you a faint Idea of how things have been going on with us. I see George B has accepted the Nomination for President and if I was a civillian I would say what I thought about it but at present I think it better to keep silent.

Give my love to all the folks and tell Lizzie not to worry about Asher for he is as well off as a man can be in this army. I will write you more fully next time.

Yours & C
Jack

* * * * * * * * * *

Camp Battery "A" Mass Vol Arty
Harrisonburg Rockingham County Va
Sept 26th 1864

Dear Brother

Haveing a little spare time I thought I would improve it in writeing you a short letter and let you know that I am still alive. We arrived at this place last night and are now waiting for our trains to come up with us. Whether we shall advance any farther or not I dont know but I expect that Early has left us in the lurch and I think he has done some damn tall travelling for we have made very good time but did not march quick enough to catch him after our last fight at Strasburg or if we did catch him he would not stop and fight us for I think he has got a belly full this time. At least the people of this part of the Country think so and I think that very good evidence. I shall not write any particulars of our battles[6] for Asher told me he should write you a good long letter and I think he will give you a better Idea of it than I could. I have not seen the Boy to day but have seen him most every day on the march and he may be here now before night. I sold him a uniform Jacket that I had fixed up for myself but either that grew to small or else I did too large and I could not wear it. I told him he need not pay me for it for I thought I could settle that with you. Was that right? Well I suppose this Battery will be smashed the 3d of next month and the men are to go to the ninth Mass Capt Bigelow. I am sorry for it but the War Department will not consent to have it filled up as it will be below the minimum as there will be only 77 men present and absent. The Capt has applied to have the non commissioned officers mustered out but I hardly think he will make a go of it but of course I would,nt object for if he is going I want to go too. But I shall try and meet my fate let it be what it will for I always did and always intend to try and do my duty. The Capt offered to reccomend me for a Commission but I dont see it. None of that for me at least not at present. I shall take my chances elsewhere first and I shall try and get a berth somewhere that I think will suit me better.

You must excuse my not writeing you before but I coaxed Asher to write twice and I thought that would answer every purpose. We have been quite busy lately as there is a good deal of writeing and work to do to get things squared up for the end of all things. I dont want you to write me again at present as I dont know how or where I shall be. When I get things fixed or get fixed myself I will let you know and shall try and keep you posted as to my whereabouts &C. I suppose when the 36 men who went home left us they thought we should be unfit for service as some of them thought they were the makeing of this Co But I am happy to say that the Battery never did better than in the last two fights and received the praise of our Gen

[6] On September 19, they were engaged at the Battle of Opequon Creek (or Third Winchester), and on September 22, they fought the Battle of Fishers Hill, near Strasburg.

General Philip H. Sheridan LC

Wright. He and Sherry were right in the Battery a great part of the time and Sheridan Put it in position once himself telling the Capt he was going to take him where he could get some horses killed but as good luck still follows us we did not but had one Seargeant wounded in the head with a peice of Shell. Little Sherry as the boys call him is the biggest man out these times with the 6th Corps he is.

[unsigned]

We expect the train to night and if it dont come you will have to wait for this letter— —.

* * * * * * * * * *

Camp 5th Maine Battery
Harrisonburg Virginia
Oct 5th 1864

Dear Brother

Asher was down to see me to day and shew me a letter from you in which you complain of my not writeing to you but I have written you twice since the date of your letter. The fact is I have had but little time to write lately and then again our mail is not very regular neither going or comeing Therefore I think take everything into consideration you should not blame me too much. As you will probably learn before this reaches you the First Mass has gone up[7] and myself with 37 men are attached to the 5th Maine Battery. We

[7] The First Massachusetts Battery was dissolved on October 3, 1864, when most of the men's three-year enlistments expired. They returned to Washington and then went on to Boston.

have two of our old Guns and I am in command of the Section and thus far I like very much. The Capt is a fine man and the rest of the officers and men are regular down easters and good fellows all of them and for my own part I am not anxious to see the order for our transfer to the 9th Battery for I dont care about going to Petersburg for I had rather remain with the old 6th Corps and take my chance under Sheridan than to go there under Grant but I suppose that I shall have to do as they tell me too. The rest of our men with the Q M Seargeant are attached to the 5th U S Battery and they dont seem to like the change quite as well as the squad that is with me. The Battery is a regular one and the most of the men are Dutchman.

I gave Conway a letter to take to you and he and Brooks said they would call and see you. If they do tell Frank to write me and direct his letter to the 5th Maine Battery Capt Stevens. We had quite an illumination here last night. Gen Sheridan burnt three villages to pay them for Shooting his chief Engineres and I think if they get his Irish up strong he will burn the whole valley. A great many of the Inhabitants are leaving and going North and our trains are loaded with them every time they go back for supplies. Asher has been paid and he paid me for my Jacket to day so that settles that affair. I dont

Captain Stevens's Battery, by Alfred Waud LC

know as I can write you any news for I expect Asher keeps you posted on our movements here in the valley. But I will say that you may send one of my shirts as soon as you can after you get this without you hear that we have gone to Petersburg. If so wait until you hear from me again. I will try and write oftener than I have done as I have not much to do now and shall have more time. But I will close for to night hopeing if the train comes up tomorrow I may hear from you. (Good night).

Strausburg Va Oct 9th

I thought I would get a chance to write you more in this letter but have only a moments notice as the mail goes right away. I received a letter from you and will write again soon. We have fell back to Strausburg and the talk is we are to remain here a while.

Love to all.
Yours &C
Jack

I saw Asher day before yesterday. He is well.

* * * * * * * * * *

Camp 5th Maine Battery
Newtown Virginia
Oct 16th 1864

Dear Brother

I suppose you have received a letter from me before this that I sent by Conway and I hope ere this that shirt is on the way for I am about Played out of that article and the weather is getting decidely cool out here in the valley. Since I wrote you last we have been on the move. First to Front Royal and then we were ordered to Petersburg and got as far as Ashby,s Gap when orders came from Sheridan for us to come back and here we are and I hope they will let us remain for I dont want any part of Petersburg. I have not heard any thing about our transfer yet and I am not anxious for I am very

Battle Near Upperville below Ashby's Gap, by Alfred Waud LC

well contented where I am. I have command of the Centre Section which is composed of the men who formerly belonged to the old Battery and thus far I like very much. I have heard rumors here that the Battery was to be reorganized but dont pay much attention to such stories and in fact dont worry much about them any way for I think I can get along some how the rest of my time. But I should like to get located somewhere so I could get paid as there is most four months pay due us now.

I had a letter from Mary a few days since. She is in better health than she was. Had been on a journey down east and sent to me for some money to pay the bills but not haveing it to spare I wrote her that I would request you to send her some and you may send her 15,00 when you can. I expect if she continues to gain that she will go to Boston this fall but I told her she better wait untill cold weather. I expected if the Battery had continued in service to come home this winter but I dont know how it will be now for there is no knowing where I shall be. But if it is so I can I shall try and get there. I shall not write any War News for I expect Asher keeps you posted on that subject. I have not seen him since we came back here for I have been orderly officer of the week and have had no chance to go away but if we are here tomorrow I shall try and hunt him up as I am off duty then. Politics runs high here in the army but I dont trouble myself much about them but they will draw me out now and then and when they do soon find out that Chase is for the little Hero and always was.

If you see any of the old boys tell them Chase still lives and hopes too long enough to see this thing through and the old Union restored.

Give my love to all inquireing friends and write me when you can and dont think hard if you dont hear from me as regular as you use to for our mail does not run very regular here and I shall always try and keep you posted as to my whereabouts &C.

So Good Bye for this time.

Yours as ever
Jack

Direct to 5th Maine Battery
Artillery Brigade
6th Corps

Tell Joe that I will try and get him some root and if I have a chance will send it to him.

Our train came up this Afternoon but no mail for the 6th Corps so I will send this and write again when I get a letter. Please give this letter for Green to Johnny Newton. He may know where he is. I dont.

* * * * * * * * * *

Camp 5th Maine Battery
Strasburg Virginia
Oct 22nd 1864

Dear Brother

I have not heard anything from you for some time but as we have been in another battle I thought you would be anxious to hear from me and I should have written before but have not had an hour to spare since the Battle and to show you that I have been pretty busy I will give you a few details. (First) On the morning of the 19th as I was quietly reposeing in my shelter tent I was awakened by a furious musketry fire in the direction of the 8th Corps which was the right of our line and before I could get out of bed I heard the big guns open and our bugle blowing boots and Saddles and Chase began to think it about time to rise. I rose and what a sight I saw. The plains was covered with the Skedadlers of the 8th and 19th Corps and it was an impossibility to stop them. It seems the rebs surprised them in there camp and before our Corps could get into position the rebs were on us. We went into position right in camp and opened fire but the morning being very foggy we could not see much but after fireing a few rounds the fog lifted and we could see the Rebs advancing in two lines of battle and comeing on the double quick. Our Infantry was forced back and we limbered up but the rebs shot our horses and my Section being the last to Limber we lost both our guns as the rebs were so snug we could not get them off by hand and for about two hours the 6th Corps held the whole rebel force but not without falling back. But about Noon Gen Sheridan who was away in the morning arrived and took his Cavalry and drove the cowards of the 8th & 19th Corps back and told the Boys he was going to have them back in there old camps that night and take back our captured Artillery. We could hardly see it but we knew if anybody could do it that man was Phil Sheridan and as the papers have informed you before this he done it and we were in our old camp at dark after being drove over two miles. After we got our supper being the first meal I had had for the day and began to think about going to bed our bugle sounded the Assembly and we went into line and our order was read for us to take our teams and go and haul in 48 peices of Artillery

Sheridan's Ride, by Alfred Waud LC

taken from the rebs and the boys wanted no second order. We went and worked all that night getting the stuff back and for once I saw what I have often read about (that is) the roads strewed with guns cassons waggons and every thing belonging to an army and among the rest was our two guns and to day I have hauled them into our camp. The next day after the fight our Battery was sent here on picket But I stopped back to look after our wounded of which we had 28—5 of them being some of the old Battery and after I got through with this I was detailed to help sort over the stuff we had captured and arrange it so that the different Batteries could make good there loss and I have not been to the Battery untill to night. So you will see that my chance of writeing has been rather small and you must not find fault because I have not written before.

I suppose the papers will give you full accounts of the battle and I will only say that if the 6th Corps had gone to Petersburg at the time it was ordered there I think the 8th and 19th Corps would have been in Richmond before this time and I will say that a more disgraceful skedaddle I never saw. And I will say of the 8th Corps as Gen Wright did the first time we went up to Snickers Gap and that was they were not worth the powder it would take to blow them to Hell and I begin to think the 19th is not much better and I dont wonder that Banks red river campaign turned out as it did if all his troops were like them. They have been trying ever since the Winchester fight to make out that they did not break that day and have written a small volume of letters to the different papers and I

General Horatio G. Wright NA

think it will take all of two volumes to get back there reputation this time. But however I will not condemn them too hard but it is damn rough to see men running away and leaving the smallest Corps of the army to stand the whole brunt of battle. Our Artillery Brigade suffered very severely. The Brigade has 24 guns all told and we lost 7 of them and had 110 men in the Hospital and 20 killed on the field makeing 130 While the 19th Corps has 24 peices lost 16 of them and had 35 men in the Hospital and there whole loss was about 40. These are the facts and you can draw your own conclusions. I dont write this to brag at all but then I want you to know the facts and as we have no Newspapers to blow for this Corps I thought I would write it. It was the hardest fight I ever was in for a short one and the first time I ever ran from the Johnnies but after finding I could not save the guns I just made good time out of it I tell you.

I have not seen Asher since we came from Harrisonburg as we have been away from his Corps all the time but I shall try and look him up if we remain here. I hope you have sent my shirts as I have my last one on and the weather is getting decidely cool here in the mountains. A good many of our Boys lost all there Clothes but what they had on and are suffering for want things to keep them warm.

If you see Brooks or any of the old Boys tell them that Charley Appleton is dead and Joseph Morean Rick and Isaacs is missing and Estabrooks and Sherman wounded. Tell Benny to write me if you see him.

Sunday Morning

I could not finish last night as my candle burnt out and I had no more but I dont know but what I have written more now than you will be able to read and I will draw to a close by saying that Phil Sheridan is a brick and when he and Custer and Torbett[8] cant whip the Rebs its no use for any one to try. You must give my love to all the folks and tell them the 6th still lives and hopes to for a while longer. You must excuse my paper as that article is getting rather

[8] Generals George A. Custer and Alfred T. A. Torbert.

scarce with us at present.

Write soon and I remain

Yours as ever
Brother Jack

* * * * * * * * * *

Strasburg Virginia
Oct 28th [1864]

Brother Sam

I dont see as I am ever going to hear from you or any one else but I thought I would send you this account of the last battle and I think it the best description I ever read for as far as I know it is true as Gospel. I saw Asher day before yesterday he is all right but told me he lost his Clotheing in the last fight. I will write one of these days but should like to get a letter first.

Yours &C
Brother Jack

[Enclosed is a newspaper clipping of three columns from *The Philadelphia Inquirer* headlined "Cedar Creek" and with a subheading "Particulars of Sheridan's Victory," with an account of the battle.]

* * * * * * * * * *

Camp 5th Maine Battery
Strasburg Virginia
Nov 2nd 1864

Dear Brother

Yours of the 23d I have just read and it is now 8 o clock in the evening and I have got to rise at 3 in the morning and go to Martinsburg with a lot of horses. A job that will take me four days before I get back. So I thought I must write to night So that you might send my Shirts for I am about naked and dont see any chance to draw any and I dont feel like paying 14,00 a pair for them. That is what the Sutlers ask us here. You can send one at a time and if you let the Postmaster know that it is clotheing it will not cost much more than it would to Express them. Besides I shall be likely to get them much quicker As the nearest office is at Martinsburg which is 37 miles from here. I presume you have got my letter giveing you an account of the late fight. If so you will know that we lost our guns but I dont feel ashamed of it in the least for the Capt and all the officers who saw it say that the men of that Section done all that human hands could do and if we had the least support from our Infantry we could have saved them but it was not to be and all I have to say is that I feel very thankful that no more lives were lost for the men had bullet holes all through there clothes and it seems a miracle that no more were hurt. I feel satisfied that the Section was just as well fought as it would have been if Billy McCartney had been there And again I know that in all the fights the Battery ever was in it never was in such a damn hot place as it was that day. If mine had been the only guns lost I should have felt worse but there was 8 lost out the Brigade and my Section was the last to leave the field and that I can prove by a Brigadier General if any body wants it.

Asher was up to see me yesterday and I gave him a pair of socks as the boy had none to his feet and I happened to pretty well supplied with that Article. As to French and McCartney,s Niggerism they probably have an axe to grind and all I have to say is they went off here in a damn mean manner and I shall take the trouble to tell them so if I ever happen to meet them. As to my comeing home I am no ways anxious to get out of the service and if they will let me stay where I am I will be perfectly satisfied for I have a man over me now that I can respect for he is a Gentleman and that is more than I could say of some of my Superiors in the old Battery. But I must draw to a close and when I get back from my journey I will write you a good long letter if I have time. Give my love to all the folks and tell them Chase still lives and believes the Lincoln Party is capable of anything that is mean to carry this Election. I have seen the workings myself slightly but it is not for me to talk much you know about these times.

Good Bye.

Yours as ever
Jack

* * * * * * * * * * *

Camp 5th Maine Battery
Near Winchester Va
November 12th 1864

Dear Brother

I have not heard a word from you since yours of Oct 23d But thought I would try and write and let you know that I was still around. We came back here last Wednsday and things look as if we should remain here a while. That is if the Rebs let us. They have some force in front of us and Our pickets were skirmishing with them yesterday and to day our folks are very busy (throwing dirt). I dont hear anything about our transfer But one of our Boys had a letter from one of the Boys at home. He said the Capt told him he had written to me twice but if he has I never have got the letters and I guess he only dreamt he wrote. I dont want to misjudge the man But I have reasons to think that it is damn little he cares for those who are left here. He has got his own ends answered and we may go to H___ for all he or any of the rest of them cares. Its the same old story. You are a damn good fellow as long as you are of any use and then you can go But I think I can live without any help from any of them and if they will only let me stay where I am I am perfectly satisfied Although I pity those who are in the Regular Battery. I have heard it rumored the Battery was to be reorganized But I dont know how true it is. I wish they might that is if they would give us the right kind of officers. We have a pretty good crowd of men left yet and I think they could easily fill it up if any one would set about it in earnest. There are now present for Duty 71 men and the whole number Present and Absent is 82 So you see we make quite a respectable squad yet. If you are acquainted with any of the powers that be I wish you would ask them about it for I am inclined to think if the thing was properly represented there might be something done about it and the First Mass once more be numbered with the liveing. I feel most damnably oblidged to Brooks for leaveing that letter at Mr Fillebrowns Store and if [I] can do anything to accomodate him I will Not. He promised me faithfully he would call and see you. If he had not I would sent it by some one else But I thought it would not be any trouble to him as he lived so handy And if you should happen to see him you can tell him to go to Hell for me. I believe I accomadated him last winter But I suppose he dont think of that. I never have heard from any of them that went home but Billy Coye. He has written me twice. But however I am not anxious to hear from many of them but have a few dollars invested with some of them that I would like but rather guess I shall have to charge it to profit and loss.

I suppose you have got all through with politics by this time. They had great times here voting. A good many of the old Regts went for Mac but I guess Abe is ahead in the army But I have not seen any reliable return of this Corps. This Battery went for Lincoln two to one but a great many of the McClellan men did not vote. They are of the weak kneed kind. But if they had given us a chance to vote I think we could cast a few votes for George but we had no chance to vote at all. I saw Asher the day we moved down here. He is well and Hearty and thinks he shall try and get a Furlough soon and I think if we go into winter quarters here he will stand a good sight. I hope you have sent those shirts for I had to beg one to put on. So you see I am not worth the Shirt on my back now. But I must stop for the present for they have gone at it again and our Battery has got to go into position And I will finish some other time——.

Monday Nov 14

The mail has just arrived and I received a letter from you informing me you had sent my Shirts by Express. I was in hopes you would Send them by mail. I wrote you to do so but Suppose you did not get the letter somehow. The mail dont seem to go as regular as it did from the Potomac army. I have had a good many find fault about it But such is life. I hope I shall get them soon for I am suffering for them. I shall send to Martinsburg to day to see if they have got along.

I see by the papers that Abe is to be the next President so I suppose that long agony is over and they will now turn there attention to putting down the rebellion once more and I think if they would be half as much in earnest about it as they have about makeing a President the job would a short one. All is quiet in our part at present. We got a small ration of Prisoners yesterday and two peices of Artillery.

You must give my respect to all who wish to hear from me and remember me at Thanksgiveing. I wish I could be there with you But its no use but I shall try and get home this winter if nothing happens. I have not seen Asher since the day we came down here but shall try and get over there this week.

So Good Bye.

Yours as ever
Jack

* * * * * * * * * *

Friday Nov 16th [1864]

Dear Brother

I am not going to write a letter for it is a raining here right smart and cold as Greenland and I have no fire and a poor show for a Shelter But as I received one of my shirts this morning I thought I would just let you know that it came all right. I was looking for it by Express as you wrote me you should send it that way but I am glad you sent it by mail for I think I shall get them sooner. Send the other the same way if you have not done so already. We were to have a Grand Review to day But the rain came and stopped It and I am glad of it.

I went over to see Asher the other day but he was not at home and I did not see him. Shall go again as soon as I get my Shirts fixed up for we are ordered to build Winter Quarters but I dont believe we shall stop in then for I dont see no Winter Quarters yet but would be perfectly willing too. Give my love to Lizzie and all the rest of the folks and if you dont send the other shirt untill you get this put in a pair of Suspenders with it.

Enclosed you will find two 24 cent stamps. They are no good to me and I thought perhaps you might change them for 3 cent ones.

Yours &C
Jack

* * * * * * * * * *

Camp 5th Maine Battery
Kearnstown Virginia
Dec 3d 1864

Dear Brother

Yours of the 28th I received this morning with the other shirt. I was very glad to hear from you. Also to get my shirt. I was over to see Asher yesterday. He had not got his valise. Neither had he received the letter with the receipt But I guess he will get it all right for you know Express matter is very uncertain in the army. He showed me a letter from you in which you said you had not heard from me for two weeks. I dont see why it is for I write as often now as ever I did and all my correspondents are complaining that they dont hear from me but it is not my fault I assure you. The first Division of this Corps went away from here Thursday and the 3d moved this morning I expect we shall go tomorrow or next day. I have no Idea where we are going but I expect down to help Sherman[9] for I have no Idea that Grant wants us at Petersburg.

We had just got fixed up in good shape for winter and got the best quarters I ever had and was building us a nice stable. But I suppose we must go and leave it now and I suppose it will be good bye for a chance to get home this winter. I dont know whether the other Corps

[9] General William T. Sherman's army had taken Atlanta and was marching in a column up to sixty miles wide toward Savannah.

will go or not. They have not received any orders as yet and I partly think they will go. But then you know the 6th are supposed to be tough Cusses and can stand most anything. I dont think Levi need care if he dont see any fighting for I dont believe he would care for it after one or two good ones. But still I had rather be in the field and take my chance than to be at Camp Barry.[10] To much Fourth of July Soldiering there for me. As to recruiting the old Battery in case they should do so I suppose if I could get a 2nd Lieut berth I should take it but still as far as I am concerned if I was sure of remaining just as I am I would rather do so but there are some of the Boys in the other Battery that I would like to see out of it for it is a perfect Hell on earth to be there.

And another thing I dont want to go to any other Mass Battery for I want to Stay in this Corps for I have been [in] it ever since I was in the army and I want to stay in it for I consider it the best damn Corps there is in the Show I do myself. I shall keep quiet untill the first of January for I want to get paid for we have not been paid now for 5 months and I am about broke but after that time I shall see if something cannot be done for the Boys. That Letter you speak of I sent by Conway and Brooks said he would see that you had it. But damn the odds I dont ask any thing of him. He can go to H___ his own way. I suppose in case the old Battery is recruited I could get a recomendation from McCartney. He offered to give me one before he went away but I was looking for something else that time and now I have lost that chance all by haveing a little too much red tape on my arm but however I guess it will all be for the best in the end. At any rate I am not going to worry about it.

You must give my respects to all Inquireing friends and I will write and let you know where we are as soon as I find out.

Yours as ever
Jack

* * * * * * * * * *

[10] The Sixteenth Massachusetts Battery had garrison duty at Camp Barry, defending Washington, D.C.

Camp 5th Maine Battery
Near Winchester Va
December 24th 1864

Dear Brother

I dont know but what you will begin to think that I have forgotten you But I have not but the fact is I have been waiting to hear from you and to day a letter came mailed the 12th of December. In that you ask if I should like a position in the Battery in case it is put into shape again. I wrote you a letter in which I stated that I should and I think you must have got that before now but then there has been no regularity about our mail lately. We got no mail from the 4 of this month untill the 22nd for our Corps has all gone from here except this Battery and we are now attached to the 19th Corps and yesterday one of the coldest days I ever saw in this country. We had to pack up and move camp and you better believe that Gen Grover and all the rest of the 19th Corps got damned slightly for we had just the best camp and best quarters there was in this army but fortunately for us we moved in where a Brigade of Infantry had just left and found very decent shanties. My tent now is within a stones throw of Ashers and I have been there to night to see him. The Boy is quite Busy these days and as yet has not got his valise but expects it tomorrow as there is a lot of Express matter at Winchester for the Corps.

Asher looks first rate. I never saw him look better and he says he never felt better. I dont know how long we shall stay here but I hope not long for if I have got to fight I want to be in the old 6th for then I am at home. In fact I want to get out of the valley army for I dont like there style. It has done very well as long as we could forage but the past month I have lived meaner than ever I lived in the Potomac Army and haveing got out of money it makes it rather tough. We have not been paid since July and they owe me 6 months pay. If they should raise the pay again I should not expect to ever get any But as Elder Piper use to say I have a faint hope left.

I see by the papers that Abraham has made another call and I think now is the time to recruit the old First Mass, for I think the Veterans deserve that much. McCartney promised us last winter to stick by us, and if he had tried he could have kept the Battery up, but then he found he could do better Elsewhere and let it go, and he dont probably care a damn what becomes of us. I want you to write as soon as you get this and if there is no chance that way I am going to try another move and see if we cannot get the old boys together somewheres.

Give my love to all inquiring friends tell them I still live and thats about all.

Yours as ever
Jack

I got my shirts all right. When you write send me some stamps and Direct to

5th Maine Light Battery
Artillery Brigade
19th Corps

* * * * * * * * * * *

Camp 5th Maine Battery
Stevensons Station Va
January 7th 186[5]

Dear Brother

Yours of Jan 1st I received this morning and if the weather will permit I will try and answer. We came to this place last Friday and since we have been here we have had but one decent day. It has snowed blowed and rained and we have had some of the coldest weather I ever knew in Virginia and it has been what I call damn rough. We are trying to get us up quarters but the weather is such that we make slow progress. I thought when I Reenlisted last winter that they could not rough me any more than I had been in the old Potomac Army But I must say that Phil Sheridans beats me for I never lived so poor as I have this winter and we have put up winter quarters this makes four times and I expect as soon as we get these done we shall have to move again a few miles just enough to lose them.

I have not seen Asher since we moved. I started out yesterday morning to hunt him up But I could not find Head Quarters But I did find the 2nd Division a loading on the cars and leaveing and I understood that Grover left the day before. I dont know where they have gone but I suppose Asher will let you know. When you write him tell him to write and let me know where he is. I hear they are granting Furloughs and I suppose he will be likely to get his. Our Captain is going next week and will be gone untill Feb and he told me when he got back he would try and get me one but I dont intend to count much on it untill I get Started for I have been disapointed so many times lately that I have got used to it. I am glad that Col Burrill is moveing. In the matter of the old Battery they have sent 25 of the men that were here with me to Battery D first Rhode Island so that we are now scattered round in three Batteries and I think it a little mite rough to say the least to have men belonging to a Mass Company scattered all through the army.

I would write to Mac if I knew his address but I dont. I wrote to French to let me know but as yet have not heard from him But I can get a Recomendation and a good one when it is wanted. Only let me see a prospect of the Batterys being built up and I will send you the Recomendation. Four good men too. When you see Mrs Church you can tell her "Barkis is willing"[11] but I think if she should take me she would be about as bad off as her mother was when she got Mr. Walker for I dont feel as if I could make a young woman very happy about this time but perhaps I might improve if the weather was warmer. At any rate I am willing to try. I have been expecting that they would cut off my State aid for Mary as I knew she was beyond the age But thought I would not say anything as long as they did not. The postage stamps came all right and I am glad you did not send the money for if I had it I should spend it and I will try and make out untill I get paid which I am in hopes they will do soon.

[11] From Charles Dickens's novel, *David Copperfield.*

You must give my love to all the folks that wish to hear from me and I am in hopes to come and see you between now and Spring. So hopeing this will find you more comfortable than I am.

I Remain yours &C
Jack

* * * * * * * * * *

Camp 5th Maine Battery
Frederick City Maryland
Jan 17th 186[5]

Dear Brother

I have not heard any thing from you for most a fortnight but as you will see by this we are now in Maryland once more. We with the 17th Indianna Battery and the Waggon train of the 2nd Division of the 19th Corps were ordered to this place and arrived here last night leaveing our good quarters which we had just got done and now we are turned out into a field and suppose if we stop here we shall have to build Barracks and Stables. I have got most tired of building quarters as we have built three times this winter and had to leave them.

As I see no signs of getting paid I want you to Send me some money as soon as you get this. Send me 10 dollars if you please and if you have heard from Asher let me know where he is. I sent a list of the men belonging to the old Battery to Mac to day. Part of our old men are in Camp Barry and Mac and the Hon Alexander Price was up there to see them. I am anxious to hear from you to know if they have done any thing about us.

There is no news and will Close.

Direct to 5th Maine Battery
Washington D C

Yours &C Jack

It is too cold to write much.

* * * * * * * * * * *

Camp 5th Battery Maine Vol
Frederick City Maryland
Sunday Jan 29th 1865

Dear Brother

Yours of the 20th with $10,00 enclosed I received last night. The reason I did not get it sooner was we have had no mail for several days. I was very glad to get it for I had nary red and here in a Christian Country a leetle tin is very handy to have in the house. We expect to get into Barracks tomorrow When I hope we shall be a little more comfortable for the weather has been extremely cold. The people here tell us the coldest they have had for ten years. Yesterday was the coldest day I ever saw in the Army. I froze my ears and quite a number of the Boys have froze some part of them. The past two weeks It has been what I call damn rough But then you know its all for your County. I am glad to hear that Asher is haveing such a good time. I dont expect that I shall get home very soon if at all for the Capt will not get back untill the middle of February and perhaps by that time Furloughs will be played out. I was reading in the papers yesterday that Sheridan is appointed to the command of the Potomac Army and the same paper thinks he will knock spots out of Lee in about a minute But I dont see it. When they whip Lee I think John Henry will be about gone up. They all thought Grant was going to raise H___ and perhaps he has but he aint got Richmond And I fail to see what great things he has done I do. But then my eye sight is getting poor.

Our Boys here are enjoying themselves. They have a Singing and Danceing School at a place called Shookstown about a mile from Camp and then a good many of them are off to parties every week. I dont go out of camp. Have not left it since we first came here. Dont you think I am getting Steady? I have heard nothing more from Mac and I dont care a damn whether I do or not. If they will only let me stay where I am I am perfectly contented and they can go to Thunder with there Mass Batteries. I have come to the conclusion that all they care for there Soldiers in the field is damn little after once getting them on there quota.

Give my love to all the folks. Tell Joe I would like to be there to help eat that Chowder but its no use.

Good Bye and write soon.

Yours &C
Jack

Next time you use two sheets of paper please leave one Blank.

* * * * * * * * * *

Camp 5th Battery Maine Vol
Frederick Maryland
Feb 7th 1865

Dear Brother

Yours of the 2nd came to hand yesterday and I was very glad to hear once more from you for I have not had a letter from any one since the last I got from you and I began to think all hands had gone back on me. Sorry to hear that you are troubled with boils but I believe that,s an old complaint of yours. We have got moved into our Barracks but the boys are rather crowded and we have plenty of music. There is to day fiddling dancing boxing and most any kind of sport that you can mention going on. I have a room about 10 feet square that I occupy with our Clerk who is one of the craft and a good fellow. He was down to the Lodge last night. They have a very large one here. The largest in the State. There is plenty of Morgans here and some of the right stamp too— —. I would liked to have been there to Joe,s Chowder Party and I want you to write the particulars of that Presentation for I think it will be a rich one.

I dont know as I shall get home this winter as there is a lot of Furloughs in now and I cannot go untill they get back at any rate. We have not seen the Paymaster yet nor is there much signs of it But I manage to live and keep hopeing he may come. I think [he] will have a hard time to get to his Division for they make no difference between Bounty jumpers and honest men at such times and I think it a damn shame. I have heard enough from our Boys who have been away from the Battery to make a man swa<u>re</u>.

Did Asher get his valise? We are haveing an old fashioned snow Storm here to day and the prospect is we shall have a hard one and get enough for Sleighing. I had the Traveller with Bens Speech in it and I have seen Porters reply and I think one or the other of them must lie and I am rather of the opinion that Butler is the man. I never thought much of him as a Warrior for I dont think thats his Forte I dont. I hear nothing more from Mac But I have heard that we were transfered to the 9th Battery but if such is the Case I should think that some one would try and have us sent to it. I am satisfied where I am and all I ask is to be let alone now.

Give my love to all and dont forget to write about that Presentation.

Yours as ever
Jack

* * * * * * * * * * *

Camp 5th Maine Battery
Frederick Maryland
February 13th 1865

Dear Brother

I seat myself at this time to write you a few lines and let you know that I am still alive although I can hardly say kicking for I am pretty well used up with a cold and Rheumatis. Sunday we were out to a Review and the snow was about 10 inches deep and the wind blowed beautifully. It was one of the coldest days we have had But our Cheif of Artillery did not see fit to countermand his order and out we had to go. Several of the men froze themselves slightly but then you know it,s all for the glory of the country and I expect that Review done a good deal towards crushing the Rebellion but I have an Idea that I would like to crush Major Bradbury and all the rest of the damn fools of officers. Tomorrow 8 men start on Furlough and when they get back I am in hopes to get a chance. They should have gone a week ago but there Furloughs got misplaced and did not get back untill to day. I had a letter from Pricilla last week. She write she paid a good visit to Lynn and I think she did and I should thought she would made them all glad twice.

I want you to send me $15,00 by mail as soon as you get this. Perhaps you had better have it registered and direct it to Frederick City. I dont see any signs of getting paid and I have got tired of liveing the way I have been lately. The fact is we are in a Christian Country and I want a little money so that I can make myself decent to go around amongst folks and live like a Christian. I see by the papers that the old 6th has been moveing down to Petersburg and I think if Grant has good luck he will get into Richmond about a week from fall.

Give my love to all inquireing friends and I hope this will find you enjoying warmer weather than we are here.

Yours as ever
Jack

* * * * * * * * * *

Camp 5th Maine Battery
Frederick Maryland
February 17th 1865

Dear Brother

Yours of the 12th I received last night and was much pleased with the account of the "Chowder Party" And think you must have had a Bully Time and wish I could have been there with you. I had made up my mind that I should be there the 17th of March as I was expecting to come home on Furlough the first of the Month But to night the Capt received an order from the War Department ordering us to the Army of the Potomac and there to join the 9th Battery. So you see that after being knocked about all winter we have got to start off again and for the next fortnight or three weeks I dont anticipate much comfort. We shall Probably leave here the first of the week for

Washington and then go to City Point and if we are lucky shall probably get to the Battery just in time to be to late to get Mustered for Pay the last of this month and have the fun of being done out of our pay for the next two months. I am in hopes to get that money I sent to you for before we go but if I dont I shall have some one here to look after it So that it will be safe. I never wanted money more in my life than I have the past month but have been all the time thinking we should get paid therefore I did not like to send for it. I think if I had known what I should have to passed through when I became a Veteran that I should have respectfully declined but then I am glad its no worse and it may all come out right in the end. At any rate it will settle the question of what is to be done with us and that is worth something. You did perfectly right in letting the money go towards the organ and I guess you better make it 5,00.

I will try and keep you posted in regard to my whereabouts but I dont want you to write untill you hear from me again.

Give my love to all the folks and I hope this will find you in better spirits than it leaves me.

Yours as ever
Jack the unfortunate

* * * * * * * * * * *

Camp 5th Maine Battery
Frederick Maryland
Feb 18th 1865

Dear Brother

Yours of the 14th with one enclosed from Mary I received to night. I also received one from Mary in which she stated that she had written to you for money but did not inform me what she wanted of it only that she wanted to get some thing. But I know she has been unwell and if what she wants is anything that will help her I want her to have it but if it is anything in the shape of dress &C I am not very particular about it. God knows that I would willingly suffer any privation if it would help her any But then I think I might know for what the money is to be spent for but however you may send her $10,00 and perhaps I may get some information before that is gone. I dont expect to see any pay for some time to come but still I shall try to get paid in Washington on our way to the Potomac Army. Somehow it seems to me that when I am short of money there is a loud call and God only knows what would become of the Children if I only had my monthly pay to depend upon. But then its no use to "arguer the question" as the Gen used to say But I will try and get along as well as I can. I live in hopes of getting home some day and then I can talk but now its no use. You probably have sent the money I asked for. If not its no matter (about it).

In my last I told you not to write untill you heard from me But if you wish to write you can direct to the 9th Battery for I think We shall have no trouble in going direct there.

Remember me to all Friends and dont forget (Jack).

* * * * * * * * * *

John Chase's Travel Routes in Chapter 9:
February 1865 to April 1865

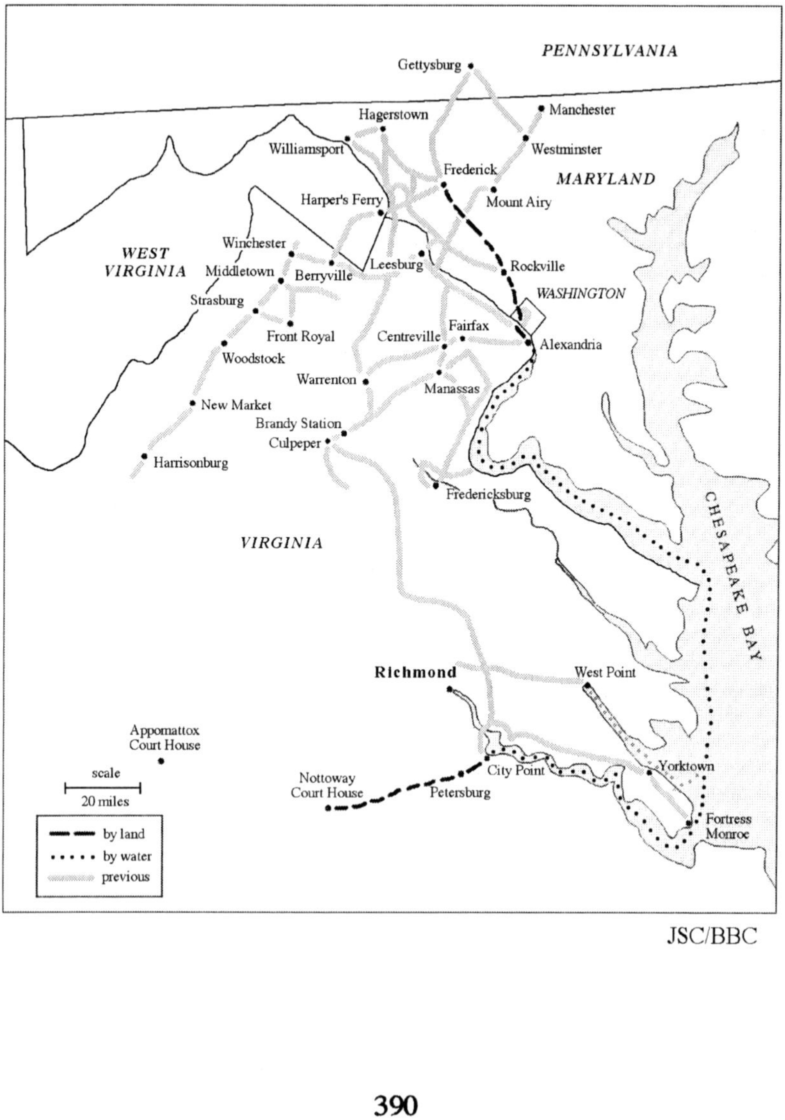

JSC/BBC

CHAPTER 9

Petersburg

Transferred to the Ninth Massachusetts Battery, John Chase rejoins the Army of the Potomac as it continues its siege of Petersburg. When Petersburg falls, the war soon ends, and Chase awaits his discharge from the army.

Camp 9th Mass Battery
February 25th 1865

Dear Brother

We left the 5th Maine last Tuesday[1] and arrived here last night but what is to be done with us now is more than I can tell. They dont want us here for they have more men now than they can muster. The Capt here tells us he will do what he can for us So that we can get some pay. He seems to be a very fine man. His name is Milton[2] and he belongs out to Jamaica Plains West Roxbury. I saw Capt Mac in Washington. He said he would do what he could for us. They are trying to keep us in the 6th Corps But I dont think they can make a go of it. Capt says he is going to write Gov Andrews and see if the Battery cannot be reorganized But one thing I am not going to fret if I can only get my pay and rations I will rest contented and think it served me right for reenlisting.

Things have changed much since we were here last summer and it seems quite natural to hear the Pickets fireing nights But as yet I

[1] February 21.

[2] Captain Richard S. Milton, who had recently replaced Captain John Bigelow.

have heard no heavy guns to speak of. We are haveing a cold rain to day but thank God I am Sheltered. We had a pretty rough time getting here and I was pretty well used up but begin to feel a little more limber now. Write as soon as you get this and let me know if you sent that money I wrote you for for I would like a little just to look at.

Give my love to all the folks and I remain

Yours &C
Jack the unfortunate

Please send me some Stamps.

* * * * * * * * * *

Camp of the 9th Mass Battery
Near Petersburg Virginia
March 5th 1865

Dear Brother

Yours of the 2nd I received last night and was very happy to hear once more from you. I also received the money you sent to Frederick all right. You did not say in your letter whether you sent that money to Mary or not. If you have and only sent 10 dollars I wish you would send her ten more as she wishes to get some things for George. I am in hopes now that we have got things so fixed that we will get paid when this Battery gets paid for I have made out our Muster and Pay rolls and sent them in with theres. I am now at work on the Muster in Rolls so that we can have the Consolidation finished. As it is now we keep two morning reports one of there own Battery and one of Battery A. We have discharged three of our men since we came here and have had two recruits join so that we now number 86 men present and absent. Capt Milton thinks that the old Show may come together yet But I dont see it But if I am going to stop in the service I wish it would or else they would send me back with the old 5th. I had as lieve stay there as not but I dont fancy this institution much although Capt Milton seems to be a fine man and I should think a good officer. I saw Capt McCartney when I came through Washington and he promised to do something for us and I think he will. At any rate I shall continue to wait for the waggon. Things remain all serene here. The usual amount of Picket fireing and some Shelling every day. Grant is running troops to the left on his Rail Road But what he intends to do he keeps to himself But then it is so muddy here now that I dont think he could make much of an advance if he should try But then I think that something will drop before a great while. You I suppose keep better posted on War matters than I do for I dont see the papers every day. Sherman seems to be doing well and according to the papers Sheridans Cavalry is on the move towards Staunton and I think Custer will do something to speak of before he gets back. He is a tough Cuss and death on Rebs.

Remember me to all the folks and write soon. After we get things fixed I will try and write a letter but untill then you must make short ones do.

Yours as ever
Jack

* * * * * * * * * *

Camp of the 9th Mass Battery
March 15th 1865

Dear Brother

I received yours of the 11th this morning and as they are talking about moveing here I thought best to write to day. I dont know about this moveing but then the Sutlers are ordered off and they are sending the sick away. They have been expecting an attack from the Rebs in front of the 9th Corps and yesterday they had quite a smart Artillery duel for a little while and I rather think that something will drop before long. We continue to hear good news from Philip and I rather expect he will make his appearance here before long And I think that everything looks bright for our side. Pray God our success may continue. I was up to the front Monday and took a view of the works on both sides and saw a Review of a Division or near as I

Siege of Petersburg, by Alfred Waud LC

could judge of Rebels. Could see them quite plain. It was in front of the 6th Corps and the works are not more than 2000 yards apart so you can judge how near the picket lines must be. If they do get up a general fight along the lines I dont care to have any hand in it for I think it will be a warm old place both sides and as I am situated at present I think I shall stand a chance to keep out of it but if I have to go in I shall try and do my duty and take the chances— —. I suppose that now the 1st mass is part and parcel of the 9th but they are trying to do something and there object is I suppose to keep We poor Non Coms in the Service for by existing orders we are entitled to our discharge. But I make no doubt they will keep us if they can for there is Officers in this army that dont give a damn for a mans rights. If they can beat him they will. I have made an application for mine but shall be disapointed if I [don't] get it. I am glad you sent Mary the money but as I have not heard from her I dont know whether she got it or not. I received a letter from Langdon a short time ago. He spoke about her sending for it but she had not got it then. I shall probably hear in a day or so. I should tried and come home this spring if I had been settled down anywhere but shall not think of it now untill I find out what they are going to do with me. I like Capt Milton very much. He appears to be willing to do all he can to help us but you know a Capt dont amount to much in this Show.

Give my love to all the folks that wish to hear from me. I wish I could be there to the dedication but as I cannot must depend on you for an account of the Proceedings. So hopeing I shall have some good news to tell of the next time I write I will Close for this time.

Yours as ever
Jack

* * * * * * * * * * *

Front of Petersburg
Sunday April 2nd 1865

Dear Brother

Yours of the 26th I received yesterday and was glad to learn that every thing was lovely. There is a Big Fight going on here to day. It commenced in our front last night about 11 o clock. This corps has got possession of three Rebel Forts and at this present moment they are makeing a fearful charge to retake them but I think if we have no serious pull backs that Petersburg goes under this time or I am a Sugar eater. I can lay back and look on. The first I ever had that priveledge. But as you will probably get a full account of the fight before you get this letter I will not try to give you any account of it. The whole army is at work and Phil has gone off with his troopers and is doing his part of the work. I am in hopes by next Sunday if nothing happens to see you and then I will tell you all about it. Dont let any one know that I expect to come home for I want to see if I cannot surprise them. Dont write again without you hear from me again.

3 PM Every thing is going on finely thus far and I think we have got them where the wool is short.

Good Bye.
Yours &C
Jack

I wish you were here with me. You could see a fight without being under fire. Aint that Bully— —.

* * * * * * * * * *

On the Road Va
April 5th /65

Dear Brother

I hardly thought when I wrote you Sunday that our victory was going to be quite so complete but So it is. But I suppose you know more about it than I do consequently I will not undertake to write anything about it only to say that I have had the pleasure of marching through the City of Petersburg and are now about 15 miles beyond towards Lynchburg. When I wrote you Sunday I expected to start for Boston this week but now I dont know when I shall come for everything is on the go and everybody is looking for the end of the war and if half the Stories we hear are true I think it must be near at hand. I thought I would write these few lines just to let you know that I was all right and never felt better in my life.

Give my love to all the folks and dont write until I ask you too without you have some thing special to write about—For I think I shall get off in the course of a week or so.

Yours as ever
Jack

* * * * * * * * * *

Nottoway Court House Va
April 11th 1865

Dear Brother

Good news still comes pouring in. Sunday I saw Gen Ewell[3] with 8,000 Prisoners pass this place and last night we had the Surrender of Gen Lee read to us and we have come to the conclusion that this War is about over. I expected to have been on my way home before this. My papers are all made out but we have been shifting about so much that I cannot get a Mustering officer to Muster me out But I am in

[3] Confederate General Richard S. Ewell, who had lost a leg earlier in the war.

hopes to get off before long. However I dont find any fault for I have had plenty of fun the past week. It is sport here to see the darkies and hear the remarks they get off. Better than Morris Brothers[4] a heap. This Corps the (9th) are guarding the Rail Road from Petersburg to Burksville and this Battery is with the 3d Division at this place. A good soft thing. Nothing to do and plenty of help in a good country. Plenty to eat and heaps of tobacco. Remember me to all the folks and I remain

yours &C
Jack

[Enclosed is an old court document written in brown ink that reads:]

Nottoway County to wit,

Mary Epes plaintiff complains of William Bevill defendant, in custody &C for this that the said defendant on the ______ day of _______ in the year of our lord ______ in the County being then an unmarried man proposed to the plaintiff, a single woman to contract with him, to marry him, the said defendant, which she consents to do that in consequence of the said proposition the said plaintiff avers that she and the said defendant mutually agreed and contracted together to marry each other, that in consequence of the said agreement the said defendant gained the entire confidence of the plaintiff and by his insinuations and asservations of fidelity and honour aver pursuaded The said plaintiff to admit him to her bed, ~~as if husband so soon as he had gained~~ and soon after he the said defendant left the said plaintiff in a state of pregnancy and refused to carry his aforesaid contract into effect by marry the said plaintiff, and contracted matrimony with another person Wherefore the said plaintiff saith that by the violation and breach of the said contract injured by the loss of her marriage with the said plaintif and deprived of the prospect of contracting

[4] The Morris Brothers was a minstrel troupe.

matrimony with any other person and has sustained damage to $10000:00 therefore she sues G. Bland Jr.

[On the reverse:]

Epes
vs } Nar
Bevill

We of the Jury find for the Plaintiff and assess
her damages to the sum of $191,66,___
Wm Perry

[Next follows a list of dates beginning March 1813, listing all the hearings and depositions, and finally, the verdict on March 8, 1817, and assessment of court costs of $76.52 in October 1817.]

* * * * * * * * * *

Camp 9th Mass Battery
City Point Va
April 24th 1865

Dear Daughter

I have just read yours of the 16th and hasten to reply although I dont know where to direct a letter so that it will find you but I shall run the risk and send it to Samuel as I see yours is mailed at Charlestown. Therefore I suppose you have already arrived at Boston I will send to Sam to let you have some money but I wish I had known of it before as it will take some time for a letter to reach him. I dont expect he has much money of mine in his hands as you know I have received no pay now for ten months but then I think he has some left yet. I am willing to spend all I can earn if it will be any benefit to you and I hope that this Dr will help you. I should have been home before this but for circumstances over which I had no control. Everything for the past six months seems to have gone wrong with me but I am in hopes that my luck will turn before long

But I suppose I shall have to take it as it comes. I write you a letter last week. At that time we were at the Court House at Nottoway but came back here yesterday where we are in the Artillery Reserve of this Army. I dont know what they intend to do with the army. There is 25 Batteries here doing nothing and costing Government a heap to keep them and I cannot see as they have any use for them. I shall send this letter to Sam and write him at the same time and I want you to let me know as soon as you get it. Also let me know what the Dr thinks of your case. I have no news to write except what you probably have heard. Every thing here is quiet as Sunday. I have not had a letter from any body but you since last March and begin to think that every body has forgotten me.

Give my love to all the folks and believe me.

ever your Aff Father
John W Chase

[The envelope is addressed to Mary L. Chase; the letter is on U.S. Christian Commission stationery that is captioned:]

"This is a faithful saying, and worthy of all acceptation, that Christ Jesus came into the world to save sinners; of whom I am chief."

* * * * * * * * * *

Camp of the 9th Mass Battery
City Point Va
April 24th 1865

Dear Brother

I suppose you still reside in Roxbury and I hope this will find you well but I expect you have got tired of looking for me. At any rate I have got tired of trying to get home. I think I have made all of 100 miles but as yet have failed to accomplish my object for the reason that we have been shifted about so much and I might add with justice because of the negligence of the proper officers but then its no use for me to borrow any trouble about for I find that does not help the matter a particle. We arrived here last night and are now in the Reserve Artillery. There is 25 Batteries here doing nothing and I think if the Govt wants to save money they better discharge them. I sit down to write to day because of a letter I received from Mary. She is going to Boston to see a Dr about her cough &C and wanted me to let her call on you for some money. I dont know how much money you have of mine. Neither do I know how much she wants But I suppose Doctoring like everything else comes high in war times. When she comes you can let her have what you think proper if you have it for I dont see no signs of my getting any here untill I am discharged and that day I expect is far off for at the present time there is no Mustering officer here and the 9th Corps has turned us off and they have gone to Washington. If I ever do get home I will give you my experience and I think you will agree with me that there is some very Slow Coaches connected with this Army.

I should like to hear from you and if you dont hear from [me] in 3 days after you get this I wish you would write.

Give my love to all the folks. Tell Lizzie I expect she will be looking for Asher in a few days. I was in hopes that I should get home first but I guess not now.

Yours as ever Jack
9th Mass Battery
Washington DC

* * * * * * * * * * *

[John Chase was mustered out two days later on April 26, 1865, at City Point, Virginia, as a supernumerary noncommissioned officer under provision of Special Order No. 254, Headquarters Army of the Potomac, Series of 1864.]

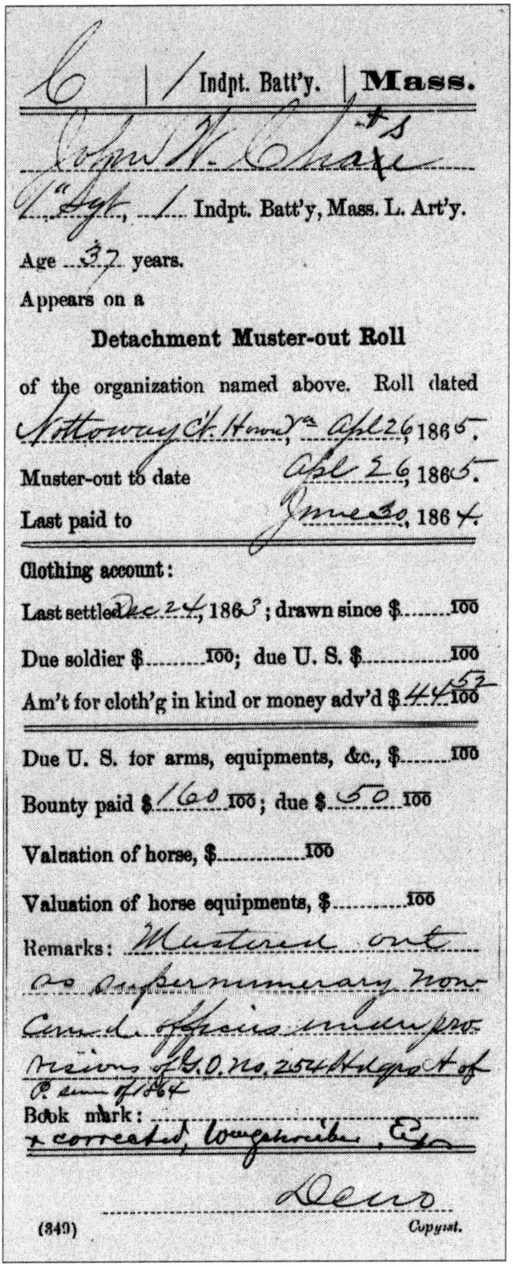

C | 1 Indpt. Batt'y. | **Mass.**

John W. Chase

1st Sgt., 1 Indpt. Batt'y, Mass. L. Art'y.

Age 37 years.

Appears on a

Detachment Muster-out Roll

of the organization named above. Roll dated

Nottoway Ct. House Va. Apl 26, 1865.

Muster-out to date Apl 26, 1865.

Last paid to June 30, 1864.

Clothing account:

Last settled Dec 24, 1863; drawn since $.......100

Due soldier $.......100; due U. S. $.......100

Am't for cloth'g in kind or money adv'd $44 52/100

Due U. S. for arms, equipments, &c., $.......100

Bounty paid $160 100; due $50 100

Valuation of horse, $.......100

Valuation of horse equipments, $.......100

Remarks: Mustered out as supernumerary non-comd. officer under provisions of G.O. No. 254 Hdqrs A of P. series of 1864

Book mark:

x corrected, Longshore, Eg.

Dews

(349) Copyist.

Muster-out Roll, April 26, 1865 NA

Epilogue

John W. Chase returned to Roxbury after the war and joined the Boston Police force as a patrolman in 1865. He was a station captain from 1868 until his death in 1880. He married Sarah A. (Dearborn) Stuart, a widow, on June 12, 1870. John died of cancer at his home in Roxbury on July 27, 1880, at the age of 56. He is buried with his

Boston Police Department Station Captain, John W. Chase TGM

Gravestone of John W. and Sarah D. Chase JSC/BBC

second wife at Forest Hills Cemetery, near Roxbury, in Boston. His headstone is inscribed with the words, NO CROSS NO CROWN. Sarah received a widow's pension from the federal government of $8 per month from 1890 until her death in 1897. See Appendix I for newspaper obituaries.

Sarah F. Chase CFC

John's first wife, Sarah Frances (Marston) Chase is buried in the Chase family plot in the cemetery behind Stratham Community Church. The inscription on her gravestone reads:

Rest dear mother rest
the battles fought, the victory won.

John's daughter, Mary E. (Lizzie) Chase, married Charles Waterhouse, was widowed, married Daniel Edwin Huntington, and was widowed again. She died in 1931, at age 83. She is buried next to her second husband, not far from the grave of John Greenleaf Whittier, in the Friends Yard of Union Cemetery in Amesbury, Massachusetts. She had no surviving children.

Mary (Chase) Huntington CFC

Charles H. Chase CFC

John's son, Charles H. Chase, became a farmer and married Cora Bell Humeston. Charles died at age 75, in 1926. He is buried next to his wife in Exeter Cemetery in Exeter, New Hampshire. They had no surviving children.

John's daughter, Sarah F. Chase, died November 30, 1863, at age six. She is buried next to her mother in the cemetery behind Stratham Community Church. The inscription on her gravestone reads:

A light is from our household gone
A voice we loved is stilled
A place is vacant at our hearth
which never can be filled.

George W. Chase CFC

John's son, George W. Chase, became a dairy farmer in Stratham, New Hampshire, where his farmhouse and barn still stand on Portsmouth Avenue. He married Mary Parker Smith in 1881. They had four surviving children, Russell, Pearl (Johnston), Mary (Hatch), and Hugh. George died at age 70, in 1924. He, his wife, as well as his children, Pearl, Mary, and Hugh, are all buried in the cemetery behind Stratham Community Church.

John's brother, Samuel S. Chase, continued working as a carpenter in Roxbury after the war. He was also a noted tenor singer and musical conductor and was connected with the Handel and Haydn Society for 40 years. He and Lizzie moved to Stratham about 1874. Sam died in 1898, at the age of 80; Lizzie died in 1907, at the age of 88. They are buried together in Forest Hills Cemetery in Boston. Sam's obituary is also in Appendix I.

Samuel S. Chase TGM

Sam's son, Asher M. Chase, became a letter carrier in Roxbury after the war. He married and had two children, but died in 1875, at the age of 33 of "slow paralysis and softening of the brain." He is buried in Forest Hills Cemetery, in Boston, next to his wife, Jane Weston Chase, his parents, and his sister, Elizabeth, who died in 1859, at age 16. Asher's symptoms suggest that he may actually have died of multiple sclerosis. See Appendix IV, Asher Chase, for more information.

John's tent-mate, Benjamin F. (Ben) Winslow, was discharged on disability on December 15, 1862. He died April 4, 1864, at the age of 33, in Bridgewater, Massachusetts, of chronic diarrhea and consumption (tuberculosis).

Benjamin Winslow CFC

Charles French USAMHI

John's friend and fellow soldier in the First Massachusetts Battery, Charles W. (Charley) French, died on March 9, 1871, at the age of 35. He too is buried in the cemetery behind Stratham Community Church. The inscription on his gravestone reads simply, "Rest."

A monument was erected on the Gettysburg Battlefield to commemorate the actions of the First Massachusetts Light Artillery. It is located on Cemetery Hill, to the rear or east edge of Gettysburg National Cemetery. The west face is inscribed with the Sixth Corp's insignia; the east face is inscribed:

FIRST
MASSACHUSETTS
LIGHT BATTERY
ARTILLERY BRIG. 6th CORPS
JULY 3, 1863

First Massachusetts Light Artillery Monument at Gettysburg JSC/BBC

APPENDIX I

Obituaries

Boston Post

WEDNESDAY MORNING. JULY 28, 1880.

CAPT. JOHN W. CHASE

of Police Station Nine died at his residence, No. 114 Thornton street, Roxbury, at 9 o'clock on the evening of July 27. Capt. Chase was born in Roxbury July 12, 1824 [sic], and was a carpenter by trade. At the beginning of the war he enlisted in a Massachusetts battery, and served nearly four years, during the latter part of which he had the rank of sergeant. He joined the police force on Jan. 1, 1865. In 1868 when Station Ten was formed, he was promoted from a patrolman, to be captain of the new station, which position he filled with credit until the reorganization of the police force in October 1878; when he was removed from Station Ten to Station One. About this time he began to be troubled with a cancer on the inside of his right thigh, but was able to continue his duties until about eight months since, when he was confined to his bed. About two months since he was transferred from Station One to Station Nine, but has been unable to do duty at the latter station, owing to his illness. He has always been regarded as an able and efficient officer and an upright and honorable man.

The Boston Daily Globe

BOSTON, WEDNESDAY EVENING, JULY 28, 1880.

A Police Captain Dead.

Captain John W. Chase of Police Division 9 died at his residence, 155 [sic] Thornton street, at 9 o'clock last evening of a cancerous affection of one of his legs. Captain Chase was born in Roxbury, July 12, 1824 [sic], and consequently was fifty-six [sic] years and fifteen days of age at the time of his death. He performed honorable service in a Massachusetts battery during the war of the rebellion and was detailed in the quartermaster's department a portion of the time. After serving his term of enlistment he returned to Roxbury and was appointed a police officer of that city, January 1, 1865. Soon after the annexation of Roxbury to Boston Police Station 10 was built, and Mr. Chase was promoted to the captaincy of it, which position he held until the commissioners reorganized the force, at which time he was placed in charge of Division 1, at the North End, commencing his duties there October 21, 1878. He received a fall on an icy sidewalk after being transferred to this division, injuring his leg, which, it is thought, superinduced the disease that ended his life. He was ill during the summer and fall of 1879, but performed his duties nearly all of the time until eight months ago, when he was confined to his house and has been obliged to stay there ever since. At the last transfers in the superior officers of the department Captain Chase was transferred to the captaincy of Division 9, but he never assumed his duties. Captain Chase was an outspoken and kind-hearted man, and never knowingly injured a person in his life. He leaves a wife and several children. He was highly esteemed and respected by the police officers and officials and the community in general, as well as by a large circle of friends and acquaintances. His record throughout is an honorable one. It is expected that he will be buried Thursday and that there will be a large number of policemen in attendance.

The Boston Herald

BOSTON, WEDNESDAY EVENING, JULY 28, 1880.

Death of Capt. John W. Chase of Division 9.

Capt. John W. Chase whose death occurred about 9 o'clock last evening at his residence, No. 114 Thornton st. Highlands, after many months of intense suffering, was born in Roxbury, July 12, 1825, and was about 55 years of age. He was educated in the Roxbury schools and was a carpenter by occupation till the civil war broke out. In the fall of 1861 he enlisted as a volunteer, and was mustered into the service as first sergeant [sic] of the 1st Massachusetts battery of light artillery, Sept. 2, 1861, and served with credit. He reenlisted Dec. 23, 1863, and was transferred March 12, 1865, to the 9th Massachusetts battery of light artillery, and was honorably discharged April 26, 1865. On the first day of June following he was appointed a patrolman on the police of the city of Roxbury. After the annexation of Roxbury to Boston, when station 10 was built he was promoted to the captaincy of that division on account of his many sterling qualities, which position he held till the reorganization of the department under the police commission Oct. 20, 1878, when he was assigned to station 1. May 29, 1880, Capt. Chase was transferred to station 9. He was a member of Washington lodge, F. and A. M., and was a man of firm character, decided in his opinions and blunt in the expression of them. He was a man of great sympathies, and was respected and beloved by his superiors in rank, his subordinates and the citizens generally, who have shown their regard for them during his long illness in many ways, and whose sorrow at his loss will be severe. Death was caused by a cancerous disease. He leaves a widow and three adult children. His funeral will probably occur on Thursday.

Boston Police Department
Records Center & Archives

Thursday, July 29th, 1880—A meeting of the Board of Police Commissioners was held this day Commissioners Jones and Gargan being present. The following business was transacted by the Board: Vis.

Voted:

That the following order be issued to the Department and that the office of the Commissioners be closed at 11:30 o'clock Friday, July 30, 1880.

General Order No. 59

The Board of Police Commissioners are pained to announce to the Department the death of Captain John W. Chase of Division No. 9 who, for the period of the last fifteen years served as an officer in the Police Department of the cities of Roxbury and Boston; and for the eleven years last past filled the position of Captain of Division.

During his long service he has been a faithful, able, and discreet officer cheerfully performing every duty to which he was assigned.

As a mark of respect to his memory the Commissioners direct that the office at Police Station No. 9 be draped in mourning for thirty days and that such officers and patrolmen as desire be permitted to attend his funeral, subject to the discretion of Commanders of Divisions.[1]

---

[1] Records of the Police Commissioners. Series 1. Thursday, July 29th, 1880. Boston Police Department Records Center & Archives, Boston, Mass.

The Boston Daily Globe

BOSTON, FRIDAY EVENING, JULY 30, 1880

FUNERAL OF CAPTAIN J. W. CHASE.

Services Held at the Roxbury Universalist Church Today.

Funeral services over the remains of Captain John W. Chase of Police Division 9 were held at 12 o'clock today in the chapel of the Roxbury Universalist Church and were largely attended. Brief services were held at the residence of the deceased, at 155 Thornton street, at 11 o'clock, after which the remains were conveyed to the chapel. About sixty members of the police formed at the house of Division 9, and marched to the chapel under command of Superintendent Adams. Nearly all of the captains were present, and all of the members of Divisions 9 and 10 not required to be on duty. Commissioners Jones and Gargan were also present together with sixteen members of Washington lodge of Masons, and several members of the Massachusetts First Battery Veteran Association, of both of which organizations the deceased was a member. The remains were dressed in a captain's full uniform, and were enclosed in a black broadcloth casket. The floral offerings consisted in part of a mounted cannon and caisson complete by the battery association, a badge by the police, a star by the police of Division 10, a mound lettered "Our Captain" by the police of Division 9, a square and compass by the Masons, and a pillow lettered "J. W. C." by friends. There were several other rich and tasteful tributes. The pall-bearers were Captain Ayers of Division 15 and Captain McDonald of Division 13, for the police, Dr. W. H. Emery and Captain Hawley Folsom of Division 10, for the Masons, Otis S. Neal and A. A. Young for the battery association.

The services were conducted by Rev. Mr. Blanchard of the Shawmut-avenue Universalist Society, and consisted of singing by a Masonic quartet, Scripture reading, brief address and prayer. The remains were followed to Forest Hills cemetery by the above-mentioned organizations, and at the grave a Masonic service was performed by Rev. Dr. Dadman.

The Boston Daily Globe

BOSTON, MONDAY MORNING, OCTOBER 17, 1898.

CAPT. S. S. CHASE DEAD.

Was Well-Known Citizen of Stratham, N H.

He Was Formerly Alderman from Ward 5, Roxbury, Mass.

During His Early Days Was Captain of Roxbury Military Company.

EXETER, N H, Oct 16—Capt. Samuel S. Chase, 81 years old, one of the most prominent residents of Stratham, died at his home in that town Saturday night of paralysis.

Capt. Chase was born in Stratham May 3, 1817, son of Andrew Chase. His family was of English origin. His great grandfather, Thomas Chase, settled in Stratham over 150 years ago. When Capt. Chase was but a year old he went with his parents to Roxbury, Mass. There he acquired his education, afterward becoming captain of the Roxbury militia company. He learned the carpenters trade with his father. After his father's retirement, Capt. Chase carried on the business of contractor and builder in Roxbury, and was connected with the building interests of that place for many years previous to its annexation to the city of Boston.

In 1874 he returned to Stratham where he has occupied a part of his father's farm. While a resident of Roxbury, he was a member of the board of aldermen from ward 5. He was also upon the board of engineers for some time, and served as assistant engineer for six years. During his residence in Stratham he was active in public affairs, and served the town one year as treasurer.

He was one of the oldest choristers for miles around. At one time he was a member of the Handel and Haydn society of Boston, and at the time of the peace jubilee led and directed the chorus in Exeter. Last winter at an entertainment given in Stratham by the grange, Capt. Chase, then over 80 years of age, sang a solo. He was a Mason, having been initiated in the Rockingham lodge of Roxbury, Mass.

On June 4, 1840 Mr. Chase was united in marriage to Elizabeth Curtis of Dover. On June 4, 1890, Mr. and Mrs. Chase celebrated their golden wedding. He is survived by his wife. Mr. Chase was a lifelong democrat.

John Chase's Travel Routes:
October 1861 to April 1865

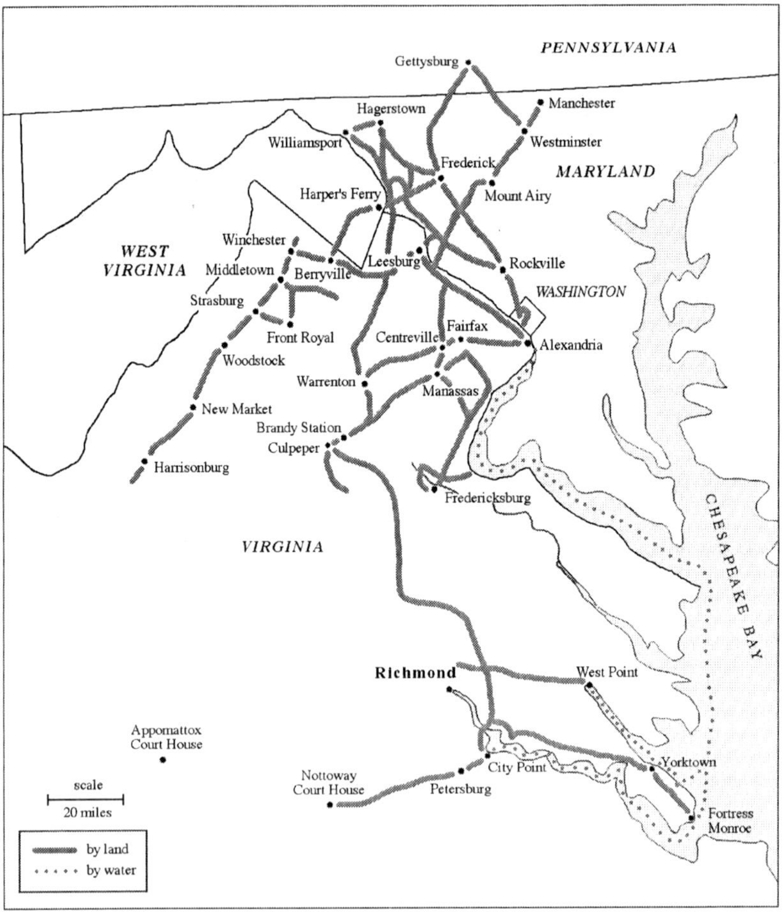

JSC/BBC

APPENDIX II

A Chronology of John W. Chase's Role in the War

1861

Aug. 28 John Chase enlists in Roxbury, Massachusetts at the age of 36, in the First Massachusetts Light Artillery under Captain Josiah Porter. They train at Camp Cameron, North Cambridge, Massachusetts, with five officers and 152 men.

Oct. 3 The battery takes the train to Fall River, Massachusetts, a steamer to New York City, marches down Broadway, takes a steamer to South Amboy, New Jersey, and a train to Philadelphia, then to the Susquehanna River. They move by train ferry across the river, by train to Baltimore, march across Baltimore, take a train to Washington, arriving on the 6th, and camp in the city.

Oct. 9 John Chase is appointed corporal.

Oct. 14 The battery marches down Pennsylvania Avenue, across the Potomac River to Fairfax Seminary, near Alexandria, Virginia. They drill and set winter quarters at Fairfax Seminary.

1862

Mar. 10 They march to Fairfax Court House, then back to Alexandria.

Apr. 5 They march to Centreville Heights to Manassas

	Junction toward Bristoe Station, countermarch toward Manassas, and then back to Alexandria.
Apr. 27	They take a steamer and two schooners down the Potomac and Chesapeake Bay to Ship Point, south of Yorktown, to join McClellan's Peninsula Campaign.
May 4	They are towed up the York River in a barge to the mouth of the Pamunkey River.
May 7	They engage the enemy at West Point, Virginia.
May 8	The battery becomes part of General Slocum's First Division, Sixth Corps, under General Franklin.
May 17	They march to Cold Harbor, then to Gaines Farm.
early June	They move to Mechanicsville, then to Cold Harbor.
June 25	Engagement at Oak Grove—the start of The Seven Days' Battles.
June 27	Engaged at Cold Harbor, they then withdraw toward the James River.
June 30	Battle of White Oak Swamp—Charles City Crossroads.
July 1	Battle at Malvern Hill, then they withdraw to Harrison's Landing on the James River.
Aug. 20	They fast march across the peninsula to Williamsburg, to Yorktown, then to Hampton.
Aug. 26	The battery sails to Alexandria.
Aug. 30	They march toward Fairfax Court House, to Cub Run, where they reinforce the retreating Union army following the Second Battle of Bull Run. They then countermarch to Centreville.
Sep. 1	They again march to Fairfax Court House, then back to Alexandria, across the Potomac, through Georgetown to Tenleytown, then into Maryland to Rockville, then to Beallsville.
Sep. 12	They leisurely march across Catoctin Mountain to Burkittsville.
Sep. 14	Battle of South Mountain at Crampton's Gap.
Sep. 17	Battle of Antietam.

Sep. 23	They march from Sharpsburg to Bakersville near Hagerstown.
Oct. 1	Captain Porter resigns, Lieutenant McCartney is placed in command.
Oct. 9	They march to Hagerstown.
Oct. 17	They march to Williamsport to guard the ford across the Potomac River.
late Oct.	They march to Berlin (now Brunswick), cross the Potomac, continue south to New Baltimore near Warrenton, Virginia.
Nov. 7	General Burnside replaces General McClellan in command of Army of the Potomac.
mid Nov.	They march to Stafford Court House, north of Fredericksburg.
Dec. 6	They move to near Belle Plains, east of Fredericksburg.
Dec. 10	They move through White Oak Church to the Rappahannock River across from Fredericksburg.
Dec. 13	Battle of Fredericksburg—the Sixth Corps crosses the Rappahannock two miles southeast of town.
Dec. 14	They retreat back across the Rappahannock at night.
Dec. 17	They go into winter quarters at White Oak Church.
late Dec.	Battery commander Lieutenant William McCartney is promoted to captain.

1863

Jan. 20	The battery gets bogged down in the infamous Mud March.
Jan. 26	General Hooker replaces General Burnside.
Apr. 28	The Sixth Corps under General Sedgwick moves to the Rappahannock River below Fredericksburg.
May 2	Battle of Chancellorsville—the battery crosses the Rappahannock and moves through Fredericksburg.
May 3	Battle of Salem Church.

May 4	Heavily engaged all day, they retreat across Bank's Ford at midnight.
May 9	They return to White Oak Church.
June 5	They cross the Rappahannock and establish fortifications.
June 9	John Chase is promoted to sergeant.
June 14	They march to Stafford Court House, to Occoquan, to Fairfax Station, to Bristoe Station.
June 25	They march to Centreville, to Dranesville, to Edwards Ferry, cross the Potomac River to Maryland, move to Barnesville, to New Market, to Mt. Airy, to Westminster.
June 28	General Meade replaces General Hooker as head of the Army of the Potomac.
July 1	They arrive near Manchester then move back through Westminster toward Gettysburg.
July 2	They arrive at the Battle of Gettysburg in early afternoon. The infantry is sent into action, the batteries replace reserve batteries, which are sent into action.
July 3	Relieving the First New Hampshire Battery on Cemetery Ridge, the First Massachusetts Battery is heavily engaged, helping repulse repeated attacks of charging infantry while under fire from enemy batteries.
July 5	They march from Gettysburg to Emmitsburg to Frederick, then west to Middletown on the 9th, then on to Boonesboro, through Funkstown toward Hagerstown, then on to Williamsport on the 14th, then backtrack to Hagerstown, Boonesboro, and Middletown to reach Berlin on the 17th.
July 18	They cross the Potomac at Berlin, then move up the Shenandoah Valley and across the mountains to near Warrenton in August, and then on to Culpeper in September.
Sep. 7	John Chase is promoted to first sergeant.

Oct. 10	They march north to Manassas, countermarch south to Brandy Station, then north again to Centreville, then south again to Warrenton.
Nov. 7	Engagement at Rappahannock Station (now Remington)—they then move south to near Brandy Station.
Nov. 26	They move south, cross the Rapidan River at Jacob's Ford, and engage the enemy at Mine Run. Choosing not to attack, they retreat north on Dec. 2.
Dec. 5	John Chase is notified of the death of his youngest child, Sarah, age 6. He takes a furlough home.
Dec. 23	John Chase reenlists as a first sergeant at Brandy Station, Virginia.

1864

Jan.	The battery goes into winter quarters near Brandy Station. John Chase takes another furlough home as a bonus for reenlisting.
May 3	The battery moves south as the Overland Campaign begins.
May 5	Battle of the Wilderness.
May 12	Battle of Spotsylvania Court House.
May 23	Battle of North Anna River.
May 26	They move south along the Pamunkey River.
June 1	Battle of Cold Harbor—Chase is slightly wounded in his neck; his horse is shot from under him.
June 12	They move south across the Chickahominy and the James rivers to the front near Petersburg.
July 9	They move to City Point, embark on a steamer, steam down the James, up the Chesapeake Bay and the Potomac to Washington to help defend the city against attack from General Jubal Early.
July 13	The battery marches up 7th St., then west to Poolesville, Maryland, then to White's Ford.

July 16	They cross the Potomac, move through Leesburg, Virginia, march west over Snicker's Gap to beyond the Shenandoah River, then march back to Leesburg, past Dranesville to Arlington Heights, and then move north to Tenleytown in Washington on July 22.
July 26	They march north to Frederick, Maryland, then to Jefferson, to Halltown, near Harpers Ferry, West Virginia, on July 29, then back to Frederick, then back to Halltown.
Aug. 10	The battery is put under the command of General Philip Sheridan's Army of the Shenandoah. They march south through Charles Town to Berryville to Strasburg, then back north to Halltown.
Aug. 28	They move south to Berryville.
Sep. 19	The Battle of Opequon Creek (Third Winchester).
Sep. 20	They move south to Strasburg.
Sep. 22	Battle of Fisher's Hill—they move south to Woodstock, New Market, and Harrisonburg.
Oct. 1	The battery makes an expedition to Mt. Crawford, then back to Harrisonburg.
Oct. 3	The First Massachusetts Light Artillery is disbanded at the expiration of the three-year enlistment of most of its members. They march north to Winchester, then to Martinsburg, then take the train to Baltimore, Philadelphia, New York, to Boston. John Chase is reassigned to the Fifth Maine Light Artillery in the Nineteenth Corps at Harrisonburg.
Oct. 10±	Ordered to Petersburg, they move to Front Royal, then east to near Upperville; then, ordered back, they move to Middletown near Cedar Creek.
Oct. 19	Overrun at the Battle of Cedar Creek, they retreat, then counterattack, regaining what they had lost.
Oct. 20±	They move south to Strasburg.
Nov. 9	They move north to Kernstown, just south of Winchester.

1865

Jan. 6	The Fifth Maine Battery moves north to Stevenson Station, just north of Winchester.
Jan. 16	They arrive in Frederick, Maryland, where they set winter quarters.
Feb. 17	John Chase is reassigned to the Ninth Massachusetts Light Artillery in the Ninth Corps.
Feb. 21	He leaves Frederick for the camp of the Ninth Massachusetts Battery near Petersburg, arriving on Feb. 24th.
Apr. 2	Assault on and fall of Petersburg—they move west in pursuit of Lee's army.
Apr. 10	The battery arrives at Nottoway Court House to guard the railroad.
Apr. 23	After Lee's surrender, they arrive at City Point to await orders to go home.
Apr. 26	John Chase is mustered out as a supernumerary noncommissioned officer at the age of 39.

The First Massachusetts Light Artillery lost during their service six enlisted men killed or mortally wounded, and fifteen enlisted men from disease.[1]

The Fifth Maine Light Artillery lost two officers and sixteen men killed or mortally wounded, and fifteen enlisted men from disease.[2]

The Ninth Massachusetts Light Artillery lost two officers and thirteen enlisted men killed or mortally wounded, and four enlisted men from disease.[3]

[1] Frederick H. Dyer, *A Compendium of the War of Rebellion*, Dayton, Ohio, Morningside, 1979.
[2] Ibid.
[3] Ibid.

APPENDIX III

Battery Organization

The First Massachusetts Light Artillery originally referred to Major Asa M. Cook's Boston Light Battery of ninety-day volunteer militia. They served from April 20 until August 2, 1861. The battery, with six brass six-pound guns, ten tons of ammunition, and seventy horses, traveled from Boston to New York City by train, then by steamer to Fortress Monroe, Virginia, then back to Annapolis, Maryland, where they were quartered at the Naval Academy. In May, they moved to Relay House to guard the stone Thomas Viaduct that carried the B & O Railroad over the Patapsco River. In June, they were ordered to Baltimore, where they remained until August, when the men were mustered out of the service.

Its officers were:

Major Asa M. Cook
1st Lieutenant Josiah Porter
2d Lieutenant William H. McCartney
3d Lieutenant Caleb C. E. Mortimer
4th Lieutenant Robert L. Sawin

After the ninety-day term of enlistment expired for the men of Cook's Battery, Lieutenant Josiah Porter led the recruitment to reorganize the battery with men who enlisted for three years. He became its captain and other officers from the earlier unit became its officers. The first hundred men were mustered in on August 28, 1861, and were sent to Camp Cameron in North Cambridge for drilling.[1]

[1] James L. Bowen, *Massachusetts in the War 1861–1865*, Springfield, Mass., Bowen & Son, 1893.

Guarding the Bridge at the Relay House NA

The officers and staff were:

Captain Josiah Porter
Senior 1st Lieutenant William H. McCartney
Junior 1st Lieutenant J. Henry Sleeper
Senior 2d Lieutenant Jacob Federhen
Junior 2d Lieutenant Robert L. Sawin
Sergeant Major J. W. B. Wright
Quartermaster Sergeant John B. McCartney

There were six *Chiefs of Pieces* with the rank of sergeant, including Charles W. French of Stratham, New Hampshire, six *Gunners* with the rank of corporal, six *Chiefs of Caissons* with the rank of corporal, including John W. Chase, six *Artificers*, including blacksmiths, wheelwrights, and harness makers, two *Buglers*, one *Wagoner*, and a *Clerk.* Most of the men were from Boston, others were from elsewhere in Massachusetts or nearby states and Canada,

First Lieutenant Josiah Porter USAMHI

and a few were from Great Britain, Prussia, and Bavaria.[2]

The battery left for Washington on October 3 with six pieces of artillery, six caissons, one ammunition wagon, one army forge, and three baggage wagons. The guns and caissons were each drawn by six horses, and the others were drawn by four. Including the officers' horses, there were a total of 125 horses. The battery was composed of 152 men and five officers. The average age of the regiment was 25. When the battery arrived in Washington, it exchanged its two rifled and two smooth-bore 6-lb. guns for four rifled 10-lb. Parrott guns, but kept its two 12-lb. howitzers. The battery later exchanged its guns for six smooth-bore 12-lb. Napoleon guns. The battery became part of Franklin's Division, which was made up of twelve regiments of infantry, one regiment of cavalry, and four regiments of artillery.[3]

In 1893, James W. Kenney, who had been a gunner and then a sergeant in the First Massachusetts Light Artillery, wrote a description of his experiences in the war to his nephew and namesake. The following descriptions are from that document.[4]

> There are 14 carriages in a Battery, 6 Gun carriages with a Gun mounted on the hind wheels and a Ammunition chest on the front wheels. The trail of the Gun hooks on the Axle of the front wheels when on the Move, but rests on the ground when in action. [There are] 6 caissons which carry Ammunition, two chests on the hind wheels and one on the front wheels. The front and rear parts of the caisson couple together the same as the Gun carriage and are alike and can be exchanged when wanted. Thus in action the caissons are left in a sheltered place when convenient and if the Ammunition of the Gun limber [the front assembly] is

[2] Bowen, *Massachusetts in the War 1861–1865.*

[3] Andrew J. Bennett, *The Story of the First Massachusetts Light Battery*, Boston, Mass. Deland & Barta, 1886.

[4] James W. Kenney, Civil War Miscellaneous Collection (Sergeant's letters and diary, 1861–65), Manuscript Archive, U. S. Army Military History Institute, Carlisle, Penn.

running low, the limber of the caissons come up and takes its place and the Gun limber returns to the caisson and refills from the rear chests, ready to exchange again. There is an extra wheel on the rear of the caisson, an extra pole under the carriage, a Shovel, Axe, Pick, Water Buckets, &c. [There is a] carriage called "Battery Wagon" with a half-round top to carry Extra Feed bags, parts of harness, halters, saddler's tools, wheelwright's tools, and various stores. [There is a] carriage called a Forge or traveling Blacksmith shop for shoeing horses and doing iron work of all kinds.

The Battery is divided into three Sections, two guns and two caissons each, with a Lieutenant in charge of each Section. Each Section is divided into two Gun Detachments, one gun and caisson each, with a Sergeant in charge of each Gun Detachment.

There is a driver to each pair of horses and he rides the nigh [left] one when on duty. They take care of their horses, cleaning, feeding, and driving, also take turns standing guard over the horses at night.

I will now give you the duties of the Gun Squad with the Gun unlimbered and in position, the limber in the rear of the Gun, horses facing the rear of the Gun, the drivers dismounted and "Standing to Horse" holding them by the bridle, the Pole Driver holds the Sergt's horse when firing, he being Dismounted and in charge of the Gun. Standing in the rear, 8 men and the Gunner is a Gun Squad. The Gunner, [with a rank of Corporal, receiving orders from the Sergeant, sights the gun and] gives the orders to load, cut the fuse, fire, &c. The men are numbered 1 to 8. No. 1 is on the right of the muzzle and Sponges and rams the Gun. No. 2 opposite him and he inserts the cartridge and shot or shell, having one in each hand. No. 3 on the right. He thumbs the vent, then steps to handspike in end of the trail and moves the Gun to right or left for the Gunner, then pricks the cartridge and steps to place. No. 4 is on the left and he fixes a friction primer to the lanyard, inserts it in the vent, stepping back to place ready to pull at the order to "fire." No. 5 is on the left and half way between No. 2 and the limber. He takes the Ammunition from his position to No. 2. No. 7 stands on the left of limber and takes it to No. 5. No. 6 stands at the rear of Ammunition Chest, cuts the fuse and delivers it as ordered to No. 7. No. 8 is the 2d Corporal of the Gun Squad and in charge of the caisson and remains with it and attends to any order received. If to pack any Ammunition from rear chest to Limber, he would dismount his drivers and set them to work. The men are drilled at all the duties on Guns and Horses, also drilled to work short-handed, one man doing the duty of two, three or more.

As I have not given you a description of our Ammunition before I will now. For a Light 12 or "Napoleon Gun" we carry 12 Solid Shot rounds weighing

A Light Artillery Gun Detachment at Drill NA

12 lbs each, 12 Case Shot, being a shell filled with Small Balls (about 60) and a charge of Powder inside and a Metallic fuse. It is marked in seconds, half and quarter seconds, cutting it at Marks required with fuse gauge. It lights on leaving the Muzzle of the Gun and burns back entering the shell and exploding it. It is intended to use on Infantry Exploding in front of line acting as a discharge of musketry. 4 Shell, being thicker than case shot and filled with a charge of Powder only, that also has a fuse . . . also "canister," looking like a tin pail with a cartridge attached to it. Some of the cans have 27- 5 oz balls in each can and some 72- 3 oz balls in each can. This is used at short range, say up to 300 yards. At shorter range double shot, breaking off the cartridge from the second shot and putting in with the other, which would be 864- 3 oz balls or 324- 5 oz balls at each discharge of the Battery. A bad thing for a line of Infantry to run against. Thus you see we carry 32 rounds to each chest, 128 to each gun, and 768 to the Battery. Ammunition trains follow us to keep up the supply.

I Will give you an account of what some of our camp duties were. 1st Call in the Morning at 5:30 when we get up, put on our boots, and are dressed, 5:45 fall in for Roll Call and served with a dipper of coffee, 6:00 fall in again and clean around the Horses also clean and feed them until 7:00, then breakfast. 8:30 Guard Mounting when the old guard are dismissed and the New Guard go on for 24 hours, they are divided into 3 Reliefs and go on for 2 hours and off for 4 hours. 9:00 Water Call, when the drivers take the Horses to water. 9:30 Sick Call, when the sick report to the Dr's tent. 12:30 Dinner. 3:30 Stable Call, when the stables are cleaned, also horses fed and cleaned. 5:30 Evening Roll Call. 8:00 Tattoo Roll Call. 8:30 Taps, when all lights are put out no noise or talk after that, also about 5 hours Drill beside, if the weather is good. Every day Field

Drill, Gun Drill, or Sabre Drill. . . . We had large "Bell" tents called "Sibley Tents" that would hold 12 men each, while in Winter camp, but when we received Marching orders we also received orders to turn them in and draw small ones called "Shelter tents" one half tent to each man. They would button together.

APPENDIX IV

Asher Chase

Asher Moore Chase was the only son of Samuel and Elizabeth Chase. He was born in Boston in 1841, and grew up in Roxbury. He and his uncle, John W. Chase, were apparently close friends, and John was obviously concerned for his welfare when Asher enlisted in the Seventh Massachusetts Light Artillery in May 1862. The regiment served garrison duty in Yorktown, Virginia, and in Washington, D.C., until January 1864, when it went to New Orleans and western Mississippi. It was when the battery was in Washington that Asher was taken seriously ill with typhoid fever. He was hospitalized for several weeks, but recovered sufficiently to travel with the battery to New Orleans and then participate in the Red River Campaign. He later transferred to a clerk position with the Second Division Headquarters of the Nineteenth Army Corps, first in Louisiana, then in Virginia, and finally in Savannah, Georgia, where he mustered out in May 1865. Following his army service, Asher returned to Roxbury where he received an appointment as a letter carrier at the Roxbury Post Office. He married Jane M. Weston in 1867, and they had two sons, Charles E. B. and Asher H. S. Chase. Unfortunately Asher was not completely healthy when he returned from the war, and his health gradually deteriorated until he had to give up his job. He moved to Warren, Maine, with his wife and children, where he died in January 1875, at the age of 33 of "slow paralysis and softening of the brain." His wife filed for a widow's pension in 1882, which required her to submit evidence that his illness and death were caused by his service in the war. Among the evidence submitted were the following letters documenting his original illness, and depositions describing his health before and after his military service.

The following four letters are to Asher's father, Samuel S. Chase, from Lieutenant Charles H. Williams, one of the officers in Asher's battery.

Camp Barry D.C.
Dec. 16th 1863

Mr. Chase
Dear Sir;

At the request of your Son Asher I have the painful duty of informing you that he is sick in the Hospital at this Post. He has not been well for the last week or two and day before yesterday he went to the Hospital; he is very weak and can only sit up a few minutes at a time.

He wishes me to say to you that if you have not started a Christmas Box for him, that you need not send it, for he does not think that he will be able to enjoy the contents of it, and it would only be an unnecessary expense. I do not think that he is dangerously ill, but his constitution is slightly shattered, and it will take time to recruit his strength up to its maximum standard. If he fails any I will let you know immediately, but I do not think that I shall have that painful duty to perform. I will write you day after tomorrow and let you know how he is progressing.

Do not give yourself any uneasiness about Asher, for he has the best of care and anything that he wishes I will see that he has it.

Please give my best respects to Mrs Chase and to all inquiring friends.

Hoping that these few lines will find you and your family well,

I remain
Your Obd't. Serv't.
C. H. Williams
1st Lt. 7th Mass Battery

* * * * * * * * * *

Camp Barry D.C.
Dec. 19th 1863

Mr Chase
Sir;

I wrote you a few days ago concerning the sickness of your Son Asher.

I was at the Hospital again this morning and he is no better, the Doctor says "that he thinks he has got the Typhoid Fever, and it will take some time before he will be able to leave the Hospital," he is pretty sick and has lost considerable flesh.

The Doctor "said that he would give him the best of care," and I will see that he needs nothing.

Give my best respects to all inquiring Friends and to Mr & Mrs F.

I am Sir
Your Obd't Serv't
C. H. Williams.

* * * * * * * * * *

Camp Barry D.C.
Dec. [30] 1863

Mr Chase
Dear Sir;

Your Son is about the same as he was the last time I wrote you, he has every care that can be afforded him for it cannot be expected that he will receive the attention and care which would be given him were he at Home. He is in the Camp Hospital about a stones throw from my quarters.

It would be impossible for him to be moved as far as Roxbury in the condition he is now in, for he is very weak and I think that the journey would impair his health greatly.

I have not yet received Asher's Box but shall send down for it tomorrow if it arrived. There is not very good accommodations out here for Mrs Chase, although if she wishes to come out here I think that I can find a place for her to stop.

Asher sends his love to you all.

Give my love to Mr & Mrs F. and to all inquiring Friends.

Do not be alarmed about Asher for if there is any sign of his failing I will let you know.

I am Sir
Your Obd't Serv't
C. H. Williams.

* * * * * * * * * *

Camp Barry D.C.
January 1st 186[4]

Mr Chase
Dear Sir:

I have the pleasure of acknowledging the receipt of your Box to day. I went up to see Asher about it and found him well enough to have a good dinner, he was dressed and the Dr says that the fever has left him and all he wants now is to get strength. Mr Mills has gone Home on a thirty day furlough he having reenlisted. We have 10 of the old . . . [missing] . . . as I am very busy and could only spare a few moments to write. Give my best respects to your next door neighbors and tell them that I am well and happy. Give my love to my Mother if you see her and to all inquiring Friends. Asher is well.

If you write to me direct to C. H. Williams New Orleans Office Chief of Art'y.

Hoping that these few lines will find you and your family well.

I remain
Yours Truly
Charley

* * * * * * * * * *

The following letter is from Asher to his parents.

Post Hospital Camp Barry
Washington Jany 2d 1864

Dear Parents

I am still in the hospital as you will see by the heading of my letter. I am gaining slowly the fever has all left me and all I want now is to regain my strength this will probably take three or four weeks. I got off of my bed yeasterday for the first time for over a fortnight and it was just as much as I could do to stand, but after a while I got out as far as the stove where I got a chair and I sat there till I was tired when I went to bed again. The Dr tells me to persevere so I am up again today, and I thought I would improve the time by writing to you. I cannot write a great amount for I am too weak. When Mr. Downs wrote I particularly told him to write for Mother to come out, I had had a talk with the Capt, and he was going to let her have his room, and he was going to move with one of the other officers. I do not know why he did not do as I requested, at that time I was very low but I suppose it was all for the best. Charley has been to see me a number of time since I have been sick. The box did not arrive in time for Christmas, but it got here for New Years morning so that I was able to enjoy the contents, I gave the boys one of the turkeys, one of the puddings, and the fixings to go with them. I also gave them some of the pies. The preserves I kept my self. The doctor told me that I could eat them also the other turkey, the only thing that he objected to was the pudding but he says that I may eat that in two or three days. Everything came all right but the apples, they rotted so that they were not fit to eat. Tell mother that I want a pair of good knit woolen gloves. I should like some money for there are a great many things that the Dr says I may eat that I cannot get at the hospital, in fact all that we get to eat here is dry toast and tea without milk or sugar, sometimes they give us mush and milk, about half a pint to a man. We are so hungry here that we are half crazy. We can buy as much as we want to provided that it will not hurt us and the Dr inspects everything that comes into the hospital. So that nothing hurtful has a chance to get in here. I dont think of any thing more to write, give my love to grandmother, and my thanks to all who contributed to the fixing of my box. Hoping to hear from you soon, I remain,

your aff Son
Asher

* * * * * * * * * * *

This letter, on Campbell Hospital letterhead, is from the Reverend W. M. Gaylord to Henry B. Metcalf, of Boston, Massachusetts.

Campbell Hospital,
Washington, D.C.,
Jan 3d 1864

My Dear Metcalf

I have just returned from Camp Bary (Some 3 miles distant from our Hospital) & am happy to state that your young friend is rapidly recovering. He is free from fever and will be able before many days to return my call. The Sergeant in charge accompanied me in my call at the Camp Hospital and seemed a very kind & attentive gentleman. Mr Chase knew me & seemed delighted to know that he was so well remembered by his friends. He is looking forward impatiently to the time of his release from the Service for though he has recovered from the severe attack of Typhoid fever & will be able to go on duty before long he feels that his constitution is broken and that it will be time for him to go home when the term of his enlistment expires. I was much pleased with him & made him promise to come and see me as soon as the Dr would allow.

I hope you will understand why I have so long delayed this visit. 1st your letter was delayed & since its reception every moment of my time has been employed.

Very truly
Yours
W M Gaylord

* * * * * * * * * * *

The following four letters are from Asher to his parents.

Post Hospital, Camp Barry
Washington, DC January 11, 1864

Dear Parents

Yours of the 6th instant received yesterday and you may believe I was glad to hear from home. It is very tiresome lying here in the hospital with nothing to do, and when I receive a letter, it is as gladdening as in the oasis in the desert to the weary and thirsty traveler. My health is tip top, but I do not gain strength very fast. I do not gain as fast as I ought to. I think it is now a week or more since I left my bed, two days after that event I was able to walk out to the cook house to eat my meals, but I had to be very careful, or my knees would give way under me and I have not gained any more strength since, but I am waiting patiently for it to return. In regard to the box you sent me I do not know what the contents were, but Charley sent up to me a turkey, part of a pudding, two pies, the cranberry sauce, and pears, and the rolls, the rest of the eatables he gave to the boys. If it had not been for the turkey and other things I believe I should have starved if it had not been for them, for they keep us on low diet here and my appetite is terrific. The doctor has given me leave to eat all I want, but I can't get enough at the cook house, so I have to depend on the sutler. I bought a chicken of him today, and I am going to have a chicken broth for dinner tomorrow, there will be enough for four or five men, and I am going to give some of it to a couple of the boys in the ward, who gave me some broth when I was very sick, they sent me some twice. The chicken weighs five pounds, and costs only fifty cents. The hospital cooks are going to cook it for me. You want to know what I want sent me in your next box. Well to tell the truth I hardly know, I have got all the clothing I want. Enough I think to last me as long as I am in the service. You might send me a few pies, for I only got a half a pie out of the two you sent or at least that Charley gave me. I gave the rest to the boys in this ward with me. I hated to set down and be eating pie, and see the rest trying to satiate their appetites with a slice of dry toast and about a half a pint of tea, without either milk or sugar. You know about what I like and anything you may send will be gratefully received. The three dollars that you sent I received, and I bought the chicken with part of it. Please return my thanks to Mrs. Eastman for her kindness in sending me so handsome a gift, and you may be assured it will not be spent foolishly. Only for eatables shall I spend it. The Rev Mr Gaylord was here to see me last Sunday. He stopped and talked with me some time, and when he left, gave me a very pressing invitation to come and see him when I was able at the Campbell Hospital. Uncle John was here to see me also last week, he did not stop more than half an hour but I tell you it did me good to look on his familiar face. Mr. Ritchie has not been to see me yet, although I have been looking for him every day. There is one thing I forgot to mention, among the rest of the things that Charley sent me from the box was some lemons and oranges. The turkey lasted me a week and I eat two meals a day off of it, besides giving some to the other boys in the hospital. I was sorry when it was all gone for I never enjoyed eating a turkey so well, before in my life. The turkey and other fixings that I gave the boys on the piece took them quite by surprise, they did not expect such a new years dinner, and were highly delighted with it. Some of them were up to see me the next day, and they said that there was plenty for all hands. You told me before that John had re-enlisted. I am glad that he gets so much money but it will take a much larger sum than the state would like to offer to get me to re-enlist. This sickness of mine has knocked all notions of re-enlisting out of my head. I don't believe I could stand it another year in the army. I have nothing more I believe to write, give my love to grandmother also my best regards to John Leet, tell him I am very grateful for the manner in which he has kept you posted in regard to my health. With love to all I remain as ever

Your aff son
Asher

PS I came near forgetting the most important thing of all. Please send me some navy tobacco in the box.

* * * * * * * * * *

Post Hospital Camp Barry
Washington DC Jany 13th 1864

Dear Parents

As Charley is going home to-morrow, I thought I would write a few lines, knowing that you would be pleased to hear from me, even if I did not write any thing very interesting. I do not gain any as yet and I have come to the conclusion that I shall have to spend the largest part of the winter in this place. I would ask the Dr for a furlough, only that I am afraid that he would laugh at me, for my health is just as good if not better than it has been for some time, it is my weakness only that troubles me now. Mr Ritchie has not been to see me yet, and I guess he does not intend to, or he would have before this. There has been some changes in the battery since I have been in the hospital, first and foremost we have received twelve new recruits, and second Lieut McCurdy has resigned, and goes home with Charley. I am sorry that he has left us, for he was a fine officer, and much liked by the boys. I received two papers last night from Mr Furguson, for which return my thanks. Since I have been in the hospital Charley has bought for me a dozen lemons and a small drum of figs, when he calls if you will pay him, I will repay you when we get paid, which I hope will be in a few days. I had my chicken cooked to-day and it was first rate. I had all I could eat for my supper, besides I gave away considerable to the sick in this ward, some to the cooks to pay them for their trouble, and have more than enough left for my breakfast. This is doing pretty well I think. I believe this is all that I have to write, give my love to grandmother and tell her that I often think of her and of the many kindnesses she has shown me, since I have been away, I shall never forget them as long as I live. Also give my regards to all who may inquire for me, if any such there be, and think of me, as ever,

your aff son
Asher

Will you please to send me all of Miss Thompsons letters in the box when you send it.

* * * * * * * * * * *

Post Hospital Camp Barry
Washington DC Jany 21st 1864

Dear Parents

It is now about a fortnight since I last heard from you. I have written twice within that time; one letter I sent by Charley. I suppose you have written, but the letter has not reached me as yet. I now wish to inform you, that we leave here to-morrow for New Orleans, I have not got much strength yet and my diarrhea still continues, though not as bad as it has been. I suppose I shall have to go with the battery, but I expect I shall have a hard time of it during the voyage. We are going to turn in our horses to-morrow to the Quartermaster, so we shall not have them to take care of on the trip, and our harnesses and battery are going to be packed at the Arsenal, and sent to Baltimore, and loaded on the transport before the company leaves here. They will be sent to-morrow morning and we are going to follow the same evening. The name of the transport is the Arago. If you have not sent the box when you receive this, do not send it. If you have you can easily regain it by speaking to the express Co. If it has started it will never reach me for the express will never themselves to find out where we are. They will keep it until it is called for, if it is three years. I dont like the idea of taking such a trip as it will be to N.O. in the condition that I am in, but if the Dr thinks that I can stand it, why I shall have to go. And thats the end of it.

Hoping that I shall soon hear from you I remain as ever
Your aff Son
Asher

"Love" to "Grandmother."

* * * * * * * * * *

Head Quarters, 2d Division,
19th ARMY CORPS.
Morganza La May 23d 1864

Dear Parents

We have just received the mail, the first we have received for over a month, and in it was two letters from you, one from Aunt Priscilla and one from Hattie Coye, also four papers from you. The letters were no's 1 & 2, in one was two postage stamps, in the other some more stamps, and a two dollar Greenback. In one of the letters which I have written you, and which, from what you say I suppose you have never received I acknowledged the receipt of 80 cents in postal currency and several stamps. I also stated in one of the letters that I have written, that I wrote to you every week, and that if you did not receive them, It was not because I had failed to write, hereafter I shall adopt your plan of numbering every letter that I write. I suppose the papers have kept you pretty well posted in regard to the doings in this quarter, we were for a month completely blockaded, so that we could not receive supplies nor mail. We had to come down to half rations, and had a pretty tough time of it generally. We might have got away by land before we did, but that Gen Banks would not leave until he had got the iron clads down over the rapids, to accomplish this two dams were built across the river, so as to raise the water on the rapids to the required depth, this was done after seventeen days labor, and as soon as the boats were safely over, the army commenced its march from Alexandria to some point, the Lord only knows where. We have had more or less fighting all the way to this place, but only two battles are worth mentioning, that of Marksville Plains fought on Sunday the 15th inst [instant] and that of Mansura the day following. The loss on our side was very small, but the rebs suffered severely, prisoners say that at the fight at Mansura Gen Walker was killed by a shell from Battery L. 1st U.S. Artillery. Our Division commanded by General Grover was in the Advance all the way, and behaved splendidly. The Battery was engaged and at the second days fight, fired 240 rounds of shell and cannister. This is the first time that the recruits of our battery have been under fire, and they stood up to it without flinching, although the rebs kept up a furious fire from about twenty pieces of Artillery, the shot and shell flew about our ears rather uncomfortably I can assure you. I was with the General all the time, and followed him wherever he went. He is the coolest man under fire I ever saw, and is just the man for me to serve under. We have taken over 500 prisoners. There was but one man killed on our side in these two days fighting, although a great many are badly wounded. Col Lucas comdg one of the Cavalry brigades made a splendid charge in the first days fight, with only two Regts, the 6th Mo. & 1st La. he charged a line of rebel cavalry 4000 strong, and drove them from the field. And speaking of cavalry makes me think of one thing, and that is Col Dudley has been relieved from the command of the 4th Brigade of Cavalry, and ordered to report to his Regt. cause, poor management of his Brigade at the fight at Pleasant hill. I saw him as he passed through Alexandria, and had a talk with him, he was very glad to see me and sent his regards to you. I have written you before of this, but as you have not said anything about it in your letters I thought I would write it again. Our Division was not in the fight at Pleasant Hill, so I cannot tell you much about it, only this, that Banks got licked, and lost the best battery in the U.S. Service, the 2d Mass (Nims). Our Corps is now lying here awaiting transportation, and I hope we shall soon leave here for I want to get to some civilized place again. I see by papers which we received at this place that Grant is doing gloriously in Virginia, I only hope he will continue as successful as he has begun if he does this thing must cave. And it cannot do so any too quick. I read the account in the Gazette of the mining operations in R. Have the people of R gone crazy or what is the matter with them. I should think they were getting decidedly luny. I have not yet received the letter you sent by Granville Dudley. But I suppose I shall sooner or later. The letter you sent me while in the Hospital at W. with money in it I have never received. I wrote to Frank some time ago and have wondered why I did not receive any answer, but as you write me that he has gone to New York, it is easily accounted for, he, very probably has not received my letter. I have not the least doubt but what you felt relieved when Priscilla left, although she is as nice a woman as ever lived, She has not the firmness required to manage a family of children, and this very want of control over her children will some day or other be the means of giving her great pain if not suffering. We are having the [illegible] kind of hot weather here, it is impossible to live out in the sun some of the time, a great many of the troops have died of sun stroke. Blackberries are ripe and plenty, also strawberries, I have had several messes of green peas since I have been on this march and they tasted tiptop. I forgot to tell you that I have had a horse to ride, this trip he was taken with a Johnny Reb on his back and turned over to me for my use. So you see I have been able [remainder missing].

* * * * * * * * * *

The following deposition, from Asher's father, was submitted in evidence of Asher's disability.

Deposition A Case of Jane M. Chase No. 293890

On this 4 Dec, 1889 at Stratham, County of Rockingham state of NH before me, Chas Fairbanks, a special examiner of the pension office, personally appeared Samuel S. Chase, who being by me first duly sworn to answer truly all interrogatories propounded to him during this special examination of aforesaid pension claim deposes and says:

Am 72 years of age P.O. address as above. Occupation farmer Asher M. Chase late of 7th Battery Mass Vols was my son. He was a sound young man at enlistment. He wrote me frequently while in the army (once every two weeks) on an average. I cannot remember dates but the letters which I sent to my son's wife at Warren Me will show when I first knew that he was sick. (Here the soldiers letters were shown deposed) Yes sir I recognize these letters as the ones received as to my sons health in the service. After my son was discharged he stopped there on four months in Savannah Ga and was clerk in a hotel. The "Palmer House." Don't know who kept said house or who my son worked for. About three or four months after his discharge he came home to Roxbury Mass and remained with me untill he got married. He did not do any thing until he got a position as letter carrier in Roxbury. When he first came home he appeared ill was complaining of fever in his head & occasional dizzy spells that he had suffered from very severe and at times he appeared singular was troubled to remember. He also complained of numbness in his legs & was clumsy in walking by spells. This was his condition when he came home and he did not seem to gain but decline gradually untill he had to give up his position as letter carrier. He could not remember where to deliver his mail. He remained in the post office too long. The postmaster was John Backup and was very friendly towards my son and kept him longer on that account. Before he gave up his position he was fractious and irritable and very nervous. His appearance at discharge was entirely different than when he enlisted. The pain & dizziness of head worried him. He thought he had rheumatism in his legs. My wife was worried about him and applied local remedies. She is now in Roxbury Mass # 52 Mt Pleasant Ave. My son died at Warren Me. in Jan 1875. I attended the funeral he was buried in my lot in Forest Hills Cemetery, Roxbury, Mass. I have no means of stating exact date of his death I saw him during his last sickness in Aug 1874 and in Dec 1864 [1874]. He was then unable to talk and partially demented he did not recognize facts. He nodded to me as though he knew me. His mental faculties were much impaired for the two years prior to death.

He was treated by Dr. Jackson (now dead) in Roxbury. I took my son to Dr. Hammond of NY City and he informed me that he could not help him. Said the brain was affected.

I don't know that my son had paralysis. I always thought that he did have some disease as he had numbness in his limbs. I considered that my son's ill health was acquired by his army service as he was sound at enlistment & came home in a broken down condition and never recovered. I don't know that he had any other disabilities than as stated. He had the Varioloid [a mild form of smallpox] when 14 or 15 years of age but came out all right.

Don't recall that I ever heard him say that he was sun stroke in the army.

I have no interest in the prosecution of this case.

I have understood your questions & my answers have been correctly recorded.

Saml S. Chase

* * * * * * * * * *

The following deposition from Jane M. Chase, Asher's wife, was submitted in evidence of Asher's disability.

Deposition A Case of Jane M. Chase No. 293890

On this ninth day of October, 1889 at Warren, county of Knox state of Maine, before me, Samuel Wood, a special examiner of the Pension Office, personally appeared Jane M. Chase (claimant), who, being by me first duly sworn to answer truly all interrogatories propounded to her during this special examination of aforesaid pension claim, deposes and says her age is 49; milliner; p.o. Warren, Knox Co Me.

I am the claimant in this case as the widow of Asher M. Chase, late private 7th Battery Mass Light Artillery. He died here in Warren on January 12, 1875 of slow paralysis and softening of the brain. I was married to him Dec 5 1867 at Warren—this place—by Rev Ira Leland, in the Congregationalist Church neither had been previously married I have remained his lawful widow since his death. We had two children only the first, Charles E. B. Chase was born Feb 8 1870 in Roxbury, Mass the other, Asher H. S. Chase was born Nov 8, 1873 at Roxbury, Mass. Both are living. The physician who attended at the birth of both children, Dr. William Jackson, of Dudley St, Roxbury is dead. My sister, Sarah Weston, was near me when Charles the elder boy was born; she was with us when Asher was perhaps two weeks old. Mrs. Fanny Taylor, wife of Joseph Taylor, who lives on Cliff St, Roxbury, though not present when Asher was born, was then a near neighbor; knew of the circumstance and was in and out. The nurse who attended me, Betsey Gardener, died in the old ladies home in Boston. I have a family record of the ages of the children both are yet under my care. I knew Asher M. Chase for perhaps four years before he went into the army. He lived in Roxbury Mass. I was then in Boston tending store for my brother in law William Tufts. He is a confectioner and caterer at 513 Tremont St Boston in the Odd Fellows building. His wife, my sister, Eunice knew of the birth of my son Asher at the time though not present when he was born. My husband—that was afterward—appeared to be in perfect health prior to going into the army.

I didn't correspond with him while he was in the service we had a little tiff and I lost track of him—beyond knowing that he was in the service—until after his discharge. It was in Nov 1865 that our acquaintance was renewed and we "made up." Shortly afterwards he invited me to go in the theater with him, but instead of coming for me he sent me a note stating that he had taken cold and was home with rheumatism. He appeared to be in fairly good health from that time except for occasionally complaining of being a bit lame—from rheumatism he supposed. From what I have since known I am positive that this was paralysis because he never complained of any pain with it it seemed to be a heaviness in the right leg. He would describe it as in the state of a persons limbs or feet when they say they are asleep. I didn't hear anything about a prickling sensation.

My husband was a person who complained very little even in his last sickness.

After marriage we went to Roxbury Mass boarded with his parents two or three months; went to housekeeping in March 1868 in Roxbury. He was then a letter carrier in the post office and he continued in that employment until about a year before he died. He had left a little more than a year; about a year and a half, I think, as he had quit in July or August 1873 and died in Jan 1875. Looking back now I do not see how he worked there at all during at least 2 1/2 years before he left the office. He was generally well liked and a great deal of forbearance was exercised on his account or he would have been compelled to give up his position long before he did. I knew of him stumbling and falling while on the street a number of times. The first one I recollect of was in the summer of 1870. He had fallen through dizziness he said and he'd dropped his letters but thought he had gathered them all up again. I know the date—not the exact date—but it was in May or June 1870 on account of the fact of my son Charles being a baby and a sister of mine was visiting me. Several times during the last two years he carried letters, letters that he had dropped were brought to the house. I suppose he must have dropped them stumbling and then the report got around that he was drinking. That seemed to hurt him he was a man who did not drink intoxicating liquors.

As to his condition between his discharge and the time he was appointed letter carrier part of the time I only know of it by his own statement. I saw him almost immediately on his return to his home in Nov. 1865 He then told me of some of his army experience and that he had had a fever, and didn't feel able to come home at the time of his discharge. He said that he had stopped at the house of an old lady and her son in Savannah. That he would have gone in business there but did not feel able and so he had come home. He looked thin at that time. He never was a fleshy person at any time. I think he said it was a sort of brain fever that he had in the army. I do not know exactly when he was appointed a letter carrier at Roxbury, but it was before we were married, and I think it must have been in the summer of

1866 that he received that appointment. Until we went to keeping house, we boarded with his father and mother at Roxbury. They now live at Stratham, NH. His father's name is Samuel S. Chase I don't believe that his parents ever understood him—his troubles—and in fact I don't think any of us really understood my husband, Asher's troubles until after Dr. Hammond explained it to me. He was examined by Dr. William Hammond the famous surgeon of New York city (we forgotten his address now) in the month of September 1873. He charged $20.00 for his examination I think. Dr. Hammond then told me that my husband had slow paralysis and softening of the brain and he gave me a slip of paper to show to Dr. Jackson of Roxbury (since dead). Dr. Jackson died before I presented a claim. I have written to Dr. Hammond 5 or 6 times I think and have never received any reply from him. I think that if Dr. William Jackson of Roxbury lived, I should not have had any trouble in proving my claim to pension.

As to Dr. Jackson treating my husband, I do not know, and have no means of knowing whether or not he treated him before we were married except in conversation with Dr. Jackson he told me of having advised him to give up attendance at the commercial college and to get outdoor employment. My husband had commenced at the college almost immediately upon his return home. I know that Dr. Jackson gave him treatment but just for what except that he called it rheumatism, I don't know during the first winter after our marriage—the same winter, the winter of '67–'68. He lived in the neighborhood my husband used to go to him and call on him I don't know that Dr. Jackson ever really understood—yes he did though—for when I showed him the paper I got from Dr. Hammond he said "I thought so: that what was I was afraid of but I hadn't the heart to tell you so." He then called to my mind having been called to attend my husband in the winter of 1869 when my husband suffered the bad rheumatism in the right leg and that there was no pain, no swelling, and only inability to move the leg on account of numbness.

There was no symptom as to his condition of which I never understood the significance until I had seen Dr. Hammond and that was that my husband's mouth used to twitch my attention was called to it by his mother speaking to him about it soon after we were married. She called it nervousness. She'd say "Asher, do you know what you are doing: stop twitching your mouth. You get so excited and nervous reading that you don't know what you are doing." I supposed then that it was nervousness; that continued ever afterwards and his mouth seemed to draw down at the corners during the last few years of his life. The most marked symptom was the numbness and deadness of the right leg; that was only at intervals at first, but got worse and took in the whole side until for a long period before his death he was unable to even feed himself. There was no pain in the leg that he complained of and no swelling—only a gradually increasing helplessness. There was also a growing loss of power of attention and an apparent confusion of ideas and great forgetfulness for at least two years before he died. There was a stuttering and stammering and hesitancy long before he quit work as a letter carrier but I cannot really date it when I first noticed it.

No one else except Dr. Jackson treated him while he lived at Roxbury (except the visits to Dr. Hammond of NY) and Dr. Jackson never gave me any satisfaction as to what ailed him until I had found out from another source. Dr. Jackson had always told me that my husband "was played out, also there was a general breaking up." I recollect that before my second boy was born I asked Dr. Jackson what did ail my husband and he said that there was a general breaking down and there was a brain trouble with it, but that it puzzled him. At this time when he could come in he would seem to be so entirely exhausted as to be unfit for anything and he had no appetite. There was a tendency—when he sat down—to fall right to sleep. It made no difference where he was. When he had leisure he'd go right to sleep, but towards the last of his life he couldn't sleep at all. My husband never had any fever or other sickness after service except this prostration. Sometimes he'd be off work one or two weeks at a time. At times he would limp but it was more of a drag and unsteadiness in his gate than a limp. He used to get better after bottle of Kennedy's Rheumatic Liniment and use it under the impression that it was rheumatism.

We moved to Warren Me in April 1874 and his first physician was Dr. Benjamin Baxter (dead). He treated him for paralysis but my husband didn't improve under his treatment. Then I got Dr. Eveleth of [illegible] and he attended him during the last of his sickness. He said that he couldn't do him any good but could simply give him something to quiet him. My husband's reason was totally gone at times, for several weeks before he died, though, there was no time but what he appeared to know me. He was so thin that I could lift him out of bed in my arms he had become pretty emaciated.

Questions understood & answers correctly recorded.

Jane M. Chase

Sworn to and subscribed before me this 9 of October 1889 and I certify that the contents were fully made known to deponent before signing.

Samuel Woods

* * * * * * * * * * *

In 1889, Jane Chase wrote a letter to her attorney, who was handling the pension request, expressing her frustration with requests for further evidence "in regard to the nature of the disease from which my husband suffered at the time of his discharge from service." She further wrote the following:

> A British Soldier scribbled these lines on the walls of Delhi, after its capture from the mutineers, and when the payment of prize money was delayed.
>
> When War is rife and danger's nigh,
> "God and the Soldier" is all the cry.
> When War is o'er, and danger righted,
> God is forgotten, and the Soldier Slighted.

Jane Chase was granted a widow's pension in April 1890, effective January 1875, of $8.00 per month plus $2.00 per month for each child until they reached the age of sixteen. Her pension increased to $12, $20, and finally $40 per month in 1928. Jane M. Chase died in October 1931, and is buried next to Asher in Forest Hills Cemetery, in Boston.

Index

The North's Civil War Series

Paul A. Cimbala, series editor

1. Anita Palladino, ed., *Diary of a Yankee Engineer: The Civil War Story of John H. Westervelt, Engineer, 1st New York Volunteer Engineer Corps.*
2. Herman Belz, *Abraham Lincoln, Constitutionalism, and Equal Rights in the Civil War Era.*
3. Earl J. Hess, *Liberty, Virtue, and Progress: Northerners and Their War for the Union.* Second revised edition, with a new introduction by the author.
4. William L. Burton, *Melting Pot Soldiers: The Union's Ethnic Regiments.*
5. Hans L. Trefousse, *Carl Schurz: A Biography.*
6. Stephen W. Sears, ed., *Mr. Dunn Browne's Experiences in the Army: The Civil War Letters of Samuel W. Fiske.*
7. Jean H. Baker, *Affairs of Party: The Political Culture of Northern Democrats in the Mid-Nineteenth Century.*
8. Frank L. Klement, *The Limits of Dissent: Clement L. Vallandigham and the Civil War.* With a new introduction by Steven K. Rogstad.
9. Lawrence N. Powell, *New Masters: Northern Planters during the Civil War and Reconstruction.*
10. John A. Carpenter, *Sword and Olive Branch: Oliver Otis Howard.*
11. Thomas F. Schwartz, ed., *"For a Vast Future Also": Essays from the* Journal of the Abraham Lincoln Association.
12. Mark De Wolfe Howe, ed., *Touched with Fire: Civil War Letters and Diary of Oliver Wendell Holmes, Jr.* With a new introduction by David Burton.

13. Harold Adams Small, ed., *The Road to Richmond: The Civil War Letters of Major Abner R. Small of the 16th Maine Volunteers.* New introduction by Earl J. Hess.
14. Eric A. Campbell, ed., *"A Grand Terrible Dramma": From Gettysburg to Petersburg: The Civil War Letters of Charles Wellington Reed.* Illustrated by Reed's Civil War Sketches.
15. Herbert Mitgang, ed., *Abraham Lincoln: A Press Portrait.*
16. Harold Holzer, ed., *Prang's Civil War Pictures: The Complete Battle Chromos of Louis Prang.*
17. Harold Holzer, ed., *State of the Union: New York and the Civil War.*
18. Paul A. Cimbala and Randall M. Miller, eds., *Union Soldiers and the Northern Home Front: Wartime Experiences, Postwar Adjustments.*
19. Mark A. Snell, *From First to Last: The Life of Major General William B. Franklin.*
20. Paul A. Cimbala and Randall M. Miller, eds., *An Uncommon Time: The Civil War and the Northern Home Front.*
21. John Y. Simon and Harold Holzer, eds., *The Lincoln Forum: Rediscovering Abraham Lincoln.*
22. Thomas F. Curran, *Soldiers of Peace: Civil War Pacifism and the Postwar Radical Peace Movement.*
23. Kyle S. Sinisi, *Sacred Debts: State Civil War Claims and American Federalism, 1861–1880.*
24. Russell L. Johnson, *Warriors into Workers: The Civil War and the Formation of Urban-Industrial Society in a Northern City.*
25. Peter J. Parish, *The North and the Nation in the Era of the Civil War.* Edited by Adam L. P. Smith and Susan-Mary Grant.
26. Patricia Richard, *Busy Hands: Images of the Family in the Northern Civil War Effort.*
27. Michael S. Green, *Freedom, Union, and Power: The Mind of the Republican Party During the Civil War.*
28. Christian G. Samito, ed., *Fear Was Not In Him: The Civil War Letters of Major General Francis C. Barlow, U.S.A.*